BAYLY'S WAR

BAYLY'S WAR
The Battle for the Western Approaches in the First World War

STEVE R DUNN

Seaforth
PUBLISHING

Dedication

For my friend Stephen Greensted

First published in Great Britain in 2018 by
Seaforth Publishing,
An imprint of Pen & Sword Books Ltd,
47 Church Street, Barnsley S70 2AS

www.seaforthpublishing.com

British Library Cataloguing in Publication Data
A catalogue record for this book is available from the British Library

ISBN 978 1 5267 0123 7 (HARDBACK)
ISBN 978 1 5267 0125 1 (EPUB)
ISBN 978 1 5267 0124 4 (KINDLE)

Pen & Sword Books Limited incorporates the imprints of Atlas, Archaeology,
Aviation, Discovery, Family History, Fiction, History, Maritime, Military,
Military Classics, Politics, Select, Transport, True Crime, Air World, Frontline
Publishing, Leo Cooper, Remember When, Seaforth Publishing,
The Praetorian Press, Wharncliffe Local History, Wharncliffe Transport,
Wharncliffe True Crime and White Owl

Typeset and designed by Mousemat Design
Printed and bound in Great Britain by CPI Group (UK) Ltd, Croydon, CR0 4YY

CONTENTS

List of Plates   7
A Note on the Structure and Intent of this Book   11
Preface   13
Prologue   16

Part One: The Coast of Ireland Command until April 1917   **19**
  1. The Western Approaches and Queenstown   21
  2. War, 1914   28
  3. 'It was just murder', January – July 1915   40
  4. A New Broom, 1915   53
  5. New Ships, New Tactics, July and August 1915   60
  6. Bad Blood and First Blood, August and September 1915   69
  7. The U-boats Return: January – April 1916   81
  8. 'A Terrible Beauty is Born', April 1916   89
  9. The Calm Before the Storm, May – December 1916   102
  10. Unrestricted Submarine Warfare, 1917   116
  11. April is the Cruellest Month, 1917   129

**Part Two: The Royal Navy and United States Navy
under Bayly's Command**   **141**
  12. The Americans Arrive, 1917   143
  13. 'Pull Together': Joint Operations Commence, 1917   155
  14. *U-Boot-Falle,* 1917   164
  15. The Fight Continues, 1917   175
  16. The Americans are Blooded, 1917   189
  17. A Strange Sort Of Life   197
  18. Difficult Times, December 1917   206
  19. The Turning Tide, January – June 1918   214
  20. The War from the Air   235
  21. A Hard Road, July – September 1918   240
  22. Victory, 1918   251

Part Three: Bayly's Leaving and Achievements   **257**

   23. Pain and Pleasure: An Admiral Takes His Leave   259

   24. Considerations and Conclusions   267

   25. Envoi   275

Appendices

   1. The Principal Queenstown Sloops and their Commanders   278

   2. The Queenstown VCs   279

   3. Why Was It So Hard to Find a U-boat?   280

   4. U-boats Sunk in the Western Approaches
      by Vessels under Bayly's Direct Orders   283

   5. Auxiliary Vessels based on the Coast of Ireland
      and Irish Sea, 1 January 1918   284

   6. Principal German U-boat Types   285

Author's Note   286

Notes   287

Bibliography   293

Index   296

List of Plates

Plate section located between pages 128 and 129.

John Redmond. (Author's collection)
Edward Carson. (Author's collection)
Skipper James Hagan of the *Daniel O'Connell*. (Courtesy of Arklow Maritime Museum)
Skipper Edward White of the drifter *Elizabeth*. (Courtesy of Arklow Maritime Museum)
Eamon de Valera c.1920. (Author's collection)
Woodrow Wilson. (Author's collection)
Admiral William S Sims USN. (Author's collection)
Admiral William Sims raises his flag at Queenstown, taking command while Bayly has a holiday. (Courtesy of Alamy Ltd)
Admiral Sir Lewis Bayly. (Author's collection)
A postcard of Queenstown c.1900. (Author's collection)
Queenstown in 2016. (Author's collection)
Admiralty House. (Image reproduced courtesy of the National Library of Ireland)
A pre-war view of Haulbowline Island and dockyard. (Image reproduced courtesy of the National Library of Ireland)
HMS *Adventure*. (Author's collection)
RMS *Lusitania*. (Author's collection)
The painting 'The Return of the Mayflower', depicting the arrival of the US destroyers at Queenstown, by Bernard Finegan Gribble. (Author's collection)
The USN depot ship USS *Melville* at Queenstown. (© Imperial War Museum Q 18793)

The destroyer USS *Paulding* at Queenstown. (Author's collection)

The sloop HMS *Zinnia*. (© Imperial War Museum Q 75459)

The *Beagle*-class destroyer HMS *Wolverine*. (© Imperial War Museum Q 109160)

The 'M'-class destroyer *Mary Rose*. (© Imperial War Museum Q 20404)

The old cruiser HMS *Drake*. (Courtesy Library of Congress, USA)

The *Canopus*-class battleship HMS *Ocean*. (Author's collection)

An album cover made for USN base Wexford. (Author's collection)

A programme of a typical entertainment at the USN recreational facility at Queenstown. (Author's collection)

Bayly's deployments to protect the South-western and Western Approaches in March 1917 (taken from Naval Staff Monographs vol XVIII, May 1933)

The memorial designed by Jerome Connor in Cobh dedicated to the victims of the *Lusitania* sinking. (Author's collection)

The gravestone in Cobh Old Church Cemetery of Captain Frederick Parslow. (Author's collection)

The memorial plaque commemorating the US Navy's arrival in Ireland. (Author's collection)

'The part that Queenstown played in the Great War is not generally known, by reason of the very necessary veil of secrecy that was drawn over its work. Someday the full story will be told and it will prove to be thrilling and amazing, for some of the most daring exploits were performed by the craft based on this port.'

The Times, 17 June 1919.

'I have never seen a brave man. All men are frightened. The more intelligent they are, the more they are frightened. The courageous man is the man who forces himself, in spite of his fear, to carry on.'

General George S Patton, *War as I Knew It*
(Bantam Books, 1980), p 322.

'I have met perhaps a dozen or so of VCs and in every case they explained that they did the first thing that came into their head without worrying about alternatives. One man headed a charge into a mass of Afghans ... and cut down five of them. All he said was; "Well, they were there and they wouldn't go away. What was a man to do? Write a note and ask 'em to shift?"'

Rudyard Kipling, 'Winning the Victoria Cross',
Windsor Magazine, 1897.

A Note on the Structure and Intent of this Book

Bayly's War is divided into three sections. Part One covers the Coast of Ireland Command from before the outbreak of the First World War until the declaration of war on Germany by America in April 1917. It examines the pre-war development of Queenstown as a naval base and its role in the war under two admirals.

Part Two focuses on the period from the arrival of the American forces in Ireland to the end of the war, all under Admiral Bayly's leadership.

Part Three examines Bayly's leaving of the command and the Royal Navy, his continued bitterness at his treatment and his legacy and remembrance. It concludes with a critical analysis of the tactics used during Bayly's time in post and the results obtained.

First and foremost, it is the intention of the author to tell a story; a true story of sacrifice and quotidian bravery. The method is to use individual incidents which build to a whole hopefully greater than the sum of the parts. This book is not a day-by-day history but a story compounded of many separate actions. Neither is it a biography, although Lewis Bayly, as the presiding admiral for most of the period covered, clearly provides a linking theme and his character and role are important to the telling of the narrative. The recounting of the Queenstown command is also tied to the story of Ireland and its growing nationalism during the war. This interrelationship is related here primarily from the perspective of the British forces and politicians and is not intended to be seen as an unbiased treatment; it reflects what the men on the ground and in the ships believed.

It is difficult to exactly assess the sinkings of merchant tonnage and ships caused by U-boats in Bayly's area of command. In some

11

case, the author has used available sources to make estimates but asks the reader to consider these as indicative rather than absolute.

Finally, in the writing of the book, I became much better informed as to the role played in the war by the merchant sailors, British and of other nations, and their largely unrecognised contribution. This book, I hope, goes some way to making their part clearer and more appreciated.

The 24-hour clock is used for convenience and consistency.

Preface

As an island dependent on imports for both food and manufacturing, Britain was extremely vulnerable to the disruption of its supply chain in times of war. Nowhere was this more true than on the nation's Atlantic coast. Food and munitions (and later soldiers) from North America, men and goods from Canada and the Caribbean, Africa, Australasia and India, ores and raw materials from South America – all passed through the 'Western Approaches', the tract of the Atlantic Ocean to the west and south of Ireland, on their way to Liverpool or the Channel ports and London. Here was to be fought the greatest sea battle of the war – the fight for survival, as Germany's U-boats targeted trade in the Atlantic in an attempt to drive Britain to submission through lack of food and *materiel*.

The problem was, very few people had expected to fight such a war. A war on commerce was certainly anticipated but it would surely be fought using regular naval cruisers and armed merchant cruisers (AMCs), armed civilian ships, crossing and counter-crossing the trade sea lanes in search of prey. This was no cause for alarm: British cruisers and AMCs would deal with them.

In any case, such a war would be fought openly, under prize rules, gentlemanly rules of cruiser warfare, internationally agreed, which stated that warnings should be given before firing at passenger or merchant ships, their crews and passengers should be allowed to disembark before sinking their vessels and they should be taken or sent to a place of safety (and a lifeboat was not deemed a place of safety). Moreover, the war would be short and a decision would swiftly be arrived at after Britain's magnificent Grand Fleet of dreadnought battleships had swept the German High Seas Fleet from the seas.

But the Germans failed to show up for their ritual slaughter. Hamstrung by the Kaiser's edict that his beautiful ships should not be risked in battle,* and politically held back by Imperial Chancellor Bethmann-Hollweg (who believed that the best use of the fleet was as a bargaining counter at some future peace conference), to the immense frustration of the High Seas Fleet's architect, Tirpitz, the German fleet skulked in harbour at the outbreak of war, whilst British, Indian, Australian, Canadian and other Imperial soldiers crossed the seas to France.

Few German cruisers and AMCs managed to escape to the open sea and by the beginning of 1915 they had been largely swept from the oceans and trade routes. Instead, and with increasing savagery and success, the German Navy turned to the submarine; cheaper than a warship, certainly more stealthy; and largely neglected by the Royal Navy.

The submarine was seen by many as a coward's weapon; ideal for poorer countries, with no naval tradition, but not for the British navy. Possibly suitable for coastal defence purposes, but too slow to work with the Fleet, they were often dubbed 'toys' before the war. And in any case, how could they be an effective weapon against trade and shipping when they were by their very size and design, unable to operate well under the accepted Prize Rules. These perceived disadvantages proved no barrier to the German Navy, however. By early 1915, German U-boats were sinking British and neutral shipping all around the coast of Britain, including in the vital Western Approaches.

Amongst the Royal Navy officer class there were few who had thought rigorously about the prosecution of a modern war with modern weapons. The Navy had not been called upon to fight a fleet engagement of any magnitude since Trafalgar in 1805. Since then its role had been to act as a sort of gendarmerie. As one such officer put it: 'I don't think we thought very much about war with a big W. We looked on the Navy more as a World Police Force than as a warlike institution.'[1] The historian Arthur Marder, moreover, judged that by the end of the nineteenth century the Royal Navy was 'in certain respects a drowsy, inefficient, moth-eaten organisation'.[2] Even the reforming genius of 'Jacky' Fisher (Admiral Sir John Fisher, First

---

* Kaiser Wilhelm II saw the fleet as his personal property; 'Willie's toys', as King Edward VII once called them. 'The Kaiser ignored [von Tirpitz's] urgent request that he be granted a free hand in directing the operations of the fleet and retained in command Admiral von Ingenohl, an officer of mediocre ability, who owed his advancement to the personal friendship of the Supreme Warlord and to prolonged service on the Imperial Yacht' (Bywater, *Strange Intelligence*, p 43).

Sea Lord 1904–10), would struggle to completely reform such a navy in time for Armageddon.

Thus, when U-boats started to sink British trade with seeming impunity, the strategic and tactical responses were often haphazard and sometimes inept. The Royal Navy was having to learn the rules and the game at the same time.

Nowhere was this more so than in the Western Approaches, an area defined by the academic geographer Sir Halford John Mackinder as 'the marine antechamber of Britain', where British trade and supply chain were so vulnerable. U-boats wreaked havoc here throughout the war and a determined battle was fought to keep the sea lanes free for Allied supplies of food and *materiel* of war. It was waged by a small and dedicated group of men; initially British and Commonwealth, latterly American too, with inadequate weapons, instant tactical doctrine and huge amounts of personal determination and bravery.

The battle for the Western Approaches became a war within a war. Lose it and the Allies would likely lose the global conflict. Indeed, in mid-1917, Admiral Sir John Jellicoe, the First Sea Lord, thought that Britain was in danger of losing the war, such was the level of U-boat predation. But the men of the Coast of Ireland Station (later the Western Approaches Command) based at Queenstown (now Cobh), County Cork, never wavered in their efforts, and driven on by a hard-pressing, old-fashioned and unlikely leader, the war in the seas around Ireland was eventually decided in their favour. Along the way, they had to fight the Atlantic weather, the Irish revolutionary movements and much of the Irish population, the Admiralty in London, and the increasingly competent and capable German submarines and submariners.

This book is the story of the war waged by the men of the Queenstown command. It is a tale of heroism, misfortune, tragedy, revolution and revolutionaries, strategies and tactics, and ships and weapons. It examines the lives and actions of men, often volunteers, who fought this climacteric battle in the wastes of the Atlantic Ocean. This book also recognises the sacrifice made by the merchant ships and sailors, many of whom were lost in the cold seas around Ireland. At the story's centre is an admiral, a man who surprised his peers and seniors, and who, for three of the four years of the Great War, drove his men and vessels to heights of bravery and effort neither they (nor anyone else) had ever imagined achievable.

Prologue

The house stood high above the harbour. The main entrance was from the road, past a gatehouse, and a steep climb from the sea below. To the rear, the house looked south out over the Atlantic Ocean and the garden running downhill towards the sea.

It had been built in 1886, anachronistically in a hybrid style of Georgian meets Regency, and when the Gothic Revival cathedral to its south and west was half complete. The four-storey south elevation sported a *piano nobile* built over a rustic and reached from the garden by twin limestone stairs. Seven regular bays divided the wall space on two principal floors, filled with long plate glass Regency windows which doubled as pairs of doors to a cast-iron veranda with cast and wrought-iron railings. To the west was attached a large conservatory. Above the fourth and final, plainer, storey was a hipped slate roof with rendered chimneystacks; cast-iron rainwater guttering and drainpipes sported lion-head motifs. It was an imposing place, immediately visible from the sea, a symbol of wealth and power.

Through the first-floor veranda doors could be seen a long ballroom, which had been divided into two separate rooms, one large, one small, by a makeshift wooden panel. In the larger of the two rooms stood a billiard table, long unused and covered by a piece of deal on which were placed little replicas of ships and submarines, over a rough map of the Irish Atlantic coasts. The room was untidy, some desks scattered around it, piles of papers and signal flimsies littered about.

Standing in front of one of the veranda doors was a man. He was of no more than average height, an impression reinforced by a slight stoop of the shoulders. In build he was slim, almost scrawny. His face was weather-beaten and swarthy and his black hair was turning grey. He was hatless but wore a uniform jacket which seemed a size too big for him and rather hung away from his spare frame.

The man in the too-big jacket was staring out to sea. It was a fine day, although the week had had the usual sprinklings of soft rain that drifted in from the Atlantic and wetted the streets he could see below. But the streets held little interest for him. His eyes were fixed on the limits of the horizon. Like the sea, his eyes were grey; but they also had a piercing quality, eyes that were used to looking at seas and ships, eyes that skewered men who were judged inept or at fault.

A more than casual observer would also have noticed movement on the roof of the house too. A young woman, carrying a telescope, was standing leaning on the ironwork roof terrace balustrade. She too was staring out to sea.

The man below her abruptly moved away from the windows and looked at the billiard/map table. Then with a small harrumph he walked back to his observation point. 'Jellicoe is wrong', he muttered under his breath, they would win this war and they would conquer the U-boat menace. 'Why', he mumbled, 'I've been doing that since 1915; but they must come and they must come soon.'

He turned and paced away from the veranda again. The dull light caused the rings on his jacket sleeve to briefly catch aglow; one thick, two narrow, the rank insignia of a vice admiral in the Royal Navy.

It was Friday 4 May 1917; the man in the too-big jacket was Vice Admiral Sir Lewis Bayly. And he was waiting for some Americans.

PART ONE

The Coast of Ireland Command until April 1917

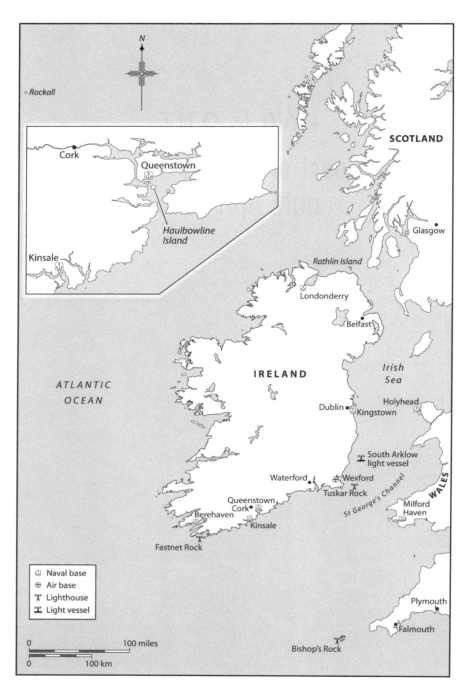

Queenstown and the Western Approaches.

1

The Western Approaches and Queenstown

The island of Ireland lies across the trade routes to England like a giant earthwork or ravelin. It breaks the prevailing westerly winds, takes the brunt of the Atlantic storms and offers an outwork to defend the British coast from attack or invasion. It was thus considered important that Ireland be defended from the enemies of Britain.

So it was that, at least since Elizabethan times, Ireland had been thought of strategic worth to Britain and to her enemies. It was a vulnerable back door during the many European struggles of the sixteenth to nineteenth centuries. Given the prevailing westerly winds, the south and west coasts of Ireland were more accessible from Spain, for example, than from Southern England where the bulk of the Royal Navy was then located. Twenty ships of the Spanish Armada were wrecked on the jagged rocks of northern and western Ireland, blown there by Atlantic gales. Revolutionary France targeted the coasts of Wicklow and Cork for invasion, pinpointing them as Britain's weak underbelly.

With the acquisition by Britain of an empire based on trade, Ireland gained an even greater strategic importance. The sea lanes of communication between Europe and America run mainly south of Ireland, through the area colloquially known as the 'Western Approaches'. As the historian Ben Wilson has noted, 'Naval strategists, from Drake onwards, had seen the value of keeping a squadron in the Western Approaches. Ships placed far out to sea between Fastnet (at the southernmost tip of Ireland) and Finisterre could keep a watch for enemy fleets. They could convoy merchantmen. They could cover Ireland.'[1]

Ships bound for the key ports of Liverpool, Bristol, London, Portsmouth, Plymouth and Southampton had to transit this area, passing Kinsale Head and the Fastnet Rock* as they navigated towards the St George's Channel or the Irish Sea. For the defence of trade, and of necessity, in the late eighteenth century the harbours of the Irish coast became important naval centres. The wars with France over control of North America following the American War of Independence and then the Napoleonic Wars produced half a century of naval development and construction all round the Irish littoral. And with good reason; only the gales of December 1796 prevented a French invasion force of 16,000 men from landing in Bantry Bay.

Initially the epicentre of Royal Navy activity was at the port of Kinsale, but this had to be abandoned in favour of Cork. The latter, possessed of the second largest natural harbour in the world by navigational area, offered better shelter and anchorage for the increasing number of naval ships deployed on the station. And after the introduction of the Compulsory Convoy Act of 1798 compelled all British merchant ships sailing to and from British ports in time of war to sail in convoy, under the protection of Royal Navy ships and in return for the payment of a fee for that service, Cork became the point of assembly for westbound convoys. Its magnificent harbour was well suited to this task but in turn this new-found importance meant that better protection for the port was necessary. Thus new forts were regularly constructed during the late eighteenth and early nineteenth centuries downstream from the city. A fort was built on Spike Island (later to become Fort Westmoreland) and a number of Martello Towers and other fortifications were added or improved nearby.

A need for better naval supply and ordnance facilities became apparent and in 1805 a start was made on building a base at Haulbowline, an island in the mouth of the Lee estuary, lying to the south of the small fishing village of Cove, itself on an island known as 'Great Island', and close to Spike Island. Construction continued in a desultory fashion until it was finished in 1821. An ordnance yard was established on the westernmost part of the island, separated from the rest by a large stone wall. By 1808 a pair of magazines had been erected on nearby Rocky Island with capacity for 25,000 barrels of gunpowder. East of the wall a victualling yard

---

* Known as 'Ireland's teardrop' as it was the last fragment of their homeland seen by departing emigrants.

was laid out, where there were six large storehouses, three grouped together around a quay on the north side of the island, and three along what was then its eastern edge. Behind these was a large rectangular rainwater tank (which collected fresh water for the ships), on top of which was a quadrangular cooperage complex. To the south were mast and boat stores, at the top of a slipway.

The area was now placed under an admiral, entitled Commander-in-Chief, Cork Station, until 1848 and then Commander-in-Chief, Queenstown (from 1849 until 1876), Senior Officer Coast of Ireland Station (until 1911) and then Admiral commanding Coast of Ireland Station. Its main roles became anti-smuggling patrol and fishery protection. Convict hulks and transportation also featured in its remit. And following the rise of Irish nationalist agitation led by Daniel O'Connell, the station assumed peacekeeping duties as well. However, it seemed the Navy had rather lost interest in Ireland and the naval yard was closed in 1831, but ten years later it was reopened. During the dreadful famine of 1846, the yard was utilised to store and distribute milled corn (and was so used again in 1863 and 1880).

In August 1849, Queen Victoria visited the complex and the town of Cove. In honour of her visit the town was renamed 'Queenstown' and that became the name of the naval command based there. The port became a major departure point for emigrants seeking a new life in America and Canada (by the 1850s a quarter of all survivors of the potato famine born in Ireland had moved abroad), bringing both wealth and new inhabitants to the town. The 1850s saw a spate of new building, including, terraces of gracefully classical villas, a Presbyterian church and the Royal Cork Yacht Club, built in 1854 to the designs of Anthony Salvin, the go-to architect for the minor aristocracy, and reputedly the oldest yacht club in the world.

The second half of the nineteenth century saw a renewed concern that war with France was imminent. In the 1860s a Royal Navy Dockyard was established on Haulbowline Island, for warship repair and construction. To accommodate this new industrial complex the island was doubled in size to a total of around sixty acres. A large basin was constructed with a 408ft dry dock at one end (later extended to 600ft). Coaling facilities were added and a hospital built. At the same time as this work was being progressed, the harbours at Berehaven and Lough Swilly were developed, both deep and sheltered waters and suitable for the protection of the Western Approaches.

But then the likely enemy changed. The growth of German industry and power after unification in 1871, and Germany's rapid development of a blue water navy, meant that it was the Scottish harbours of Invergordon and Scapa Flow and the North Sea ports of eastern England which took precedence. As the navy centralised under Fisher's reforms, and with the need to face Germany, the station reduced in importance; in the 1860s the admiral in charge at Queenstown could call on over twenty gunboats; by 1905 there were only two. In the 1890s an old line-of-battle ship was provided as harbour guardship; by 1905 there was none. And the dockyard on Haulbowline Island stood idle. This state of affairs was still the same in 1914 when war broke out. Queenstown was, in naval terms at least, a quiet backwater.

*　　*　　*

At the commencement of hostilities against Germany, the commanding officer at Queenstown was Vice Admiral Sir Charles Henry Coke. He had been in charge since 1911, with a temporary suspension of duty between April and May 1914. Sixty years old and with a neat pointed beard, he had previously been in command of the Sheerness Gunnery School and had not served at sea since 1907. He was not considered an intellect. Coke had attended the War College Course in 1908 where he had been assessed as 'slow'.[2]

His residence was in Queenstown itself, in the grand Admiralty House, high on the hill above the town. The house dominated the harbour, with only St Colman's Cathedral, a little lower down the hill, competing for architectural bragging rights. In the House's magnificent ballroom, Coke was used to giving lavish dinners, balls and other such entertainments, as befitted a senior officer abroad on His Majesty's service, whilst his staff officers, under Flag Captain Hugh Thomas Hibbert (who had also been appointed in 1911), kept the work away from his desk.

For service in Ireland was not like service at home in England. It was much more akin to a foreign station despite the common language. An elite of British administrators – the lord lieutenant, generals commanding, admirals, lord mayors, bishops – dominated a population which, for the large part, sullenly resented them. The Protestant Ascendancy supressed the Catholic majority who, in the main, wanted independence from Britain and the freedom to direct their own affairs. The toxic legacy of the famines of the previous century and the religious and political differences between Ireland and her Imperial mistress made it a posting not without its share of difficulties.

In London, H H Asquith's Liberal government had only held onto power after the General Election of 1910 by relying on the support of the Irish Nationalist MPs under the leadership of John Redmond, who had led the Irish Parliamentary Party since 1900. Their agenda was an independent Ireland and Redmond used his leverage to persuade Asquith to introduce the Third Home Rule Bill in April 1912, which would grant Ireland national self-government. But Home Rule was vehemently opposed by many Irish Protestants, the Irish Unionist Party and Ulster's Orange Order, who feared domination in an overwhelmingly Catholic state. It was also opposed by many in the House of Commons, the *soi disant* Unionists, who were concerned both by the likely economic impact from an independent Ireland but also resented the breakup of Empire.

Many saw real danger in any change in Ireland's relationship with England. Admiral Lord Beresford, himself a member of Ireland's Protestant Ascendancy, wrote of 'an Ireland ruled by a disloyal faction [which] would easily afford shelter to the warships of the enemy in her ports ... thus lodged a fleet or squadron would command the main trade routes to England and might inflict immense damage on a short time'.[3]

Within the island of Ireland itself civil war threatened. The more industrial and Protestant enclave of Ulster armed itself to fight Home Rule (forming the Ulster Volunteer Force – UVF). British army officers based in Dublin threatened mass resignation if they were called out to put them down (the so called Curragh Mutiny of March 1914).[*] The Irish Nationalists armed too (forming the Irish Volunteers) and in 1914 many formed the breakaway Sinn Fein. Ireland in August 1914 resembled a boiling cauldron of mistrust and mutual antipathy. It was not an easy place from which to go to war.

Fortunately, the Navy did not think that Queenstown needed to. At the outbreak of war, apart from the hulked depot ship *Colleen*, Coke had

---

[*] The threat of 'mutiny' was not confined to the Army. Captain Francis Martin Leake RN, who will be met again later in this narrative, was ordered in to Irish waters in March 1914 at the time of the potential civil war and Curragh misgivings, in the light cruiser *Pathfinder*. He felt bound to state that in the event of hostilities with the Ulster Volunteers, he would be unable to participate in subsequent operations. News of his message quickly leaked to the press, much to the annoyance of Churchill at the Admiralty, who sent him a blistering note of chastisement. It did not, however, affect Leake's determination.

only four antiquated torpedo boats* under his command, with which to defend the harbour from potential attack. Built in 1886, armed with a single torpedo, two 3pdrs and two Maxim guns and commanded by 51-year-old William Ahern, a Queenstown-born retired warrant officer who had been recalled to duty, they would no doubt have fought bravely but would be no match for a determined enemy squadron. But none came. The German High Seas Fleet remained in harbour, hamstrung by the Kaiser's order that it should not yet be risked in battle.

To go with a potentially diffident native population and a lack of modern resources, the position of the Navy in Ireland was further hampered by a divided command structure. Coke ruled at Queenstown, but he was not alone. There were other admirals holding commands at Larne, Kingstown (Dublin), Milford Haven and the Scilly Isles, all of whom had to play a role if the Western Approaches were to be defended. Co-ordination and co-operation was thus made administratively difficult.

All of which suggests that the Navy had either forgotten the importance of the Western Approaches in history or not yet realised the threat to Britain that could be mounted there. They may be in part excused this omission, for few people expected a long war and many thought that the German fleet would come out, be defeated by the Royal Navy, and that would be that!

Deeper thinkers realised that Britain stood at great risk if its incoming trade could be disrupted. This was not new. Walter Raleigh had known it when he wrote 'there are two ways in which England may be afflicted. The one is by invasion ... the other by impeachment of our trades.' Britain in 1914 was just as vulnerable. She imported nearly two-thirds of her food supply and did not keep more than a month to six weeks' worth of food and raw material supply on hand. As Marder noted 'It was therefore of the most vital importance that those necessities continued to reach British shores'.[4] Meat and wheat and other cereals flowed in from the USA, Canada and South America; other foodstuffs came from the sons of Empire in the Caribbean. Australian, New Zealand and South African produce all came through the area. During the five-year period 1909–13, imports had accounted for 78.7 per cent of wheat and flour consumed in Britain and 56.2 per cent of cereals and pulses overall; and imports accounted for 35.7 per cent of meat, 43.4 per cent of butter and 74.2

---

* T050, T052, T055 and T058.

per cent of cheese consumption. On top of these requirements, Britain would suddenly need to receive large amounts of guns and ammunition from manufacturers in the Americas, ores and raw materials from South America and fighting men from Canada, Newfoundland and other far-flung parts of the Empire. And all of this traffic would have to come through the Western Approaches.

The writer Sir Arthur Conan Doyle was amongst those who recognised the problem. He wrote a short story for *Strand* magazine in July 1914 which depicted a Britain brought to her knees by a German severing of her supply chain. Reviewing it, Arnold White (author of *The Navy and its Story*) stated that Sir Arthur had 'placed his finger on the neuralgic nerve of the British Empire – i.e. the precarious arrival of our food supplies'.[5] The great 'Jacky' Fisher knew this too. He noted 'it's not invasion that we have to fear if the navy is beaten, it's starvation'.[6]

As the countdown to war started, Queenstown began to stir. On 3 August, a man was arrested on suspicion of spying. He had sketches of ships and fortifications in his possession. At a meeting of the Queenstown regatta committee the members adopted the resolution 'that in view of the ominous happenings which have intervened since our previous meetings, the proposed regatta and fireworks of the season be abandoned until a happier future'.[7] They further decided to send a copy of the resolution to Admiral Coke.

Back in London, John Redmond, speaking in the House of Commons on 3 August after Sir Edward Grey had made his speech outlining why Britain would go to war with Germany, committed that the government could withdraw all its troops from Ireland and that the Irish and Ulster Volunteers would defend the country from invasion. The speech electrified the Commons and Redmond was applauded. His objective was to nail the Home Rule Bill into the statute book. Back in Ireland, however, he was regarded by many as having betrayed his country.

And old Admiral Sir Percy Scott, an iconoclastic moderniser whilst in the Navy, and a burr under the saddle when out of it, wrote to the *Times*. 'In war the purpose of the enemy is to crush his foe. To arrive at this he will attack where his foe is most vulnerable. Our vulnerable point is our food and oil supply. The submarine has introduced a new weapon of attacking these supplies. Will feelings of humanity restrain our enemy from using it?'[8] Time would tell.

2

War, 1914

The Royal Navy was not sure about the submarine. They were a relatively new and much reviled and distrusted class of ship. Many sailors thought them a cowardly, dishonourable and underhand weapon, suitable only for weaker nations and only then for coastal defence. At the 1899 Hague Convention, Russia had tabled a motion to ban them completely.

Nonetheless, Britain launched its first submarine in 1901 (*Holland 1*). But it was very much on the basis that it was a learning experience, an experiment, and there was great uncertainty as to its usefulness. There was another consideration too; the submarine changed the rules of warfare. It was much cheaper than a battleship or cruiser, required only a small crew and was difficult to detect. And a torpedo, just one, could sink a large warship. The submarine offered newcomers to any naval race an entrée hitherto closed to what Kipling had called 'lesser breeds'.* Therefore the world's largest navy did not want to promote and develop a weapon which could pass an advantage to a weaker power.

It is probable that the first successful use of a torpedo was in 1878 during the Russo-Turkish War when a torpedo was fired from a 'fast boat'. But it is certain that the first battleships to be badly damaged by torpedo attack were the *Retvizan* and the *Tsesarevich*, which were put out of action for weeks, as was the protected cruiser *Pallada*, when Japanese torpedo boats attacked the Russian fleet at Port Arthur on 8 February 1904. Two years later, on 14 December 1906, Germany commissioned her first '*unterseeboote*', or U-boat, *U-1*.

---

* In his 1897 poem *Recessional*.

In Britain, submarines found a champion in 'Jacky' Fisher. He influenced the Admiralty to appoint the brilliant Captain Reginald Bacon to the position of Inspecting Captain of Submarines in 1901 and Bacon prepared the first wholly British design for a submarine, *A1*. Bacon laid the groundwork for the growth of the submarine arm when Fisher gained the First Sea Lord's office. As First Sea Lord between 1904 and 1910, Fisher drove the development of the submarine. He recognised that the advent of the torpedo-armed submarine meant that the narrow waters of the North Sea and English Channel became a very high-risk environment for large and expensive capital ships. Rather than risk battleships in such a situation it was better, he argued, to police those waters through 'flotilla defence', using large numbers of torpedo boats, submarines and torpedo boat destroyers to render the waters uninhabitable for enemy battleships, potential invasion fleets and the like.

But many in the Navy were unconvinced by Fisher's enthusiasm. His successor as head of the Navy, Admiral Sir Arthur Wilson VC, First Sea Lord in 1910–11, thought them a dastardly weapon and once argued that their crews should be hanged as pirates if captured. Whilst in office he did much to hamper the development of the weapon for the Royal Navy, in part because he did not want to set an example which would be followed by smaller, foreign navies. 'Playthings' was the common view of submarines and was held by well-known admirals such as Francis Bridgeman, First Sea Lord in succession to Wilson. He thought them inaccurate and undeveloped weapons. Rear Admiral Horace Hood wrote to a friend 'really these submarines are the devil. It is a great misfortune they were ever invented.'[1]

And the submarine's utility was questioned too. Admiral Lord Charles Beresford (who called submarines 'Fisher's playthings') opined as late of July 1914 that 'the submarine can only operate by day and in clear weather, and it is practically useless in misty weather' to which he added 'a submarine cannot stay any length of time under water, because it must frequently come into harbour to replenish its electric batteries'.[2] And Captain Herbert Richmond, Assistant Director of the Operations Division of the Admiralty War Staff, wrote 'the submarine has the smallest value of any vessel for the direct attack upon Trade. She does not carry a crew which is capable of taking charge of a prize, she cannot remove passengers & other persons if she wishes to sink one. Therefore she will not affect direct action in attack, which must be made by cruisers & other surface travelling vessels.'[3]

Richmond's comment pointed to another problem for submarines to surmount. Both sides in the conflict expected to wage a war on each other's trade. The prevailing law of the sea recognised a code of behaviour under which a commerce raider should operate. Commerce warfare was supposed to be conducted under these 'cruiser' or 'prize rules'. These, originally drafted at the Treaty of Paris in 1856 and subsequently re-ratified at the Hague Convention of 1899 and 1907, stated in essence that passenger ships could not be sunk, crews of merchant ships had to be placed in safety before their ships could be sunk (lifeboats were not considered a place of safety unless close to land) and only warships and merchant ships that were a threat to the attacker could be sunk without warning. Alternatively the vessel could be taken by a prize crew to a port where passengers or crew could be discharged and the cargo inspected.

Fisher saw that submarines would find adherence to prize rules impossible for a simple practical reason: a submarine could not capture a merchant ship, for it would have no spare manpower to deliver the prize to a neutral port; neither could it take survivors or prisoners aboard, for lack of space. There was nothing a submarine could do except sink her capture. He expressed these views in a letter to Winston Churchill, First Sea Lord, written on 24 June 1912. Fisher also noted 'this submarine menace is a terrible one for British Commerce and Great Britain alike for no means can be suggested at present of meeting it except by reprisals.'[4] But nobody believed him. Churchill himself did not think that such a course 'would ever be done by a civilised Power'.[5]

The consequence of these prevalent views was that the submarine arm was undeveloped by the time war broke out. On 5 August there were fifty-four boats ready for action (with three refitting) from the 'A' to 'E' class but no one was exactly clear what to do with them. And, critically, because submarines had not been taken too seriously, neither had anyone thought too deeply of how to defend against them. Anti-submarine measures and tactics were primitive and undeveloped. As retired Admiral Percy Scott noted '[at the outbreak of war] we had ... no anti-submarine precautions ... our torpedoes were so badly fitted that in the early days of the war they went under the Germans ships instead of hitting them'.[6]

Germany had twenty-one U-boats in commission and available at the outbreak of war. And she knew how to use them.

Initial dispositions

The Royal Navy made its dispositions around the British coast at the outbreak of war. The Grand Fleet headed up the east coast of Britain to its bases at Rosyth and Scapa Flow. The 5th, 6th, 7th and 8th Battle Squadrons (consisting of pre-dreadnoughts) went to Sheerness to defend the crossing of the British Expeditionary Force to France against German surface attack, an attack that never came. The 6th Destroyer Flotilla went to Dover to close the Channel to enemy commerce. At Harwich, the Harwich Force of destroyers and light cruisers gathered to patrol the North Sea. The 7th Cruiser Squadron began its patrolling of the 'Broad Fourteens' off the Dutch coast. The 12th Cruiser Squadron (Western Channel Patrol) of four old cruisers (supported by a French squadron of eight cruisers and one light cruiser) went to close the St George's Channel. The northern gateway, around Orkney, Shetland, Norway and Iceland, was patrolled by the 10th Cruiser Squadron. And the 11th Cruiser Squadron, also known as the West of Ireland Coast Patrol or Cruiser Force E, and comprising the elderly *Juno* (Flag), *Doris, Isis, Minerva, Venus* (and later *Sutlej*) all under Rear Admiral Robert Stewart Phipps Hornby, was speedily despatched to Queenstown as reinforcements. They were instructed by the Admiralty to patrol the approaches west of Fastnet (and on the 5th captured two small German sailing vessels there) but were soon withdrawn to more distant duties in the English Channel. On 13 August, for example, they escorted the Vth Division from Dublin, Queenstown and Belfast to Le Havre, patrolling with the Armed Merchant Cruiser (AMC) *Caronia* between Queenstown and the Scillies to guard against minelaying and incursion; and on subsequent occasions they made forays into the Atlantic to escort large passenger vessels. They would not in any case have been of much use against a determined enemy. Laid down between 1893 and 1895, they were protected (rather than armoured) cruisers carrying guns no bigger than 6in and were slow by modern standards, with a design speed of around 19 knots which they rarely reached after some seventeen years of service. However, they were stationed around Queenstown until mid-1915, after which they were sent to the Persian Gulf.

The Germans too were making their opening plays. Korvettenkapitän Hermann Bauer was in overall command of the U-boats based with the High Sea Fleet, as *Führer der Unterseeboote* (FdU). Two days after the declaration of war he sent ten U-boats into the North Sea to find British warships and sink them. They proceeded in line abreast, 350 miles up the middle of the waters, and found nothing. They had expected the sea to be alive with warships seeking to impose a close blockade, but only on the 8th did *U-15* sight three battleships which, although she fired a torpedo at them, disappeared unharmed. That same day she was surprised on the surface by HMS *Birmingham*, rammed and sunk.

Another of the U-boats, *U-13*, was lost without trace, two developed engine trouble and returned to base and not a single enemy ship was sunk. It was a poor start. But they were soon up and running. The light cruiser *Pathfinder* was sunk by *U-21* on 5 September, with the loss of 259 of her crew. On the 22nd three old British cruisers, the *Aboukir*, *Hogue* and *Cressy*, were all sunk in the space of minutes by *U-9*. The death toll was 1,460 men and boys.

On 20 October the 866-ton steamer SS *Glitra*, proceeding off the coast of Norway, became the first British-flagged merchant vessel ever to be sunk by a submarine. The German commander, Kapitänleutnant Feldkirchner in *U-17*, conducted the affair under cruiser warfare rules. Operating on the surface, he hailed the ship and ordered her to heave-to, sending over a boarding party. The *Glitra*'s crew were allowed ten minutes to take to their boats and, after 'giving an exhibition of hatred for the British flag', the little ship's seacocks were opened and she sank without loss of life. Feldkirchner even towed the lifeboats towards the Norwegian coast. It was all very correct – and slow, laborious and dangerous to the submarine. All was quiet at Queenstown however. The dockyard was actually less busy than in peacetime. But the war was about to come to Ireland.

The Germans had made immediate use of mines, laying fields in the Channel, the North Sea and, on 23 October, off the coast of Ireland. SS *Berlin*, a 17,324grt passenger liner converted for use as a minelayer, dropped mines close to, and north of, Tory Island (nine miles off the north-west coast of County Donegal). Three days later, SS *Manchester Commerce*, outward bound for Quebec City, hit one of the Tory Island mines. She sank immediately, taking her master and thirteen of the crew with her and achieved a certain fame in becoming the first merchant ship of the war to be sunk by a mine.

Two days later the same minefield accounted for *Audacious*, a new battleship (launched in 1912) in the 2nd Battle Squadron. The second-to-last man to leave the sinking ship was Vice Admiral Lewis Bayly, commanding the 1st Battle Squadron at Scapa Flow, who had gone out to see if he could assist in the salvage operation. As for *Berlin*, it was to be her only mission. Damaged in a storm whilst trying to return to Germany, she sought shelter in Trondheim and was interned by the Norwegians.

And the war arrived in Queenstown on 31 October. The ex-Bibby Lines ship *Oxfordshire*, now a hospital ship, sailed into harbour with 700 wounded officers and men from the Western Front. She was met at the quayside by Coke and Hibbert, with local dignitaries, and trains then carried the casualties to hospitals in Dublin, Cork, Waterford, Limerick and other parts of Ireland.

Meanwhile, the minefield laid by the *Berlin* proved hard to locate and harder still to sweep. It was eventually found to consist of 200 mines running north-east to south-west. Requisitioned trawlers and paddle-steamers were pressed into service as minesweepers (the Royal Navy had only ten minesweepers in service at the start of the war). By the end of April 1915 they had swept only forty-five mines. It took until July to finish the job. In the meantime, it continued to claim victims. On 13 January 1915 HMS *Viknor*, an AMC with the 10th Cruiser Squadron, previously the *Viking* and originally RMS *Atrato,* was on passage for Liverpool for leave and refit. She was a beautiful, almost luxury yacht-like liner in peacetime, built for the Royal Mail Steam Packet Company, and she became the next victim of the Tory Island minefield. Hitting a mine was fatal for ships like these, an eventuality unprepared for by their builders. She sank like a stone, taking all twenty-two officers and 273 crew with her. There was not even time to get off a radio message. However, she was carrying a very unusual cargo. Two days earlier, whilst on patrol, she had intercepted the *Bergensfjord*, a regular war contraband runner between the USA and Norway, north east of the Faroes where that vessel had been trying to sneak through to the north in the dark. Amongst the large number of passengers on board was one Rosato Spero, travelling on a Mexican passport. Spero was taken unawares, in the act of burning his private papers. He was, in fact, none other than Count Botho von Wedel, Privy Councillor to the Kaiser and chief of the German spy bureau. And now, thanks to information provided from British intelligence agents in the USA, he was a prisoner. *Viknor* was ordered to take on board the Count and seven German stowaways, escort the prize to Kirkwall and then to convey the prisoners to Liverpool for interrogation. So the German mine not only killed British sailors, it also took with it a vital part of the German espionage effort.[*]

ss *Dacia* and maritime law

On 3 November 1914, Britain had announced, in response to the discovery of a German ship laying mines off the English coast, that the whole of the North Sea was to be designated a military area, which would be mined and into which neutral ships proceeded 'at their own peril'. Similar measures in regard to the English Channel insured that neutral ships would be forced to put into British ports for sailing instructions or to take on British pilots. During this time they could easily be searched for contraband (war goods intended for the enemy) as well. This represented a distant blockade of Germany, intended to prevent a range of goods, from mineral ores to foodstuffs, from reaching German hands.[**] German-flagged ships were captured and taken into ports and neutral ships were intercepted and searched as they attempted to enter the North Sea from either its northern or southern openings. Ships registered to Germany discovered the oceans barred to them and the vessels themselves confined in neutral ports. And German shipowners found that they owned expensive floating dormitories, of which no use could be made.

This not only inflamed German opinion but that of neutrals too. America was extremely vocal against such British presumption, not least because it put at risk the huge earnings made by a vociferous lobby group, the cotton famers of the southern states. The American government argued that such interception and detention of neutral ships with cargo consigned to Germany, or that might be intended for her through other neutral countries, was illegal. Likewise if German vessels were reflagged as neutrals, America and other countries argued that the British had no right to intercept them, irrespective of the destination of the cargo.

[*] 'Spero' means 'I hope' in Latin; 'Rosato' means 'Rosy'; so 'Rosy Hope'. The author wonders if von Wedel was expressing his optimism or pessimism.

[**] See S R Dunn, *Blockade: Cruiser Warfare and the Starvation of Germany in World War One* (Barnsley: Seaforth Publishing, 2016).

On 25 January 1915, both Admiral Coke at Queenstown and the Admiralty found themselves faced with a difficult problem which directly related to these arguments. Where on earth was ss *Dacia*? She was a former Hamburg-America Line vessel, and her owners had been trying to sell off their expensive, idle assets at discount prices rather than risk sailing them into the blockade. Germany had begun the war with the world's second-largest merchant fleet, but most of those ships were now condemned to sit at anchor in neutral ports. An opportunist by the name of Edward N Breitung Jr had purchased *Dacia* for the bargain price of £33,000, loaded her with cotton insured for £10,000, and consigned her, flagged as an American ship, to Rotterdam for onward shipment to Bremen in Germany. The worry for the Allies was that Breitung's action set a precedent for Germany to regain its maritime trade through the sale of German-flagged interned vessels to private parties, who could then re-flag them as neutrals and then claim exemption from blockade under International Law. It was thus essential that she be intercepted and the claims of the law of the sea tested in a Prize Court – an Allied one, of course.

The Admiralty telegraphed Admiral Coke, Captain George B Hutton, Senior Naval Officer (SNO) Cruiser Force E (11th Cruiser Squadron), off Queenstown and Admiral Rosslyn Wemyss, Cruiser Force G (12th Cruiser Squadron) in the St George's/Bristol Channel. 'Have you any knowledge of *Dacia*'s course or position?'[7] Coke replied the following day; he passed on information received from the master of the British merchant vessel *Bolivia* giving a description of the *Dacia* and adding 'several Germans abroad having taken out naturalisation papers'.[8] But he didn't know where she was. The *Times* newspaper was worried. 'If she [*Dacia*] sails, she must be stopped, and the novel point of international law which she threatens to raise must be brought to a definite decision' a leader writer thundered.[9] And in faraway Melbourne, Australia, the *Argus* – commenting on the principle at stake – noted 'the opinion is held generally that since the German Government are confiscating wheat supplies they may be regarded now as the sole importers of wheat, in which case the Allies will be justified in seizing every ship carrying food for Germany, under whatever flag'.[10]

On 27 February the *Dacia* was found nearing the St George's Channel where three British and six French cruisers were on patrol. Given the unease between the USA and Britain over the blockade, it was decided that she should be intercepted by a French warship operating with Cruiser Force G, to show Allied solidarity, and taken before a French Prize Court. Unsurprisingly, the French court did not recognise the transfer of belligerent vessels in wartime (on the legal basis that such transfers had been forbidden under the Treaty of London in 1909) and condemned her as a prize; she was to end her days under the French flag, blown up by *U-38* on 6 November 1915.

The U-boats reach Ireland

Meanwhile, armed yachts and (especially) trawlers were assigned to Larne and Queenstown with orders to seek submarines. With a maximum speed of only 9 knots and operating in the rough seas off the Antrim coast, the trawlers found it hard going. Quite how they were expected to chase a surfaced submarine was not explained. Armed trawlers were also sent to Kingstown to patrol the Irish Sea and Milford Haven was similarly reinforced.*

The U-boats began to roam further afield. They penetrated the English Channel, despite the establishment of a net barrier; in January 1915, *U-21* traversed the Dover straits at night, sailed the full length of the English Channel and turned up in the Irish Sea. Off the Mersey she sank three British ships (two steamers and a collier) and then returned by the same route to her Wilhelmshaven base.

The potential advent of submarines around the Irish coast clearly confused and dismayed merchant shipowners and naval officers alike. At Queenstown, advice was given that vessels should only put out to sea at their own peril. On 1 February, the Admiralty sent Coke an admonitory letter. 'It is most undesirable that vessels should be informed that they are only allowed to proceed to sea at their own risk. If vessels entered in the War Risk Clubs put to sea they will remain covered for war risks ... Such an order can only have the effect of frightening owners and leading to serious congestion at ports.'[11] Keeping trade moving was paramount to the British economy and war effort; ships and cargoes sitting in ports afraid to leave because of the financial risk (never mind the human

---

* Ireland's fisher folk had cause to thank the Admiralty for their impressment of steam trawlers and drifters. Almost three-quarters of the British fishing fleet was eventually to be on naval duty, and all of the Irish steam fishing fleet too. But the majority of Ireland's fishing craft were sailing ships and the war years would prove a bonanza for the Irish fishing industry, which benefitted from the sharp reduction in the available British vessels.

one) would swiftly cause financial chaos. It was for this very reason that the day Britain declared war on Germany, Chancellor of the Exchequer David Lloyd George announced to Parliament the immediate institution of a War Risks Insurance Scheme. The scheme, originally conceived as a means to ensure security of the food supply chain, allowed the government to control the supply of marine insurance during the first two years of the international confrontation.*

In response to the British declaration of a military area in the North Sea and its blockade of German trade, on 4 February Germany announced that from the 18th of that month all of the waters around Britain and Ireland would be deemed a war zone. Any merchant ship, neutral or otherwise, which was found in the area would be sunk; and they would not necessarily apply prize rules. The rate of loss of merchant ships increased and a sudden burst of sinkings struck the Irish Sea; ships were sunk off the Isle of Man, Point Lynas in Anglesey, the Liverpool Bar, Ilfracombe and County Down. But the real shock to Ireland came on 14 March 1915, when ss *Atlanta* was attacked by a U-boat off the coast of County Mayo. Rather than waste an expensive torpedo, the U-boat crew set her on fire. The *Connaught Tribune* noted that:

> This is the furthest distance yet recorded of a submarine's voyage from her base, and this is also the first time an engagement with a German submarine has taken place off the West Coast of Ireland, so far as is known.
>
> After the crew had been put off in boats, the Germans set fire to the ship, and as the sailors were rowing for Inishturk, they saw the submarine making off at full speed in a south-westerly direction. In the afternoon, the crew landed at Inishturk, where they were most hospitably entertained by the islanders, who provided them with bread and bacon and eggs.[12]

And on 28 March *U-28* began to operate off the south-east Irish coast and sank the 5,000-ton Elder Dempster Lines passenger and cargo ship RMS *Falaba* near to the Coningbeg lighthouse (off the coast of

---

* The scheme operated in two ways. For the ships themselves, the government provided an automatic 80 per cent reinsurance for any British ship insured by a British underwriter grouped under the Liverpool and London War Risk Insurance Association or the North of England Association, accounting for about 80 per cent of British overseas tonnage. With regard to cargo, a State Insurance Office was established which offered a flat rate for all merchant voyages on British ships.

Wexford). The U-boat surfaced and ordered the British ship to stop. Initially, the U-boat commander allowed for evacuation before sinking the ship, but when *Falaba* started sending wireless messages and fired distress rockets for help, he cut short the time to evacuate the ship and fired a single torpedo which sank her. The Germans claimed that they allowed twenty-three minutes for evacuation; the British counter-claimed that they were only given seven. Over 100 people died, including an American citizen, Leon Thresher, a mining engineer headed towards the Gold Coast in Africa. The submarine sailed amongst the survivors, jeering them without offering any assistance to those dying in the water. The American press denounced the sinking as a massacre and an act of piracy, but the US government took no action.

The war had come to Ireland and to Queenstown. U-boats could now travel into the Atlantic and operate in the Western Approaches. Queenstown was now at the centre of a new and immense challenge. The crucial question was how to stop U-boats destroying Britain's supply chain in the thirty-two million square miles of the Atlantic Ocean?

Ireland's call
How did the people of Ireland respond to the outbreak of hostilities? Following Redmond's statement of support in the House of Commons, on 3 September the Unionist leader Edward Carson, speaking at the Ulster Unionists Council in Belfast, urged the 35,000 Ulster Volunteers to enlist in the new Ulster Division (later the 36th Ulster Division).* 'England's difficulty is not Ulster's opportunity' he told the delegates, 'however we are treated and however others act, let us act rightly'.[13] Redmond too was forced to make a similar appeal to his party, as he had gained his wish and the Home Rule Bill had passed into law on 17 September (but was immediately suspended for the duration of the war). On the 20th he called upon the Irish Volunteers to enlist in the existing Irish regiments of the British Army.** Redmond himself truly believed that Imperial Germany's hegemony and military expansion threatened the

---

* The 36th Division took heavy casualties during the first two days of the Battle of the Somme, some 5,500 men out of a total of 16,000 with approximately 2,000 killed. The Somme thus became part of the Unionist movement's mythscape.

** Many Nationalists eventually became part of the 16th (Irish) Division which also suffered heavy losses at the Somme in the September.

freedom of Europe and that it was Ireland's duty to fight against it, having achieved future self-government. The Catholic Church too came out in favour of the war, under the slogan 'Save Catholic Belgium'.

The Irish Volunteers, numbering some 180,000 members, were divided by Redmond's support for the British war effort. A majority followed him, forming the National Volunteers, of whom around 25,000 went on to serve in Irish regiments during the war. However, a rump of 10,000 members, led by Eoin MacNeill (Chief of Staff of the Irish Volunteers) declared they would keep their organisation together, and in Ireland, until Home Rule was passed. A further 100,000 or more men, who were not members of the National Volunteers, enlisted from all over Ireland.

However, the more radical fringe of Irish nationalism, the remaining Irish Volunteers who had followed MacNeill, and the secretive Irish Republican Brotherhood, rejected Irish participation in the war on Britain's side. They actively opposed enlistment and, in secret, elements of them prepared an armed insurrection against British rule in Ireland. Their slogan made their position very clear: 'England's Extremity is Ireland's Opportunity'.[14] Here was stored up much trouble for the Queenstown command.

Loyalties were strained as a result. On 6 May, the armed yacht *Zarefah* received instructions to investigate the sighting of two or three U-boats in the Shannon estuary; on arriving there, none could be found. Nor did the subsequent police report make any mention of them leaving.[15] And for those members of the British armed forces based in Ireland, it did not feel as if they were either welcome or wanted. As one Irish historian has noted, 'those serving in the Royal Navy in Irish waters were no exception to this rule. Many felt that they were serving in a hostile country, where none of the native population could be trusted'.[16] The sight of the Irish Volunteers openly parading with arms in the streets of Cork or Dublin, and the political stance of Sinn Fein, merely served to reinforce such views.

But such hostility was not universal. Lieutenant Commander Alan George Despard Twigg, serving on board HMS *Doris* in Cruiser Force E, noted in his diary that 'one lady there [in Queenstown] has given us the offer of three beds and later ... five beds to any officer ... who wants a good meal and a night in bed'. Duty, however, supervened. 'I am afraid that it can't be managed' he added.[17]

3

'It was just murder', January – July 1915

One of the problems for the Royal Navy in trying to intercept German submarines in Irish waters was that of a divided command structure in the seas around the coast. Apart from Coke, the Larne, or North Channel area, was commanded by 67-year-old Admiral 'Billy' Barlow, a retired officer who had re-joined the navy as a commander Royal Naval Reserve (RNR); the Kingstown, or Irish Channel area, belonged to Rear Admiral Evelyn Robert Le Marchant, also reinstated from the retired list; and the Milford area, which included the St George's and Bristol Channels, was the responsibility of Vice Admiral Charles Holcombe Dare, another re-activated officer. At the same time, Liverpool was constituted as a separate area and entrusted to Rear Admiral Harry Hampson Stileman, yet another officer brought back from retirement. There was additionally an independent squadron of six armed yachts at Belfast for service wherever it was needed.

Moreover, the Royal Navy of the First World War had an unreasoning conviction in the benefit of anti-submarine nets. Because salmon could be caught in nets stretched across river estuaries it was believed that U-boats (just a bigger fish after all) could be caught in bigger nets stretched across larger waters. In early 1915 plans were laid for net barrages across the Dover Straits, the Otranto Strait and the Irish Sea. A rectangular area thirty miles long and twelve miles wide, which extended from the Mull of Kintyre to Rathlin Island, was completely closed to navigation by the laying of nets from 23 February. A small passage three miles wide was left between Rathlin and the coast of mainland Ireland through which all traffic, neutral and Allied, had to pass, and then only between the hours of sunrise and sunset, and where it could be stopped and searched as necessary. Meanwhile, another squadron of drifters and trawlers based on Milford Haven maintained a watch and dragged their nets in places where submarines were likely to congregate in the St George's Channel, and an inner defence was provided by another auxiliary flotilla which maintain a line of patrols between Kingstown and Holyhead.

On 2 April, the Rathlin Island barrier became the responsibility of Rear Admiral the Honourable Robert Francis Boyle who took command at Larne (replacing Barlow) with (eventually) 130 drifters, managing a continuous net barrage across the North Channel, closing the northern entrance to the Irish Sea. They towed their nets back and forth, 1,500 men on board. In the deep waters, the aim was not so much to entangle the U-boats but to force them to dive and stay submerged, thus exhausting their batteries. Boyle deployed nine sections of drifters with at first nine, and afterwards twelve, drifters in each together with an armed yacht squadron from Belfast and three armed trawlers, two destroyers and the armed boarding steamer *Tara*. But it was a complete failure, the success rate of the barrier against submarines being precisely nil.

If the nets could be said to be a less-than-successful passive device against submarines, the active tactic of constant patrolling was equally suspect. As one officer put it, 'it was extremely rare for patrols to be in the right place at the right time in the right force to repel an attack on a merchant ship, still less to find the enemy before he attacked'.[1] This belief in anti-submarine patrolling was slow to die. Even in 1916, an officer as clever as Herbert Richmond, former Assistant Director of Operations on the Admiralty's Naval Staff, could write that 'the way to protect trade is to cruise constantly in certain areas through which trade passes'.[2]

As a result armed trawlers and yachts cruised around the coast of Ireland looking for U-boats with nothing more useful than the Mark One eyeball. Unsurprisingly, the Germans proved hard to find. U-boats hunted for their prey on the surface, where their superior speed would allow them to overtake most merchant ships; and when submerged, they simply disappeared. Their preferred mode of attack was to use gunfire to sink the captured vessel or to board the victim and set charges to destroy it. Torpedoes were limited in number (generally six), impossible to replace until back at base and expensive. There were saved for more difficult targets and standing orders required U-boat commanders to save two for the voyage home.

Occasionally the active patrols got lucky. On 24 May the trawler *Norbreck* came upon a stationary barque under whose quarter lay a U-boat. *Norbreck* opened fire, the submarine replied and then, using its much superior speed, made off. A week later, another trawler, *Ina Williams*, patrolling off the Fastnet Rock, spotted *U-34* on the surface some three miles away. She made all speed and opened fire but then the gun jammed; by the time it was cleared the U-boat had dived to safety. And on 5 June the same thing happened to her, except the gun didn't jam this time.

There was additionally an imbalance in the relative capabilities of the likely opponents at this time. Trawlers generally carried either a 12pdr or a 6pdr gun and a few rifles. The 12pdr was a 3in calibre weapon, capable of firing fifteen rounds per minute, each round weighing, as the name would suggest, 12lbs and with a maximum range of some 11,000yds; the 6pdr Nordenfelt or Hotchkiss gun of 2.24in calibre fired around twenty-five rounds per minute with a range of some 5,000yds.

U-34, as an example, was a *U-31* class vessel, a type generally armed, apart from torpedoes, with one or two 7.5cm (3.0in) or 10.5cm (4.1in) deck guns; the latter fired a 38lb shell some 14,000yds. Its submerged speed was 9.7 knots which was faster than the trawler could make on the surface; surfaced the U-boat had a design speed of 16.4 knots. This was definitely asymmetrical warfare and this particular submarine lived to sink 119 ships with a total of 257,652 tons. It is perhaps hardly surprising, therefore, that – despite the expenditure of considerable resources and manpower – by the end of April 1915, no U-boat had been sunk around the coast of Ireland or in the Western Approaches.

The loss of *Lusitania*

By May 1915, the 11th Cruiser Squadron was again conducting patrols in the Western Approaches, trying to intercept ships carrying war contraband, and now under the command of Rear Admiral the Honourable Horace Hood with his flag in *Juno*. Anti-submarine efforts on the south coast of Ireland were restricted to ten armed trawlers and two small motor yachts. Hood was not sanguine about the chances for his ships as submarine activity increased. Indeed he wrote to a friend 'I don't see how *Juno* can escape [being torpedoed]'.[3] Hood was nearer the truth than he knew. Early on the morning of 7 May his old cruiser had been sighted by *U-20* which had manoeuvred for a firing position but failed to achieve one; now Hood was ordered to return to Queenstown by the Admiralty which had issued a submarine warning for the area.

This was patently true for on the 5th the 132-ton schooner *Earl of Latham* and been sunk south of Kinsale Head, the *Cayo Romano* attacked off Queenstown and two 6,000-ton cargo ships were sunk off the Waterford coast a day later, south of the Coningbeg light vessel. One of the latter was SS *Centurion*, 5,945grt, torpedoed fifteen miles south of the light without warning at 1300hrs on Thursday 6 May, whilst on passage from Liverpool to Durban. All forty-four of her crew took to their boats and, after ten hours at sea, landed on the Barrels Light Vessel from whence they were taken by *Fleswick* of Liverpool to Rosslare and safety. All had been the victims of *U-20*. And on the morning of the 7th, the motor yacht *Seagull* had observed a submarine near the Fastnet; having no radio, she had to put into Baltimore harbour to report the sighting. Conditions were not good. *Juno*, at sea, recorded 'thick fog' in her log at 0045hrs, then 'fog clearing' at 0835hrs. She increased revolutions and zigzagged continuously on her way back to Queenstown (she eventually moored to No 2 buoy at 1430hrs).

And now, in the early afternoon of 7 May, the Cunard liner *Lusitania*, 30,396 tons, on passage from New York to Liverpool with 1,959 passengers and crew aboard, came speeding into this danger zone. She had left the USA on 1 May, the warnings placed in newspapers by the German embassy of the possibility of attack on British ships by U-boats ringing in her passengers' ears. Since her departure, the six days following had resulted in twenty-six ships sunk in the war zone. The day previously the Admiralty had sent a message to the *Lusitania*'s master, William Turner, that there were submarines active in the area (three had indeed been sent to the Irish Sea and Bristol Channel). Turner was a careful man. He had the lifeboats swung out, the watertight doors closed and the number of lookouts doubled.

Sometime before 1100hrs, the liner had run into fog and Turner slowed his speed to 15 knots. He also wanted to take a sight using the lighthouse on the tip of the Old Head of Kinsale; and he may have hoped to delay his arrival at Liverpool so as to cross the bar at high tide. *U-20* had three torpedoes left. She sighted the big ship at 1320hrs, when the U-boat was on the surface; given that standing orders required her to keep two torpedoes for her return journey, she could only fire once. Kapitänleutnant Walther Schwieger ordered a dive and began to manoeuvre for a firing position. A chance starboard turn by the *Lusitania* helped him and at 1410hrs he fired a single G-type torpedo at a range of only 700m; he couldn't really miss.

On the bridge, Captain Turner suddenly saw the torpedo. 'I immediately tried to change course but was unable to manoeuvre out of the way of it' he told the *World* newspaper.[4] The explosion in her side mortally wounded the big Cunarder. Her radio operators sent out an SOS ('Come at once. Big list. Ten miles south of Old Kinsale Head')[5] and the crew endeavoured to launch the lifeboats, but the conditions of the sinking made doing so extremely difficult, and in some cases impossible, due to the ship's severe list. All of the lifeboats on the port side could not be launched and those on the starboard side were now very high above the water because of the 30° list the ship had quickly taken. In all, only six out of twenty-two regular lifeboats, together with a number of her twenty-six collapsible rafts, were launched successfully. Eighteen minutes after the torpedo struck, she sank.

The sea was full of terrified men, women and children, floundering around. Some sailors tried to help them. Able Seaman Leslie Morton, one of the lookouts, and another seaman, Joseph Parry, found themselves in the water next to a collapsible raft and manged to tear off its canvas cover. There were people thrashing in the water on all sides of it and the two seamen tried to pull some of them to safety. In this way they saved eighty souls. Later Morton would save twenty more from an overturned lifeboat.[*]

At 1513hrs the Admiralty received news of the calamity, via Admiral Coke. '*Lusitania* torpedoed eight or ten miles South East Galley Head. Tugs *Warrior* and *Stormcock* and the Examination Steamer and all available small craft despatched' he telegraphed.[6] 'I have also sent *Juno*. Sea calm, weather very fine.' His despatch of an old cruiser with 450 valuable men on board was too much for the Admiralty. At 1615hrs they ordered 'Urgent. Recall *Juno*'[7] to which chastened Coke replied 'have despatched every craft available … I recalled *Juno* before she got outside [the harbour].' In fact, when the SOS was picked up at Queenstown, Horace Hood had just reached

---

[*] For his heroism, Leslie Morton was awarded the Silver Board of Trade Medal for Gallantry in Saving Lives at Sea.

port. He immediately put to sea again in advance of Coke's order to assist the rescue attempt. Just south of Roche's Point at the mouth of the harbour and only an hour from the site of the sinking, he received the recall and returned to base. 'I felt it was my duty to go' he wrote later.[8]

The nearest vessel to the stricken liner was the Isle of Man fishing boat *Wanderer*, out hunting mackerel. They saw the ship go down and, making for the area, pulled 160 survivors out of the water. The Queenstown lifeboat saw distress rockets and launched: its crew rowed themselves to exhaustion trying to get there quickly. An armed trawler, *Indian Empire*, arrived and was able to pick up 200 survivors from the water. Three torpedo boats were sent from Queenstown. William Ahern in *TB 052* was amongst the first to arrive and picked up a number of survivors, three of whom died during the return to shore.[9] Another trawler rescued Captain Turner; he had been four hours in the water. More ships arrived. But it all took too long. Exposure kills quickly and silently. Bodies floated around the rescue flotilla like so much flotsam. Seagulls feasted on the dead. The Ellerman's Line passenger liner *City of Exeter* informed the Admiralty that she was proceeding to assist and would arrive at 1900hrs. The Admiralty merely told Coke to tell her to 'keep out of submarine area'.[10]

And the Navy contrived to make things worse, not better. The Arklow-based trawler *Daniel O'Connell* and the drifter *Elizabeth* had each picked up survivors and were headed into Kinsale, thirty minutes away, when they were intercepted by Commander Shee in the tug *Stormcock*. He demanded that the survivors be transferred to his vessel and taken to Queenstown, a much longer voyage in waters that many of the survivors feared were U-boat infested. There was an argument and tempers flared but Shee eventually got his way and the Navy subjected the bedraggled ex-passengers to a long and probably unnecessary trip. Skipper Edward White of the *Elizabeth* was particularly incensed by Shee. His motor drifter had towed lifeboats with eighty passengers on board them for twelve miles and had reached the mouth of Kinsale harbour when intercepted by the Commander.

The Foreign Office were more concerned with the 'Captain's secret books'. On the 8th they telegraphed Coke asking if he had been saved and where they were. And on the 10th Coke was instructed by the Admiralty that no statement should be made at the inquest regarding the instructions given to merchant vessels in avoiding enemy submarines, for fear that they would be of help to the enemy.

The American Consul in Queenstown was one Wesley Frost, originally from Ohio. He became dissatisfied with the efforts being made to recover the bodies from the sinking and told his Lords and Masters so. On 11 May he sent to the Secretary of State in Washington 'Matter of search for *Lusitania* corpses on scene disaster not well managed ... if drastic enquiries advisable will cable promptly'.[11] That same day Coke received an unwelcome missive from the Admiralty. 'United States Embassy disquieted by report that search for bodies of persons lost in *Lusitania* is being slackly managed. Alleged that patrol boats passing scene of disaster are instructed to look out for corpses but that no special vessels detailed for that express purpose.' The last thing the British government needed at this time was a further reason for relations with the USA to be worsened. Thus Coke was further ordered; 'Very desirable that all efforts be made to recover bodies and special unarmed vessels should be engaged for this purpose so long as may be necessary. Report immediately action taken and what more can be arranged on these lines, conferring with American Consul.'[12]

Stung, Coke replied by return. At 1623hr he telegraphed 'Dockyard tug will be sent as soon as possible as there is no privately owned vessel in port. Clyde shipping tug however due, she will be taken up, sent to assist, so two vessels will be used for this duty as long as necessary.'[13]

When the final reckoning was made, 1,198 men women and children had died in the sinking. Civilians, about their everyday business in the main. Ninety-four of the victims were children, thirty-five out of thirty-nine babies on board drowned. Also among the dead were 128 American citizens. They included writer, philosopher and publisher Elbert Hubbard, theatrical producer Charles Frohman, multi-millionaire businessman Alfred Vanderbilt, and the president of Newport News Shipbuilding, Albert L Hopkins. Hubbard and his wife had deliberately returned to their cabin so they might die together. Frohman (who had a bad leg and could not have jumped into a lifeboat) and Vanderbilt tied lifejackets to Moses baskets containing infants who had been asleep in the nursery when the torpedo struck, before linking arms on deck and awaiting the end. Hopkins was travelling to Britain to negotiate contracts for the manufacture of armour plate for battleships. Only 289 bodies were recovered. They were buried in twenty private graves, and three mass ones, in the Old Church Cemetery at Queenstown.

The tragedy caused an outrage; the press in both America and Britain brought down curses on German heads and there were anti-German riots in both countries. A typical headline appeared in the *Daily Mail*; 'British and American Babies Murdered by the Kaiser' it thundered.[14] The Cork coroner J J Horgan suggested that the coroner's jury return a verdict of 'wilful and wholesale murder' against the officers of the submarine.[15] The Germans defended themselves, claiming that the *Lusitania* had been carrying contraband of war and also asserting that, because she was classed as an auxiliary cruiser, Germany had a right to destroy her regardless of any passengers aboard. They added that the warnings given by the German Embassy before her sailing, plus the February note declaring the existence of war zones around Britain in which all ships were at risk of sinking, relieved Germany of any responsibility for the deaths.

The British felt that the Americans had to declare war on Germany. However, President Woodrow Wilson had other ideas and, perhaps more importantly, an election to win the following year. But the heat generated by the subsequent debate fuelled the first beginnings of America's eventual entry into the war. Most people thought the same as Rear Admiral Hood who wrote to a friend in America 'It was just murder'[16] Captain Turner certainly agreed. 'It was cold blooded murder' he told the American press.[17]

Change at the top

In a prime example of shutting the stable door after the horse has bolted, the Admiralty sent eight Scottish steam drifters to Coke's command. They were tasked with laying nets across likely headlands to entrap submarines in transit. Armed trawlers continued their anti-U-boat patrols; but they were far too slow to catch a submarine on the surface and Coke's repeated requests for speedy destroyers to support his efforts fell on deaf ears.

And the sinkings continued. On 21 May, the old sailing vessel *Glenholm* was torpedoed sixteen miles off Fastnet rock. Sailing ships were easy prey for submarines; wind power was variable and capricious. She had been stuck in the vicinity of Mizen Head for seven days unable to make progress and when she finally got moving with all sails set, the cloud of canvas was a beacon for a U-boat.

Then on 25 May, ss *Nebraskan*, American-owned and in ballast from Liverpool to New York, was south of Ireland when an unseen submarine torpedoed her, bursting open No 1 hold and throwing the derrick 30ft in the air. But she didn't sink and there was no follow-up attack. The armed yacht *Seadaun* took in her SOS and another armed yacht, *Aster*, was despatched from Berehaven. It took them six hours in the heaving Atlantic swell to find the damaged ship and the three ships were then able to inch their way back to safety and the port of Liverpool. More sinkings followed during May and June, amongst them four barques and two schooners, sailing ships all, and various steamers. In total, the Allies lost 120,000 tons of shipping in May, a threefold increase in the rate of destruction compared to the period prior to the German declaration of its 'war zone'.

In fact the war was not being won anywhere. The fighting in France had become a stalemate of trench warfare. Churchill's grand scheme of Gallipoli had turned into farce and failure. And Fisher's disgust at Churchill's meddling in what he regarded as his affairs brought both men down. Churchill's arrogation to himself of the powers which had traditionally belonged to the First Sea Lord had become a matter of great contention between the Sea Lords, Churchill and for Fisher himself. The Dardanelles affair brought things to a head. Churchill increasingly issued orders for ships and equipment to be sent without Fisher's prior consent. At 0500hrs in the morning on 15 May, Fisher received four minutes from Churchill calling for yet more reinforcements for the Dardanelles. It was the straw that broke the camel's back. Before he ate his breakfast, Fisher sent his resignation to both Churchill and Prime Minister Asquith.

Fisher's resignation set in train a run of events that Churchill and Asquith found themselves powerless to resist. His departure, coupled with the breaking news concerning a shortage of high-explosive shell, threatened to topple the Liberal government.

To stave off Opposition attacks on his government and the progress of the war, Asquith was forced to agree to a coalition. And the Conservative Party's price for coalition included the sacking of Churchill. On the 20th Asquith wrote to Churchill asking him to leave the Admiralty, a departure which Churchill reluctantly agreed to the following day. Admiral Coke wrote to him on the 23rd expressing his regrets; 'Only a few lines to say how very sorry I am that you are leaving the Admiralty ... personally I have to thank you for much kindness ... I wish you every success in the high office which will doubtless be offered you.'[18] It was always good to keep friends in high places.

The coalition government was formed on the 25th, with the ex-prime minister A J Balfour as First Lord of the Admiralty. As his First Sea Lord he had a compromise candidate, Admiral Sir Henry Jackson – a good administrator but lacking much verve. The change in administrations did not change the course of the war, however. Sinkings continued; another 130,000 tons of shipping was lost in June. But sometimes the victims did not go to their end without a fight.

ss *Anglo-Californian*

Anglo-Californian was owned by the Nitrate Producers Steam Ship Co Ltd (The Anglo Line) and was normally engaged in the South-American nitrate trade. In 1915 she was chartered by the Admiralty to carry 927 horses – for military use – from Montreal to Avonmouth. On American Independence Day, she was some ninety miles SW of Queenstown when, at 0800hrs, she was intercepted by *U-39* whose commander ordered 59-year-old Islington-born Captain Frederick Daniel Parslow to stop. Parslow's ship was unarmed but she was fast and he decided to run for it. By manoeuvring to keep his stern to the enemy, Parslow held the enemy off, despite the U-boat opening fire with her deck gun. Parslow's son, also Frederick, was the vessel's second officer and he steered the ship while his father ordered course changes based on the German's fall of shot. Some shots went home, nonetheless. All the while, the *Anglo-Californian* was transmitting SOS signals. Eventually, after some ninety minutes and tiring of the game, the U-boat hoisted the abandon ship signal and Parslow, conscious of his responsibility to his 130-man crew, decided to obey. At that very point he received a reply to his SOS from the destroyers *Miranda* and *Mentor* (on detached duty at Devonport) asking him to delay abandonment as they were on their way and for him to continue to transmit as a sort of homing beacon. However, when it became apparent to the U-boat that Parslow had no intention of stopping, she opened a withering fire on the bridge and when out of ammunition, closed and fired on anything that moved with rifles. By now, Captain Parslow was dead, literally blown apart by a shell, which removed his head and arm, but his son remained at his post, steering the ship by lying prone on the deck and moved the spokes of the wheel from its bottom. Just in time the destroyer cavalry arrived, drove off the submarine and escorted the limping, but still afloat, transport into Queenstown. Captain Parslow's dismembered body was brought ashore in a gunny bag. Parslow Jr was given a commission as sub-lieutenant in the Royal Naval Reserve and awarded the Distinguished Service Cross. His father was awarded the Victoria Cross, one of the oldest men to receive it, in 1919, the award delayed because of his civilian status; his citation for the medal stated that he had set 'a splendid example to the officers and men of the Merchant Marine'.[19] Thirty horses and thirty men were killed in the attack and the latter, including Captain Parslow, were buried at Queenstown.

Change of command

The new men in charge at the Admiralty surveyed the situation around the coasts of Britain with some concern. The U-boat menace in the Western Approaches was growing all the time and the existing command structure was clearly not delivering results. No U-boat had yet been sunk in the Western Approaches or round the coast of Ireland.

Coke had proved less than effective during *Lusitania* and *Dacia* crisis and was failing to get results in the war against the U-boats. Indeed Jellicoe was to say of him later (and in a different context) 'I am sorry he was not up to the job, but he is of course aging rapidly'.[20] Jellicoe's advice was sought on the situation and in reply he noted that 'it should be the sole business of one officer and staff to watch submarines that are located and to get every available craft to them on their probable course'.[21] Admiral Beatty, commander of the Battlecruiser Fleet, weighed into the debate too. 'The gravity of this submarine menace has now increased to such an extent that new measures and more drastic actions are imperative ... I recommend that all the forces for hunting submarines be under the direction of one man.'[22] Both men stressed that a forceful and energetic officer was needed. And both men recommended Vice Admiral Sir Lewis Bayly. 'He is wasted at Greenwich' wrote Jellicoe.[23]

Bayly was languishing as President of Greenwich College, nursing a grievance and frustrated with his lot in life. In early July he was summoned to the Admiralty to see the new First Lord and First Sea Lord. Balfour, tall, languid and with a habit of lying in his chair with his legs thrust out in front of him, Jackson, neat, organised, efficient; they were a study in contrasts. They put it to Bayly that they were very concerned about the rate of merchant sinkings by U-boats and about the *Lusitania* affair and asked him if he had any suggestions for checking the submarine campaign. Bayly didn't hold back. 'If I am given a light cruiser I will go and do it with my base at Queenstown.'[24] He drew a circle on a map that which circumscribed the area he wanted control of. It stretched from the Sound of Mull to Ushant, covering all of the Western Approaches including the Irish Sea, the coast of Ireland, St George's Channel, the Bristol Channel and the entrance to the English Channel. He also asked for an air force in Ireland and Wales and control of Liverpool. Balfour and Jackson pondered. Then they gave him everything he had asked for, except Liverpool. All of the disparate Irish commands would become part of a new organisation based in Queenstown.

And so, on 12 July 1915, Coke was ordered to haul down his flag. He had been fired. And rather to the surprise of the Navy, Bayly now had the job of delivering against his bravado as the admiral responsible for the Western Approaches. He commanded at Larne, Kingstown, Berehaven, Belfast, Milford Haven and the Scilly Isles. He would soon have something like 450 vessels under his orders. He asked for, nay demanded, as many small craft as could be spared and first options on the new sloops then building. Here was the saviour.

Coke was less than delighted; and even more upset when he failed to receive any recognition for his services in the New Year's Honours list at the end of 1915. He wrote to First Sea Lord Henry Jackson from his home in Exeter on 9 January 1916, after the latter had refused to give him a personal appointment.

> I am greatly disappointed that my services in Ireland were not recognised in the New Year's Honours. Most of the other Vice Admirals have been and I thought that you would kindly tell me the reason why I was not recommended to His Majesty.
>
> Ireland was in a very disturbed state, gun running was rife and I was specially sent back by the First Lord for 'as long as Ireland was unsettled' … the work was most strenuous and although my health suffered from want of rest I should have loved to remain until the end of the war.

It does seem strange that after forty-seven years of faithful service ... I should not be considered worthy of their Lordship's recommendation for a mark of His Majesty's appreciation.[25]

4

A New Broom, 1915

Vice Admiral Lewis Bayly, known in the Navy as 'Luigi', was nearly fifty-eight years old when he went to Queenstown. He was the third son of a captain in the Royal Horse Artillery. His mother, Henrietta Charlotte, was the daughter of General Charles George Gordon (of Khartoum fame) and he was the great-great-nephew of Admiral Sir Richard Keats, who had achieved prominence at the Battle of Algeciras Bay. He had joined the Navy in July 1870, not quite thirteen years of age, and his career had followed the usual progression with service at home and abroad, including the Ashanti Wars of 1875 and the Egyptian campaign of 1882.

He was a hard man with a mania for efficiency and discipline and with an unbending, unsmiling demeanour; in the service he was considered a 'character' who did not tolerate fools gladly. He drove himself and others hard. When studying for his torpedo lieutenant's exams in 1883, and being short of money, he set himself to pass out first in the class as there was a £80 prize for the person who did. He established a monastic schedule of study, eleven hours a day, six days a week, never smoked before 2200hrs, walked at least twenty miles on Sunday, played tennis for an hour at 0630hrs and ran round Greenwich Park at 1730hrs. Perhaps unsurprisingly, he won the money.

Bayly gained the rank of captain on New Year's Eve 1899. Edward Harpur Gamble, his captain on his last ship (the brand-new cruiser *Talbot*), disliked Bayly's fanaticism and had been unwilling to recommend him for promotion. Fearlessly, Bayly went to see the First Sea Lord, Admiral Walter Talbot Kerr, in person, despite neither knowing the other, and laid out the reasons why advancement should be his. He gained the coveted elevation.

His first posting was as naval attaché at the British Embassy in Washington. Bayly found this uncongenial. An attaché was meant to seek out naval intelligence to send back to the Admiralty and this was a time when the American navy was beginning to stir back to life, under the prompting of President Theodore Roosevelt. The role involved much schmoozing, dinner parties, eavesdropping and general low-level espionage. It was, Bayly later wrote, 'a very unpleasant position for a naval officer who has not the detective instincts'.[1] His direct questioning and bull-in-a-china shop approach did not go down well and he was recalled after two years at the personal request of John Hay, the US Secretary of State. His successor, Dudley de Chair, noted that 'he had been recalled, owing to his rather indiscreet conduct there'.[2]

Back home, Bayly gained a reputation for running a 'tight ship'. In 1906, when he was captain of HMS *Queen*, Admiral Bridgeman wrote into Bayly's service record 'ship is exceptionally clean, organisation excellent, ship as a whole is a credit to the service', and Admiral Lord Beresford added at a later date 'was second ship in British Fleet at battle practice, is a model of what a British man-of-war should be'.[3] However, some thought that he 'extracted good service from his subordinates because they were afraid of him'.[4]

Promotion to commodore of the Eastern Group of Destroyers in the North Sea followed in 1907. Destroyer tactics were little studied at the time and Bayly was credited with the development of new ones, including the use of smokescreens. Certainly he worked his charges hard, exercising in all weathers and at all times. He told Lord Tweedmouth, First Lord of the Admiralty at the time, that '[he] did not expect to lose more than one every six months'.[5] His Lordship was horrified. In November 1908 Bayley was appointed to command of the Royal Naval War College. Edmond Slade, a predecessor in the post, told Admiral George King-Hall that 'he did not think Bayly a good choice'.[6]

From there, and now a rear admiral, Bayly took charge of the 1st Battle Cruiser Squadron, where he came to First Lord Winston Churchill's notice. They developed a close relationship, Churchill admiring Bayly's 'can-do' attitude. And in 1914 he went to command the 1st Battle Squadron in the Grand Fleet and, after the declaration of war, to Sheerness in command of the Channel Fleet.

Bayly was a strong character and a man of fixed opinions. Among his *idee fixe,* and in common with many of his contemporaries, he had a 'slight contempt for the submarine ... he just would not believe in [them]'.[7] This character trait was to be his undoing and cause his career to come off the rails. Personally in command of the 5th Battle Squadron on exercises off Start Point, Bayly failed to take precautions against U-boat attack. As a result, the old battleship *Formidable* was torpedoed and sunk by *U-24* on New Year's Day 1915 and nearly 600 men and boys were killed.[*] Bayly had not taken the submarine threat seriously.

Bayly was severely censured by the Admiralty for the mishandling of his squadron. Fisher was particularly strident in his criticism and Commander Kenneth Dewar, an eyewitness to the sinking, spoke for many when he stated 'I do not think it would have been possible to take greater risks than were taken on that night'. He continued, 'there is no doubt that *Formidable* was sacrificed to the gross stupidity of a very ignorant man – and long before the incident occurred both officers and men criticised the folly of taking such risks for no reward whatsoever ... In peacetime he has continually shown himself as ignorant of the personnel as he is of the material ... no one thought he would be employed again until Winston Churchill gave him command of the 3rd Battle Squadron.'[8] Dewar's friend, Captain Herbert Richmond, Assistant Director of the Operations Division at the Admiralty, weighed in too. 'It looks like some lunacy of Bayly's' he confided to his diary. 'So I should expect it to be. The man has no judgement, is as obstinate as a mule, and is too stupid to convince.'[9]

Bayly asked for a court martial but this was refused and on 17 January he was relieved of his command of the Channel Fleet by Vice Admiral The Honourable Sir Alexander Bethell and was made President of the Royal Naval College, Greenwich, a position not at all to his liking for martial activity, but one Churchill probably arranged for him to keep him 'on ice' until the *Formidable* situation calmed down. Richmond was pleased. 'Lewis Bayly has been relieved of his command. Thank goodness! Bayly had entirely forfeited the confidence of his officers and men by his idiotic cruising which led to the loss of the *Formidable*,' he noted.[10]

At Greenwich, Bayly simmered, refusing to accept his culpability and resentful of the denial of any opportunity to clear his name. As he wrote much later 'I asked for a court martial and was refused – I

---

[13] For an account of this disaster, see S R Dunn, *Formidable* (2015).

have never known why. It sounds like a fairy story, seeing what happened during the war, and presumably was done to encourage other admirals.' However, he tried to effect a stoic detachment; 'It is well to remember that in a disciplined force an essential of that discipline is facing injustice with a smile,' he noted.[11] Had Fisher not fallen, Bayly may have languished there for the rest of the war, for Fisher disliked him and once accused him of arrogance and improper behaviour. But the fall of Churchill and his First Sea Lord in May 1915 opened the door for further active service. And thus he came to Queenstown.

Bayly arrived at his new command accompanied by his personal coxswain, Chief Petty Officer G F Wade, a faithful companion since 1908, his Marine servant Murray, a spaniel called Patrick, and his niece, Violet. In July 1892 the 35-year-old Bayley had married Henrietta Mary Ives Stella, née Voysey, six years his senior and mother to two children, Giuseppe and Cecile. Henrietta had married an artist, 43-year-old Giuseppe Stella, in 1870 at the age of nineteen but was subsequently widowed. She was the cousin of the famous architect Charles Francis Annesley Voysey and brother to one Annesley Wesley Voysey, who had emigrated to Australia where, in 1880, he sired a daughter Violet Mary Annesley, who thus became Bayly's niece by marriage.

It would appear that Bayly's marriage did not prosper. He makes no mention at all of his wife, or even of the fact of his marriage, in his autobiography and there were no children from the union. Possibly the austere Bayly was a little difficult to bear after an Italian love match; they separated.* By 1912, Violet was acting as his housekeeper at his home in Ebury Street, London. And when Bayly took up the Queenstown command, Violet came with him; an unmarried, 35-year-old, Australian chatelaine.

First steps

Bayly arrived with virtually no staff. No flag lieutenant, no staff commander; he, Wade and Violet would handle all the basic administrative work that was required. He thought that anyone who was good enough to be on his staff was good enough to be at sea fighting the war and therefore did not request any support.

---

* Some authorities (Marder and those who followed him) state that Bayly was a widower but this was not the case. Henrietta died in Italy on 29 July 1934.

And the staff he inherited did not please him. Captain Hibbert was removed in early August* and replaced on the 7th of the month by Captain Charles Douglas Carpendale as Flag Captain Queenstown and officer commanding *Colleen*. And he received the promised light cruiser, *Adventure*, under Acting Captain George Hyde. Hyde had been a Merchant Marine apprentice, joined the Royal Navy as a lieutenant and, in Bayly's words, '[risen] entirely by his own energy and ability'.[12]

Bayly was, however, unimpressed with his new command. Writing to First Sea Lord Henry Jackson he noted 'the place here and the situation generally is gradually getting organised and systematised. I hope things will be in proper working order soon; the naval officers seem keen but as their duties were all mixed up, the situation was difficult.'[13] He lost no time in making his mark. His first signal informed one and all that social calls should be considered to have been made and returned. Additionally, he declared that there would be no further social events at Admiralty House; only officers and dockyard mangers were to be seen there in future. Alerted by the Admiralty that there was a leakage of information from the station, he immediately replaced the pre-existing system of communication with the harbour. Previously this has been carried out in plain-language semaphore from the gardens of Admiralty House, obvious to anyone who cared to look: Bayly immediately adopted a system of cypher and a private cable to a signal station he caused to be built on Haulbowline Island, for onward coded transmission to his ships. Furthermore, no one was to be allowed on any ship unless in Royal Navy uniform; this effectively banned calls by curious civilians. He also established a boom defence net to protect the harbour entrance.

In Admiralty House itself, Bayly ordered that the large ballroom/lounge be divided by a bulkhead, one-third to be used as a common room and two-thirds as the command centre. The billiard table was covered with boarding by the dockyard hands and used as a chart table.

The dockyard concerned him too. He felt that it was congested and too small, and far too dilatory. One dockyard official told him that 'they were not accustomed to work Saturday and Sunday'.[14]

---

* In 1916 Hibbert was told that he would be forcibly retired unless he applied to go voluntarily onto the retired list. He was only fifty-three.

That soon changed, but he also proposed to Jackson that the Navy was going to take in hand repairs itself too, clear of the civilian-run dockyard, 'as they are so slow' taking Rushbrooke Dock, further up river, for the purpose. He ended the practice of weekly dockyard meetings to prioritise the work required and instead ordered that all ships should signal their maintenance requirements ahead of entering harbour so that they could be dealt with straight away. Employment at the dockyard began to boom, from less than a hundred to thousands by the end of the war.

The vessels under his command did not please him either. Of the armed trawlers he noted 'even as escorts they are of little use ... I had no idea what poor things the armed trawlers were ... to catch submarines they are wanting.'[15] But he showed a touching, and rather unexpected, concern for his men. He ordered two bedrooms in Admiralty House to be kept permanently ready for use by officers returned from patrol who needed a good night's rest and created a private rose garden in the grounds of Admiralty House where officers could relax away from the stresses of their normal environment. There was also an adjacent tennis court for more vigorous activities.

Admiralty House was located close to the Cathedral Church of St Colman, diocesan church of the Roman Catholic see of Cloyne. Building had begun in 1868 but it was still unfinished and when war broke out was lacking, inter alia, bells for its carillon. The bishop was the Most Reverend Robert Browne, seventy-one years old at the time of Bayly's appointment. Bayly was fully aware that there was a possibility that the two major forces and personages in Queenstown – the bishop and the admiral – might pull in opposite directions, to the detriment of both, especially as nearly all the dockyard workers were Catholics. Bayly had eschewed all social calls but he made an exception for the bishop and paid him a visit. 'I called on him and asked him, as the most prominent man there, if we could not work together,' Bayly later noted. 'Luckily for me he was a great gentleman and ... never failed to help me when I asked for his assistance.'[16] Bishop Browne was concerned about his bells, or rather the lack of them, which were stuck at Liverpool awaiting shipment. Bayly was able to offer some help. 'I ... suggested that we adopt the scriptural injunction to watch and pray; he should pray and I would watch. This was agreed to and the bells arrived safely at Queenstown.'[17] The forty-nine bell carillon first rang out in May 1916.

Bayly shared Haulbowline Island with the Army, a fact which displeased him. He held the traditional Royal Navy disdain for the soldiery and needed their space, so he embarked on a campaign to rid himself of them. 'It was not easy,' he wrote, 'but eventually I succeeded and so had the whole of the Island.'[18] By mid-August, he felt that he was making some progress. Writing to Jackson, he commented 'at last the place is getting organised and we are getting able to take stock and see where we are … soon I will be able to look at the command and see what can be done to improve matters. Up to now, Queenstown has taken all of my energies.'[19]

Bayly was, in fact, an indefatigable letter-writer, always in longhand, never typed and always personally penned. His handwriting gave something of the character of the man. It was small, crabbed, but neat and legible. He often started his correspondence with the injunction 'on condition that you do not bother to reply I propose to drop you a line now and then to keep you informed [about] this far flung corner'.[20] He used this form with Jackson (and later with Jellicoe). It would appear to be a way of ensuring that he got his ideas in front of the key decision-maker without going through the normal bureaucracy.

He also manged to lighten his administrative load by making a direct approach by telegram to Paymaster H Robert Russell who had served as secretary to Admiral Milne, CinC Mediterranean Fleet until October 1914, and had been Bayly's secretary when he commanded the 1st Battle Cruiser Squadron. Now he was languishing with the Grand Fleet at Scapa. Russell had a reputation for organisation and a thorough technical knowledge of navy 'business'. He arrived, worked from 0900hrs to 0200hrs most days and lessened the administrative load that had previously fallen on Bayly and Violet. Bayly said of him that 'he never failed me' and added that 'no one ever went to ask for help from Russell and went away empty handed'.[21]

The new broom had made a start but still no submarine had been sunk around Ireland, yet.

New Ships, New Tactics, July and August 1915

The new and enlarged command which Bayly now presided over included three auxiliary patrol bases at Larne, Kingstown and Milford Haven, which had been separate commands, and the Scilly Islands submarine base, which had been part of the Falmouth command. The Bristol Channel also became a separate auxiliary patrol area with a base at Swansea. Holyhead too came under Bayly's sway; a new patrol area was formed there which included the eastern half of the Irish Sea. But his basic problem was simple – there were no vessels in his command which could be reliably expected to prosecute an anti-submarine war.

Trawlers, steam and motor yachts he had in abundance and a few old torpedo boats too, but he considered them to be wanting in all respects, writing to Jackson on 12 August 1915:

> Our method of defence by trawlers [against submarines] does not seem to me to be a serious one, except where they are situated near the coast ... and in ordinary weather. On the open sea it is doubtful that they are much use; few have W/T and what there is, is weak. Their speed is absurdly slow; their gun is easily seen from a considerable distance so that they are easily recognised and avoided. I should imagine that they are bad gun platforms.[1]

And he had little faith in some of their crews in any case, commenting of the trawlers 'it seems to me that the weak point of our scheme is the personnel. It is hard to prove weakness or laziness [and is] so difficult to know what the trawlers do when out at sea.'[2]

He went on to note that a submarine had been entangled in nets laid outside Castle Haven (at the southern tip of Ireland) but cleared itself while the trawler watching the nets did nothing. Such strictures were perhaps to overlook the point that these vessels were manned by fishermen, plucked from their peacetime employment, and thrust into a war for which they had neither training nor, possibly, aptitude. Nonetheless, in Bayly's eyes there was clearly not much hope of sinking U-boats if the status quo pertained.

But help was on the way. In his initial discussions with Balfour and Jackson, Bayly had been promised an allocation of the new patrol vessels that were coming into action. And shortly after his appointment they began to arrive.

The sloops

The 'Flower'-class sloops were a series of ships named after flowers and originally designed as minesweepers, but they were hurriedly pressed into service as patrol vessels as the scale of the U-boat threat became apparent. Bayly had been promised twelve and the first of them arrived with his command in July. They were simple ships, based on merchant-ship plans and built in ordinary commercial yards which were accustomed to such designs. They had been constructed in double-quick time (the first batch ordered in December 1914 were commissioned in May 1915 for service with the Grand Fleet) and lacked either comfort or subtlety. But beggars could not be choosers. Initially armed with two 12pdr guns (later classes had 4in), very economical on coal and capable of 16 knots, they were lively in a seaway with a tendency to pitch. But they proved to be durable and capable. The sloops were often commanded by senior lieutenants or lieutenant commanders, fresh from the Grand Fleet, and the 'sloops provided first-class opportunities for any ambitious young officer who was bored with spending the war as a watch-keeper swinging round a buoy at Scapa Flow'.[3]

Bayly himself had initially doubted their potential and wondered 'how they would get on in the heavy gales off the coast'.[4] But he soon expressed himself proud of their performance and that of the officers and men who commanded them. By the end of the war, he was to emphasise the 'great value that they were to the nation in guarding trade, assisting torpedoed ships ... and saving valuable lives. They performed many acts of splendid seamanship, doing these things as a matter of ordinary duty, in spite of gales, fogs and enemy submarines'[5] (see also Appendix 1).

Sub Lieutenant Robert Goldrich RN of HMS *Poppy*, not yet twenty-one years old when he joined his ship, described what it felt like to be part of the sloop force at Queenstown: 'Those were the days and no mistake! Exec officer of a small ship in the thick of the submarine campaign, with the organisation of the ship and the comfort of some eighty men to supplement my regular watchkeeping duties. What a motley crowd our officers must have seemed as we lounged around the roaring stove which gave a semblance of comfort to our tiny steel wardroom.'[6] Goldrich went on to describe his fellow officers. The captain was a lieutenant commander from China gunboats, the navigator an old merchant sailor RNR, the warrant officer in charge of mines and minesweeping a grizzled regular and the doctor a surgeon probationer. These were the men who would wage the anti-submarine war.

As soon as the first sloops arrived, Bayly devised a new system of patrolling, a sort of rough inverted triangle. He stationed sloops along the entire south Irish coast from the Tuskar to the Fastnet, each vessel tending an area fifty miles north to south and thirty miles west to east. This soon proved to be fruitful. On 14 August, the sloop HMS *Lavender* saw and chased a U-boat and two days later *Veronica* did the same. But there were still no sinkings.

Bayly now had five sloops under his orders but they were far from perfect. He was concerned about the officers who 'suffer from a want of domestics and cooks. Their meals are half-cooked and most of them live on bread and cheese ... and clean up their own cabins.'[7] Some RNR Merchant Marine officers may have let slip a wry smile at such comments. Bayly also 'made a point of asking those officers who had no belongings on shore to dine and sleep at Admiralty House during the short time they had in harbour',[8] no doubt a welcome break from a damp sea-cabin.

And the ships themselves showed problems of design and the rough and speedy nature of their construction. W/T was a problem; 'of five sloops, two were speechless and have since come in with their [wireless] in a state of ruin,' Bayly wrote to First Sea Lord Henry Jackson on 17 August. The propulsion plant was not all it could be either. '*Lavender* tells me her engines are walking about the engine room and want re-securing to their beds.'[9] They also suffered badly from vibration problems 'owing to having no governor in their engines'.[10] On the 10th, two of them were in the harbour repairing their engines. They would easily ship water in heavy seas. Often a sloop would return to Queenstown with a foot or two of water in the wardroom and the seamen's quarters flooded out. Moreover, Bayly was getting little support from the Constructor of the Dockyard in repairing his defects. He told Jackson 'I have asked for the Constructor to be invalided.' But the Chief Engineer there was much more to his liking; '[He] eats out of my hand and is forgetting what it is to have an evening off.'[11] But overall the little ships pleased him. 'I could easily do with eighteen sloops', he wrote to Jackson, 'if you have another six to spare after I have got my twelve.'[12] In fact, Bayly was lucky to get the twelve he had been promised; as they became available, they were often snaffled up by Jellicoe for use as minesweepers with the Grand Fleet. As Chief of the Admiralty War Staff Henry Oliver confided in his memoirs, 'as soon as I got a sloop to hunt submarines, Jellicoe would want it'.[13]

Bayly was not above going out on operations himself, in support of his sloops. He kept *Adventure* at two hours' notice and on 14 August suddenly set sail because he felt there was 'something in the air'.[14] His seaplanes were out too and one sighted a U-boat on the surface. *Adventure* made for her at high speed – but it proved to be one of the command's own trawlers.

The prospect of serving under Bayly, whose reputation in the service for discipline, efficiency and duty was legendary, in these hastily-constructed warships put fear into the hearts of many ships' officers when they were assigned to his service. The 31-year-old Lieutenant Commander Salisbury Hamilton Simpson RN was appointed to command of HMS *Jessamine*, a newly-built *Azalea*-class sloop (4in guns instead of 12pdrs), in October 1915 and assigned to Queenstown. He suffered 'from a cold shiver'[15] at the news and wondered how long he would last in post under the martinet that Bayly was reputed to be. His new ship was at Wallsend and the trip to Ireland was made in terrible weather which tested her machinery to the full and, on arrival in Queenstown, Simpson's engineering officer told him they would need a week in harbour to fix the manifold defects exposed in the vessel's first voyage. The young commander toiled up the hill to Admiralty House to pass this news onto the Admiral, whom he found working in the garden with his niece. Bayly fixed him with a gimlet eye. 'You will proceed to sea at eight o'clock tomorrow morning. Good day to you sir.'[16] Simpson left chagrined. How his engineer felt was not recorded.

Simpson soon discovered that the enemy was not just the

U-boats. The weather too was a constant problem. *Jessamine*'s log recorded one of their first patrols at sea. On 4 November, Simpson noted 'vessel pitching and straining heavily'. Later that same day, 'reduced to 90 revs, vessel straining heavily and pitching violently'. The 5th brought no relief; 'steering gear very unsatisfactory'. And on the 10th, 'mercurial barometer apparently damaged by rolling'. By the time the 12th came round he was an old hand, content merely to record 'weather assuming threatening appearance'.[17] This was in fact the onset of a cyclonic storm which lashed Ireland with the worst such weather since 1861. On one small estate over 1,000 trees were blown down and fallen trees blocked the roads around Queenstown and Berehaven for three days. The mountains around the coast were covered in snow.

Jessamine was in the midst of it. From the bridge, 40ft up, it was impossible to see over the oncoming wave tops. But the sloops proved themselves to be 'hill-climbers', riding up each wave to the top before crashing down again. Because of their shallow draft the single propeller would come out of the water causing the engine to suddenly race and the engineers to curse. And then, in the middle of the storm, the telemotor steering gear gave up the ghost. Immediately the little ship went broadside-on to the enormous waves. She started to roll to 40°. Water poured into her, drenching the living quarters and causing even heavy furniture to float around the wardroom. Somehow the alternate steering arrangements were connected and it was a very damp and down at the bows *Jessamine* that eventually regained Queenstown harbour.

The sloop *Zinnia* was also at sea during the storm. Her logbook records the battle to survive. '1600; hove to ... wind increased to hurricane force ... so that ship became unmanageable. 2100; wind NNE, force 10-11. Very rough sea, driving hail and rain. 2300; at last got away and steered east by north ... the foremost gun carried away securing chains, demolished training stops and kept crashing against foremast, shaking ship throughout. Engines racing dangerously. Speed through water about 3 knots.'[18] She steamed in to harbour the next day missing her wireless aerial and with one of her starboard boats stove-in. But all the little ships survived; they had proven excellent sea boats.

The sloops settled down to the monotony of patrolling. *Jessamine*'s log for 21 November gives an idea of her daily duties, patrolling and escorting. First thing she was off Kinsale Head where she met ss *Patella*, an oil tanker, and escorted her to Queenstown. She resumed her patrol and passed Fastnet lighthouse, Galley Head and the Old Head of Kinsale, where she stopped for some engine room problem. At 1525hrs, *Jessamine* rendezvoused with another oil tanker, the *Silvership* and escorted her back to base. Next she intercepted ss *Barnson*, again bound for Queenstown with oil and questioned her, checking her *bona fides*. And *Jessamine*'s day ended with the Fastnet abeam once more.

Not all was stress and storm or quotidian patrolling however. The advent of the sloops occasioned a bout of competitive gardening in the private garden which Bayly had created at Admiralty House for his officers to enjoy and relax in. Each sloop's commander saw it as a matter of honour that the flower whose name his ship bore should be represented there. Before long a veritable nursery of herbaceous plants delighted the eye and officers fought to maintain the precedence of their own ship's namesake flower.

Q-ships

The problem remained that hunting patrols seeking U-boats suffered because the submarine could see them and submerge or flee but the patrol could not see the enemy. But if the enemy could be caused to surface and come close to a ship, then it might be possible to fight it. How could this be achieved?

False-flag deception was as old as maritime trade. Pirate ships would sail under friendly flags to deceive an intended victim, and in times of war, sailing vessels would voyage under the flag of their enemy or some other nation not involved in the war in the hope of getting close enough to surprise and capture an enemy ship. In fact false-flag deception was so common that it was recognised in international treaty, with the proviso that the offending vessel should raise its proper flag immediately before any engagement. In 1914, such disguise came of age as the Q-ship. A Q-ship was an everyday merchant vessel, a tramp or similar down-at-heel maid of all work, sailing under false colours and carrying concealed weaponry. The intention was to cause a U-boat to surface to investigate the ship, or to attack it with gunfire rather than expensive torpedoes. Once close enough, the Q-ship would raise the White Ensign and open fire with its hidden guns.

Bayly was not the originator of the concept (some authorities ascribe that to Churchill[*]) nor were the Admiralty very enthusiastic about it. When Captain Richmond, in the Admiralty's Operation Division, wrote a minute dated 26 November 1914 advocating the use of disguised ships he was slapped down with the response that a gun-armed vessel was no use against a submarine.[19]

But as an admiral without a suitable weapon to fight U-boats, Bayly became an enthusiastic 'early adopter' of Q-ships, assisted by the fact that he had his own dockyard at Haulbowline in which alterations to suitable merchant ships could be made (and which, anecdotally, gave the such vessels their name).

Once their use had been accepted by the Admiralty, the vessels were identified only as 'Special Service' ships and their existence regarded as a great secret to be kept from the Germans. They were given numbers and a variety of ship's names, which changed regularly, and were kept hidden from general view where possible.

On 11 December 1914, two such vessels were fitting out at Belfast. Over Churchill's signature, Admiral Jellicoe at Scapa was instructed to ensure that their original names were removed and that it was essential that they were not detected. They were to be hidden in the Wash or the Swin until deployed. They were to be fitted with smoke-making apparatus so that 'they could draw a veil over their nakedness' and armed trawlers should be used to usher away the curious.[20] When three Q-ships were despatched to the Mediterranean in February 1915, the Admiralty telegrams referred to them as 'battlecruisers' and the SNO Gibraltar was instructed not to attempt to contact them.[21] Special Service Ship No 12, sent in the April to patrol off the coast of North America, was to be referred to as the battlecruiser *Queen Mary*.[22] Over Fisher and Churchill's signature, the Admiral commanding the North America and West Indies Station (Vice Admiral Sir George E Patey) was instructed to 'use your discretion how to mislead the enemy or neutrals and be careful not to expose the true character of the ship'.[23]

The first Q-ships to be officially part of the Queenstown command were two colliers, *Glendevon* and *Chevington*, both of around 4,000grt. They had been sent by the Admiralty to Bayly, who was dismissive of them. 'They were too large' he commented 'and were filled with coal. The only apparent use of the coal was to

---

* It is certainly true that in the early days of the war Churchill sent a telegram to Admiral Hedworth Meux, Commander-in-Chief Portsmouth, asking him to send a disguised steamer to 'trap' a submarine preying on shipping off Le Havre.

enable them to sink at once if torpedoed, and so save the crew from the trouble and discomfort of trying to prolong their lives by staying on board.'[24] He sent them instead to Montreal to unload their cargo and fill up with wood, to act as a flotation device. In the process, however, he lost one as Admiral Patey requisitioned it for his own use.

Bayly decided that he needed to choose his own ships, suitable for operations off the Irish coast; not too big and not requiring many men. He sent out a naval officer and a constructor from the Queenstown dockyard to identify suitable candidates and then gained permission from the Admiralty to buy them. In this way he was to amass some thirty vessels,[25] which he deployed between Ireland, Finisterre and the Scillies. They were converted at the Queenstown yard (or sometimes at Devonport), in great secrecy, and afterwards kept moored in the remotest parts of the harbour until ready to sail. It was from this activity that the 'mystery ships' came to be called 'Q-ships', Q for Queenstown. As the war continued, some 'Flower'-class sloops were redesigned and re-designated to be Q-ships as were many of the later coastal sloops, otherwise known as P-boats (or PC-boats when built as Q-ships).

The duty was dangerous. When the Germans found out about the ships they declared that the crews would be treated as pirates and shot out of hand; perhaps unsurprisingly, the crews of the Q-ships, also known as 'mystery ships', were all volunteers. Demonstrating his respect and concern for these men, Bayly agitated with the Admiralty to ensure that they were paid over and above the norm with 'hard lying money'.* Crews were also entitled to prize money. The bounty for sinking an enemy submarine was £1,000, divided into shares of £1 18s 1d, each perhaps worth around £100 today. An officer who played a significant role in an action could gain fifty such shares.

Other anti-submarine plans

Bayly did not stop at revamping the operations of his new command at sea and on land. In his first month in post he also took it upon himself to suggest new general strategy to the Admiralty.

---

* On 30 November 1916 Bayly wrote to Admiral Marx that the 'Admiralty have agreed to give Q-ship officers and men submarine pay' (2009.39/1/31, NMRN). It was not until 20 July 1916 that the Admiralty allowed war service badges to be worn by Q-ship officers and ratings. Later certificates were added. Both actions were intended to prevent the crews, if captured, being executed as *franc tireurs*.

Before the war, Bayly had been assigned to the Admiralty by Churchill to work on a plan favoured by the latter to take the island of Borkum (largest and westernmost of the East Frisian Islands in the North Sea) in the event of war, the idea being that this would be an advantageous place to intercept the German vessels operating from The Jade and Heligoland and form a close blockade of the Heligoland Bight. The then CinC Home Fleet, Admiral George Callaghan was dismissive; 'This policy of close blockade was considered a few years ago and abandoned as impractical. As it appears to be still more impractical now it is useless to consider it,' he wrote.[26] And Herbert Richmond, assigned to evaluate Bayly's Borkum plan at the end of 1914 wrote 'It is quite mad ... I have never read such an idiotic amateur piece of work as this outline in all my life.'[27]

Now, with the idea of interdicting German U-boats, Bayly once more pressed his idea. On 12 August he wrote to First Sea Lord Henry Jackson about it, adding 'I want to do it.'[28] On the same day, he sent a separate note recommending that the exits from the U-boat bases now established at Zeebrugge and Ostend should be blocked up. Bayly then addressed the issues of confusing U-boats navigation and spotting them early by suggesting that six navigation lights in the Irish Sea be extinguished and naval ratings posted to offshore islands to report any U-boat sightings. A harassed Jackson passed these suggestions to Oliver, who replied a few days later. 'I do not think it worth asking for the definitive plans [for blockading U-boat bases]' he noted 'as we will get so many of their plans and they usually are made regardless of our resources.'[29] Jackson did not give Bayly a reply. And so summer passed into autumn and Bayly came to grips with his command. The hard work was just beginning.

6

Bad Blood and First Blood, August and September 1915

August 1915; the war had been in progress for a year. No one except the dead had, as the Kaiser once expected, 'come home before the leaves fall'. Neither had it been 'all over by Christmas' as many in Britain had predicted. From the French coast to the Swiss border, Europe was bisected by a line of trenches behind which men eked out their lives, killing and being killed.

At sea it was no better. The failure of the naval campaign to take the Dardanelles had further damaged the Royal Navy's reputation and precipitated the downfall of Churchill, Fisher and the Liberal government, which was now incorporated into a Grand Coalition of parties. On 28 July, the anniversary of the Austro-Hungarian declaration of war against Serbia, Asquith announced to the House of Commons that the British total of men dead, wounded and missing since the war began was 330,995, including 9,000 from the Navy. And August 1915 was a bad month for merchant shipping in Bayly's Irish command. Just three U-boats were causing chaos in the Western Approaches and the Irish Sea.

The month had started badly for the admiral. On the 1st, *U-28*, operating some thirty to fifty miles south-west of Ushant under Kapitänleutnant Freiherr Georg-Günther von Forstner, sank three merchant ships in the day; the Stag Lines cargo vessel *Clintonia*, out of Marseilles for the Tyne in ballast, ss *Benvorlich*, from Manila heading for London and the Ellerman and Bucknall Lines ship *Ranza*. All three were captured, the crews forced to abandon ship and then the vessels sunk by torpedo, unusual at this time, for most commanders preferred to use gunfire or explosive devices and keep their expensive torpedoes for more difficult prey. A day later, von Forstner despatched the fleet messenger *Portia* by gunfire and then, on the 3rd, the *Costello*. *Midland Queen* was sunk the following day. Satisfied with his work he then returned to his home base.

Now *U-38*, Kapitänleutnant Max Valentiner (who was to become one of Germany's most successful U-boat commanders), entered the lists; between the 11th and the 23rd he sank twenty-one merchant vessels for a total of 65,039grt. These included cargo vessels, coasters, colliers and even the little three-masted schooner *Martha Edmonds*, 182grt.[*]

U-24 was cruising to the south of Ireland. On 19 August she sank by gunfire the sailing vessel *St Olaf*, 277grt, and the *New York City*, 2,970grt, forty-four miles south-south-east from Fastnet. Now she was searching for her next victim. That same day the White Star Line passenger ship *Arabic* was on passage from Liverpool to New York. She was well known at Queenstown, a regular stopping point for her from her first voyage on the route in 1903. On board she had 133 second class and 48 third class passengers, together with 243 crewmen. Her captain, William Finch, had ordered a zigzag course and was steaming away from the normal sea lanes about fifty miles south-west by west from the Old Head of Kinsale.

At around 0915hrs Captain Finch noticed in the distance the steamer ss *Dunsley* under attack from a surfaced submarine. He immediately ordered the crew to get his passengers into their lifebelts, but it was already too late. The submarine left its doomed prey, dived and attacked the newcomer. As one newspaper later put it 'When the passengers saw *Dunsley* being attacked in the distance they rushed to the life-preservers but had only adjusted these when the *Arabic* was struck. Many scrambled on to a number of rafts that had been thrown over the side, and many fell in the water. Fifteen of the *Arabic*'s sixteen lifeboats were launched successfully.'[1] *Arabic* had been torpedoed by *U-24* under Kapitänleutnant Rudolph (Rudi) Schneider, the destroyer of Bayly's nemesis *Formidable* on the previous New Year's Day; the liner went down in under ten minutes.

An American passenger, a Mr Nebeker, commented 'that the crew of the *Arabic* worked splendidly, and that but for the discipline shown there would have been hundreds of fatalities'.[2] In fact forty-

---

[*] Valentiner sank 147 ships (303,032grt) during his career with six ships damaged (33,151grt). After the war, he was listed as a war criminal by the British authorities.

four passengers and crew, of whom three were American, were killed. Amongst the ships in the area which picked up *Arabic*'s distress calls, one did not immediately rush to provide assistance. She was a 4,192grt 'three-island' steam cargo liner built in 1901 and which had until the war pursued an uneventful peacetime career with Bucknall Steamship Lines. In 1914 she had been requisitioned by the Royal Navy as a supply ship and then converted to a Q-ship at Barry Docks in 1915. Now named ss *Baralong* she was cruising in the Western Approaches offering herself as a tempting U-boat target. If she found one, her three 12pdr guns, hidden in concealed mountings, could at last be used in anger. And there was a lot of anger. The *Lusitania* incident had whipped up a firestorm of public indignation in Britain and America; and now another liner had been seemingly attacked without warning too.

As part of her disguise, *Baralong* was flying the Stars and Stripes of neutral America. Her captain, Commander Godfrey Herbert, a submariner turned Q-ship captain and disguised as a merchant master with the alias Captain William McBride, thought that he would move towards the sinking liner to see if he could find the attacker. But then his wireless operator picked up an SOS message. A freighter, *Nicosian*, with a cargo of mules and horses, was being attacked just nine miles away. There were clearly two submarines and Herbert now ordered full speed, a stately 10 knots, towards the second one.

Herbert was a 'character'. A big man, ginger-haired, loud and unruly, he had already had a brush with death when serving aboard the submarine *A-4* in 1905. She sank, full of water and grounded at 90ft. In a hull full of chlorine gas and seawater, he and his commanding officer somehow got her back to the surface. When serving on the China station he invented a midget submarine, only to be told by the Admiralty that they had no use for it; he then blotted his copybook by entering Kowloon harbour lashed to the periscope of his just-submerged submarine giving the impression of walking on water and much to the disturbance of the native onlookers. His admiral was not amused.

At the outbreak of war, Herbert was in command of the submarine *D-5*. However, on 4 November 1914 and whilst in pursuit of elements of the High Seas Fleet, *D-5* hit a mine; nineteen men died, only those on the bridge being saved. He then served on the French steam-powered submarine *Archimède* but that too foundered and its French commander wanted to head for internment in Holland. Herbert disagreed and somehow persuaded the crew to get the ship functioning properly, bailing like fury, and sailed it to Harwich and safety.

With no submarine command offered to him (he thought that the Admiralty regarded him as 'unlucky'), Herbert transferred to a decoy ship, RMS *Antwerp*, but had no success in finding a U-boat to attack. Invited by the Admiralty to choose a vessel to convert to a Q-ship, he picked up the *Baralong* and in that ship was cruising off the coast of Jersey when the *Lusitania* was torpedoed. His ship picked up her cries for help and he had sailed to assist. He was at Queenstown when the bodies came ashore; he and his men saw the terrible tragedy of civilian deaths. To men brought up in the Victorian/Edwardian world of chivalry and fair play, the killing of non-combatants seemed an atrocity, an uncivilised slaughter. Herbert and his crew took an oath that they would show no mercy to any U-boat crewmen who fell into their hands. But up until now, they had not been so lucky.

U-27 had been patrolling near to Bishop's Rock. She had already sunk the 3,359grt cargo ship *Gladiator* and had now caught up with ss *Nicosian*, boarded her and ordered the crew to take to their boats. As *Baralong* drew closer to the freighter, the crew saw men in boats and a U-boat, *U-27*, shelling the ship. Herbert raised a flag signal indicating that he was coming to rescue the freighter's crew and quickly altered course to starboard, placing the *Nicosian* between him and the submarine. He knew *U-27* would appear from behind *Nicosian*'s bow ready to fire at him, so he posted Royal Marines with rifles in *Baralong*'s bow. When the submarine cleared *Nicosian* the Marines were ready. They opened an incessant rifle fire and killed several of the U-boat's gun crew before it was possible for them to retaliate. At the same time Herbert ordered the main guns cleared of their camouflage and opened fire with the 12pdrs. Some thirty-four shells were fired to good effect. The submarine sank in just over a minute, leaving her commander and a number of men in the water. These men swam to the pilot ladder dangling from the side of the abandoned *Nicosian,* clambered aboard and disappeared.

Herbert was concerned that they might attempt to carry on the fight from there for he was aware of the cargo and that the *Nicosian* also had some rifles and ammunition on board; he feared that any German sailors on board might seek to destroy the cargo by setting fire to the fodder or might even attempt to scuttle the ship. Herbert ordered twelve Marines to board the freighter; they hunted the German sailors through the ship, shooting them dead as they found them.

At last a Q-ship had proved its worth; but there were complications. The American muleteers on the freighter had witnessed what had happened. On return to the US they spoke to reporters. It was suggested that the US flag she was flying might not have come down before *Baralong* opened fire; it was argued that the German sailors on board *Nicosian* had been murdered in cold blood. The Germans saw an opportunity to lay a charge of atrocity against Britain, demanding that Herbert should be tried for murder and pointing to both the deaths and the misuse of the US flag. The Admiralty awarded Herbert the DSO. Nonetheless, in just one month four U-boats had sunk thirty-five vessels representing 111,974grt of valuable British merchant shipping in the Western Approaches and killed seventy-eight sailors and passengers.

RMS *Hesperian*

September started as August had finished. On the 4th *U-33* despatched the *Mimosa* and then at 1230hrs attacked the tanker SS *Cymbeline*, just twenty-nine miles from Fastnet. The U-boat opened fire on the tanker whilst her crew of thirty-seven were attempting to launch the two lifeboats. Gunfire destroyed one boat, causing the deaths of six men. The survivors were taken into the second boat, which now contained thirty-one men, four of whom were seriously wounded. It was to be sixteen hours before they met a sailing vessel which towed the little lifeboat to within three miles of the Irish coast; and another six-and-a-half hours before they were able to reach the shore.

The Royal Mail Steamer *Hesperian* was a single-funnel, double-screw passenger vessel originally belonging to the Allan Line but since 1910 chartered to Canadian Pacific. Built in 1907, 485ft long and 10,920grt, as designed she could accommodate 210 passengers in first class, 250 in second class and 1,000 in third class. At 1900hrs on 3 September 1915 she had left Liverpool bound for Quebec and then Montreal under the command of Captain William Main with 814 passengers and 300 crew; two American nationals were on board.

Her passengers were an eclectic group. One was Mrs Ellen Carbery from St John, Newfoundland who, in 1887, had broken the male domination of the department store trade in that city by establishing Ellen Carbery's Ladies' Emporium, which proved to be a commercial success. Now aged seventy she had made her annual buying trip to England in February and was now returning with her wares. War or no war, trade must go on. Elizabeth Fisher was a single young lady, up until now a chambermaid, who was *en route* to Canada to marry one Jesse Would. They had met in England; now he had sent for her to join him in his new promised land. Marjorie Campbell Robarts from Ontario was another young lady but of a very different station. Daughter of Aldham Robarts of Ontario she had travelled to Britain two years previously to stay with her Aunt and Uncle Campbell. Now aged eighteen she was returning to her home, in a first class stateroom. Just before she sailed her Aunt Flo abjured her not to join any partying on board but to return to her cabin immediately after dinner. It wasn't what she wanted but on the second night of the voyage she did as she was instructed. The majority of the passengers, however, were wounded Canadian soldiers, returning home from the Western Front. Amongst them was Major Percy Guthrie of the 10th Battalion, who had been fighting in the Battle of Festubert on 25 May 1915. A shell exploded at his feet and he was wounded in eleven places. Now he was being invalided back to Canada.

At 2030hrs, approximately eighty-five miles SW by S of the Fastnet, the liner was hit by a torpedo fired by *U-20*, Kapitän-leutnant Walther Schwieger, the destroyer of the *Lusitania*. For the second time, he had attacked a large passenger liner without warning. The liner shuddered throughout her length and came to a stop. Witnesses reported that a column of water and debris was thrown up into the night sky to a height of 100ft above the bridge, falling back onto the decks. The hatches on No 2 deck were blown off and considerable damage was done to the second class cabins and bridge decks. The ship quickly took on water, developing a bad list to starboard, and began sinking by the head.

Captain Main sounded the 'boat stations' signal on the steam whistle and ordered his chief officer to get the passengers into the boats, ordering 'Women and children first'. The alarms rang out all round the ship. There was no panic; the crew loaded passengers into lifeboats and tried to get them away. Ellen Carbery was placed in one of them. Marjorie Robarts ran up from her stateroom and found herself ushered into another. Her erstwhile dining companions were less fortunate. They had gathered altogether on the other side of the liner as they had been directed and were all put into one lifeboat. But the liner's list meant that the hull projected out under their lifeboat. As Marjorie's dinner friends were being lowered down the high sidewall of the hull, the lifeboat banged against the ship, upsetting it and projecting its occupants into the dark ocean. They were never seen alive again. Elizabeth Fisher lost all of her belongings except the clothes she was in and a money belt round her waist. She had been conducted down a ladder and a rope into a lifeboat already in the water, damaging her finger in the process. But she was alive and recovered sufficiently to make it to Canada and her beau.

An SOS had been successfully broadcast and soon rescue ships began to arrive. Among them was HMS *Sunflower*, one of the Queenstown sloops under Lieutenant Commander John Claud Cole-Hamilton. She rescued over 100 survivors. But they were too late for Ellen Carbery who died of exposure and shock just before dawn. Major Percy Guthrie was luckier, for he had taken to the water and was plucked from it floating with the aid of his crutches.

It was a miracle that only thirty-two people were killed, largely due to the efficient procedures of Captain Main's crew who evacuated the vessel within an hour. The ship's watertight bulkheads had kept the ship afloat and Captain Main and several other officers had remained on board as a skeleton crew, hoping to beach the ship or have her towed to Queenstown. It was all in vain. On the 6th she sank, still some thirty-seven miles from land and not far from where the *Lusitania* wreck lay on the seabed.

And the shade of one victim of the *Lusitania* attack may well have given a wry smile. *Hesperian* had been carrying the casket and embalmed body of Frances Stephens, widow of a Canadian politician, who died in the sinking of the *Lusitania*. Mrs. Stephens thus achieved the rare, if not unique, distinction of being sunk twice by the same commander in the same submarine.

Baralong again

U-20 had not finished her work of destruction; the day after attacking *Hesperian* she sank *Dictator*, 4,116grt, and *Douro*, 1,604grt, both by gunfire off Fastnet and Bishops Rock. Then she returned home, although not – as shall be seen – to the hero's welcome that Schwieger had probably expected.

And *U-33* too had one last hurrah before departing, sending the *John Hardie* to the bottom, around 100 miles from Cape Finisterre. And then there was quiet. Until along came *U-41* under her commander, Claus Hansen. Since taking command of his submarine at the beginning of May, Hansen had sunk twenty-eight merchant ships, damaged one and taken one as a prize. On 23 September, *U-41* had sunk three merchant vessels, *Chancellor*, on passage from Liverpool to New Orleans with a 2,500-ton general cargo, *Hesione* and *Anglo-Columbian,* sailing from Quebec to Avonmouth with a cargo of horses. Now she was shelling the Wilson Lines 6,651grt steamer *Urbino,* returning to Hull from New York and positioned about sixty-seven miles SW by W of Bishop's Rock. Her crew had taken to their boats, jeered at by the German sailors, when the *Baralong,* now renamed *Wyandra* and with a new captain, Lieutenant Commander Andrew Wilmot-Smith, hove into view. Once again she was flying the American flag. Kapitänleutnant Hansen saw an opportunity for another kill and manoeuvred towards the newcomer when Wilmot-Smith dropped his disguise and opened fire. *U-41* sank rapidly as she tried to dive after being hit at the base of her conning tower. Two of her thirty-two man crew survived, but this time it was fairly certain that Wilmot-Smith had not lowered the US ensign before commencing his attack and this added to the outrage which the Germans felt about Q-ships in general. Nonetheless, Wilmot-Smith was awarded the DSO (gazetted 19 November 1915)[*] and a £170 bounty.[**]

Bayly's faith in the type had been vindicated; after a long wait,

---

[*] The listing in the *London Gazette* made no reference at all to the action which had warranted the award. The Admiralty was concerned to keep the actions of the Q-ships top secret.

[**] The Germans were fond of striking medals to mark events in the war, either patriotic or condemnatory, which were sold on the streets to raise war funds. *Baralong's* successes against *U-27* and *U-41* in 1915 led to two medals struck by Karl Groetz. With an insouciant disregard for the activities of their own U-boat commanders and their sinking of civilian ships, both medals sarcastically made the *Baralong's* victories out to be underhand and uncivilised. On the first a bearded figure in a plumed hat is depicted, pinning a decoration onto a sailor who is holding a knife; a female figure wearing a tiara holds a wreath with an inscribed ribbon 'DENKULTUR KAMPFERN' (the champions of culture). They represent George V and Queen Mary. On the reverse another picture carried the legend 'BARALONG MOERDER.' (Baralong Murder).
The second shows a fist rising out of the sea pointing at the White Ensign with 'U', '4' and '1' placed each in the three empty squares of the flag. The legend says 'ALBIONS EHREN – FLAGGE.' (Albion's Flag of Honour.) On the reverse are two men in a boat armed with guns and carrying a sail, one pointing a revolver at a man in the water. Propaganda has never, of course, had much truck with unbiased commentary.

the fightback in the waters of the Western Approaches had started. Some measure of revenge had been extracted for *Lusitania*, *Arabic* and *Hesperian*. And in October there were no losses to U-boats at all in the Coast of Ireland Command; indeed there were no U-boats. What had happened?

The Germans withdraw
The sinking of *Lusitania* and the loss of American lives had caused outrage in the neutral United States. The American government protested at the deliberate attack on non-combatant vessels and the loss of its citizens. A sharp exchange of diplomatic notes ensued and the temper of the country at large was inflamed. The protests of the US government did, in fact, cause some concern in Berlin, for the Kaiser and many of his ministers wished to keep America neutral and out of the War. President Woodrow Wilson condemned the killing of Americans stating 'no warning that an unlawful and inhumane act will be committed can possibly be accepted as an excuse of palliation'. Anti-German rioting broke out in American and British cities, with property worth over £40,000 destroyed in Liverpool alone.

However, these protests did not manifest themselves in any change of strategy and the Germans justified the *Lusitania* and other sinkings as reprisals for the British blockade of the German coast which was causing severe food shortages.[*]

The loss of *Arabic*, and more American lives, exacerbated the situation. On 22 August US President Wilson's press officer issued a statement which in essence stated that the White House staff was speculating on its course of action if an investigation into the causes of the loss of *Arabic* indicated that there had been a deliberate German attack. If true, it was possible that the US might sever diplomatic relations with Germany. If it was untrue, negotiations about leaving neutral ships and passenger liners unmolested and American diplomatic intervention with the Allies were possible. The Germans obfuscated and suggested *Arabic* had hit a mine. But more diplomatic notes crossed the Atlantic and the German ambassador to Washington, Count von Bernstorff, was informed by Secretary Lansing's assistant that if Germany abandoned submarine

---

[*] They also claimed that ship had been carrying arms and ammunition and that it was actually equipped as an auxiliary cruiser and was therefore a legitimate target (see Chapter 3).

warfare, Britain would be the only violator of American neutral rights.

The American government's diplomatic protests had been so pointed that the Kaiser and his chancellor, Bethmann-Hollweg, felt constrained to act. Bernstorff was told to inform the US government that, until further notice, all passenger ships would only be sunk after a warning and the saving of passengers and crews, a message he passed to Lansing at the end of August. German naval opinion was not in favour of such concessions and von Tirpitz, State Secretary of the Imperial Navy Office, offered his resignation in protest. It was declined by the Kaiser.

There was thus considerable embarrassment in Germany when the news of Walther Schwieger's sinking of *Hesperian* reached their ears. Washington was confused and annoyed. Newspaper headlines reflected this; the *Atlanta Constitution* of 6 September was typical. 'Germans torpedo liner *Hesperian* without warning; Washington hears of dead with unconcealed surprise.'

Schwieger was ordered to Berlin in order to justify his actions and apologise officially. He was accused of having sunk another unarmed passenger liner without warning, despite the explicit directions given to submarine commanders not to do so. Schwieger himself complained about his treatment, which he thought unfair, but to no avail (although he seems to have been forgiven by 1917 when he was awarded the '*Pour le Mérite*' – the 'Blue Max').

The instructions to U-boat commanders were further reinforced. The German Navy was prohibited from attacking liners of any nationality without giving due warning and ensuring the safety of passengers. As this was considered to expose the U-boats to unacceptable risks of attack and loss, the decision was taken to withdraw them from western waters altogether. They were concentrated instead on the Mediterranean, where the chances of meeting liners with Americans aboard were considered small.

Bayly wanted to go after them. In November he wrote to Jackson 'Why not send me with my flag in *Adventure* taking the sloops ... to work between Gibraltar and Malta to stop and sink submarines ... we could be there in ten to twelve days.'[3] Perhaps more than a little concerned at leaving Ireland undefended, Jackson declined the offer. Bayly was never far from a gripe. In November, he was having trouble with various of his officers. On the 4th he wrote to Jackson beseeching him to get rid of Captain Robert H Travers, who was

Senior Naval Officer at Berehaven. Bayly, ever concerned for the welfare of his men, wanted to build a YMCA hut there for their use in their leisure hours. Travers appeared to be a stumbling block; 'I know him of old many years ago,' Bayly told the First Sea Lord 'he does not help and I have had to send Carpendale [Captain Charles Carpendale, Flag Captain Queenstown] to smooth difficulties. If you could take Travers away … you would do a kindness.'[4]

And the reorganisation which had led to the expanded command that he now controlled had obviously not gone down well with everyone. The Scilly Isles command held by Commander William O Oliver and now in Bayly's purlieu had previously reported to the captain in charge at Falmouth, Captain Valentine E B Phillimore. Now Bayly complained that he had stopped sending orders to Oliver as 'he does not know where he is and neither do I … Orders are sent to Oliver by Captain Phillimore.'[5] And he still did not want any staff, saying he would rather wait for a good person than take anyone the Admiralty offered. 'I don't want a flag lieutenant until Dix is ready', he wrote.[6]

In November, as in October, no merchant vessels were lost in the territory of the Coast of Ireland Command. And just four were sunk in December in a brief spasm of activity. One was ss *Van Stirum*, sunk on Christmas Day by *U-24*. Two men were killed by the explosion of a torpedo as they tried to get their lifeboat lowered to the sea. And then on 28 December 1915 the tanker *El Zorro* (5,989grt) was ten miles off the Old Head of Kinsale, five miles from the very spot where *Lusitania* had been sunk and on passage from Port Arthur, Texas, to Dartford, when a submarine surfaced beside her and demanded her surrender. Her master rang down for full speed to escape and simultaneously radioed to Queenstown for assistance. But she could not outpace a surfaced U-boat and was soon taking in a hail of shells, one of which killed her chief engineer. A torpedo hit finally stopped her and the crew took to their boats. It was yet another kill for *U-24* and Rudi Schneider.

At Queenstown, Bayly had sprung into action. He sent the armed yacht *Greta* to the rescue, despatched two old torpedo boats and then ordered his flag raised in *Adventure* and put to sea at 0800hrs. At 1245hrs *Adventure* picked up a further SOS, from the brand-new Leyland Lines cargo vessel *Huronian* (8,766grt), heading for Liverpool from Galveston, Texas, with a cargo of grain and cotton. She had been torpedoed, Schneider again, and her forepart shattered by the explosion. Bayly ordered a speed of 22 knots and fifteen minutes later had found her, driving the U-boat away. More sloops were summoned to the scene and *Begonia* and *Camellia* were able to escort the wounded, but not crippled, ship into Berehaven and safety, her valuable cargo saved. Meanwhile, *Greta* and six trawlers and tugs in company were striving to get *El Zorro*, and her 8,000 tons of badly-needed oil, to harbour. The sea was high and vicious and near Daunts Rock Light Vessel it was decided that the men would need to be taken off the stricken tanker. In terrible conditions, an east-south-easterly gale and high, short sea, and in an act of great seamanship by the skipper, the trawler *Freesia* took off all but one man who perished trying to jump onto the trawler's deck. It was all in vain. In the storm that night, the tanker dragged her anchor and drove ashore, broke in two, spilled all her oil and was wrecked forever. It was not a good way to end the year.

7

The U-boats Return: January – April 1916

America in 1916

American pressure had caused the German U-boat campaign in the Western Approaches to be largely paused. Germany was worried that America might come into the war on the Allied side and did not wish to provoke her. Britain likewise was worried that if the USA took a resolutely neutral stance, it might actually work to the detriment of Britain, France and their allies.

The US President Woodrow Wilson, a Democrat, had come to power in the elections of 1912, largely because Teddy Roosevelt had run as an Independent and siphoned votes away from the Republican candidate. Wilson was an idealist, a pacifist and an academic who had studied history, political science and the German language. He was in many ways the antithesis of Roosevelt, the creator of America's Blue Water Navy, a belligerent enthusiast for war and who was to become the first and only American president to be posthumously awarded the Congressional Medal of Honour. Already the holder of a Nobel Peace Prize, Roosevelt's double distinction remains unique. Wilson was anti-war and pro free trade and the freedom of the seas. His government had reacted vigorously against Britain's declaration of November 1914 that all shipping in the North Sea and beyond would be stopped and searched for 'war contraband'.

American patience with this policy began to fray towards the end of 1914. To begin with the US government framed their demands for the freedom of the seas in the language of the impact on American trade. At the end of December 1914 the American ambassador to the Court of St James, Walter Hines Page, was instructed to deliver a note prepared by the Secretary of State, William Jennings Bryan, but given its final form by President Wilson himself. In this note the British government was asked to make such arrangements as will 'discourage the search of ships without evidence and seizure on suspicion'. The communication went on to suggest that American industry was suffering as a result of the policy, as exporters were reluctant to ship goods that might be detained or forfeit, and stated that America viewed with concern the detention of scores of American cargoes conveyed to neutral ports. In this, there was more than a hint of past arguments, the War of 1812 having been caused in large part by Britain's perceived infringement of America's maritime rights and the impressment of American seamen.

Immediately before the delivery of the note, the influential German-American lobby in Washington had been making strong representations to President Wilson that he needed to act or else he would face a backlash in the forthcoming elections. As the delivery of the communication became public, the German-American supporting newspapers celebrated it. The forthcoming election of November 1916 was a sore trial for Wilson; he wanted to win it and he thought that his best platform was to be 'the man who kept us out of the war'. There were some in America who wanted to join the Allies, largely amongst the East Coast elite; but there was also a substantial number who didn't. Amongst these could be ranked the number of foreign-born Americans who came from those countries now in opposition to Britain, France and Russia; not to speak of those who had their own reasons for a hatred of the British Empire. Wilson himself was Scots-Irish and no friend of Britain's imperial past. And out of a population of 92 million, 2.5 million were first-generation foreign-born German, 1.7 million foreign-born Russian and Finnish, 1.3 million born in Ireland, 1.3 million in Italy and 1.2 million in Austria-Hungary. And this does not reflect the size of the 'hyphenated' American population; there were 4.5 million Irish-American voters, for example.[1] Between 1820 and 1914, over 5 million Germans had emigrated to America together with some one million Austro-Hungarians. When Wilson visited Milwaukee in January 1916 the New York *Evening World* headlined 'Milwaukee Germans Cheer Wilson; 15,000 Give Him Rousing Welcome'.[2]

There was another, and grubbier, reason for America to stay out of the war. She was making a fortune from it. Despite the British blockade, American exports to all participants were booming. By the end of 1914 direct American trade to Germany had all but been extinguished, but a substantial amount still went through the Nordic and Scandinavian neutrals. And exports to Britain and France rose from $750 million in 1914 to $2.75 billion in 1916.

The sinkings of the *Lusitania*, *Arabic* and *Hesperian* had a profound effect on American public opinion, but not on Wilson's. 'There is such a thing as being too proud to fight'* became his watchword. 'There is such a thing as a nation being so right that it does not need to convince others by force that it is right'.[3] The moral high ground Wilson held was so high it must have given him a nosebleed. It wasn't high enough for Secretary of State William Jennings Bryan, however, who counselled an even-handed policy, treating Germany and the Allies just the same. Bryan resigned in June 1915, protesting '… Why be so shocked by the drowning of a few people, if there is to be no objection to starving a nation.'[4] He was replaced by Robert Lansing, a lawyer specialising in the international law of the sea.

Perhaps unsurprisingly, those in Britain and France who saw themselves fighting for civilisation itself were unimpressed. The *Sydney Sunday Times* referred to American policy in the war as 'a diseased itch for money'.[5] Pictures of President Wilson screened in cinemas or music halls in Britain provoked hissing and booing.

And so it was that both sides in the conflict had a beady eye focused on the USA and its likely reaction to further disruption to the freedom of the seas.

The U-boats return

Whilst the end of 1915 had been a quiet time in Bayly's command, U-boat attacks had continued apace in the Mediterranean and other areas. Over 153,000 tons of shipping had been sunk by U-boats in November and 123,000 tons in December. But in the Atlantic, the Germans relied on their surface raiders, especially the *Möwe*, under her charismatic commander Korvettenkäpitan Nikolaus Burggraf und Graf zu Dohna-Schlodien. In a mission lasting from the end of December 1915 to 5 March 1916 she sank fifteen merchant ships for a total of 57,520grt and tied up significant British naval resources in looking for her.** One of *Möwe*'s victims, the last of this first cruise, was ss *Saxon Prince*, captured and sunk by scuttling charges at the

---

* Wilson first used this phrase in an address in Philadelphia on 10 May 1915.

** Her three separate cruises are described in Dunn, *Blockade*.

extreme edge of Bayly's territory, 620 miles west of Fastnet. Her crew were all made prisoners.

But in March, the U-boat peril returned to plague Bayly. He redoubled his patrols and sent his Q-ships out. *U-32*, *U-70*, *U-28*, *U-43* and *U-44* were all at large in his waters. During March they sank twelve vessels between them for a total of 48,638grt. These included the tanker *Teutonic*, 4,823grt, inbound to Avonmouth with a cargo of American distilled oils, the tiny sailing ship *Willie*, 185grt, sunk by gunfire off Fastnet, tankers and a collier. SS *Englishman* (what a pleasure sinking a ship of that name must have been for *U-43*'s commander, Hellmuth Jürst) was on passage from Avonmouth to Portland, Maine, when she was torpedoed thirty miles north-east of Malin Rock on 24 March; ten men were killed.

On 29 March, *U-44*, commanded by Paul Wagenführ, was on patrol south of Ireland. In four days of operations she had sunk two ships; then Wagenführ spotted the sloop *Begonia*, under Lieutenant Commander Basil Stratford Noake. At 1345hrs he fired a torpedo which hit the sloop on the port side by the boiler room. This might have been a fatal wound to many ships but the 'Flower'-class sloops had been designed to withstand the impact of a mine forward and the magazine was placed aft: so, for now at least, she floated. Noake spotted a periscope 500yds to port and opened fire on it, forcing *U-44* to go deep and then resurface 200yds away to fire a second torpedo. This fortunately passed under the ship. The U-boat then stood off some five miles and awaited developments.

Begonia was in a sorry state with a large hole in her side, a 20° list, her main steam pipe carried away and her wireless out of action; additionally she had suffered one man killed, one man wounded and one missing. But her luck was in. Around 2000hrs the American-flagged SS *Siberia* came alongside and relayed her request for help using her own wireless. Of their own volition, the commanders of *Snowdrop* and *Zinnia* made for *Begonia*'s position and Bayly sent the tug *Warrior* and an armed trawler from Queenstown. Around 0300hrs the next day, *Snowdrop* managed a fine feat of seamanship and secured a tow, in the dark and with a rising sea, on her wounded sister. The sorry convoy limped back to Queenstown where *Begonia* was docked. The dockyard at Haulbowline then performed a seeming miracle; bit by bit the little ship was rebuilt, not as originally designed, but as another Q-ship to add to Bayly's fleet. As *Q-10* she was relaunched in August the following year. But her loss to active operations in 1916 was a blow to an already limited force.

On 31 March *U-44* went on to claim two significant victims. The tanker *Goldmouth,* belonging to the Anglo-Saxon Petroleum company and defensively armed with an old naval gun, was captured, sunk and her master taken prisoner. She had been inbound to Falmouth with a load of much needed oil from Tarahan. Then the *Achilles* was torpedoed without warning ninety miles west-north-west from Ushant; she had sailed all the way from Sydney, Australia, via Cape Town and was headed for London and Liverpool with a cargo of cereals and cotton. Five merchant seaman died in the attack.

But Bayly's fightback continued nonetheless. He deployed the trawlers to work inshore, looking out for submarines or ships to be escorted. The drifters worked nets off places which it was important to keep clear, his few submarines operated one at a time off the south-west coast; and the sloops (from 1 January 1916 there had been twelve on station) patrolled specific assigned areas on the trade route past the south of Ireland, five days at sea, two in harbour. But his ace in the hole was still his Q-ships.

Farnborough

Lieutenant Commander Gordon Campbell was an undistinguished officer, newly promoted from lieutenant and of limited achievements in the war so far. One of eleven sons and five daughters, he had gone to Britannia College in 1900 aged thirteen, and passed out unremarkably. Academically he did not shine, with four second class passes and two 'thirds' in his lieutenant's exams, and the outbreak of war found him commanding the old destroyer *Bittern*, a 'C'-class '30-knotter' dating from 1897 and now serving in the Devonport Local Defence Flotilla. He was one of many lieutenants assigned to the old and hard-worked destroyers which patrolled the coasts of Britain. His frustration with his lot reached its apogee when he and his ship chased an unknown vessel which had ignored his signals. *Bittern*'s engines, pushed to their limits, blew up and he had to hobble back to harbour at 4 knots. His temper was not improved by the discovery that the mysterious ship he had wanted to apprehend was a Royal Navy seaplane carrier.

Salvation was at hand. Consequent with his promotion to the extra half-stripe, in September 1915 he was appointed for 'special service' at Queenstown. He was to join Bayly's private Q-ship navy. Campbell took little comfort in the remark from a fellow officer that Bayly would either make him or break him. As he later noted, 'Although I didn't know Admiral Bayly personally, I knew his reputation for being a man who understood war and would tolerate neither fools nor red tape.'[6]

SS *Loderer* was a collier of 3,207grt built in 1904. She was taken up by the Navy early in the war and in 1915 sent to Devonport dockyard for conversion to a Q-ship. When she emerged she was Q-ship No 5, and named *Farnborough*. A 12pdr gun was hidden in a fake steering house aft, with two more concealed behind hinged flaps on either side of the main deck and another two guns in dummy cabins on the upper deck. A 6pdr was hidden at each end of the bridge and a Maxim placed in a 'hencoop' amidships. It was a formidable armament and for good measure she also carried some depth charges. Campbell was in command, and was the only RN officer on board, with another ten RNR officers and fifty-six crew. On 21 October he commissioned her and took his new command to Queenstown.

On 20 March 1916, Campbell was at sea to the south-west of Ireland when he received a message that a U-boat had been sighted nearby. He turned his vessel in the direction of the sighting, heading north, just another tramping ship about its everyday business. At 0640hrs on the 22nd Campbell spotted through the murk a U-boat just above the surface. He sounded action stations and signalled to Queenstown, but otherwise did not react. Twenty minutes later, his crew saw a torpedo wake on the starboard side; everyone tried to look relaxed, and were so when it passed harmlessly by. Then a submarine surfaced on their port side and a shot rang out ahead of *Farnborough*. In Morse, Campbell sent to Bayly that he was being fired on. A carefully-rehearsed and deliberately amateur 'abandon ship' drill was now put into practice by Campbell's crew, even down to one man pretending to be the master and carrying a (stuffed) parrot in a cage. As this 'panic party' took to the boats, Campbell and a carefully-chosen group of engineers, gunners and officers remained on board, hidden from sight. The submarine was lulled into a false sense of security and presented its full length, ahead on the port side of *Farnborough*, 800yds away. The U-boat fired again, just missing *Farnborough*'s magazine. It was time to act. Campbell blew a whistle, the White Ensign ran up the masthead, the concealing panels fell away and a withering fire blazed out at the enemy. *Farnborough* fired twenty-eight rounds into the U-boat as she tried to dive. Campbell drove his ship at the spot where she had gone down and rolled out his two primitive depth charges. With a roar of escaping air, *U-68* rose vertically from the water and then sank, never to reappear. There were no survivors. Kapitänleutnant Ludwig Güntzel and his thirty-seven crewmen would never now get the chance to chalk up their first 'kill' and had unwillingly become the first submarine victims of a depth charge attack.

Victorious, Campbell signalled at 0745hrs to Bayly 'Have sunk enemy submarine'. And at 0810hrs 'Shall I return or look for another?'[7] He was ordered home. And when *Farnborough* docked in Queenstown at 0700hrs, Bayly sent his admiral's barge with a handwritten letter of congratulations and a basket of fresh-laid eggs, a considerable luxury in wartime. Two hours later, the admiral himself arrived and congratulated the crew in person.

For this exploit, Campbell was awarded the first of the three DSOs he would eventually win; he had found his metier. And, at Bayly's urging, he was promoted to the rank of commander over the head of 700 lieutenant commanders above him on the Navy List.

April

ss *Zent* was an Elders Line refrigerated vessel of 3,890grt, inbound with a cargo of meat. On 6 April she was attacked and torpedoed without any warning by *U-66*, slightly south-west of Fastnet. In their panic to escape, the crew manged to overturn every lifeboat and raft; *U-66* observed them in the water and then sailed away. Forty-nine merchant mariners died that day; only the master, Captain Martin, and ten crewmen survived to be picked out of the Atlantic Ocean by a passing steamer.

Indeed, April proved to be a shocking month for British-flagged ships in the Coast of Ireland Command. Five U-boats accounted for nineteen merchant ships with a total of 66,485grt. Ninety seamen lost their lives including two masters. At this time, sailing ships still formed a substantial part of the mercantile fleet and they were easy prey for submarines. The barque *Inverlyon* was sunk by gunfire from *U-73* on the 11th. A Russian-flagged barque, *Schwanden*, was scuttled by *U-69* four days later. The same submarine accounted for the fully-rigged sailing ship *Cardonia* on the 16th, just twenty miles south of Fastnet while *U-67* put paid to *Ravenhill*, another fully-rigged sailing vessel. And on the 22nd the French-flagged four-masted barque *Chanaral* was sunk, again by *U-67*, sixty miles from Bishop's Rock. For all Bayly's patrols and Q-ships, they seemed unable to prevent the carnage. And then it stopped again. Why?

The *Sussex* affair

Still fixated by the issue of potential American intervention, the Germans had announced a new campaign on 11 February 1916 in which only enemy merchant vessels within the designated war zone would be considered as fair game; outside they could only be sunk without the application of international rules if armed, and passenger liners were not to be interfered with in any way. As can be seen above, this edict was often honoured in the breach.

On 24 March *UB-29* torpedoed and sank without warning the French-flagged passenger steamer *Sussex*, crossing between Dieppe and Folkestone. She was carrying 53 crew and 325 passengers, including American citizens. The ship was severely damaged, with the entire bow forward of the bridge blown off. Some of the lifeboats were launched, but at least two of them capsized and many passengers were drowned. In total at least fifty lost their lives. Several Americans were injured. *Sussex* remained afloat and was eventually towed stern-first into Boulogne Harbour. Following on from the promises extracted by the US government from Germany, this further breaking of their undertaking with regard to passenger vessels enraged public opinion in the United States, and caused another heated exchange between the two governments. Panicked by the strength of the American diplomatic notes, which implied that America would break off diplomatic relations if Germany did not immediately comply with International Law, on 4 May 1916 Germany issued a declaration, the '*Sussex* pledge', which effectively once more brought about the suspension of the U-boat campaign.

The government instructed the Naval Staff to prohibit all attacks outside prize rules. Angry and frustrated, on 24 April Admiral Reinhard Scheer (CinC High Seas Fleet) ordered his U-boats to port. Trade flowed freely again. In the first two weeks of May, seven merchant ships were lost in the Western Approaches. In the next two weeks, none. But meanwhile, Bayly had been much preoccupied.

'A Terrible Beauty is Born', April 1916*

The unrest which had been simmering in Ireland before the outbreak of war was not dissipated by it. Indeed the reverse was true, with many revolutionary-minded Irishmen seeing opportunity in Britain's troubles. When the London government introduced conscription on 2 March 1916, Ireland was specifically excluded to avoid inflaming the ill-feeling and nationalist ardour which lay just beneath the surface, particularly in the south and south-west of Ireland, although attempts at voluntary enlistment continued apace, if not in peace. The *Morning Post* of 16 March, for example, urged the government to act firmly against 'Irishmen who are opposing recruitment', adding 'the anti-British activity of the Sinn Fein Society is blamed for much of the agitation. An organised campaign against recruiting in the south and west is carried on. It includes the distribution of pro-German pamphlets.'[1]

However, the Nationalist leader John Redmond tried to maintain the position he had set out in 1914. Responding to a call for a mass meeting to object to increases in 'war taxation' in Ireland (which applied in the rest of Britain too) imposed in Chancellor of the Exchequer Reginald McKenna's March budget, Redmond declared to prominent Nationalists that 'the best interest of Ireland lies in a speedy termination of the war', pointing out that for citizens to 'obstruct recruiting in Ireland and other pro-German efforts would result in merely the prolongation of the war'.[2]

---

* It is not the purpose of this book to give a detailed description of the Easter Rising in Ireland. It is now part of the Irish mythscape and many great authors have written about it better than this one ever could. This chapter deals only with the role of the Coast of Ireland Command and Admiral Lewis Bayly in the events that followed the outbreak of the rebellion.

Some Nationalists thought otherwise. In a similar fashion to another part of the British Empire, India, and the nascent Indian Independence Movement, the Irish rebels collaborated with their Indian counterparts and mutually sought help from Germany during the war. They also called on their compatriots in America for arms and money. They modelled themselves on the Boers, whose revolt at the turn of the century was much admired, even to the point of affecting their commando slouch hats and calling themselves 'De Wets' after one of the leaders of the Boer insurrection.

The capture of the *Aud*

A necessary precursor to a revolt was to obtain weapons and, even better, military support. The Irish patriot and former British consular official, Sir Roger Casement, who had become treasurer of the Irish Volunteers in 1913, had travelled first to America where he had met the German ambassador Count von Bernstorff in New York, to propose a mutually beneficial plan: if Germany would sell guns to the Irish revolutionaries and provide military leaders, the Irish would revolt against England, diverting troops and attention from the war on Germany. Bernstorff appeared generally sympathetic and paved the way for Casement to visit Germany itself.

Accordingly, in October 1914 Casement then voyaged to Germany, via neutral Norway, and met with Arthur Zimmermann, then Under-Secretary of State in the Foreign Office, and with the Imperial Chancellor, Theobald von Bethmann-Hollweg. Here he obtained a declaration that Germany would assist any planned insurrection and that he could attempt to recruit an Irish Brigade from POWs held in German camps; this was a failure, with only fifty-five men enlisting. Amongst other things, Casement also asked for a U-boat to sail up the Liffey and a blockship to be sunk at the entrance to Dublin harbour.

Then in March 1916 Germany offered the Irish nationalists 20,000 Mosin-Nagant M1891 Russian rifles, captured on the Eastern Front, ten machine guns with accompanying ammunition and explosives, but no German military advisers. It was much less than Casement had wanted or expected, but he made arrangements for the weapons to be shipped to Ireland.

ss *Castro* was a 1,062-ton steam cargo transport built for the Wilson Line of Hull, in 1907. At the beginning of the war she had been impounded by the Imperial German Navy in the Kiel Canal.

Renamed *Libau*, she remained inactive until 1916, when she was offered as the vessel to carry Casement's arms shipment to Ireland and given yet another name; ss *Aud* (the name of an actual Norwegian ship).

Commanded by Karl Spindler and crewed by twenty-two Imperial Navy sailors, all volunteers, she left Lübeck on 9 April 1916, bound for the south-west coast of Ireland. By skill and good fortune, she evaded patrols of both the British 10th Cruiser Squadron and coastal defence auxiliary patrols and battled through violent storms off Rockall. On 20 April, *Aud* arrived in Tralee Bay, County Kerry, for Fenit harbour where she was supposed to meet with Casement (who had travelled separately by submarine and arrived in the early hours of the 21st) and men to help transfer the arms. Having no radio (the German navy had refused to so equip the vessel), Spindler did not know that the rendezvous had been put back to 23 April. Nor did he know, as Casement had not until very recently, that the rising was planned for the 24th. Casement, thinking that there were not enough arms and that they should be unloaded and secreted away for another time, now decided to try to stop the revolt taking place.

What neither Casement nor Spindler knew was that Bayly knew that they were coming. Room 40, the Admiralty's signals intelligence operation, had intercepted more than thirty messages from Bernstorff and Berlin indicating German support for the rebellion. In early April they decoded a signal from the Count informing his masters that the uprising was planned for Sunday 23 April. And Room 40 told Bayly (and the First Lord, Balfour, who told the Cabinet, which didn't believe it and took no action). Bayly increased the guards on naval installations, as well as the frequency and intensity of the patrols of his sloops and trawlers, and waited; and the Admiralty sent him the cruiser *Gloucester* with four attendant destroyers.

Spindler, having failed to find anyone to welcome him, stayed out in the bay. At 0500hrs the armed trawler *Setter II* came alongside and sent a boarding party to inspect the ship. But Spindler was able to bluff that he had engine trouble and removed a hatch cover to show merchandise that was certainly not military, but pots and pans and other such stuff, as described in his manifest. The trawler departed unsuspecting.* If he thought he might have got away with

---

* Her skipper was subsequently court martialled.

it, Spindler was wrong; at 1300hrs he saw the large armed trawler *Heneage*, commanded by an RNR officer, not a fishing skipper as had been *Setter II,* coming into view. She had been warned of a suspicious vessel by the Loop Head signal station nearby.

It was enough for Spindler. He ordered that his cargo should be thrown overboard and set off with all the speed his ship could muster. *Heneage* followed but her quarry was faster and pulled slowly away toward the wide Atlantic. Lieutenant W H A Bee in *Heneage* might not be able to catch up; but he had a radio and friends who might. His message was taken in by the sloops *Zinnia* and *Bluebell* who immediately moved to intercept. Bayly ordered *Aud* to be taken and brought to Queenstown for inspection. It was *Bluebell* who took her in; she found the German vessel ninety miles to the south-west of Ireland and signalled *Aud* to follow. When Spindler was dilatory, a shell fired across his bows changed his mind. Just outside Queenstown harbour, at around 0925hrs on Good Friday, *Aud* suddenly stopped, the crew hastily abandoned ship and she blew up. Spindler had sunk the evidence and tried at the same time to block the harbour entrance. He failed in both attempts.

Bluebell picked up the German crew and took them into harbour, where Bayly sent his admiral's barge and CPO Wade to bring Spindler to him. Wade offered to carry the German officer's suitcase, an offer rudely rebuffed. The reason was not far to find – it was full of English gold sovereigns. Three rebel leaders had been sent from Dublin to Limerick by train to supervise the unloading of the weapons. On arrival it was night and they hired a car and driver for Fenit, telling their chauffeur they would direct him. This they did – off the edge of a wharf where they were all drowned, excepting the driver.

Casement, ill and unable to travel, had been discovered on the beach near to where he had been landed and arrested, also on Good Friday*. And back at Fenit Harbour in Tralee Bay, 240 motor cars waited to collect arms which were already at the bottom of the sea. Bayly noted 'when *Aud* was driven off the coast ... there were motor cars from Cork, Waterford, Limerick, the whole south and west

---

* Casement was arrested by a policeman in a ruined fort (McKenna's Fort) just off the beach. The constable had been alerted to suspicious activity by the discovery of a boat and close by, three revolvers and a large supply of ammunition, three flash lamps, maps, a cipher code, and the green and gold flag of the Sinn Fein Republic. Casement was later convicted of treason and hanged in Pentonville prison on 3 August 1916, despite many pleas for clemency from Ireland and the USA.

principal towns for the arms that never came'.[3] With sardonic glee he added 'one considerable factor of success was that the three principal organisers of Sinn Fein for Limerick were the three that were drowned in a motor car ... and suffered the fate of the Gadarene swine'.[4]

The Germans did, however, provide some support designed to distract the British response in Ireland. On 24/25 April Scheer arranged for six airships to attack Norwich, Lincoln, Harwich and Ipswich while a battlecruiser squadron shelled Great Yarmouth and Lowestoft. The Times headlined this as 'all apparently part of a concerted German plan'.[5] Maybe it was. But British intelligence had certainly meant that the Aud's fate was sealed well before it reached Irish waters. As Bayly himself wrote 'the sinking of the Aud was beautifully stage managed; my niece was on the roof and saw her go down'.[6]

To the British, it seemed that they had nipped the rebellion in the bud. With Casement captured and the arsenal provided by the Germans gone, all that was necessary was to round up the ring leaders. They decided to wait until Monday to do so. But they were wrong.

The Rising
The Easter Rising was intended to take place across all Ireland; however, a variety of mishaps resulted in it being effective primarily only in Dublin. On 24 April 1916, Easter Monday, the rebel leaders and their followers, many of whom were members of the rump of the nationalist organization, the Irish Volunteers, or of small radical militia groups, such as the Irish Citizen's Army and the Irish Revolutionary Brotherhood (IRB), seized the city's General Post Office and other strategic locations. Early that afternoon, from the steps of the post office, Patrick Pearse, one of the uprising's leaders, read a proclamation declaring Ireland an independent republic and stating that a provisional government (comprised of IRB members) had been appointed. It was war.

Dublin
At the beginning of the nineteenth century, the Royal Navy had decided to establish a base at Dublin, just south of the city at Dunleary, and construction was authorised in 1816. On the occasion of the visit of George IV in 1821 the harbour's name was changed to

Kingstown (today Dún Laoghaire) but like Queenstown it was moribund by the start of the war. Early in 1915 Kingstown was reactivated as a base for minesweeping and patrolling trawlers (fifty of them by 1918) with the depot ship *Boadicia II*, an armed yacht built in 1882 and fitted with one 12pdr and one 6pdr gun. From January 1916, the port had been under the Senior Naval Officer, a retired captain reactivated for war duty as a commander RNR, Henry F Aplin.

In April 1916, Aplin's command was light in firepower, comprising *Boadicea II* and six armed trawlers (designated 'Unit 66') and another six trawlers with the armed yacht *Helga*, equipped with two 12pdr guns and named 'Unit 67'. Built in 1908, she had previously served as a 'fisheries cruiser' for the protection and policing of the fishing grounds around Ireland and had been taken up by the Navy in March 1915 and converted in Dublin dockyard. The primary duty of both groups of vessels was the protection of the daily mail boat route to Holyhead and of troop convoys when they sailed. On 5 March, *Helga* had been sent to investigate a suspicious vessel off the Codling light vessel, but found nothing; and on the 27th she was despatched to look for a floating mine fifteen miles east of Dublin, but again there was nothing to report. Other than that, March and April was an ocean of ennui and routine.

That changed around 1400hrs on 24 April, when an army officer in civilian clothes arrived at Kingstown by bicycle, asking that a message be sent to London urgently. At 1430hrs, this message informed the powers that be that an uprising had taken place and communications from Dublin to the rest of Ireland were cut. Aplin immediately signalled Unit 67 to return to Kingstown. At around 1700hrs he was informed by the military that 'large bodies of Sinn Feinners were gathering on the banks of the Royal Canal, evidently expecting the arrival of a boat with ammunition'.[7] They asked that a naval vessel be sent up the Liffey and Aplin went himself with a trawler and *Helga*. He found nothing, and left to return to Kingstown, leaving *Helga* commanding the River Liffey with *Sealark II*, an armed trawler pulled out of the dockyard where it was being repaired. Army reinforcements began to arrive and occupied the north bank of the river, whereupon *Helga* was requested to take a party of men across the water to guard the Pigeon Point power station. A trawler was also despatched with seventy-five men to defend Kingstown, where all confidential books and codes had been placed in a trawler which was moored in the middle of the harbour, and a passing coastal sloop was commandeered to come into Kingstown and keep the harbour illuminated through the night with her searchlight.*

No one in London really knew what was going on and reliable news from Ireland was hard to come by. On the instructions of Andrew Bonar Law (Secretary of State for the Colonies), his fellow Canadian Max Aitkin (later Lord Beaverbrook) managed to gain access to the only working telephone line to Dublin and somehow reached Irish right-wing Catholic Nationalist Tim Healy. 'Is there a rebellion?' he demanded. 'Yes' was the reply. 'When did it begin?' asked Aitkin. 'When Strongbow [Richard de Clare, 2nd Earl of Pembroke] came over to Ireland.' 'When will it be over?' 'When Cromwell gets out of hell' a drunken Healy roared back.[8]

Meanwhile, at Queenstown, at 2155hrs Bayly ordered Captain Hyde to take *Adventure* to Kingstown to cover the landing of two infantry brigades being sent from Liverpool and ensure W/T communication if the rebels put the W/T station there out of action. In difficult weather conditions (Force 7 from the south-east) she made her best possible speed and arrived in Kingstown harbour at 0750hrs. Known as a touchy character, Aplin maintained that he did not need any additional help, but Hyde trained his guns on the approaches to the pier and wharf and stayed where he was. It was just as well for at 0815hrs the rebels cut off the power to Kingstown W/T station, as Bayly had predicted they would, and *Adventure* now became the only radio link to the mainland (via the Fishguard W/T station). The expected reinforcements began to arrive from Liverpool, starting with the mail steamer *Ulster* at 2200hrs on Tuesday, and followed by five more transport vessels escorted by three destroyers, sent from Queenstown by Admiral Bayly.

Meanwhile, reports came in of trouble in the Skerries (north-east of Ireland, just off Portrush, County Antrim) and that the W/T station there was to be attacked at midnight. Bayly and Aplin sent *Boadicia II* with orders to use her gun if necessary but not to land any men. She arrived at 1300hrs on Wednesday and her advent persuaded the local rebel commander to call off his planned raid on the communications buildings. Later the destroyer *Dee* (based at Liverpool and originally sent to Kingstown as transport for the GOC

---

* Most accounts give this as *P-50* but it could not be as she had not yet been built.

Irish Command) arrived with 170 troops and that effectively ended any possibility that the Skerries could fall into rebel hands.

There were about 1,000 Irish Volunteers at Enniscorthy (on the River Slaney), seventy miles south of Dublin, where they had cut the railway line and threatened a nearby munitions factory. The local military commander asked for assistance and Bayly ordered Admiral Dare at Milford Haven to send armed trawlers as guard ships. This was sufficient to deter any attack.

Back in Dublin, the *Helga* found herself in the thick of things. On Tuesday she had secured to a berth on the River Liffey, with gun crews and a rifle party on deck, and stood to. At 1415hrs she fired, as requested by the military, at Boland's Mill with her 12pdrs. That night, in response to a rumour that the rebels were attacking the Pigeon House power station, she shifted moorings and anchored off it. On Wednesday mooring she steamed up river and fired twenty-four rounds from her 12pdrs at Liberty Hall, where the rebels had established an armaments factory but which was, in fact, empty at the time. Considerable damage was caused to the Hall and to next-door Northumberland House.

That same day the Lord Lieutenant of Ireland, Lord Wimbourne, issued a proclamation by way of handbills, posted and distributed around Dublin.

The Lord Lieutenant has issued the following statement from the Vice-Regal Lodge; During the night the Royal Naval Reserve Gunboat on the Liffey shelled, and the troops subsequently occupied, Liberty Hall (Headquarters of the Sinn Fein Force). Meanwhile large reinforcements have arrived in Dublin, including detachment of 10,000 troops from England, with Artillery, Engineers and Medical Corps. In other portions of the city the situation is well in hand. Repairs to telegraph lines now being rapidly effected. By Order. Dated 26th April, 1916.

But the artillery had yet to arrive, and the army was short of heavy weapons so, also on Wednesday, *Adventure* landed a 6pdr gun which was mounted onto a horse-drawn coal wagon by her engineers. They armoured it with steel plate and *Adventure* provided two gun crews to man the contraption. It was transported to fire on Boland's Mill where the Volunteers' 3rd Battalion, under

Commandant Eamon de Valera, were ensconced. This was a key location as it controlled the railway line and the main road from Kingstown to the city centre. The mill was also taken under fire by *Helga*, which additionally shot at the Dublin Distillery buildings where future Irish President de Valera had caused an Irish flag to be flown as a decoy. The coal wagon's improvised gun actually managed to fire off eighty-eight rounds that day. That night Dublin burned. 'Large conflagration in Dublin', noted Captain Hyde.[9]

Cork/Queenstown

The Admiralty had expected Bayly to return *Gloucester* and her escorts now the *Aud* had been captured. But when news of the uprising came through he declined to part with them, informing London that he was keeping the cruiser with the destroyers *Morning Star*, *Nictator*, *Ossory* and *Onslow* and peremptorily ordered them to Queenstown.

In his autobiography, published in 1939, Bayly states that he had demanded a battleship from the Admiralty and they sent him *Albemarle*, a pre-dreadnought of the *Duncan* class armed with four 12in guns and a variety of lighter guns. She was outdated and out-classed if in combat with the German High Sea Fleet; but in Irish waters she would be a powerful asset. He says that he anchored her in the river just above Queenstown and 'propaganda ... was issued to warn the people that on the slightest trouble in Cork, she would shell the city'.[10] The only trouble with this story is that according to her log book *Albemarle* was in Murmansk, Russia, at the time. In fact it was *Albion* that was despatched to Queenstown, a *Canopus*-class ship of 1898, fresh from service at Salonika. Bayly was also sent a battalion of Royal Marines and he ordered them to dig in on Haulbowline Island. When the people of Queenstown awoke, there was a line of machine-gun emplacements facing the town, defending the dockyard from any attempt to force a landing by water.

The senior leaders of the Cork-based Volunteers had been informed of the rising two weeks before Easter. They had been instructed to march to the Cork/Kerry border on Easter Sunday and 'protect the offloading of 20,000 rifles from a German vessel'; these were to be distributed to Volunteer units in Limerick, Clare and Galway who were to form a protective screen south of the River Shannon. But 'the Rising leaders issued no back-up instructions and the units themselves were so poorly armed that any other action would be doomed to failure'.[11]

In fact, around 1,200 Irish Volunteers had mustered in Cork on Easter Sunday, but they dispersed after receiving nine contradictory orders from the Volunteer leadership in Dublin. On 26 April and much to the anger of many Cork Volunteers, their leader, Tomás Mac Curtain, under pressure from the Catholic clergy, agreed to surrender his men's arms to the Lord Mayor of Cork on the understanding that they would be returned at a later date. Mac Curtain was arrested and the arms were never returned. It was probably just as well; on the 30th, the garrison commander at Queenstown, Brigadier General Stafford, gained an additional battalion of soldiers, sent from the 179th Brigade of the 60th Division (originally a London-based Territorial unit) in England and later the rest of the 179th joined him.

Galway

The other major events of the rising took place in Galway. The SNO there was Commander Francis W Hanan, a Irishman and former naval officer who had come out of retirement for the war. On hearing of the rising in Dublin, Hanan took immediate and decisive action; he closed all the public houses – and then arrested thirteen leading Sinn Fein members and put them under lock and key.

It was found that telegraphic communications with Dublin had been severed and so Hanan established communications with London through the Marconi station at Clifden by sending messages via America. This left two primary threats to be dealt with. Firstly, a small detachment of police were besieged in their barracks at Athenry, fifteen miles to the east of Galway city itself. Secondly, an estimated 1,200 rebels seized a nearby experimental farm, which belonged to the Department of Agriculture and Technical Instruction for Ireland, the same body that had once owned *Helga*.

Commander Hanan led an attempt to rescue the embattled policemen using an armoured train which came under fire but was ultimately successful. On the Wednesday a British scouting party was fired upon as it left Galway, leading to a thirty-minute gun battle after which the Volunteers retired to Athenry and the British back to Galway. A request for military support to break the impasse had been denied by Dublin, as all available manpower was needed there. However, sea power came to the rescue. On hearing from

Hanan of the threat to Galway, Bayly sent the sloop HMS *Laburnum* under Lieutenant Commander William Wybrow Hallwright and she arrived in the morning of Wednesday 26th.

The small British garrison at Galway had taken up defensive positions to the east of the town in a cemetery. On Wednesday afternoon a convoy of motor vehicles carrying rebel fighters was observed to be approaching this defensive perimeter and someone had seemingly informed the Royal Irish Constabulary that the Claregalway and Castlegar Volunteers were marching on Galway. Others said it was men from Athenry.

From her positon in the harbour roads, and directed by an observer in the cemetery, and another on the roof of the Railway Hotel, *Laburnum* fired nine 12pdr rounds at them from her aft gun. No hits were seen and indeed it later transpired that the rebel commander at Athenry had sent no men but, whatever the threat, it was removed by the sloop's firing.*

The following day Bayly despatched SS *Great Southern* (a railway packet usually sailing on the Fishguard to Rosslare route) from Queenstown, with men from the Royal Munster Fusiliers on board and escorted by *Snowdrop*; and later the same day the cruiser *Gloucester* arrived off Galway with more troops and gave a significant boost to the seaborne artillery fire that could be provided. Galway was thus reinforced and with the collapse of the rising in Dublin, the force at Athenry faded away into the countryside.

One of the men rounded up by Commander Hanan's sweep was Frank Hardiman, a member of the IRB in Galway since 1913 and treasurer of the Irish Volunteers there from 1915. He and his fellow prisoners were transferred to the patrol trawler *Guillimot* from where they saw *Laburnum* arrive in harbour. They were transferred to the sloop where they were detained and 'cordoned off by strong canvas and slept in hammocks rigged up by the sailors – they were quite comfortable',[12] and from where they could hear *Laburnum*'s firing. Hardiman also observed *Gloucester* enter the bay, escorting a troopship with troops on their way to Galway. He was soon to become more familiar with *Gloucester* for he and his colleagues were transferred to her, where they were lined up on deck. As each prisoner's name was

---

* In his autobiography, Bayly states that it was *Snowdrop* that shelled Galway; this is incorrect.

99

called, a charge of treason was read out by a naval lieutenant. 'He told us that the penalty if found guilty would be death, and warned us that any prisoner trying to escape would be immediately shot.'[13] From *Gloucester* they were transferred to *Snowdrop* for passage to Queenstown. The sloop's brig was not designed for such numbers and their voyage was uncomfortable in the extreme. On arrival, the prisoners were transferred to *Albion* and detained there for a week before finally Bayly's flagship *Adventure* took them to Kingstown, from whence they went England and to Wandsworth Prison.

Meanwhile, in Kingstown a vessel of the Commissioners of Irish Lights, the lightship *Cormorant*, was requisitioned on 1 May for one night to confine several prisoners under guard. They were eventually sent to internment camps or prisons. The revolt was over. Some 450 people had been killed and more than 2,000 others wounded in the fighting, which also destroyed a swathe of Dublin city centre. As one eyewitness, Mary Louisa Norway,* noted 'it passed all my powers of description and only one word describes it "desolation"'.[14]

According to the official despatches, 106 British soldiers died in the rising with 344 wounded;[15] the Navy reported two ratings wounded and one killed. And he was not killed in the fighting. Robert Glaister RNR was a 45-year-old retired marine engineer from East Cote near Silloth, Cumberland. He was a reservist serving as an engine room artificer on HMS *Colleen*, Queenstown's depot ship. On 28 April, with the rising still in progress, Glaister was sitting outside the Northern Hotel on Amiens Street, Dublin with the proprietor of the hotel, Francis Gray. Glaister invited Gray to take a stroll around the area, which was quiet at the time. In the course of their perambulation, they came upon Private Henry Joseph Wyatt, serving with an Irish regiment, who was on sentry duty near the hotel. Wyatt challenged both men to halt, which they did. Wyatt pressed his rifle to Glaister's chest and Glaister pushed the rifle away. The gun discharged, hitting Glaister in the arm. Glaister and Gray rushed back to the hotel followed by Wyatt, who fired on both men but missed. Whilst the two men attempted to close the hotel door Wyatt caught up to them and placed the muzzle of his rifle on Glaister's chest and fired, killing him. He then ordered the guests in the hotel upstairs, firing at the wife of

---

* Wife of Arthur Norway, the Secretary of the Irish Post Office.

the proprietor as she took her children upstairs. According to witnesses, Wyatt was drunk.

Wyatt was court martialled and found guilty of manslaughter. He was sentenced to five years penal servitude, presumably on the basis that his actions were inflamed by the situation in the city at the time. Glaister was buried in Glasnevin Cemetery, Dublin. What a pointless waste of life.

* * *

Bayly's navy had been a deciding factor in the suppression of the revolt, providing logistics and artillery at a time of need. As he himself put it: 'We have had quite an interesting time and thanks to the captain of the *Laburnum* who saved Galway, and others, the rebels in the West were finally held.'[16]

Others were in agreement. The Earl of Midleton, William St John Fremantle Brodrick, a previous Secretary of State for War in Balfour's administration and an important Cork landlord, wrote that 'but for the prompt measures taken by Sir Lewis Bayly, all of the south would have risen'.[17] Field Marshal Viscount French of Ypres, commanding all troops in the British Isles, added his recognition in his official despatch: 'I beg to bring to your notice the assistance afforded to me by the Lords Commissioners of the Admiralty, who met every request made to them for men, guns and transport with the greatest promptitude, and whose action enabled me to reinforce and maintain the garrisons in the south and west of Ireland without unduly drawing upon the troops which it was desirable to retain in England.'[18]

The Easter Rising could hardly have taken place at all but for the landing of a cargo of arms from the Continent at Howth at the beginning of August 1914 from the yacht *Asgard,* owned and sailed by the novelist and Irish Nationalist Erskine Childers. But, 'militarily, the revolt would have been a far more formidable affair if the arms had been got ashore at Fenit'.[19] Indeed, the noted Irish maritime authority John de Courcy Ireland thought that 'the British navy retained effective control of the waters around Ireland unhindered by any Irish effort whatever'.[20] And the Irish historian Daire Brunicardi has noted that 'there can be little doubt that the navy was the biggest single asset that the authorities had at their disposal in supressing the rising, with its communications, technical support, mobility and firepower'.[21]

101

The Calm Before the Storm, May – December 1916

The rebellion may have ended but Bayly was not at all sanguine about the situation. Writing to First Sea Lord Henry Jackson on 2 May he averred that 'We are not relaxing an inch, as these people look on kindness as weakness'[1] and that 'I expect trouble on the Dingle peninsula when the arms are surrendered'.[2] To deal with this eventuality, he asked Jackson to appoint a local Justice of the Peace, Lieutenant McMullen RNR, a Kerry man, to command the drifter *Golden Effort* which Bayly had despatched to the potential trouble spot. Jackson sent the request on to the Fourth Sea Lord, Captain Cecil Lambert, with the annotation 'can this be done'. The Irish Volunteers were to give up their arms on the 6th, a requirement that was not extended to the Unionists in the north; Bayly foresaw trouble. 'The situation is interesting because in this case if there is trouble it will be in the SW of Ireland; whereas if ALL arms are called in the trouble would be in the north east.'[3] And he had decided that Henry Aplin had to go. He is 'very difficult to get on with' he told Jackson,[4] grumbling 'I asked for an admiral and got a commander'.

The loss of *Cymric*

The war had not stopped while Ireland simmered and then boiled over in revolt. Maurice Hankey, secretary to the War Council, confided to his diary on 19 April that forty-three ships had been sunk in April to date for a total of 140,000grt. Thirty-seven had been lost to U-boats. Overall, he calculated that 423 merchant ships had been sunk by the enemy during the war thus far, accounting for 1.4 million tons.[5] But then Scheer withdrew his submarines (see Chapter 7).

In the Western Approaches this meant a sudden decrease in the loss of merchant ships. In the first six days of May four British vessels, including *Galgate*, a four-masted fully-rigged vessel of 2,356grt, and two French barques were sunk. *U-20* claimed three of them and was looking for a bigger prize before making for home.

ss *Cymric* was a 13,370grt steamship of the White Star Line, built by Harland and Wolff in Belfast and launched on 12 October 1897. She had originally been designed as a combination passenger liner and livestock carrier, with accommodation only for first class passengers. However, it became clear that such a combination would not be a marketing success and so the stalls originally designated for cattle were reconfigured into third class accommodation. She sailed initially on the Liverpool–New York run, then Liverpool to Boston. When war came, *Cymric* was used as a troop and cargo transport. In August 1915, under the command of Captain Frank E Beadnell, she delivered 17,000 tons of ammunition from New York to Liverpool, one of the biggest such shipments since the start of the war, and she continued to voyage between the Atlantic coast of America and Britain, carrying cargo and passengers.

On 29 April 1916, *Cymric* finished her loading in New York and sailed for Liverpool with 112 crew on board, including only six passengers (according to the *New York Times*, members of the British Consular Service), and with Captain Beadnell still in command. On 8 May she was 140 miles west-north-west of the Fastnet when she was torpedoed without warning by Walther Schwieger in *U-20*. So much for adherence to prize rules. Three torpedoes were fired at her, one of which hit home on her port side engine room. The destroyer of the *Lusitania* and *Hesperian* had sunk another unarmed liner. Four members of her crew were killed in the initial explosion; the officers believed the ship was sinking fast and 'abandon ship' was ordered. During the evacuation Chief Steward K B Malcolm was killed when he fell into the sea and drowned. In fact the ship sank more slowly than expected and the captain and some of the crew returned to the ship and were able to send a wireless message for help. *Cymric* finally sank at around 0330hrs the following day and the survivors were rescued by a Dutch steamer and taken to Bantry, on Ireland's west coast.

Newspapers reported that 'the survivors were not allowed time to get into the boats. The submarine did not wait to assist them. The crew were left in open boats 130 miles from land, with no apparent prospect of rescue. The men had a bad blowing about in half a gale.'[6] The US government formally asked Britain if *Cymric* had been armed (she was not) which made the sinking a clear breach of the latest undertakings given to America by Germany; but, as on this occasion no Americans were involved, President Wilson did not protest.

For the rest of May no British ships were lost to U-boats in Bayly's territory. Accidental losses could not be avoided, however. The 296grt armed trawler *Carbineer*, purchased by the Admiralty while she was under construction, fitted with a 3pdr gun and used primarily as a minesweeper, was out on patrol near the Scillies. On 18 May she hit the Crim Rocks and was run ashore on Great Crebawethan, part of the Western Rocks, becoming a total loss.

Reinforcements

Until mid-1916, Bayly had to rely on his sloops and trawlers, the latter becoming maids of all work, minesweeping and inshore submarine hunting especially. But now his resources were enhanced by the addition of a new type of vessel, specifically designed for inshore anti-submarine work. These were the Motor Launches or MLs. They were the brainchild of the American Elco Company of Bayonne New Jersey, whose General Manager Henry Sutphen and Chief Naval Architect Irwin Chase conceived and designed the launches in conjunction with representatives of the Royal Navy. The first fifty were built in the USA, and then Canadian Vickers became the prime contractor to get round American neutrality issues. Once built they were sent by train to Halifax, Nova Scotia, and then deck loaded onto British freighters to cross the Atlantic.

They were twin-engined, much faster than a trawler (c. 19 knots), just about seaworthy (they were wet ships and rolled a lot), armed with one 3pdr gun (and Type D depth charges when available) plus machine guns and carrying a crew of nine, two officers, two engineers and five deckhands. They were developed as anti-submarine vessels, the precursors of the American 'sub-chaser' classes, but found themselves undertaking escort duty, boarding merchant ships and clearing mines, amongst many other tasks. And they were almost entirely the preserve of Royal Naval Volunteer Reserve (RNVR) officers,[*] volunteers and (mainly) amateur yachtsmen all.

---

[*] Among the RNVR officers who skippered these vessels under Bayly was the prolific author, journalist, playwright and yachtsman Edward Keeble Chatterton. He commanded a flotilla of MLs at Berehaven.

They were not, however, entirely without defects, the most dangerous of which were with the Hall-Scott engines. These originally used petrol, a significant fire hazard, and problems with the engines overheating resulted in a decision in mid-1916 to use a mixture of one part petrol to two parts kerosene. Another quirk of the engines was that they had to be stopped and restarted when going from ahead to astern or vice versa. Starting was achieved with a burst of compressed air from cylinders carried aboard and was not always reliable. Thus manoeuvring could be tricky on occasion. Commander F F Tower RNVR was responsible for fourteen of these vessels in Kingstown. He thought that '[they] were always an anxiety but everyone connected with them was keen and did their duty resulting in a good deal of useful work; only the constant repairs were trying, though unavoidable'.[7]

Nonetheless, Bayly came to appreciate their value and soon asked the Admiralty for twelve more for he saw that, in addition to their many patrol qualities, they would be useful to prevent the landing of guns and other armaments on the Irish coast. He noted 'they were quite wonderful at sea in weather which I should have thought quite unfit for them'.[8]

Cares and worries

Prime Minister Asquith visited Ireland on 18 May; he travelled from Dublin to Cork to meet with Redmondite leaders and the Bishop of Cork, Daniel Cohalan, and was then to stay with Bayly at Admiralty House. The local population had prepared to give him a hostile reception at the railway station (there was considerable ill-feeling over the execution of the ringleaders of the revolt), so Bayly organised that a lieutenant would take his admiral's barge upriver and bring Asquith back by water and 'got him to Admiralty House before anyone in the town knew he was there'.[9] Bayly was impressed by the grasp of the war situation that the PM showed, something that his enemies regularly claimed he was lacking. At the conclusion of the visit, Bayly returned Asquith to Milford Haven aboard *Adventure*.

By the close of May 1916, there were over 450 light patrol craft based at Queenstown alone.[10] But Bayly remained less than happy with the situation in Ireland. At the end of June, he wrote to Jackson that 'Ireland in the south and west is in a rather bad condition and the steps that have been taken up to now seem to have annoyed everyone. There is certainly a very uneasy feeling about and when the harvest is in things may happen in a desultory sort of way, such as individual shootings, blowing up bridges etc. But they seem to have a wholesome fear of the navy.'[11] Certainly he had taken precautions regarding his own security and the Royal Marines sent at the time of the Easter Rising were now in part deployed guarding Admiralty House (where one poor Marine unfortunately shot dead a donkey in the dark, mistaking it for an intruder).

The sloops, worked hard in difficult waters, were starting to concern him. '*Sunflower* will have to pay off' Bayly complained, '[her] engines are rickety on their foundations.' And there were lots of breakdowns for the dockyard to deal with. However, overall he thought 'they are wonderful little ships with exceptionally able and keen youngsters in command (bar about two)'. Perhaps because of the ongoing maintenance issues, he asked that Commander Ernest Lacey, in charge of the Queenstown dockyard, be promoted; 'He works hard and works well.'[12] It would appear that Bayly was beginning to think that he needed more staff assistance around this time. He asked Jackson for a flag commander, but then revealed his finicky streak too; 'There is so much to do, but I prefer to wait until I can get a man who suits me, like Swabey*.'[13]

And the uneasy peace held in the Western Approaches. No merchant vessel was sunk by a U-boat in the whole of June – the first such month since the end of 1914. Fretting at the absence of U-boats, Bayly again pressed his wish to take his sloops and Q-ships to the Mediterranean (and was again declined). Instead *Rosemary*, *Alyssum*, *Buttercup*, *Poppy*, *Gladiolus* and *Mignonette* were removed from him and deployed in the North Sea on minesweeping duty, the task they had originally been envisaged for. Here, on 4 July, *Rosemary* was torpedoed by *U-63*. The attack blew off her rudders, screws and much of her stern. Disabled, she was towed back to the safety of the Humber, the others of the brood gathered around her for protection. It was later decided that they were unsuited for this particular duty, as they could not sufficiently defend themselves, and returned to Ireland. Bayly may have rued his offer, as *Rosemary* was now in dockyard hands.

Bayly tried to project the persona of the bluff English sailor, hard, unyielding, and focused on duty. But in fact he was as sensitive to

* George Thomas Carlisle Parker Swabey, promoted commander in July 1913.

trinkets and baubles as the next man. In August he began a campaign to have the status of his command upgraded. Writing to Jackson on the 21st, he noted 'Scotland is a Commander in Chief [CinC Rosyth, a full admiral's billet since June 1916] and Maxwell [General Sir John Grenfell Maxwell] has been made CinC for the military in Ireland'[14] and went on to suggest that his position should therefore be made a CinC for the duration of the war. A week later he was back on the subject, writing again to the long suffering Jackson 'I shall be very grateful if they will make me CinC. I certainly have more work than many others and as this is my last command in the service it will be some satisfaction after what I have been through*' (Bayly would eventually get his wish on 4 June 1917).[15]

And at the end of August, Bayly reverted to his *idée fixe* of deploying some of his vessels to the Mediterranean. He proposed sending three Q-ships, *Q-1, 2* and *3*, at irregular intervals from the south of the Irish Channel to Malta, along the north coast of Africa and now and then to Alexandria from where they would return to Queenstown.[16] On this occasion the proposal was accepted and they sailed as he had indicated. *Q-1* (alias *Perugia* alias *Paxton*), a converted collier, was sunk on 3 December in the Gulf of Genoa by *U-63* with the loss of eight men, all stokers. Undeterred, by October Bayly was advocating sending one of his remaining Q-ships to the coast of America.[17]

The sinking of HMS *Genista*

The U-boats began to return to the Western Approaches in September and October. Merchant ships were sunk off Ushant, Finisterre and The Lizard in September and in October twelve British-flagged vessels were lost, including four carrying defensive armaments. The U-boats were out in force; on the 20th, 120 miles west-north-west of Tory Island, *U-69* sank the *Cabotia*, 4,309grt, with the loss of thirty-two lives including the master; that same day *UB-39* scuttled *Midland*, 4,247grt, off Ushant; and a day later *UB-40* sank by gunfire the little sailing vessel *Cock O' the Walk* off Guernsey.

Bayly redoubled the patrols and provided escorts for ships deemed particularly at risk. On 23 October, HMS *Genista* was escorting the steamship *Alexandria*, south-west of the Fastnet. *Genista* was a modern ship, launched only in February 1916, and

---

* '... have been through'; was he here once more expressing his resentment at his treatment over the *Formidable* affair?

under the command of Lieutenant Commander John White, who had commissioned the ship. It was his first independent command and he had endeared himself to Bayly, who considered him 'a great friend of mine and a very good seaman'.[18]

Lying in wait for just such an opportunity was *U-57*, capable of nearly 15 knots on the surface, armed with four torpedo tubes and a 10.5cm (4.1in) deck gun and commanded by Kapitänleutnant Carl-Siegfried Ritter von Georg. He and his boat had just arrived on station for their second cruise together, the first having netted twenty-one small ships in the North Sea.

Just before 1000hrs, von Georg fired one torpedo at *Genista*; it hit home and the sloop sank like a stone in the cold Atlantic waters (he claimed the kill as a 'light cruiser'). *Alexandria* increased to full speed and fled. She radioed to Queenstown that *Genista* had been hit but that she was carrying on to her destination. In this she was following standing orders, but it must have been difficult leaving men in the water to die.

Bayly instructed the two sloops nearest the broadcast position to search but they were hampered as they had been out at sea for some days and did not know exactly where they were. In these circumstances, the practice was to head for land to fix a position. At Admiralty House, Bayly paced the drawing room. He was a religious man and had a compelling sense of destiny and of providence. In his own words 'I felt a strong pressure on me telling me to go and look.'[19] *Adventure* was at thirty minutes notice; he decided to go. At 2200hrs he hoisted his flag in the cruiser and they set out to *Genista*'s last reported position, reaching it at 1000hrs the following day where they found the dead body of a sailor. Putting the wind directly behind his ship, Bayly followed the most likely course of drift; and at 1300hrs found three Carley rafts with twelve men in total, just before a gale got up that would have swamped them. As Bayly put it, 'there is no doubt that some or all of the men on the rafts had been praying hard to be rescued and that I was sent out to do it'.[20]

Seventy-nine British sailors, regular RN, RNR, RNVR, died that day. They included the captain John White[*] and 21-year-old Surgeon

---

[*] White, a Freemason, is remembered on the Masonic Memorial in London and by a plaque erected in Marylebone New Church, Marylebone Road, London; in a panel with a semi-circular top bearing a wreath and crown, with a border of oak leaves and acorns, and with a serpentine surround, it reads 'John White, d.1916, Lt Commander of the Royal Navy, killed in action while in command of HMS *Genista*, this tablet was erected by his former shipmates in HMS *Africa*'.

Probationer Alexander L Strachan RNVR. Strachan, son of a pharmacist and a medical student at Aberdeen University, had only volunteered in the spring, being in his third year of study. He had already made a fine contribution. On his way to join his ship, he arrived in Dublin in the middle of the rising and had to take charge of a hospital there. 'His skill and attention after joining his ship were thoroughly recognised, and he was the recipient of a special letter of thanks and a presentation by the officers and crew of a ship which was found in a sinking condition a few months before *Genista* was itself sunk.'[21] The loss was badly felt, for it was the first of the sloops to be sunk. But the next day the sloops were out on patrol again.

Bayly knew he worked his men hard and wanted recognition for their efforts; he requested promotions for three officers, Lieutenant Commanders Briggs, Sherston and Leslie. 'I work the fellows here hard and they reply to my demands excellently well, but beyond any occasional thanks they get nothing for it', he wrote to Jackson in November.[22] And of Rear Admiral Dare at Milford Haven he noted, in asking for him to be kept in place, 'he works hard, tactfully and well and now that submarines may become more active ... keep a good man there'.[23]

The work of the sloops was demanding but could occasionally be rewarding in a monetary fashion. 1916 was lucrative for the crew of *Zinnia*, for example, and her captain, Lieutenant Commander Graham F W Wilson. On 7 October, *Zinnia* was steaming in the Irish Sea in rough weather when she sighted an American-flagged schooner, *Samuel S Morse*. The sailing ship seemed to be out of control, so Wilson approached her and challenged by flag, to which the American responded by flying her ensign upside down, an internationally-recognised signal for distress. The weather was too rough to board, so Commander Wilson settled down to keep company with the schooner. At 1600hrs he was able to send over a boat which found the American awash to her main deck and unable to stand to. A grass warp was passed across and *Zinnia* towed her new charge all through the night to Milford Haven and the safety of a harbour.

Just two months later, on 26 December, *Zinnia* was able to perform a similar service for the Russian-flagged oil tanker ss *Terek*. She was also towed to harbour over a two-day period (and survived to become the British Tanker Company's ship ss *British Duke* in 1917). For both these services, *Zinnia* and her crew were awarded salvage money, the notice of distribution of which appeared in the *London Gazette* of 29 November 1917. It would make a nice little Christmas bonus.

But despite all the hard work and dedicated patrolling, still the sinkings continued. The last week of October 1916 was typical. ss *Rappahannock* was a familiar sight in the Atlantic. Built in 1893 she had been the last vessel to communicate with the *Titanic* (warning her of pack ice ahead) in 1912 and the following year had been involved in the rescue of survivors from the burning liner *Volturno*, from which she saved nineteen souls. On 26 October the Furness Withy Line ship was seventy miles off the Sicily Isles, on passage from Halifax, Nova Scotia, to London with a cargo of deals, wood pulp and apples, when she was torpedoed by *U-69* under Kapitänleutnant Ernst Wilhelms. Sea conditions were poor (level seven according to the submarine's own log) and the crew of thirty-seven took to their boats. None was ever seen alive again and their corpses washed ashore along the Cornish and North Devon coasts for months to come.

Two days later *U-55* accounted for the *Marina* near the Fastnet with eighteen lives lost; *U-63* sank two ships off Cape Trafalgar on the 29th. And near the Scillies an unknown assailant took down ss *North Wales*, 4,072grt, with thirty men killed.

It was not until 8 January 1917 that the body of *Rappahannock*'s third officer, 33-year-old Edward Gage, was found on the beach at Ilfracombe. His family's suffering was no doubt exacerbated by the fact that his brother Alfred had been a stoker on board hms *Good Hope*, sunk with all hands on 1 November 1914 and his younger brother was to die of wounds in late 1917 at Passchendaele. Three brothers, none of whom survived the war.

The sinking of the *Rappahannock* had caused a furore, coming as it did after the '*Sussex* Pledge' of 4 May in which the Germans had undertaken that merchant ships would not be sunk without provision for the safety of passengers and crew, in order to placate the American government. In Britain, the *Times* thundered that 'the German pledge not to sink vessels "without saving human lives" has thus once more been disregarded and another of their submarines has been guilty of constructive murder on the high seas'.[24] *

---

* The German government issued a statement in late January 1917 in which they claimed the crew had been allowed to take to their boats in calm weather and with a favourable wind for shore, a statement which was manifestly untrue and which came at a time when they had in any event already decided on unrestricted submarine warfare.

The rate of loss of merchant shipping was now a major concern to the government. Secretary of State for War Lloyd George, in a memorandum to the Joint Allied Conference of 15 November 1916, noted that 'at sea the British allied and neutral shipping, on which depends the life of the English people, its food, its munitions and those of its allies, is being destroyed at an alarmingly increasing rate'.[25]

Despite the bold claims Bayly had made on taking over the command, the arithmetic did not look good. Merchant ships were sunk with seeming impunity, now a sloop had been lost; and only three U-boats had been sunk in the Western Approaches, all by Q-ships. That was about to change.

Q-7, Penshurst

ss *Penshurst* was built in 1906 as a three-masted cargo steamer with a single funnel placed aft, making her look like a tanker. In 1915 she had been requisitioned by the Royal Navy for use as a special service vessel, or Q-ship, and was converted at Longhope, part of the Scapa Flow naval base. Here she was fitted with five concealed guns, a 12pdr, two 6pdrs and two 3pdrs, all hidden behind screens and dummy fixtures. Manned by a volunteer crew, she was under the command of Commander F H Grenfell.

Francis Grenfell was a retired naval officer, who had volunteered for service on the outbreak of war. Born in 1874 he entered *Britannia* in 1889 and was one of the last officers to serve a foreign commission under sail. When work aloft was removed from the training agenda, the Admiralty introduced physical training into the curriculum and Grenfell was appointed lieutenant in the Physical Training School at Portsmouth. Despite being short and slight, he developed such a passion for the 'Swedish System' which formed the basis for instruction that he wrote a book about it (*The Swedish System of Education for Gymnastics*) in 1905 and in the same year retired from the navy to teach the subject in the public schools, subsequently joining the Board of Education in 1909 to undertake the same mission for state schools. Aged forty on his return to the service, he held the rank of lieutenant commander on the retired list (promoted to commander in December 1914) serving with the 10th Cruiser Squadron maintaining the Northern Patrol. Tiring of 'stop and search' and seeking more action, he volunteered for special service and commissioned *Penshurst* (*Q-7*) on 6 November 1915.

Bayly regarded him as an excellent Q-ship commander, one capable of bearing the constant strain of the role exceptionally well.

Penshurst had begun her career with operations around the north coast of Scotland, without success, and then transferred in to the Coast of Ireland Command in the spring of 1916. On 29 November 1916 she came upon a submarine which was in the process of attacking the steamer *Wileyside*. Grenfell was able to come to within some 3,000yds of the action before the U-boat ordered her to stop. Grenfell's crew went through their abandon-ship evolution, with the panic party taking to the boats in chaos while Commander Grenfell remained on board with the gun crews and waited for the U-boat to come closer, which she declined to do. Losing patience, Grenfell opened fire and got several shots away before the submarine dived and despite *Penshurst* dropping depth charges, the unidentified made good its escape.

Undaunted, the following day Grenfell ordered a change in appearance and moved to a position at the western end of the English Channel. Here he encountered a submarine on the surface attacking the steamer *Ibex*. It was the minelaying submarine *UB-19* under a new and inexperienced commander, Erich Noodt, who had joined the vessel only on 4 November. In this, his first cruise as a commander, he had so far sunk five ships for a total of 5,276grt. Grenfell thought his luck was in but as he closed a seaplane flew over and attacked the U-boat with bombs, driving it beneath the water. The catalogue of errors then continued for the pilot landed his plane and when appraised of *Penshurst*'s true nature agreed to spot for her, only to crash on take-off.

As Grenfell stopped to pick up the crew, the overambitious (or just inexperienced and incautious) Noodt surfaced to attack. Grenfell waited until the U-boat drew nearer, probably seeking to identify its intended victim for the records, then opened a withering fire. Some eighty-three rounds were fired at a range of 250yds and the U-boat's attempted crash-dive turned into a death plunge. Sixteen of her crew of twenty-four were picked up by Grenfell, including the luckless Noodt, and spent the remainder of the war as prisoners.[*]

---

[*] Grenfell was awarded the DSO for his achievement.

Change at the top

Bayly had been put in post by the then-new team of Balfour and Jackson and they had left him pretty much a free hand in dealing with his command. But this was unfortunately not a dynamic partnership, Balfour being too aloof and disengaged, whilst Jackson was a workaholic technician and administrator. The Navy's reputation for caution was not disturbed by Jackson and he was replaced in November 1916 by Admiral Sir John Jellicoe, in command of the Grand Fleet since the beginning of the war. Jellicoe was not sanguine about his new appointment. On the night of 27 November, Jellicoe entertained a group of staff and other officers. He allegedly said that the submarine war was going to get so bad in 1917 that he would be blamed and not last as First Sea Lord for more than six months. Balfour was replaced too, by the Ulster politician Edward Carson, who proved to be somewhat out of his depth.[*]

Lewis Bayly was an admirer of Jellicoe and had served under him in 1914 when the latter took over the Grand Fleet. On leaving to take command of the Channel Fleet, Bayly wrote to Jellicoe 'I will joyfully serve under you anywhere or under any circumstances'.[26] Jellicoe, however, did not fully reciprocate this admiration. In 1915 he wrote 'Bayly is, I fear, occasionally a little mad'[27] and a year later, when discussing the choice of commander for the 1st Battle Squadron he noted '... I don't think Bayly will do. He had such curious fits of heroics and he proposes such impossible things that I doubt his judgement now'.[28]

Nonetheless, Bayly (who had got on well with the similarly workaholic Jackson) thought he had a friend at court still. Immediately after Jellicoe's appointment, Bayly wrote to him promoting the success of his Q-ships.[29] But as 1916 came to a close, the Queenstown command had sunk only four U-boats out of forty-seven lost in all theatres.

Another admiral

Of the strange and diverse group of individuals (and individualists) who ended up as Bayly's Q-ship captains, none came stranger than Admiral John Locke Marx. He had joined the Navy in 1866 and

---

[*] Asquith was rather pushed into appointing Carson, whom he did not hold in high regard, calling him 'ambitious, at the same time histrionic and arrogant on the surface and vacillating and infirm of purpose down below' (Cameron, *1916*, p 196).

eventually was promoted rear admiral in 1906, after a career spent afloat, mainly in independent commands. He retired in 1909 and was subsequently promoted to vice admiral and then full admiral (in 1913) on the retired list.

At the start of the year he attempted to re-join the Navy but was rejected. Refusing to take such a refusal, he camped out in the steps of Whitehall in protest, occasioning an article in his favour in the magazine *Punch*. Eventually his services were accepted and he was gazetted as a captain RNR, aged sixty-two, and given command of the ex-Russian yacht *Iolanda* (and later six accompanying trawlers) as part of the Milford Haven patrol.

Leith-built in 1908, *Iolanda* herself had an interesting career. Owned by Elizabeth Terestchenko, she had been interned by the Germans in Trondheim. But her skipper, Captain Bertun, secretly chartered the yacht to the British Admiralty in 1915, and he escaped from Trondheim on the excuse of needing dry dock repairs in Bergen, and then sailed the vessel to Southampton where she was fitted with two 3in guns. After Milford, Marx took her to the Mediterranean but there he fell foul of the authorities for his independent and less than deferential manner and was sent back to Britain. Here he was given command of another yacht, HMY *Beryl*, built in 1893 and once owned by Lord Inverclyde (the Scottish shipowner Sir John Burns, 2nd Baronet).

Finally he gained command of a Q-ship in August 1916, *Q-13 Aubrietia*, a 'Flower'-class sloop completed as a Q-ship. 'The independence of the job held great attraction' according to Gordon Campbell.[30] Marx was not impressed by his new command; 'went over her, not much catch, badly arranged … ship's company a queer lot. Not at all satisfied. No accommodation for me.'[31] A good impression of a grumpy old man!

On 26 September he sailed for Queenstown. If his ship had not impressed him, Admiral Bayly did. 'Bayly was a "hands-on" admiral'. When Marx had difficulty getting his starting stores, Bayly 'brought them on himself' in his barge.[32] It seems that Bayly liked Marx too. They were both 'old navy' and had grown up in a hard school. Bayly noted that 'no weather daunted him, no difficulty was too great. He was always ready and nearly always smiling.'[33] On 30 November he wrote to Marx explaining why he had sent him on a wasted cruise. 'So many thanks for your kind wishes which are cordially reciprocated. The Admiralty ordered me to send a Q to cruise from Lizard to Ushant one day and to Ushant to Lizard the next. A silly way to do things [Q-ships preferred to linger about] but they are my masters so I sent you.'[34] Bayly's ongoing resentment of the Admiralty smoulders through the letter. And on the penultimate day of the year, Bayly wrote 'Come and stay [at Admiralty House] when you can.'[35]

A strange Christmas

Between 16 December and 27 December 1916 *U-46*, with a crew of thirty-six men under Kapitänleutnant Alfred Saalwächter, cruised in the Bay of Biscay, sinking nine vessels of six different nationalities. Saalwächter rigidly operated under prize rules. He took a French trawler *Goulfar* as a depot ship in which to house his captives and where possible took the master of the sunken vessel prisoner. This allowed the master of ss *Bayhall*, sunk by *U-46* on 17 December in the final stages of a journey from Mauritius to Bordeaux with a cargo of sugar, to witness the strangest Christmas Day he ever saw. After sinking the French schooner *Marie Pierre*, taking her master Georges Constant prisoner and transferring the crew to the *Goulfar*, he sat his submarine on the bottom in thirty fathoms of water. There a small electrically-lit Christmas tree was produced, Saalwächter made a little speech, gave a present off the tree to each of his crew and presented his master mariner prisoners with a gift of writing paper and an indelible pencil. He then resumed his cruise, sank another British ship on the 27th, ss *Aislaby*, took her master prisoner and headed for home, having landed his prisoners, except the masters, and scuttled his temporary depot ship. In an increasingly vicious war at sea, chivalry was not quite dead.

Unrestricted Submarine Warfare, 1917

It takes all sorts to fight a war. William (Willie) Mason was a medical student at Victoria University, Manchester. Lancashire born, the son of a headmaster, he was seen as someone who 'has had a brilliant career' as a student.[1] At the end of 1916, he somewhat unwillingly entered the RNVR and on 11 January 1917 joined HMS *Laburnum* as Surgeon Probationer – its medical officer – at the princely rate of seven shillings and sixpence a day.

Mason was not much impressed by his new home. '*Laburnum* is a squat grey sloop. My cabin stores etc … a vile filthy mess.'[2] There were six officers for the ship but Mason was soon disenchanted with them. 'Officers – drink, what horrors are wrought in thy worship',[3] he wrote in his diary shortly after coming aboard. He liked his commanding officer; 'a gentleman from whom one expects and receives fair treatment' but not the first lieutenant 'a child with a child's idea of things [and] an innate sense of selfishness'.[4]

Mason was soon inducted into the sort of casework he would handle. His first patient had a mild case of gonorrhoea, which the Royal Naval Hospital at Queenstown refused to treat. He prescribed calomel cream and occasional lavage of potassium permanganate which, if nothing else, must have rendered the offending member purple. His second case was a sailor with syphilis.

On 27 January *Laburnum* put to sea. Mason, a landlubber, noted that 'the old bus rocks and rolls and tosses like Hades … she wallows in the troughs of the Atlantic rollers'.[5] He lived in perpetual fear of U-boats. 'I don't want to meet a sub [because] we are helpless against them,' he wrote, adding 'unhappily, this is just the weather for subs and since being an HMS they would sink us on sight without rising'.[6] A week later, he recorded that 'in future I am going to wear my lifebelt continuously since we seem to be sitting on top of a powder cask'.[7] He was not alone in worrying about submarines.

The submarine war

American President Woodrow Wilson had gained the Democratic nomination unopposed on 2 September 1916, having campaigned on the slogan 'He kept us out of the war.' In his acceptance speech, however, he showed a little steel, warning that submarine warfare resulting in American deaths would not be tolerated and stating that 'the nation that violates these essential rights must expect to be checked and called to account by direct challenge and resistance. It at once makes the quarrel in part our own.'[8] On 9 November he was elected President for a second term.

Before and after his nomination, Wilson continued to display his aggravation with the British blockade, and especially the seizure of mail from neutral ships and the blacklisting of firms trading with Britain's enemies, and most particularly with the British negativity towards his proposal for a post-war League of Nations. He saw acceptance of such a body by all combatants as a means of ending the war.

But on 1 February 1917, Germany declared unrestricted submarine warfare. In doing so the Imperial government knew that there was a very strong risk that America would be tipped into the war by such an action. Why did they do it? Firstly, the German high command had been convinced by some clever calculations from Department B-1(the Economic Warfare Plans group) that within five months Britain could be brought to her knees through lack of food, primarily wheat, as a result of such a campaign. But, as importantly, the morale of the German nation on the home front was at rock bottom. The 'Turnip Winter' of 1916/17 had badly damaged people's faith in their leaders and food rationing was harsh, leading to public unrest and rioting. The ongoing British blockade had brought hunger and misery to the home front and many in Germany cried out to inflict similar pain on Britain and her Allies.[*]

Indeed, the German Ambassador to the United States of America, Count von Bernstorff, wrote an exculpatory letter to US Secretary of

---

[*] As early as 19 September 1916 the *New York Sun* was stating 'reports from Berlin show that people are demanding [unrestricted submarine warfare]'.

State Lansing in justification of the new unrestricted warfare, stating that:

> A new situation has thus been created which forces Germany to new decisions. Since two years and a half England is using her naval power for a criminal attempt to force Germany into submission by starvation. In brutal contempt of international law, the group of powers led by England not only curtail the legitimate trade of their opponents, but they also, by ruthless pressure, compel neutral countries either to altogether forego every trade not agreeable to the Entente Powers, or to limit it according to their arbitrary decrees ... the English Government, however, insists upon continuing its war of starvation, which does not at all affect the military power of its opponents, but compels women and children, the sick and the aged, to suffer for their country pains and privations which endanger the vitality of the nation.[9]

It was an admission of weakness which they would much rather not have made.

Finally, Germany believed (correctly) that it would take America some time to place herself on a war footing and get men into battle in meaningful numbers. If the Allies could be brought to their knees before then, America might be persuaded to stay her hand.

Wilson felt betrayed, especially after the assurances given post the *Lusitania* and *Arabic* affairs and the '*Sussex* declaration'. Then came the revelation of the Zimmermann Telegram,[*] in which Germany attempted to enlist Mexico as an ally, promising Mexico that if Germany was victorious, she would support Mexico in winning back the states of Texas, New Mexico and Arizona from the USA. The plot had been uncovered by the British through decrypts in the Admiralty's Room 40 and was revealed to the American government on 20 February 1917.

But still Wilson was unmoved. His reaction after consulting the Cabinet and Congress was minimal – only that diplomatic relations with the Germans should be paused. The President said, 'we are the sincere friends of the German people and earnestly desire to remain

---

[*] For a full exposition of this incident, readers are directed to B Tuchman, *The Zimmerman Telegram* (London: Constable and Co, 1959).

at peace with them. We shall not believe they are hostile to us unless or until we are obliged to believe it.'[10]

Bayly's response was to have all his sloops out looking for submarines; but all they found were more U-boat victims. HMS *Laburnum* was sent to patrol near the Fastnet. SS *Warley Pickering* was cargo vessel of 4,196grt on passage from Sangunto, Spain, to the Tees, laden with iron ore. On 5 February she was torpedoed forty-six miles west of the Fastnet by *U-60*. All *Laburnum* could do was pick up thirty-five crewmen from their boats.

And four days later, the sloop was once again too late. SS *Mantola* was a new cargo liner of 8,260grt, operated by the British India Steam Navigation Company. She had left port on 4 February, destination Calcutta, carrying 165 crew, 18 passengers and 600,000 ounces of silver with a market value of £11,000 (perhaps £860,000 today). On the 9th *Mantola* was torpedoed by *U-81* when she was 143 miles south-west of Fastnet. Captain Chivas got everyone into the lifeboats but one overturned, drowning seven Indian seamen in it. The U-boat surfaced and began to shell the sinking ship but then disappeared as *Laburnum* hove into view. The sloop picked up the survivors which meant she now had over 200 rescued seamen on board. *Laburnum* took the hulk in tow but the line broke and *Mantola* sank. Eventually *Warley Pickering*'s and *Mantola*'s crews were landed at Bantry.

The German declaration of unrestricted submarine warfare had thrown other neutral countries into something of a panic. Shipowners instructed their ships to remain in port and vital food supplies to nations already badly suffering collateral damage from restricted food supplies. Eight Dutch steamers, both outbound and inbound and of 40,000grt in total, were confined to the harbour at Falmouth whilst the Dutch government tried to negotiate a free passage for them. Believing that it had succeeded in that regard, the Dutch authorities told them to sail on 22 February. Four were destined for Rotterdam with cargos of foodstuffs. Of the eight, only one made its intended destination intact. Seven were attacked thirty miles to the north west of Bishop's Rock by Otto Hersing in *U-21*, six being sunk and one damaged. Neutral opinion was outraged, especially when the German government responded to criticism by stating that it had given only conditional promises of safety.

U-50, under Gerhard Berger, was lurking around 150 miles west of Fastnet. On the 24 February he sank the cargo vessel *Falcon*. The following day he despatched the *Aries*, taking her captain prisoner. That same day, the Cunard liner RMS *Laconia* was on passage from New York to Liverpool with seventy-five passengers and a crew of 217. One hundred and sixty miles north-west of Fastnet she was also torpedoed by *U-50*, the weapon striking on the starboard side just abaft the engine room. The enormous ship, 18,099 tons, did not sink and her captain and crew struggled to save her. Berger had hung around to make sure of his kill and twenty minutes later fired a second torpedo into the engine room. This time it was fatal and *Laconia* sank at 2220hrs. Twelve people lost their lives including a mother and daughter, 59-year-old Mrs Mary Hoy and Miss Elizabeth Hoy, both American citizens. The women had been placed in a lifeboat but it was swamped by the heavy seas. Elizabeth nursed her mother, up to her knees in water, but Mary died of exposure and her body was washed overboard; the same fate befell her daughter shortly afterwards. Some of the survivors of all three sinkings were picked up by *Laburnum*. Willie Mason noted 'a full house ... but a sense of duty done'.[11] Once again US opinion was inflamed and further public pressure for war resulted.

And sailing ships continued to be easy prey for U-boats. On 27 February the three-masted barque *Galgorm Castle* was nearing the end of a long passage from Buenos Aires to Queenstown with a cargo of maize. She was a sailing ship of 1,596grt with twenty-four crew on board, including the master, Captain Frampton, and his wife. At 1645hrs she was ninety miles west of Fastnet when there was a sudden explosion of gunfire from some two miles distant and *U-49*, Kapitänleutnant Richard Hartmann, ordered her to heave to. The crew took to their two boats and Hartmann's men boarded the sailing ship and sank her with three small explosive charges. Adrift in the Atlantic, the two small lifeboats became separated in the darkness and the increasingly turbulent seas. The following day, Captain Frampton's craft was discovered by a passing steamer and all twelve people on board were saved, included Mrs Frampton. But the lifeboat under the command of the first mate, 57-year-old Nicholas Rundell, was less fortunate. During the night she had overturned, drowning four men. The other eight managed to cling to the upturned vessel until one by one they succumbed to exposure and fell back into the cold and merciless sea. Only one man, a Russian national, survived to be rescued an amazing eight days later.

By 1917 the needs of the Navy (and those of conscription from 1916) had reduced the number of experienced seamen left to man merchant ships such as *Galgorm Castle*. The RNR, Royal Fleet Reserve (RFR) and Mercantile Marine Reserve (MMR) had taken the cream of the merchant marine and the ages and nationalities of the barque's dead bore testimony to that. Of the eleven lost, five were British, two Norwegian, two American and one each Swedish and Dutch. Six of them were under twenty years of age, the youngest just fifteen, with two more of sixteen. One of those was Fred Hyde from Bury in Lancashire. He had left school and his widowed mother in July 1914, aged fourteen, and joined the mercantile marine as an apprentice. Fred's mother had already lost her eldest son, Harry, at Ypres in 1915. Now she paid another blood price at sea.

The sinkings by U-boats of British and neutral ships were significantly increased after the February declaration of unrestricted submarine war. In January, 368,521grt of merchant shipping was sunk; February, 540,006grt; March, 593,841grt, over four times the levels of the same months in 1916. The numbers for March included five American-flagged vessels, four of which were sunk in Bayly's domain. The cargo vessels *Algonquin* and *Vigilancia* were despatched near Bishop's Rock, the latter with the loss of fifteen lives. The passenger liner *City of Memphis* was sunk south of the Fastnet Rock by *UC-66* on 17 March. The U-boat surfaced and signalled for the crew to leave the vessel, whereupon she was sunk by gunfire. The tanker ss *Illinois* was despatched by *UC-21* north of Alderney and the tanker *Healdton* was sunk in the North Sea with the loss of seven of her crew. As if to bait the passivity of the American government, the newspaper *Deutsche Tageszeitung* ran an article by Count Ernest von Reventlow, one of Germany's leading naval experts, to the effect that 'it is good that American ships have also been obliged to learn that the German prohibition is effective and that there is no question of distinctive treatment in favour of the United States. Against such shipping losses there is only one policy for the United States of America as for the small European maritime powers, namely to retain the ships in home ports as long as the war lasts.'

American ships and American lives were being lost and the country taunted; surely Wilson could not fail to act. Ex-President Teddy Roosevelt, seething on the sidelines, reacted 'If he does not go to war I shall skin him alive'.[12] But Wilson had finally had enough. He called a Cabinet meeting on 20 March and opinion was unanimously in support of entering the war. The die was cast. The President called a special session of Congress on 2 April, declaring that Germany's latest pronouncement had rendered his 'armed neutrality' policy unfeasible. On 4 April, Congress passed a declaration of war against Germany with strong bipartisan support, although there was opposition from ethnic German strongholds and remote rural areas in the South. Wilson signed the declaration two days later.

While the USA was edging towards war, German activity in the Western Approaches was increasing significantly. In attempting to protect ships in the Western Approaches, the British had, since Bayly's arrival in mid-1915, tried to have incoming and outgoing ships widely dispersed in mid-ocean but protected closer to the shores. The effect of this was, of course, to force U-boats to operate further out in the Atlantic, which improved construction methods and propulsion plants rendered them very capable of doing. This led to incoming vessels being channelled into three cones of approach from around July 1916. Routes now converged on Tory Island for vessels entering or leaving the Clyde and Liverpool, on the Fastnet for ships bound for Liverpool, Bristol Channel, London or East Coast ports and on Scilly for cargoes to and from the Mediterranean and South Atlantic. By 1917, some twenty-four vessels per day were routed through the Fastnet area alone. As the German U-boat campaign grew in ferocity, Bayly thought that this traffic would prove an irresistible attraction to the submarines and attempted to deploy his forces to defend the cones of approach. His chosen weapon was again his Q-ships; five were placed in the approaches to the Fastnet, with three sloops, four yachts and twenty-four trawlers also in attendance. Seven sloops and a further three Q-ships were stationed immediately to the north of this area, defending the western approach, with a yacht and six trawlers placed at Galway (see map in plates section). Vessels based at Lough Swilly defended the northern approach. But he remained desperately short of ships, none the less.

Fortunately, the Coast of Ireland Command began to receive an entirely new class of ship around this time, the P-boat or coastal sloop, designed in part to take on the inshore anti-submarine work which had been the lot of the trawlers. Twin screws, a large rudder area and a very low freeboard gave them a small and fast turning circle and with ram bows of hardened steel they were primarily intended to attack submarines. Indeed, a resemblance to large submarines had been deliberately designed in to give the boats a chance to close the range and sink a German U-boat by ramming or gunfire. A low, sharply cut-away funnel added to that impression. They carried a crew of fifty, could exceed 21 knots and were armed with one 4in gun, one 40mm anti-aircraft gun and two 14in torpedo tubes, taken from older torpedo boats. Twenty-four ships of this design had been ordered in May 1915 and another thirty between February and June 1916, although ten of this latter batch were altered in December before launch for use as Q-ships and were renumbered as PC-class sloops. Eighteen shipyards were involved in building them and they supplemented the larger 'Flower'-class sloops.

Bayly received one in each of January, February and March, *P-46*, *P53* and *P-39,* and based them at Pembroke to look for submarines in the Irish Sea. By the June he would have five of them, one – *PC-67* – in Q-ship guise. Additionally, Ireland also gained six more sloops in February, grudgingly supplied on Jellicoe's orders by taking them from the East Coast of England. Jellicoe's view seems to be reflected in his later comment that 'six sloops were diverted from their proper work of minesweeping in the North Sea and added to the patrol force at Queenstown'.[13]

A double blow
German strategy now included the laying of large minefields off Queenstown and Kinsale in the sea lanes where all manner of vessels would be making transit. *UC-66* was one of sixty-four coastal minelaying submarines built during the war, all armed with seven torpedoes, eighteen mines and an 8.8cm (3.46in) deck gun. On 11 March she had been sent to operate in the Western Approaches and on the 16th laid a minefield off Galley Head (before sinking the *City of Memphis* the following day, see above). It was a clear danger to shipping and on the 17th Bayly sent two *Arabis*-class sloops, *Mignonette* and *Alyssum,* to sweep it clear. *Mignonette,* under Lieutenant in Command Arthur Evans was a relatively new vessel, commissioned only in May the previous year.

It was to be an unhappy St Patrick's Day for Queenstown. Whilst attempting to clear the danger, *Mignonette* hit a mine and had her bow blown off. An effort was made to tow her stern-first to harbour but she sank shortly afterwards. Fourteen crewmen, mainly stokers, were killed and Lieutenant Evans wounded.* Then the following day, *Alyssum* too hit a mine; no lives were lost but the vessel was, and Bayly could ill afford to lose such valuable ships.

The problem was that the draught of the sloops and trawlers used for minesweeping were too deep for the type of field now being laid. Bayly called a halt, ordered in MLs and drifters to do the job, and sent an urgent request to the Admiralty for shallow-draft minesweepers.

Zinnia to the rescue

The minefields continued to claim victims. On 22 March, HMS *Zinnia*, under Lieutenant Commander Graham Francis Winstanley Wilson, was escorting the Norwegian tanker SS *Malmanger* inwards towards the Fastnet. At 1225hrs Wilson considered his job done and parted company with his charge but then, noticing that *Malmanger* was steering rather close to the coast, chased after her again and signalled for her to stand clear of the coastline. It was too late. At 1255hrs, five miles east of the Fastnet, she hit a mine (her master thought she had been torpedoed). Wilson raced over and transferred her crew on board and then took her in tow, stern first at just 3 knots, a sitting target for any itinerant U-boat. It was to no avail. She sank bow-first, standing on her head such that 100ft of hull stood above the water and then slowly toppled into the sea, just three miles south of Baltimore and safety.

Six days later, *Zinnia* was escorting a British tanker, the *Gafsa*, 3,974grt, just off the Old Head of Kinsale. Wilson was taking no chances; he was zigzagging ahead of his charge at full speed, had his first lieutenant perched in the foretop looking for any sign of a periscope, and had ordered three men closed up around each gun, also on lookout. But danger lurked unseen beneath the sea. *U-57*, still under von Georg, had begun a new patrol on 22 March and had thus far sunk two vessels. Now he fired a torpedo into the starboard side of the *Gafsa* to make it three. There was a huge explosion, the magazine of the defensively-armed ship being set off, and she immediately started to sink by the stern. Wilson turned his ship to attack and dropped two depth charges a minute apart some

---

* One of *Mignonette*'s 12pdr guns was recovered in 1982 and is on display at Kinsale Museum

1,000yds from the stricken ship; he then searched for the U-boat but saw no sign. Forty-five minutes after the attack he picked up the tanker's survivors, the master and thirty-one officers and men. The explosion which sunk the ship had wrecked the engine room, killing the second engineer and six crew. As for the *Gafsa* herself, she had some 20ft of her bow sticking out above water; Wilson sank it by gunfire, to remove a danger to navigation.

The light goes out

UC-65, under the command of Kapitänleutnant Otto Steinbrinck, was having an exceptional cruise. Steinbrinck was an outstanding U-boat commander who had, a year earlier, been awarded Germany's highest military award, the Pour le Mérite. Before this, his latest cruise, he had sunk a staggering 145 vessels, 27 in 1915, 68 in 1916 and 48 to date in 1917. Starting his patrol on 24 March, he had sunk ten ships by the morning of the 28th. On this day he would sink a further seven in the cold waters off the south-east Irish coast.[*]

The South Arklow Light Vessel, known as *Guillemot*, lay ten miles south-east by south from Arklow, County Wicklow, in the Irish Sea. Since 1893 she had provided a navigation mark and light, guiding sailors past the dangers of the Arklow Bank on the south eastern corner of Ireland. Seven light keepers manned her, all employees of the Commissioners for Irish Lights. Thus far in the war, light vessels had been spared attack by either side. In the early days of conflict, there had been a convention that they were in some way neutral, there to help mariners of all nations and not partisan to one side or another. But increasingly, the Germans believed that this neutrality was being honoured only in the breach. And in large part this was true. Naval ratings were now often stationed with lighthouses and light vessels tried to warn passing ships of the presence of U-boats. Such reporting was greatly aided when the light station had a telegraphic wire connection to land, as some lighthouses and light vessels had. Others were fitted with radio but German submarines could detect warning transmissions made in this way using their own radio systems. Morse and flags were also used. Steinbrinck felt that the South Arklow Light was behaving in

---

[*] By the end of the war Steinbrinck would sink 206 ships totalling 244,797 tons with twelve more ships damaged (65,720 tons).

just such a fashion, warning off his intended prey. On 28th March he surfaced alongside and boarded her, justifying his actions by stating that he was searching for 'secret papers'.

After no secret material was found, the light keepers were ordered to leave the vessel and demolition charges were placed in the hull. But *Guillemot* wouldn't sink; this was perhaps hardly surprising as she had been built to last out any storm, with a complete steel hull, riveted and caulked, and covered with teak planking from keel to gunwale. The teak was sheathed with felt and plates of Muntz* metal, and inside the hull was lined with Portland cement. The main deck was covered with steel, with Danzig fir on top. In the end *UC-65* had to sink her with gunfire. In the whole war, only two light vessels were sunk by enemy action. Otto Steinbrinck had gained another claim to fame. *Guillemot*'s master, James Rossiter, was unrepentant, despite the loss of his vessel, later declaring that 'my duty to the British sailor was plain ... I was desirous of doing my bit, in my humble way, for the Empire'.[14] He was later awarded a medal for his bravery but reprimanded for disobeying orders.

However, this cruise could nearly have been the end of Steinbrinck's career for on the 30th, during the return trip to Germany, he attacked the newly-commissioned Q-ship, *Q-36* (aka *Peveril*) 30 miles south west of The Lizard. *Q-36*, otherwise *Peveril*, *Polyanthus* or *Puma*, was a cargo vessel built by Grangemouth & Greenock Dockyard Company in 1904 and taken up by the navy, initially as a stores carrier. She was then armed with two 12pdr guns and sent to join Bayly's merry band of Q-ships. On 30 March 1917, she was under the command of Commander G R Dolphin RNR, when *UC-65* chanced upon her. There was a good deal of muddle and confusion on board the Q-ship and her response to the attack was not vigorously pressed home. The Q-ship failed to get any hits but took punishment in return and a lifeboat of the 'panic party' capsized in rough seas with the loss of nine men; the bodies of eight of them were never recovered including nineteen-year-old Signalman Thomas Charles Croft, RNVR, from Swansea, and twenty-four-year-old Able Seaman Francis Emerson from Bury. The body of George Cawley, an officer's steward, washed ashore dead in

---

* Muntz metal is a form of alpha-beta brass with about 60 per cent copper, 40 per cent zinc with a trace of iron. It is named after George Fredrick Muntz, a metal-roller from Birmingham, and was used for protection from teredo shipworms.

a lifeboat on Jersey where, at the inquest, it was stated that the Admiralty had asked for the name of his ship to be supressed. Such were the lengths gone to in order to keep Q-ships a secret from the enemy. Both *Q-36* and *UC-65* made it safely home, however.

The subsequent court of enquiry was held at Portsmouth and chaired personally by the Port Admiral, Sir Stanley Colville. The court's findings were highly critical of Commander Dolphin, stating that he 'should be removed from command of *Q-36*. The tone of his orders is not the right spirit for the captain of a Q-ship to imbue into the ship's company and since his return he has openly expressed his views to the effect that the days of a Q-ship are dead, which opinion is the last a captain desirous of retaining his command should have expressed.'[15] Clearly, not every officer had the 'right stuff' for the demanding role of Q-ship command.

Between 7 and 13 March, nineteen merchant ships had been sunk around the coast of Ireland, plus a Q-ship, HMS *Warner*. Six were Norwegian-flagged, seven British, two Italian, one each French, Russian, Swedish and Spanish. And in the last week of March, fourteen more merchant vessels were sent to the bottom, ten merchant ships and patrols attacked.[16] It was a desperate time in the Coast of Ireland Command. Indeed, Winston Churchill later described this period as one when 'the great approach to the south west of Ireland was becoming a veritable cemetery of British shipping in which vessels were sunk regularly day-by-day almost 200 miles from land'.[17]

Bayly continued to advocate offensive patrolling, however, trying to hunt down U-boats with his sloops and other offensively-armed vessels. On 15 March he added to this a recommendation that heavily-patrolled trade routes be designated (a course of action in any case beyond his current resources) through which all commercial traffic be directed.[18] In this he was merely parroting accepted naval opinion, (see Richmond in Chapter 3 above) but the recommendation was not acted upon. The Admiralty wrote to him on 10 April, gently telling the admiral that it was impractical and required resources that they did not possess. To sweeten the pill, they added 'I am to add, however, that the moment it becomes possible you will be furnished with a flotilla of destroyers'. What the staff really thought is probably better reflected in the pencilled marginalia on Bayly's original memo, the sarcastic 'a glimmer of common sense here'[19] when Bayly alludes to some difficulties in his plan.

But there was one bright spot. On 2 April, four 'Racecourse'-class paddle-minesweepers sailed into Queenstown under the overall command of Commander Gervase W H Heaton. They were the 3rd Minesweeping Flotilla, HMS *Haldon*, *Hurst*, *Eridge* and *Epsom*, previously based with the Grand Fleet. Driven by two side-mounted paddle wheels, of 810 tons displacement and capable of 15 knots, they drew only 6ft 9in in draught compared to 11ft 9in for the 1,250-ton sloops. They were immediately put into action for, also on the 2nd, *U-78* had left Germany with a cargo of thirty-six mines which she laid between Cape Clear and the Old Head of Kinsale. Minesweeping had become an unending duty.

John Redmond, leader of the
Irish Parliamentary Party.
(AUTHOR'S COLLECTION)

Edward Carson, leader of the Irish
Unionists and First Lord of the
Admiralty 1916–17.
(AUTHOR'S COLLECTION)

Skipper James Hagan of the *Daniel
O'Connell*, rescuer of *Lusitania*
survivors. (COURTESY OF ARKLOW
MARITIME MUSEUM)

Skipper Edward White of the drifter
Elizabeth, another who rescued
Lusitania survivors. (COURTESY OF
ARKLOW MARITIME MUSEUM)

Eamon de Valera c.1920.
(Author's collection)

Woodrow Wilson who, as US
President, was focussed on winning
an election on the platform 'he kept
us out of the war'.
(AUTHOR'S COLLECTION)

Admiral William S Sims USN.
(AUTHOR'S COLLECTION)

An unusual event. Admiral William
Sims raises his flag at Queenstown,
taking command while Bayly has a
holiday. Sims is third from the right.
(COURTESY OF ALAMY LTD)

Admiral Sir Lewis Bayly in a rare posed photograph. (AUTHOR'S COLLECTION)

A postcard of Queenstown c.1900. Admiralty House can be seen top middle-right. The cathedral has yet to gain its spire. (AUTHOR'S COLLECTION)

Queenstown in 2016 showing the Crown Hotel (now renamed the 'Commodore'), where the USN made the drink expensive, and the cathedral of St Colman. (AUTHOR'S COLLECTION)

Admiralty House seen from the seaward side.
(IMAGE REPRODUCED COURTESY OF THE NATIONAL LIBRARY OF IRELAND)

A pre-war view of Haulbowline Island and dockyard seen from Admiralty House. (IMAGE REPRODUCED COURTESY OF THE NATIONAL LIBRARY OF IRELAND)

HMS *Adventure*, Bayly's flagship at Queenstown until August 1917. (AUTHOR'S COLLECTION)

RMS *Lusitania* in 1907. (AUTHOR'S COLLECTION)

The painting 'The Return of the Mayflower', depicting the arrival of the US destroyers at Queenstown, by Bernard Finegan Gribble. The original is at the US Naval Academy Museum in Annapolis, Maryland. It was purchased by F D Roosevelt and hung in the White House in 1933. (AUTHOR'S COLLECTION)

The USN depot ship USS *Melville* at Queenstown with attendant destroyers in dazzle paint. (© Imperial War Museum Q 18793)

The destroyer USS *Paulding* at Queenstown. Note the dazzle painting. (AUTHOR'S COLLECTION)

The sloop HMS *Zinnia*.
(© IMPERIAL WAR MUSEUM Q 75459)

The *Beagle*-class destroyer HMS *Wolverine*, sunk in a collision with the sloop
Rosemary in December 1917. (© IMPERIAL WAR MUSEUM Q 109160)

The 'M'-class destroyer *Mary Rose* which had the distinction of being the first RN vessel to make contact with the USN destroyers as they arrived off Ireland, May 1917. (© IMPERIAL WAR MUSEUM Q 20404)

The old cruiser HMS *Drake*, sunk by *U-79* on 2 October 1917 near Rathlin Island. (COURTESY LIBRARY OF CONGRESS, USA)

The *Canopus*-class battleship HMS *Ocean*, identical sister-ship to *Albion* (they were launched within two weeks of each other) which was deployed at Queenstown during the Easter Rising.
(AUTHOR'S COLLECTION)

An album cover made for USN base Wexford, 1 January 1919. (AUTHOR'S COLLECTION)

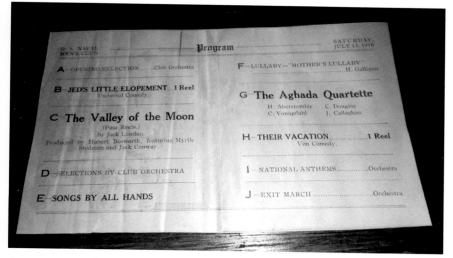

A programme of a typical entertainment at the USN recreational facility at Queenstown given on 13 July 1918. *Valley of the Moon* was an adaptation of a Jack London novel, produced in 1914.
(AUTHOR'S COLLECTION)

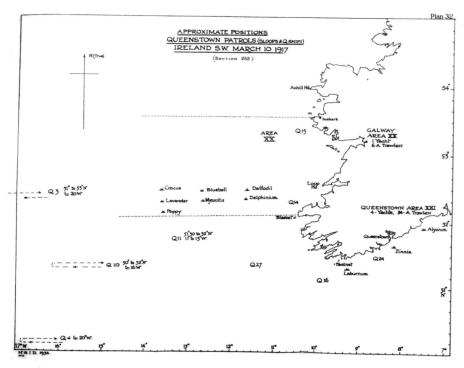

Bayly's deployments to protect the south western and western approaches in March 1917 can be seen from this map (taken from Naval Staff Monographs vol XVIII, May 1933).

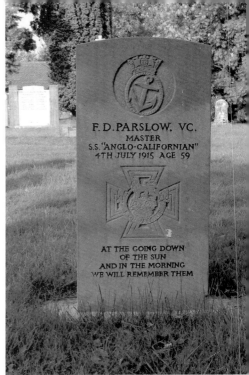

The memorial designed by Jerome Connor in Cobh dedicated to the victims of the *Lusitania* sinking. Begun in 1936, it was not completed until 1968. (AUTHOR'S COLLECTION)

The gravestone in Cobh Old Church Cemetery of Captain Frederick Parslow, master of the *Anglo-Californian*, who won the VC for his defence of his ship. (AUTHOR'S COLLECTION)

The memorial plaque commemorating the US Navy's arrival in Ireland, laid by the Naval Order of the United States at Admiralty House, 2017. (AUTHOR'S COLLECTION)

April is the Cruellest Month, 1917

In April 1917, German U-boats sank 881,027grt of Allied and neutral ships. It was the worst month of the war for losses by nearly 300,000 tons. Of this total, 516,384grt was from British-flagged vessels. U-boat activity was at its height in the Western Approaches; and mines were laid off the south Irish coast at Conninbeg, Waterford, Daunt's Rock light vessel and Old Head of Kinsale as well as Belfast Lough, Milford Haven and Barnstaple. In April alone 120 British ocean-going ships of greater than 1,600grt each were sunk, fifty-three of them in the three cones of approach off Ireland and thirty-five in the Fastnet alone.[1] It was indeed a cruel month for the Coast of Ireland Command.

The Admiralty sent Bayly four extra escorts, the destroyers *Parthian, Peyton, Narwhal* and *Mary Rose.* These were modern (1916) 'Admiralty M'-class destroyers, fast (34 knots) and armed with three 4in guns; but it was a literal drop in the ocean. Some eighty-two British flagged vessels of all types were sunk in the whole of the Western Approaches during the month. ss *Canadian,* 9,309grt, was a Leyland Lines passenger steamer. On 5 April she was on passage from Boston to Liverpool with a cargo of horses, grain and general goods when at around 2320hrs, forty-seven miles north-west of the Fastnet, she was torpedoed four times by *U-59,* without a warning. Her master, Captain H H Bullock, supervised the evacuation but, in checking that every one of his crew had got away, he went down with his ship, the only casualty of the attack. Most of the crew were fortunately picked up from their boats by *Snowdrop* only two hours later. *Laburnum* rescued some more men from rafts and wreckage and tried to save a horse, but it was impossible so the poor animal was shot.

There was a shocking example of the brutality of unrestrained warfare three days later. ss *Torrington* was a Tatem Steam Navigation Company ship, used to carry coal from Cardiff to Italy.* On 8 April she was returning to Wales to collect another cargo. At 1130hts, some 150 miles off the Isles of Scilly, she was torpedoed forward of the bridge by *U-55*. The U-boat then surfaced and opened fire on her. *Torrington*'s master, Captain Anthony Starkey ordered his men into the lifeboats but the submarine came alongside and Starkey was instructed to come on board and taken below deck. Some of his crew went on the deck of the U-boat, whilst others remained in a lifeboat. The 29-year-old Kapitänleutnant Wilhelm Werner, then commanded the submarine to dive, remarking to Starkey that the rest of his crew could swim. Some twenty men standing on the casing of the U-boat were washed off. With the single exception of Captain Starkey, all of the *Torrington*'s crew died, thirty-four men in total. Starkey was kept prisoner aboard the submarine for fifteen days before being sent to a prisoner of war camp, one of four he would eventually be held in. After the war, Werner was accused of a number of war crimes. These included sinking without warning ss *Clearfield*, *Artist*, *Trevone*, *Torrington* and *Toro* and attacking the hospital ships *Rewa* and *Guildford Castle*. These charges were eventually reduced to a single one of sinking ss *Torrington* and murdering the crew. He never faced justice, however; Werner fled Germany to work on a coffee plantation in Brazil. After some years he returned to Germany and became a National Socialist member of the Reichstag.

On the 13th, ss *Bandon* struck a mine off the Mine Head Lighthouse; twenty-eight crewmen died. *Toro* was sunk off Ushant with fourteen lives lost and the master made prisoner. *Kariba* went down in the same area with thirteen merchant sailors killed. *Queen Mary* was torpedoed without warning north-west of the Fastnet and nine men drowned. Twenty-five sailors died when *Aburi* was sunk 125 miles from Tory Island by *U-61*.

The 10,157grt tanker *San Hilario* was sunk near Bishops Rock by *U-43*. On the 25th, sixty-five people died when Elder Dempster passenger liner rms *Abosso*, 7,782grt, was sunk 180 miles west of

---

* Before the war, coal had been Britain's largest export and the shipment of coal throughout the war was an important political as well as industrial weapon. Italy had been offered preferential amounts of coal as part of its decision to enter the war on the Allied side.

Fastnet Rock by the same U-boat. She had been heading for Liverpool from Lagos with 127 passengers, 134 crew and 3,400 tons of West African produce. For some reason Numbers 1, 3 and 7 lifeboats were lowered away before Captain James Thomas Toft had given the order, for he was waiting for the ship's forward motion to stop. The three lifeboats contained forty-one passengers and twenty-three members of the crew and immediately on reaching the water, as the ship was still moving, they were swamped and all occupants lost. Two days later *U-43* also dispatched the Norwegian tanker *Hectoria*, 5,000 tons, on passage for Birkenhead from Philadelphia.

The 11,120grt ss *Ballarat* was a troopship, torpedoed without warning twenty-four miles south-west of Wolf Rock. She was a passenger liner on the Australia-England run, taken up for use as a transport for Australian soldiers. In February 1917, *Ballarat* left Melbourne on passage to Devonport with 1,602 Australian troops and a general cargo, which included copper and bullion. This was the ship's thirteenth voyage (which caused concern amongst some of the more superstitious troops). On 25 April, the Australian officers had arranged a memorial service to commemorate Anzac Day. At around 1400hrs, as the service was getting underway, an explosion blew a hole in the starboard side of the ship and the vessel started taking on water immediately. Despite the deployment of lookouts and the presence of an escorting destroyer, nobody had seen *UB-32* approach and fire a torpedo. Fortunately, the troopship was close to land and rescue vessels were able to approach quickly to take the soldiers off safely. *Ballarat* was taken in tow but it was no use. In the early hours of the next morning she sank, about nine miles south of Lizard Point. Her captain, Commander G W Cockman RNR, DSO, was commended by the Lords of the Admiralty for his seamanship in getting all his passengers off the sinking ship, and the Australian troops were congratulated on their good fortune by King George V. The U-boat, under her commander Max Viebeg, would sink eleven ships in two cruises during April.

Manchester Citizen, 4,251grt, was sunk on 26 April by *U-70*, 240 miles north-west of the Fastnet Rock. She was a Manchester Liners' ship, based on the eponymous ship canal. Her sister-ships *Manchester Commerce*, *Manchester Engineer* and *Manchester Inventor* were all sunk in the Western Approaches during the course of the war. And so it went on.

Q-ships were not immune from the carnage either. HMS *Tulip* was an *Aubrietia*-class sloop, completed as the Q-ship *Q-12*. On the last day in April she was loitering 135 miles south west of the Fastnet when she was attacked by the serially successful *U-62*, commanded by Ernst Hashagen. The first torpedo hit almost split the little craft in two and killed twenty men in the engine room. The rest of the crew took to the boats and were later picked up by a destroyer but her captain, Commander Norman McCrea Lewis RNR, was taken prisoner. He was from British Columbia, where he had gone to live after leaving the Royal Navy. Aged 40, he had returned to Britain to re-enlist when war broke out. Now he was a prisoner of war. His captors treated him decently. He was well fed and dined with the U-boat officers, which was far from always the case. Hashagen sank another eight vessels on this particular cruise.

Hard-pressed sloops
Bayly's sloops could not have worked any harder. The weeks following the German declaration of unrestricted submarine warfare stretched the already hard-pressed ships of Bayly's force to the limits. An example of the workload can be gleaned from the exploits of the sloop *Zinnia*, captained by Lieutenant Commander Graham Wilson. On 16 April she was escorting the cargo vessel SS *Cranmore** when Wilson picked up a SOS from SS *Queen Mary* (5,658grt), which was inbound from New York for Le Havre when she was torpedoed by *U-60*, 180 miles NWW from Fastnet Rock.

Wilson's report takes up the story. '*Zinnia* proceeded at full speed to assist, arriving 0200 [on the 17th] and cruised in the vicinity, showing lights at intervals. The boats were picked up at 0415; they had seen my lights from the first but kept quiet for fear it was the submarine come to capture the master.'[2] Nine men had died in the attack on the merchant ship. However, at the very point of rescuing the survivors of *Queen Mary*, *Zinnia* received a signal from SS *Kish* (4,928grt) saying she was steaming N20E (true) at 10 knots and was being chased by a submarine. Wilson now turned to intercept *Kish*, passing the wreck of the *Queen Mary* at 0440hrs, still afloat but with decks awash.

At 0600hrs *Zinnia* reached *Kish*, inbound from Norfolk, USA, to Newport, Wales, whereupon the cargo vessel reported the chase

---

* *Cranmore* was eventually torpedoed less than three months later when she was attacked by *U-66*, 150 miles north-west of Fastnet on 7 June; she was beached and refloated.

abandoned. *Zinnia* now escorted her for two hours before departing to respond to a call for help from SS *Cairnhill*, steaming southwards chased by a U-boat. But when *Zinnia* was only four and a half miles away, *Kish* was seen to be torpedoed on the starboard side by *U-67*, 160 miles north-west-by-west of Fastnet; she sank with the loss of six lives. *Zinnia* had passed a transport, *MFA 1463*, and now returned to protect the newly-arrived vessel as she was only two miles from where *Kish* had been sunk.

Meanwhile, *Cairnhill* had been captured and scuttled by *U-55* when 160 miles NW of Fastnet. She had been on passage from New York for Le Havre with a cargo of 1,000 tons of copper and 400 tons of brass.* The Q-ship *Q-14* now joined *Zinnia* to help and Wilson left her to pick up the men from *Kish*. The Q-ship then sailed to protect a large steamer which was approaching from the westward and visible on the horizon. A frustrated Wilson reported that 'nothing was seen of the submarine and I parted company with the transport to go to [map reference] T3 to pick up SS *Irishman*'.[3]

At 1248hrs Wilson sighted a U-boat on the surface 1,100yds ahead and steering west-north-west. *Zinnia* opened fire but her first shots fell short and at 1318hrs the submarine dived. Wilson altered course to intercept the U-boat's presumed position and dropped depth charges, without noticing any effect. At 1525hrs *Zinnia* parted company with *Irishman*, which passed safely on her way.

The following day, 18 April, *Zinnia* came across HMS *Peyton*, a modern 'M'-class destroyer, standing by a damaged steamer, the Cardiff-based SS *Rhydwen*, and flying the signal 'Submarine in the vicinity'. Wilson sighted a periscope at 1155hrs but it disappeared at once; Bayly now ordered him to stay in company with the crippled cargo ship but at 1425hrs she turned turtle and sank 170 miles north-west-by-west of Fastnet with the loss of six men.

All of this activity had taken place in around thirty-six hours and in the same small area of sea. Four cargo ships had been sunk despite Wilson's best efforts; no U-boats had. The war on commerce was turning into a turkey shoot. If sinkings continued at this rate during the next few months, Britain would lose the war.

Jellicoe, the First Sea Lord, realised this. On 27 April he wrote a letter to the First Lord of the Admiralty, to be laid before the War Cabinet, which included the statement:

* This would equate to some £10,000,000 at today's commodity prices.

The real fact of the matter is this. We are carrying on the war at the present time as if we had the absolute command of the sea, whereas we have not such command or anything approaching it. It is quite true that we are masters of the situation so far as surface ships are concerned, but it must be realised – and realised at once – that this will be quite useless if the enemy's submarines paralyse, as they do now, our lines of communication.

Without some such relief as I have indicated [inter alia 'the import of everything that is not essential to the life of the country is ruthlessly and immediately stopped'.] – and that given immediately – the navy will fail in its responsibilities to the country and the country itself will suffer starvation.[4]

An unlikely saviour

Admiral William Sowden Sims, USN, was the President of the Naval War College at Newport, Rhode Island. Fifty-eight years old, tall, urbane and elegant, he lived at the college with his wife Anne and his children, two boys and three girls. His career had encompassed assignments as Naval Attaché in Paris, Madrid and St Petersburg. Unlike many American sailors, he had an international world view as a result. His career had been furthered by an association with President Theodore Roosevelt and by his conspicuous success in transforming the accuracy and speed of American naval gunnery when Inspector of Target Practice. However, this brought him enemies too from amongst those who resented his youth and lack of regard for traditional methods. One American historian has described him as 'an iconoclast who did not suffer fools lightly'.[5]

He had further given his enemies cause to complain in 1910 when, as a guest at a dinner at London's Guildhall, he responded to a toast from the Lord Mayor by stating that 'if the time ever comes when the British Empire is seriously menaced by an external enemy, it is my opinion that you may count on every man, every dollar, every drop of blood of your kindred across the sea'.[6] This was definitely NOT the policy of the United States government and brought a torrent of criticism on his head with the threat of disciplinary action. Seven years later, he assumed that his career would drift to an end in his Rhode Island educational establishment.

He was therefore surprised one day in March 1917 to receive an urgent, and secret, summons to the Navy Department in Washington. In his own words:

> The orders directed me to make my visit as unostentatious as possible; to keep all my movements secret, and, on my arrival in Washington, not to appear at the Navy Department, but to telephone headquarters. I promptly complied with these orders; and, after I got in touch with the navy chiefs, it took but a few moments to explain the situation.
>
> It seemed inevitable, I was informed, that the United States would soon be at war with Germany. Ambassador Page had cabled that it would be desirable, under the existing circumstances, that the American navy be represented by an officer of higher rank than any of those who were stationed in London at that time. The Department therefore wished me to leave immediately for England, to get in touch with the British Admiralty, to study the naval situation and learn how we could best and most quickly co-operate in the naval war.[7]

Secretary for the Navy Josephus Daniels,* pacific if not pacifist, was concerned that Sims's movements should not be generally known, as America was technically at peace with Germany. Sims was to remain ostensibly as head of the War College, his wife and family were still to occupy his official residence, and he was to sail on a merchant vessel, to travel under an assumed name, to wear civilian clothes and to take no uniform. Once in Britain, he was to prepare and remit a report on the situation as he found it.

Sims took with him just one aide, Commander John V Babcock, but his attempt to remain undiscovered was unsuccessful, for he was recognised by the captain of the liner on which he travelled, the US-flagged ss *New York*. They arrived at their destination on 9 April; Sims had left his country at peace and arrived when it was at war. As proof, his ship hit and detonated a mine as it neared Liverpool harbour. The passengers had to transfer to another steamship.

At the port Sims and Babcock were met by Rear Admiral George Price Webley Hope, second director of the Operations Division at the Admiralty, to which place a special train now whisked them.

---

* Daniels, a former journalist, had managed Wilson's election publicity campaign and owed his position to a debt of loyalty felt by Wilson for his support.

There he met with Jellicoe; and here was another happy coincidence. Not only was Sims a cosmopolitan Anglophile, he and Jellicoe were also good friends, having first met when serving together during the Boxer Rebellion in China. Here Jellicoe showed him the true statistics relating to merchant shipping losses. Sims was appalled. As he later related it, the following conversation took place:

'It looks as though the Germans were winning the war,' I remarked.

'They will win, unless we can stop these losses – and stop them soon,' the Admiral replied.

'Is there no solution for the problem?' I asked.

'Absolutely none that we can see now,' Jellicoe announced.[8]

Sims met with the Cabinet and the King, and spent hours and days at the Admiralty – and came to the certain view that America had to send ships to fight the U-boats and send them now. His reasoning was Cartesian:

The British were most heroically struggling against the difficulties imposed by the mighty task which they had assumed. The British navy, like all other navies, was only partially prepared for this type of warfare; in 1917 it did not possess destroyers enough both to guard the main fighting fleet and to protect its commerce from submarines. Up to 1914, indeed, it was expected that the destroyers would have only one function to perform in warfare, that of protecting the great surface vessels from attack, but now the new kind of warfare which Germany was waging on merchant ships had laid upon the destroyer an entirely new responsibility; and the plain fact is that the destroyers, in the number which were required, did not exist.[9]

Sims drafted a note for US Ambassador to the Court of St James, Water Hines Page, to send to President Wilson, via the Secretary of State. In full it read:

There is reason for the greatest alarm about the issue of the war caused by the increasing success of the German submarines. I have it from official sources that during the week ending 22nd April, eighty-eight ships of 237,000 tons

Allied and neutral were lost. The number of vessels unsuccessfully attacked indicated a great increase in the number of
submarines in action.

This means practically a million tons lost every month till
the shorter days of autumn come. By that time the sea will be
about clear of shipping. Most of the ships are sunk to the
westward and southward of Ireland. The British have in that
area every available anti-submarine craft, but their force is so
insufficient that they hardly discourage the submarines.

The British transport of troops and supplies is already
strained to the utmost, and the maintenance of the armies in
the field is threatened. There is food enough here to last the
civil population only not more than six weeks or two months.

Whatever help the United States may render at any time in
the future, or in any theatre of the war, our help is now more
seriously needed in this submarine area for the sake of all the
Allies than it can ever be needed again, or anywhere else.

After talking over this critical situation with the Prime
Minister and other members of the Government, I cannot
refrain from most strongly recommending the immediate
sending over of every destroyer and all other craft that can be
of anti-submarine use. This seems to me the sharpest crisis of
the war, and the most dangerous situation for the Allies that
has arisen or could arise.

If enough submarines can be destroyed in the next two or
three months the war will be won, and if we can contribute
effective help immediately it will be won directly by our aid.
I cannot exaggerate the pressing and increasing danger of this
situation. Thirty or more destroyers and other similar craft
sent by us immediately would very likely be decisive.

There is no time to be lost.[10]

The note was sent on 27 April; in fact, under the influence of the
Balfour mission* to America and the previous notes sent by Sims,
the US government had already acted. On 4 May, the first American
ships arrived at Queenstown.

---

* Balfour arrived in New York on the 22nd; his task was to solicit American aid and
brief the US Executive on the war situation. Amongst his successes were to negotiate a
loan of £10,000,000 to shore up Britain's fast-deteriorating finances.

Bayly and Sims

Two more dissimilar and unlikely personalities to be thrown together in the heat of a desperate conflict could not be imagined. Bayly had been an undersized child and as an adult remained rather scrawny. He was not given to the pleasures of the flesh, eating sparingly and drinking alcohol hardly ever; Admiralty House was 'dry'. Bayly was ascetic, Calvinist, dedicated to his work and his duty. He had no children or dependents and his niece was the only female company he seemed to enjoy. Many people thought him cantankerous. Perhaps surprisingly, he was well read, 'deeply read in general literature, in history, and in science'.[11] He disliked change and revered the past, 'a conservative of the conservatives, having that ingrained British respect for old things simply because they were old'.[12]

A British officer who served with him noted that 'he never spared either himself or his men. "Know your work, do it, and keep on doing it," was his motto. Live up to that, and he would be your best friend, but God help you if you were slack or incompetent.'[13] Visitors to Bayly's office were made to wait silently whilst he'd finished whatever task was occupying him. Only then would he look up and brusquely ask their business. Once he had answered their request he would lower his head back to the business in hand. There was no chit-chat.

Bayly eschewed personal publicity. He refused to talk to reporters about himself and objected to having his picture taken; if a press photographer tried, he would turn his back. And an American reporter, trying to get to sea to report on the war, was denied his wish, Bayly telling him icily that 'this war is not a pastime'.[14]

Although as a young man he had engaged in sport, he now claimed 'I am entirely against violent exercise'.[15] He confined his exertions to walking in the hills at the back of Admiralty House every Saturday afternoon, often in the company of his paymaster, Russell, or with his niece. Occasionally he would participate in tip-and-run cricket in the garden of the big house. Every Sunday he went to church where he frequently read the lesson.

On his appointment the Admiralty offered him a car, but when it arrived the vehicle proved to be ex-RNAS and well worn. Bayly thought it ill-befitting the status of an admiral and returned it until a better one was provided. But he was not without offers of comfort. A local landowner, Lord Midleton, offered him the use of a country house and grounds which, whilst appreciated, was not taken up. Midleton also came over to Queenstown to offer his assistance during the Easter Rising; on departure he left a case of 15-year-old Irish whiskey which was enjoyed 'out-of-hours' by the officers of the command but not by Bayly himself.

Sims was a completely different personality, described by one historian as 'an Anglophile officer of great sea experience, broad views, quickness of mind and easy manner'.[16] His first meeting with Bayly was less than successful. In early April, Bayly had been summoned to the Admiralty by Jellicoe at short notice. To say he was irritated would be to put it mildly. Apart from the political situation in Ireland, which was bubbling up again, the war in the Western Approaches was taking all of his energy and he wanted to be left alone to get on with the job, not waste his time in pointless chat in London. Informed by Jellicoe that it was probable that the USA was about to enter the war, Bayly was then introduced to Sims. As he often was, and certainly as he was reputed to be, Bayly was distant and cold to Sims; the latter wrote that 'on that occasion he was as rude to me as one man can be to another'.[17] Jellicoe was horrified and offered to have Bayly removed from command, an offer Sims declined.

On his return to Queenstown, Bayly pondered how to be 'nice' to the Americans, as Jellicoe had exhorted him to. After much consideration, he decided to treat them just as he treated his own Royal Navy officers. And he wrote to Sims, asking him to come and stay at Admiralty House. Bayly had been in post for nearly two years without a break. Jellicoe wrote to him suggesting that he should take some holiday. Bayly replied that 'I am deeply touched by your taking the trouble to make my way easier in the suggestion of leave that you make' but declined the offer.[18]

Now this spare, driven, cold man was to be responsible for welcoming Britain's latest ally to the war. The thought gave many in Whitehall kittens. Jellicoe's offer of leave may not have been as caring as Bayly thought. Herbert Richmond, commanding *Conqueror* at Scapa, noted in his diary 'Bayly at Queenstown quarrels with his superiors'.[19] Nonetheless, Bayly and Sims grew to like and respect each other. 'Admiral Sims was practically an honorary member of Admiralty House', according to Bayly's later testimony.[20] On 3 May, the day before the US ships were expected, Bayly, Sims, Russell and Violet were at dinner when the sound of explosions were heard from the harbour. Almost as if they knew the Americans were coming, the Germans had mined the harbour.* Bayly merely remarked that his minesweepers were doing good work.

And so, the next day, a man in a too-big-jacket stared through the windows of Admiralty House out to sea; and above him a woman stood on the roof, searching the distant horizon.

---

* They did, Germany had extensive spy networks in the USA; Sims later wrote 'the news that our destroyers had reached Queenstown actually appeared in the German papers several days before we had released it in the British and American press (Sims, *The Victory at Sea*, p 51).

PART TWO
The Royal Navy and United States Navy under Bayly's Command

The Americans Arrive, 1917

The morning of May 4, 1917, witnessed an important event in the history of Queenstown. The news had been printed in no British or American paper, yet in some mysterious way it had reached nearly everybody in the city. A squadron of American destroyers, which had left Boston on the evening of April 24th, had already been reported to the westward of Ireland and was due to reach Queenstown that morning. At almost the appointed hour a little smudge of smoke appeared in the distance, visible to the crowds assembled on the hills; then presently another black spot appeared, and then another; and finally these flecks upon the horizon assumed the form of six rapidly approaching warships. The Stars and Stripes were broken out on public buildings, on private houses, and on nearly all the water craft in the harbour; the populace, armed with American flags, began to gather on the shore; and the local dignitaries donned their official robes to welcome the new friends from overseas. One of the greatest days in Anglo-American history had dawned, for the first contingent of the American navy was about to arrive in British waters and join hands with the Allies in the battle against the forces of darkness and savagery.[1]

The return of the *Mayflower*
Commander Joseph Knefler Taussig, USN, was captain of the destroyer *Wadsworth* and in command of Division Eight, Destroyer Force, Atlantic Fleet, which comprised *Conyngham* (Commander Alfred P Johnson), *Porter* (Lieutenant Commander Ward K Wortman), *McDougal* (Lieutenant Commander Arthur P Fairfield),

Davis (Lieutenant Commander Rufus Zogbaum) and *Wainwright* (Lieutenant Commander Fred H Poteel). They were modern vessels, 315ft long overall with a 30ft beam, armed with four 4in/50-calibre guns and four twin 21in torpedo tubes with a range of 10,000yds.

On 14 April, Taussig received orders to proceed to the navy yard at New York and equip for 'special service'. Nobody seemed to know why he was there and it took many phone calls and some heavy lifting on his part to get the necessary arrangements made for his vessels to fit out. From New York he was ordered to the Boston yard, where he arrived on 17 April, whence followed a frustrating period of 'hurry-up-and-wait'. No definite orders came through and a telephone call with the Navy's Chief of Staff brought little illumination. As Taussig recorded in his diary, 'our doctrine in the flotilla teaches us that in order to carry out instructions intelligently the commanding officer should know the reason for the issuing of such instructions. But doctrine has no weight with the [Navy] Department, which appears to go along with its eyes only half open.'[2]

On the 23rd Taussig received orders to sail 'urgently', his destination the English Channel. To this he replied that they would be ready to leave on the 25th. In the end the flotilla departed on the 24th, minus some expected pieces of kit, including their ice-making machines! His instructions required him to sail to a point fifty miles east of Cape Cod and then break open his sealed orders and act on them.

When opened, his orders instructed him to sail for Queenstown and thereafter co-operate fully with the Royal Navy. 'When within radio communication of the British Naval Forces of Ireland, call "GCK" and inform the Vice Admiral at Queenstown in British General Code of your position, course and speed. You will be met outside of Queenstown.'[3] He had already been given copies of the British and French naval code books. He and his ships were off to war.

The trip across the Atlantic came as a salutary introduction to the conditions that they would be facing on a daily basis. The weather was rough and the little destroyers rolled and took on water continuously. Taussig noted 'we have been rolling so much that the mess table has not been set up since April 25th. We have been holding our plates in our laps.'[4] *Wainwright* had problems with her condensers and they had to come to a complete stop twice for them to be repaired.

As they neared Ireland, they picked up radio messages from the destroyer HMS *Parthian*, sent by Bayly to meet them. But despite dividing his force to search for her, Taussig could not make a rendezvous; it was misty and dull and visibility was not good. Bayly sent out the *Mary Rose*, which did find them. She hoisted the international signal 'Welcome to the American colours' and *Wadsworth* answered 'Thank you, I am glad of your company'.

The following day, 4 May, the American flotilla sailed into Queenstown. An official photographer in a tug recorded their arrival. A film crew from the F W Engholm company filmed it for posterity. There were cheering crowds and the Stars and Stripes were enthusiastically waved in the welcoming crowd. High above the tumult, Lewis Bayly stood in the window of Admiralty House and watched the new ships enter harbour; as did his niece, perched on the rooftop.

The motor launches *ML-181* and *ML-325*, the former flying a pilot's flag, brought a greeting party to *Wadsworth*. There was Captain Lacy from the dockyard, asking if they needed his help; and Captain Edward 'Teddy' Evans, 'Evans of the *Broke*', a legendary destroyer captain and quondam polar explorer. He had been sent to Queenstown to help induct the US Navy in hard-learned destroyer tactics. Evans brought a letter from Jellicoe, for here was another fortunate coincidence; Jellicoe and Taussig knew each other from service (again) in the Boxer Rising. The former's letter ended 'I must offer you and all your officers and men the warmest welcome possible in the name of the British Nation and British Admiralty, and add to it every possible good wish from myself. May every good fortune attend you and speedy victory be with us.'[5]

There was also a letter from Bayly; it was short and to the point.

Dear Lieut. Comdr. Taussig [Taussig had actually been appointed Commander before he left the USA, back dated to 1916, but the documentation had not yet come through]

I hope that you and the other fine officers in command of the US destroyers in your flotilla will come and dine here tonight, Friday, at 7:45 and that you and three others will remain to sleep here so as to get a good rest after your long journey. Allow me to welcome you and to thank you for coming.

Yours sincerely
Lewis Bayly

Dine in undress: no speeches.[6]

At the Royal Naval Pier, Taussig and his captains, ferried ashore in Bayly's admiral's barge, were met by Captain Carpendale. Babcock was there too and so was the American Vice Consul Sherman, resplendent in a frock coat and top hat. The Americans exchanged greetings and made a quick visit to the US consulate, situated above O'Reilly and Sons Machine Bakery.

Formalities over, Taussig did what any good destroyer captain would do. He started to refuel.

Lessons to be learned

At their first meeting that day, after shaking hands in greeting, Bayly asked Taussig when his ships would be ready to sail. Taussig's reply was the sort that would earn the admiral's respect. Whether coached to Bayly's ways or not, Taussig replied 'We are ready now, sir, that is as soon as we finish refuelling. Of course, you know how destroyers are, always wanting something done to them. But this is war, and we are ready to make the best of things and go to sea immediately.'[7] 'You will take four days rest' Bayly replied.[8] The US Navy had passed the first test.

That night the American officers dined with Bayly and his niece. Four slept at Admiralty House, their first comfortable night since 24 April. The following morning all six USN commanders met with Bayly again. 'Gentlemen', he addressed them 'the Admiralty are afraid I shall be rude to you. I shan't if you do your work; I shall if you don't.'[9]

In point of fact Taussig's storm-tossed destroyers had a long list of defects. Additionally, Bayly wanted them fitted with depth charges and to have their topmasts reduced in height to lower their profile when at sea. This gave Bayly and his team time to try to inculcate some of the lessons learned. First the admiral set out their priorities; sink submarines, escort ships and rescue survivors, in that order. Next Bayly, Captain Evans and the staff passed on the learning that might save American sailors' lives. They must beware of submarines in disguise; they must not stop to rescue people in the water if there was a chance of finding and sinking a U-boat; periscopes should be shelled not rammed, as some were mine-laden decoys; torpedoed vessels should always be approached with the sun astern; no lights should be shown at night and searchlights never used; always zigzag and never steam at less than 13 knots; and so much more. Three days was not much time to pass on three years' experience.

On 5 May the sloop *Lavender* was torpedoed by *UC-75* whilst on area patrol south of Mine Head. Her captain, Lieutenant Commander Thomas Stephen Lewis Dorman, Lieutenant James Williamson RNR and twenty men were lost. The remainder of the crew were picked up by one of the motor launches and brought into Queenstown. Thirty-three-year-old Thomas Dorman had already been awarded the DSO for bravery in Persia in 1915 (gazetted 6 September 1916). He had been married for exactly 126 days. It was a salutary reminder for Taussig and his men of the risks they would now run.

At 1400hrs on Tuesday 8 May the US destroyers put to sea. They were as ready as they could be in the time. Now they were no longer 'too proud to fight'.

The Northern Division

With the arrival of the American destroyers, on 18 May the Admiralty reinforced Bayly's command structure by appointing Rear Admiral Francis Spurston Miller to a newly-created 'Northern Division' based at Buncrana on Lough Swilly. The northern approach to the Irish Sea near Tory Island was not well protected and now, with the added USN resources available, it was possible to strengthen the defences in the area. The same day as the US Navy forces reached Queenstown, all the 'E'-class submarines, on detachment from Harwich and up until now based at Berehaven, were sent to the new command (four destroyers were added later) with orders to patrol the narrow exit and entry route, seeking U-boats. They were based at Killibegs, on the Lough, and were designated the 'Vulcan Flotilla', six vessels strong. To this force were added three 'D'-class submarines taken from the 3rd Submarine Flotilla, designated the 'Platypus Flotilla' after the name of the depot ship. By September a further two vessels had been added.

The 'E'-class were the backbone of the British submarine fleet, armed with four or five 18in torpedoes, a 12pdr gun and capable of around 15 knots when surfaced. Conditions on board were basic and extremely cramped; there was just one bunk which the three officers shared, the twenty-seven ratings slept where they could and the heads were more often than not just a bucket. They made poor patrol vessels in the choppy waters of the Irish Sea, not least because they and their intended prey sat low in the water, giving a very limited range of vision; despite that they did sink one U-boat.

On 1 May, just before their deployment north, *E-54* sank *U-81* shortly after the latter had torpedoed the tanker ss *San Urbano*, 180 miles NWW of the Fastnet. The British submarine's captain, Lieutenant Commander Robert Henry Taunton Raikes, had form in this unlikely success for he had sunk *UC-10* in the North Sea the previous year. Raikes arrived back at Queenstown with seven German prisoners, including the U-boat captain, rescued from the Atlantic, at 0100hrs the next day and reported straightaway to Bayly, who gave him hot coffee and stayed up all night to listen to his story.

And Bayly welcomed the arrival of a new senior member of staff in Miller. He later wrote that 'Admiral Miller at Lough Swilly and Captain Charles Carpendale at Larne ran the north side of the Irish Sea so well that I was able to devote myself to the main trade routes in the south'.[10]

A united command
Rear Admiral (Vice Admiral from 25 May 1917) Sims was responsible for all American naval vessels and personnel in Britain (his official designation was 'Commander of the US Naval Forces Operating in European Waters'). But he had insisted that the destroyers sent to Queenstown should come under Bayly's operational command, as part of an integrated force. This was a sensible decision from an operational point of view but one which did not please many people both within and without the US Navy.

America had come late to a blue water navy; not until Theodore Roosevelt's 'Great White Fleet' had circumnavigated the globe between 1907 and 1909 did the world understand the America now wanted to project international power and it was Roosevelt's impetus and vision which had reenergised interest in matters naval in the first place. Additionally, the US Navy was in some ways jealous of the traditions and battle honours of the Royal Navy; many could not decide whether they admired or resented British sea power and traditions.

As a consequence, Sims' insistence on placing American ships under a British flag was contentious. His ultimate superior, Admiral William Benson, Chief of Naval Operations, was not an admirer of the British. Benson charged that the anglophile Sims had 'gone native' and that he was too much influenced by the British. In fact, Benson had warned Sims before his departure, 'Don't let the British pull the wool over your eyes. It is none of our business pulling their chestnuts out of the fire. We would as soon fight the British as the Germans.'[11] In this statement Benson was reflecting popular US dislike of the Royal Navy's blockade, as well as the view held in some quarters that America and Britain would come to blows over imperial ambitions.

Sims had made Benson aware of the immediate crisis and of the necessity to support the anti-submarine campaign. But Benson felt he needed to keep an eye on the potential future course of the war. A memorandum prepared by his staff in February 1917 concluded 'vessels should be built not only to meet present conditions but conditions that may come after the present phase of the world war … We may expect the future to give us more potential enemies than potential friends so that our safety must lie in our own resources.'[12] And the Navy Board recommended: 'Keep constantly in view the possibility of the United States being in the not distant future compelled to conduct a war single-handed against some of the belligerents.'[13]

Sims faced opposition from sections of the press too. As the admiral later noted, 'The fact that these American destroyers were placed under the command of a British admiral was somewhat displeasing to certain Americans. I remember that one rather bumptious American correspondent, on a visit to Queenstown, was loud in expressing his disapproval of this state of affairs, and even threatened to "expose" us all in the American press.'[14]

But the system worked. Bayly went to great lengths to ensure that American sensitivities were respected. Ships went out in mixed patrols. The senior man commanded, be he an USN or RN officer. Any court of inquiry was to consist of three members; for the first one, two British and one American, the next two American and one British, and so on. The presidency of such courts would be held USN/RN alternately.

Sims continued to press for more ships to be sent to Ireland. On 28 April, concerned that he had not heard that more than the first six destroyers were on the way, he cabled home, 'We cannot send too many or too soon'[15] and was relieved to learn that the United States intended to send thirty-six in total. In May, another two divisions of destroyers arrived with the destroyer tender *Melville*, designated flagship of the force.

Then, on 12 June, another destroyer division arrived along with a second tender, *Dixie*. Her commander was 44-year-old Captain Joel Roberts Poinsett Pringle. His entry into Queenstown was somewhat fraught. The harbour entrance and roads had been swept for mines the previous day but when the minesweepers went out at 0600hrs, the channel had been newly sown. Pringle was told of the fact by wireless but the signal did not reach him until he was actually in the minefield itself. Bayly, who was dressing (it was just before 0800hrs) looked out of his window and was horrified to see *Dixie* bearing down on the harbour. Pringle had decided to carry on, as it was high tide and he believed he could pass over the mines; fortunately he did.

Bayly took to Pringle straight away. He made him his US Chief of Staff and had Pringle entered in the Navy List, the first time a foreign officer had appeared in it as a member of an admiral's staff (Bayly wrote to Jellicoe re Pringle appearing in the Navy List on 1 September 1917: 'It will help him a good deal in his service and will give pleasure all round to the US officers').[16]

By the end of June there were over thirty USN ships under Bayly's command. The first arrivals had been sent out on area patrols, looking for submarines. But now they had a further task to undertake.

The doughboys

The first 'doughboys', American troops, to land in France were the 16th and 28th Infantry Regiments, who arrived at St-Nazaire on 26 June 1917. For the very last part of their ten-day journey they were escorted by French destroyers. But for a significant part of the voyage it was their own destroyers, based at Queenstown and commanded by Lewis Bayly, who brought them safely to Europe. By the end of the war, a total of 1,100,000 American troops would be transported across the Atlantic in escorted convoys, with only 637 American soldiers killed as a result of German attacks.

The introduction of convoy had been the subject of sometimes acrimonious debate. With the advent of America into the war, the safe transportation of troopship, soldiers and supplies to Europe was a key priority. Many in the Admiralty thought convoys unworkable as they believed that merchant masters would not be able to maintain the necessary sailing discipline and keep station. Others felt that it was an entirely defensive approach, out of keeping with the tradition and proper use of British warships. Yet another faction was misled by an erroneous interpretation of shipping movement statistics into believing that the Navy had insufficient vessels to make convoy work.

It was not just in Britain that this distrust of convoy manifested itself. The United States Navy Department was also somewhat reluctant to accept convoy. Benson and Secretary of the Navy Josephus Daniels put more emphasis on armed merchant ships sailing independently, at one point even suggesting the already-discredited method of patrolled sea lanes, previously put forward in Britain by such as Richmond and Bayly.

But Admiral Sims was an ardent supporter of the escorted convoy and argued strongly that this was the only safe method to transport US troops over the Atlantic. And he was somewhat contemptuous of Bayly's 'area patrol' system. As he wrote later:

> The so-called submarine patrol, under the circumstances which prevailed at that time, could accomplish very little. This little fleet of destroyers was based on Queenstown; from this port they put forth and patrolled the English Channel and the waters about Ireland in the hope that a German submarine would stick its nose above the waves. The central idea of the destroyer patrol was this one of hunting; the destroyer could have sunk any submarine or driven it away from shipping if the submarine would only have made its presence known. But of course this was precisely what the submarine declined to do.
>
> It must be evident to the merest novice that four or five destroyers, rushing around hunting for submarines which were lying a hundred feet or so under water, could accomplish very little. The under-water boat could always see its surface enemy long before it was itself seen and thus could save its life by the simple process of submerging. It must also be clear that the destroyer patrol could accomplish much only in case there were a very large number of destroyers. We figured that, to make the patrol system work with complete success, it would be necessary to have one destroyer for every square mile. The area of the destroyer patrol off Queenstown comprised about 25,000 square miles; it is apparent that the complete protection of the trans-Atlantic trade routes would have taken about 25,000 destroyers.[17]

Instead Sims argued for escorted convoy.

The advantages of the convoy were thus so apparent that, despite the pessimistic attitude of the merchant captains, there were a number of officers in the British navy who kept insisting that it should be tried. In this discussion I took my stand emphatically with these officers. From the beginning I had believed in this method of combating the U-boat warfare. Certain early experiences had led me to believe that the merchant captains were wrong in underestimating the quality of their own seamanship. It was my conviction that these intelligent and hardy men did not really know how capable they were at handling ships.[18]

Politicians such as Prime Minister Lloyd George were also strong advocates of the system and eventually the Admiralty ran a 'trial' convoy to Gibraltar. It was a success and, as Sims reported:

On May 21st the British Admiralty, which this experimental convoy had entirely converted, voted to adopt the convoy system for all merchant shipping. Not long afterward the second convoy arrived safely from Hampton Roads, and then other convoys began to put in from Scandinavian ports. On July 21st I was able definitely to report to Washington that the success of the convoys so far brought in shows that the system will defeat the submarine campaign if applied generally and in time.[19]

And so convoy became the lot of the USN ships at Queenstown. By the end of June, twenty-eight American destroyers were escorting convoys, rather than simply conducting patrols as had been the original plan. And despite their personal reservations, Daniels and Benson continued to send all available destroyers; by the end of August, the number at Queenstown had risen to thirty-five. Sims was informed by Daniels that the 'paramount duty' of American destroyers in European waters was the protection of US troop transports and that everything was secondary to that.[20] And Bayly, wise after the event for he had definitely been in the 'anti' camp, wrote 'considering that in our past wars the necessity and value of convoys were so clearly recognised it is difficult to see why they were so long delayed in the Great War'.[21]

Convoy escort was both arduous and humdrum. The incoming

convoys were met some 500 miles west of Ireland by mixed flotillas of USN and RN ships and guided to port. 'Our routine was five days at sea and three days in Queenstown' recalled Lieutenant Commander William Halsey[*] of *Benham*, 'with five days for cleaning boilers every fifth trip.'[22]

In one week in July, for example, USS *Shaw* escorted three convoys. On 21 July, *Shaw* and USS *Parker* met and escorted RMS *Celtic* (now a troopship) safely to St-Nazaire, and then to Queenstown.[**] On 24 July she was covering the outbound Convoy OQ2 and the inward HS6, in company with *Wadsworth*, *Jacob Jones*, *Ericsson*, *Burrows*, *Paulding*, *Sterret* and *Porter*, all USN destroyers. And on 28 July *Shaw*, *Trippe*, *Wadsworth*, *McDougal*, *Porter*, *Wainwright*, *Jacob Jones* and *Ericsson* formed an escort for an incoming convoy of nineteen ships. This was eventful for on the second day of the duty, USS *Wadsworth* sighted a submarine wake at 2255hrs and dropped a depth charge on it. Five minutes later, the nearby *Trippe* collided with an underwater object, which may (or may not) have been a U-boat hull, but no serious damage was done and nothing further was seen. About half an hour later the radio man on watch heard a German submarine calling wildly – as if in distress. Commander Taussig wondered if they had hit a U-boat (they hadn't). It was the same every month thereafter; days of tedious watchfulness and occasional moments of action and terror. Convoy duty was here to stay.

The two navies settled down to work together. As Sims noted 'they [the USN officers] had established cordial relations with Admiral Bayly and were prepared to trust themselves unreservedly in his hands'.[23] And Sub Lieutenant Francis Stephen Walter de Winton, serving on board HMS *Narwhal*, noted 'we got on well with the US destroyers and they found Admiral Bayly a good man to work for'.[24]

Bayly caused a sign to be made from an old U-boat signal board

---

[*] The future Second World War USN Admiral William Frederick Halsey Jr, known as 'Bull' Halsey.

[**] *Celtic* had an eventful war. Initially converted to an AMC, she was returned to service as a troopship owing to her high fuel consumption. She had struck a mine laid by *U-80*, off the Isle of Man. Although *Celtic* survived, seventeen people lost their lives. She was then taken to Belfast, where she was repaired, and returned to service around two months later as a trooper. Just over a year later on, 31 March 1918, *Celtic* was again damaged, this time by a torpedo from *U-77*, once more near the Isle of Man. She survived the attack and was repaired at Belfast. Six people were killed in the attack.

and placed against the bulkhead of USS *Melville*, opposite the main gangway; it simply said 'Pull Together'. Both the USN and the RN had successfully crossed the *Pons Assinorum*.

* * *

By early 1917 many British warships had been painted in a new camouflage scheme known as 'razzle dazzle' or 'dazzle' painting. It was a camouflage paint scheme credited to the marine artist Norman Wilkinson, who had been co-opted into the navy as a lieutenant commander in the RNVR, and consisted of a complex pattern of geometric shapes in contrasting colours, interrupting and intersecting each other. The idea of 'dazzle' was not to conceal the ship but to make it difficult for enemy submarines to estimate its type, size, speed and heading by disrupting the visual rangefinders used. Dazzle was intended to make life hard for the U-boat commander such that he may delay too long to 'take his shot', or decide not to waste a valuable torpedo on an indistinct target.

Bayly's sloops and some of the sloop Q-ships were also to be so camouflaged and when the American destroyers arrived in Queenstown it was determined that they too should be painted in a dazzle scheme. As admirals know everything, Bayly had painted *Zinnia* up in a scheme of his own devising. Wilkinson was despatched to Queenstown to supervise the painting of the American vessels and Bayly proudly showed him his design for *Zinnia*. Wilkinson was profoundly unimpressed and told Bayly so. Bayly was reciprocally unimpressed by the painter's less-than-naval manner; when Wilkinson departed for London he left his paint box on the steps of Admiralty House and arrived at the train station without his hat.*

---

* Admiral Sims was so taken by the usefulness of 'dazzle' that in January 1918 he asked for Wilkinson to be seconded to Washington DC to advise on schemes for American cargo ships. Wilkinson arrived in the USA in early February.

'Pull Together': Joint Operations Commence, 1917

The war had not been on hold while the Americans reinforcements arrived. Nor was it only British-flagged ships that suffered. On May Day itself, the full-rigged Finnish sailing ship *Imberhorne*, the Russian sailing vessel *Alide*, the American cargo ship *Rockingham*, the Norwegian barque *Ivrig* and the French fishing craft *Raymond Ester* were all sunk in the Western Approaches along with six British-registered merchant ships. And on the day Commander Taussig arrived at Queenstown, seven cargo vessels were lost in the waters of Bayly's command.

Among them was ss *Pilar de Larrinaga*, 4,136grt and owned by Larrinaga and Co of Liverpool. She was carrying general cargo and wheat from Galveston to Manchester when she was torpedoed and sunk by *U-65*, two miles south-east of the Tuskar Rock. Twenty crewmen, including the master, died in the attack. The Larrinaga company had already lost one ship, *Jose de Larrinaga*, to *U-81* six days earlier with the loss of twelve men (again including the master), 150 miles from the Fastnet.[*] The crew of this latter ship had been rescued by the sloop *Poppy* from their lifeboats on 28 April. They told their rescuers that, after sinking their ship, the U-boat 'surfaced and told survivors to "smile please" as they took a photograph.

Bayly ordered that they be brought to Queenstown and so the merchant sailors were allocated two messes in the starboard battery, with masts and sails to sleep on. Sub Lieutenant Robert Goldrich noted that '[We] fed them our fresh meat and spuds. Will run short

---

[*] They would lose another vessel, the brand-new *Richard de Larrinaga*, 5991grt, in October, torpedoed by *U-57*, fifteen miles from Ballycottin Island, County Cork. Thirty-five sailors died, the master again being one of them.

of both in two days' time and then we will all go on tinned dope together.'[1]

Zinnia claims a sub

As the American destroyers arrived, the sloops were out hunting U-boats. On 4 May Lieutenant Commander Graham Wilson and his sloop *Zinnia* were on patrol thirty miles west of Ireland. At 1520hrs they heard gunfire to the north and east of them; visibility was about five miles but nothing could be sighted so Wilson went to full speed and headed east by north. Forty-five minutes later, gunfire could be heard once more and he turned north-north-east, demanding every last knot from his engine room team.

Wilson had been in Bayly's command for over two years. He had seen the devastation that U-boats wrought all over the Western Approaches; now, at 1625hrs he saw his chance to do something about it. Dead ahead at about 8,000yds range was the three-masted Danish barquentine *Jorgen Olsen*; and shelling her from starboard was a U-boat. *Zinnia*'s tactical position was good; Wilson had contrived to be between the submarine and the setting sun; the U-boat would find the sloop hard to spot against the glare.

Wilson ordered the forward gun to open fire with 4.7in common shell; a hit was immediately observed amidships and a large explosion followed. *Aubrietia* now arrived to join in and opened fire two miles to the west-north-west of *Zinnia* but her shell fell short and broke up on impact with the water, the fragments nearly hitting *Zinnia*.

When the smoke cleared the U-boat had disappeared. Wilson thought they had killed the submarine. 'I am convinced', he wrote in his report to Bayly, 'that she must have had ammunition on board which was detonated as no 4.7in common shell could cause so large an explosion.'[2] Wilson drove his ship to where the submarine had last been sighted and dropped depth charges which seemed to raise a film of light oil. He then remained in the areas, hoping for a further sign of his victim until 2000hrs when Bayly ordered him to return to patrol.

Bayly and Wilson claimed a sinking, but the Admiralty disagreed. On 25 June they wrote to 'acquaint you that they [Their Lordships] do not consider it probable that the submarine was sunk on the occasion'.[3] And they were correct; it was *U-62*, and she and her captain, Ernst Hashagen, survived the war to sink forty-eight ships, damaging another five. By way of consolation perhaps,

Wilson was awarded the DSO, gazetted in July, 'for his good service in command of *Zinnia*'.[4]

On patrol

On 18 May, HMS *Laburnum* was detailed to escort the iron ore carrier SS *Farnham*, on passage to the Clyde, though the Fastnet danger zone. William Mason described her as 'a squat ugly old one funnel tramp …she makes like a log through the seas'.[5] She may have been ugly but the Spanish ores she carried were vital to Britain's war effort. They could only make 7 knots, which made the two-ship convoy very susceptible to U-boat attack. The following morning the vessels were about five miles off Mizzen Head, difficult seas where the cliffs rise high above the Atlantic Ocean, the currents meet from the west and south coasts and the waves from the mid-Atlantic crash into the land. At 0900hrs and just as *Laburnum*'s wardroom was finishing breakfast, *Farnham* was torpedoed by *U-57*. She sank evenly to her waterline and then broke in two. Nine out of twenty-seven of Farnham's crew were plucked from the seas by the sloop; one, a stoker, died later. Even when under individual escort, merchant ships were just not safe.

But trying to protect merchant vessels by attracting U-boats to Q-ships made a dangerous berth for a sailor. *Lady Patricia*, or SS *Paxton*, and in fact *Q-25*, was a 1,370grt steamer with a hidden armament of one 4in and two 12pdr guns. On 20 May, she was cruising about 100 miles west of Fastnet Rock. She had sighted and engaged a submarine in the morning but it had submerged and disappeared. As her disguise might well have been 'blown', she changed her colours and became the Swedish ship *Tosca Sverige*. It was to no avail. At 1915hrs she was torpedoed by *U-46* with two men killed outright. Lieutenant Commander George Osbourne Hewitt fought to keep her afloat and tried to lull the U-boat into surfacing and coming near enough to fire on it; but at 1930hrs the submarine fired a second torpedo which sank the Q-ship in four minutes. Thirty-one men died in the attack. Some were regular navy, some MMR, others RNR or RNVR. There was an officer's cook, a paymaster, a marine, trimmers, firemen, greasers, a steward and a painter. They were mainly from Portsmouth; now they lay at the bottom of the sea. Hewitt was taken prisoner along with Engineer Sub Lieutenant Johnson and saw out the war as a POW. He was awarded the DSO for his pains.

Apart from torpedoes, U-boats wreaked damage through minelaying. The task of minesweeping was continuous and often fell to the trawlers. It was dangerous duty. Two armed trawlers were lost in May. HM Trawler *Senator* was a Grimsby-based boat taken up by the Admiralty in 1915, armed with a 3pdr gun and converted to minesweeping duty. On 21 May she was sunk off Tory Island by a mine laid by *U-80*. Eleven men were killed, including skipper Robert George; they were fishermen until they and their boat joined the war, then Royal Naval Reservists, and now dead. And on 30 May the *Ina William*, another minesweeping trawler, hit a mine from *U-50* and sank two miles south of the Bull Rock Light, Berehaven. Skipper Charles Slapp and eleven of his men died, all RNR bar an RNVR signalman.

Bayly persisted in his strategy of area patrols, attempting to hunt down U-boats at sea, and escorting single vessels through the danger areas. But the demands of convoying the flow of American troops and supplies taxed his capability to do so, the more so because in July the Admiralty withdrew the four Royal Navy destroyers that had been assigned to him earlier, and sent them back to the Grand Fleet at Scapa. The American destroyers now formed the entirety of his faster vessels. Sub Lieutenant de Winton thought that the arrival of the Americans had been 'a most welcome reinforcement' but added 'no significant improvement occurred in U-boat sinkings until convoys were at last introduced from about July 1917'.[6]

Commander Taussig described in his diary a typical day on patrol.

Friday night at about eight o'clock we fell in with the British merchant steamer *Port Macquarie*, with a cargo of wheat bound for Birkenhead. Decided to escort her, so zigzagged ahead until 5 a.m. Saturday [16 June 1917] when parted company and started back for my patrol station. At noon we sighted the oiler *Cuyahoga*, and we joined her, escorting ahead until 4 p.m. when the *Jacob Jones* relieved us. I had sent a wireless to the J J, giving our position, course and speed. Returned to patrol station and was looking for the merchant steamer *Tarantia* when sighted the oiler *Cheyenne* about eight o'clock. Decided to accompany the Cheyenne as all oilers are valuable and did not know what the *Tarantia* was carrying. Remained with the *Cheyenne* and at 3 a.m. [Sunday, 17 June

1917] sighted a steamer about two miles away—steaming on nearly parallel course. This turned out to be the *Tarantia*. At 4 a.m. the *Benham* came along in reply to my wireless message and took over both ships. We are now (10 a.m.) on the way back to our patrol station ...[7]

The challenge of sailing small ships in the dark with no lights was a new one to the American captains, and accidents did happen. While USS *Jenkins* was convoying a merchant vessel at night, the sloop HMS *Laburnum* came along to relieve her. It was very dark; just before midnight on 10 June *Laburnum* saw the US ship but the *Jenkins* did not see her until they were right on top of each other. *Jenkins* slammed her engines hard astern but it was far too late. The British ship buried itself abreast the forward fireroom of the American vessel, at about 4 or 5 knots speed. The (mixed) court of inquiry found no one at fault; it was deemed to be one of those accidents that must be expected where a large number of ships are operating at night without navigation lights and in a confined area. But there was an upside for *Laburnum*'s crew; her bows had been shredded in the accident and twenty days' leave was declared while she was repaired at Haulbowline. Surgeon Probationer Willie Mason seized the opportunity with both hands. Rushing home, on 15 June he got engaged to his sweetheart, Mary; five days later they were married. Willie was aged just twenty. War makes for swift decisions; but by 2 July he was back with his ship – and made a will.

Despite the introduction of convoying, ships continued to be attacked and sunk in the Western Approaches. Some 110 merchant ships were sunk there in June. Amongst them was the troopship SS *Southland* (11,899grt), originally the *Vaterland*. On 4 June she was on passage from Liverpool to Philadelphia when she was torpedoed, 140 miles north west of Tory Island. She had already been torpedoed once, when carrying Australian troops in the Aegean but survived; this time she was not so lucky. *U-70* fired two torpedoes into her and *Southland* went down with the loss of four men.

SS *Addah* was an Elder Dempster line vessel of 4,397grt. On 15 June she was headed from Montreal to Cherbourg when she was sunk near Finisterre by *UC-69*. The submarine then surfaced and its commander, Erwin Wassner, ordered her to fire on the master's lifeboat, killing eight men. The little boat's stern was blown off, but the U-boat continued firing at the swimming men as their lifeboat was sinking. The chief officer's lifeboat was also fired on and some men in it were badly wounded. When the U-boat finally disappeared, the master and the survivors in the water swam for the second lifeboat; nine men died in the attack. Wassner sank another nine vessels during this June cruise.

And on the 20th, HMS *Salvia*, a 'Flower'-class sloop converted to a Q-ship, *Q-15*, was attacked west of Ireland by *U-94*. At about 0700hrs she was struck well aft on the starboard side by the enemy torpedo. The lookouts had not spotted the submarine and there was no opportunity to fight, as the 4in gun she carried had been blown overboard by a depth charge set off by the explosion. Additionally, her engines had been disabled. Five of her crew were killed and her captain. Lieutenant Commander Wybrants Olphert RNR was taken as a prisoner of war. Two hours later HMS *Aubrietia*, aka *Q-13* and under retired Admiral J L Marx, arrived and picked up the survivors. It took a couple of hours to locate everyone because the lifeboats and rafts had drifted apart in the rough seas.

Olphert, a New Zealander and a merchant ship chief officer before the war, had been on the Irish station since the start of the conflict. He had commanded HMY *Scaduan,* a modern hired yacht armed with a 6pdr gun, and worked off the coast of Ireland on coastal patrols On 21 June 1915, *Scaduan* had encountered a submarine off Fastnet and fired on her before she dived. After a search for several hours proved unsuccessful, it was decided by the Admiralty that it had been a hit (in fact no U-boat was sunk that day). For this action, Olphert was Mentioned in Despatches and later awarded the Distinguished Service Cross. After service in several other vessels, Olphert volunteered for duty in Q-ships and took charge of *Q-15*. Even as a POW he was able to support the war effort, for he smuggled information back to Britain via messages stuffed into a smoker's pipe.

The admiral takes a holiday

Despite the continued carnage, Bayly was eventually persuaded that Jellicoe was right and he did indeed need a holiday. Others took the same view; Admiral Marx noted that the command was taking a physical toll on Bayly.[8] The question was, who would command while he was away? Bayly knew the answer. He wrote to Admiral Sims 'If I go on leave from June 18th to 23rd would you like to run the show from here in my absence?'[9] Sims was astonished and replied immediately: 'It was the surprise of my life. I will not attempt to express my appreciation of the honour that you have done me ... '[10]

It was an unprecedented move, the first time an American admiral had commanded Royal Navy ships. Sims moved into Admiralty House, Bayly's flag was lowered and Sims USN admiral's ensign, blue with three large stars, was raised. Sims himself noted: 'On June 18th, therefore, I went to Queenstown, and hoisted my flag on the staff in front of Admiralty House. I had some hesitation in doing this, for American navy regulations stipulate that an admiral's flag shall be raised only on a ship afloat, but Admiral Bayly was insistent that his flag should come down and that mine should go up, and I decided that this technicality might be waived.'[11]

Commander Joseph Taussig also recorded this thoughts; '[Bayly] informed me during a conversation recently that he had requested the Admiralty to allow Vice Admiral Sims to take charge of the Coast of Ireland station during this period. That he was the only man in England to be trusted with the job! That is co-operation with a vengeance. And who, a few years ago, would have expected an American Admiral taking command of an important British station on the European side of the ocean.'[12]

Even the Irish were impressed with this visible act of unity to the point where those of a revolutionary tendency spread the rumour that Bayly and Sims 'had quarrelled and that Sir Lewis had gone off in anger, leaving Admiral Sims to do what he liked'.[13]

And so Bayly and Violet set off on a motor tour of Ireland in an USN Cadillac, chauffeured by an US naval rating; but Bayly made sure that the itinerary included visits to his naval bases.

A staff

Bayly had long resisted the formation of a formal staff but the pressure of work had now reached such proportions that even the tireless Russell could not keep up with it. Apart from appointing Pringle as his US Chief of Staff, the admiral now agitated for a larger team, writing to Jellicoe that he wanted two commanders, Herbert (who had already served under him in Q-ships and had commanded *Baralong*) and Douglas, to join him in Admiralty House.

Instead of Herbert he was given a Commander Kettlewell, who was not at all to his taste. Eventually he got his way in July and Herbert was appointed ashore. 'Herbert will be of great value to me'

Bayly noted.[14] He had also taken a dislike to Carpendale, his flag captain; 'He has so little sympathy with my little ships that the captains of them dislike him,' he told Jellicoe.[15] This situation was resolved on 17 June by a straight job swop. Captain Francis Martin-Leake DSO, who had recently been involved in the destruction of the German raider *Leopard*,* was appointed as Bayly's Chief of Staff and Carpendale took Leake's position as captain of HMS *Achilles*.

'The one pleasure one has in getting old', Bayly wrote to Jellicoe in July, 'is to help on the youngsters and so repay the debts of those who helped us.'[16] In this sprit he asked for promotion for Sherston of the *Snowdrop* and CBs (Companion of the Order of the Bath) for Paymaster Russell and Captain Lacy of the dockyard. But the grudge-bearing misanthrope was never far from the surface. In the same letter as he asks for these promotions, he makes the point that he has not been offered a decoration and that if he was, he would refuse it until granted a court martial for the *Formidable* affair. 'I may be stupid', he wrote, 'but I am determined on that course.'[17]

And his suspicions of Winston Churchill, who Bayly saw as the instigator of his lack of a hearing, were worn on his sleeve. 'I hear many stories that Mr Churchill and others are burrowing in order that their personal ambitions may be satisfied,' he warned Jellicoe,[18] expressing his reservations over Lloyd George at the same time. Later he would add 'I somehow feel that you and Admiral Sims will defeat intrigues; I only wish I could help you'.[19] Bayly was here referring to the many voices now being raised against Jellicoe, both in government and to an extent in the Navy, regarding the slowness of coming to grips with convoy, the continued merchant losses and the perceived overly defensive posture that the navy was taking. Lloyd George, Prime Minister since his 'coup' in December 1916, was particularly critical of Jellicoe.

Jellicoe was seen as overly pessimistic in many political quarters, not least as on 19 June he had confessed to the War Cabinet that they were losing the war. Field Marshal Sir Douglas Haig and the Prime Minister's 'fixer', Eric Geddes, met with Lloyd George over a breakfast and argued for a new administration at the Admiralty. As a result, on 6 July, First Lord Sir Edward Carson was pushed aside and Geddes replaced him as First Lord of the Admiralty. His brief

---

* See Dunn, *Blockade*.

was, as he had done with munitions and transportation on the Western Front, to shake things up.

The losses continue

July brought no respite in the war on trade. Some 113 merchant ships were lost in the Western Approaches during the month. One was ss *Ramillies*.

On 21 July 1917, *Poppy* was on patrol 120 miles west and north of Tory Island when gunfire was heard. *Poppy* sailed towards the sound of the guns and as she neared saw a submarine engaging a merchant vessel. By 0940hrs she could make out two lifeboats in the water and that the attacked ship was sinking. She was on fire aft and had several large holes in her sides. The U-boat submerged as the sloop came to her attention. The doomed vessel was *Ramillies*, 2,935grt, carrying coal from Troon to Huelva in south-western Spain. She had been chased by a large U-boat (it was *U-58*) from 0430hrs to 0730hrs. The submarine had opened fire from a range of 14,000yds which, although the *Ramillies* was a defensively-armed ship carrying a 12pdr gun, was beyond her range of reply (only 8,000yds). Neither did the British ship have wireless. The crew took to the boats when it was clear that resistance was futile and the merchant master was taken prisoner.

Poppy picked up the survivors who watched their ship finally sink at 1030hrs. Sub Lieutenant Robert Goldrich described the sinking. 'One of the first things which came to the surface was a kind of calcium light which burnt amongst the floating coal dust and wreckage like a funeral pyre on the surface of the water. For the next twenty minutes wreckage kept coming to the surface shooting high into the air before it fell.'[20] A terrible sight to watch a ship die. *U-58* did not reappear, however, and indeed sank no more ships on this cruise.

Total Allied and neutral losses in May, June and July were 596,629grt, 687,507grt and 557,988grt respectively. It looked as if Jellicoe might be right.

1 4

U-Boot-Falle, 1917

The year of 1917 was something of an *annus mirabilis* for Bayly's Q-ships.* In that year, more than any other, did they seem to justify the bravery and the sacrifice which was demanded of the men who manned them. And the German U-boat commanders came to fear them, calling them *U-boot-falle* (U-boat traps) or 'trap ships'; which, perversely, made service in them even more dangerous because submarine captains would launch torpedoes first and ask questions afterwards if they suspected that they might be engaging a disguised warship.

Bayly believed that Q-ship commanders were a breed apart and he respected them greatly. 'Slow Q-ships are the most deadly', he noted, 'but they require exceptional men to command them, such as Grenfell, Campbell and Herbert.'[1]

January

On 12 January, retired Admiral John Locke Marx was cruising off the Casquets, north west of Alderney. Nearly sixty-five years old, he was still determined to sink a U-boat in his Q-ship *Q-13*, aka HMS *Aubrietia*. She was disguised as the Danish steamer SS *Kai* and had picked up two lots of men from the water the previous day, survivors of U-boat attack; now he hoped to find the submarine responsible. At 1030hrs, *Q-13* sighted a submarine; the crew ignored it and allowed the intruder to intercept their ship and fire a shell over it, which Marx ignored. The U-boat then fired again and signalled them to stop. They did so, blew off lot of steam and in

---

* Although chronologically at odds with the rest of the story, Q-ships in 1917 will be considered together, rather than in different chapters as the timing of the actions might indicate.

response to a demand from the German, sent away a boat. The U-boat closed in, and edged round to their port beam. At 1123hrs, Marx opened fire. His first 12pdr shot hit the conning tower at its base and there was a large explosion which 'blew away the conning tower completely'.[2] A second shot hit the hull and the U-boat slipped below the waves, whereupon Marx dropped depth charges over the spot where she had disappeared.

Marx was ecstatic. He confided to his diary: 'Sunk a sub off Casquets. Thank God after trying for two years and three months and having passed over two, hit a third with my bow going 13 knots, been present when a trawler at 1,000yds has twice blown up her sweep on one, twice dropped a depth charge at another. At last we get one, blew her conning tower off.'[3]

There was only one problem. The Admiralty did not accept his claim that the enemy had been sunk. He was awarded the DSO for the action but Their Lordships decided that 'the evidence of the submarine being sunk is not conclusive'.[4] An *exempli gratia* bounty of £200 was granted to the crew only, Marx being deemed ineligible to share in it. Marx was stunned. He spent the rest of his life fighting the decision, not least for the £1,000 bounty that he and his crew would have shared (he believed that he had sunk *UB-23* but in fact she was interned in Spain in July 1917). Bayly invited him to stay at Admiralty House and was sympathetic, but there was nothing he could do.

Marx continued to command his Q-ship, but the duty, his age and perhaps his disappointment took its toll on him. On 19 September Bayly wrote to him that he had telegraphed Jellicoe to have Marx relieved. '[Bayly] said that we had lost so many Qs he could no longer take the responsibility of having me in command. I was sick but said nothing. He asked what I would like and I said anything at sea.'[5] In fact he became a convoy commodore and served in that position for the remainder of the war.

Two days after Marx had encountered his U-boat, on 14 January *UB-37* was cruising in the English Channel. She was a small submarine, with a complement of only twenty-one, but nonetheless had sunk thirty-one ships for a total of 20,504grt in five cruises. Under her commander Paul Gunther, she had already despatched that day the steamer *Norma*, on passage from Valencia to Falmouth with a cargo of oranges.

It was her bad luck that the next target that she sighted was the

Q-ship *Penshurst*, with Grenfell still in command. Grenfell affected not to see his opponent until Gunther opened fire at a range of 3,000yds. Off went the panic party, and Grenfell slowly managed to cause his ship to turn until she was broadside-on to the U-boat. However, Gunther was suspicious and crossed *Penshurst*'s bow, resuming his firing and causing damage and two casualties over a twenty-minute period. Judging that he was not going to get a more favourable firing position and worried at the injury to his ship, Grenfell opened fire and made hits with his opening shots. The U-boat sustained immediate fatal damage and began to sink; Grenfell made sure of her destruction by dropping depth charges over the point of her disappearance. *UB-37* went down with all hands. *Penshurst* lost two men, one RFR, the other RNVR.

February

The growing fear of trap ships by U-boat commanders meant that they were increasingly chary of surfacing alongside a suspicious vessel and would rather simply torpedo it and identify its precise details from the survivors.* It was thus more difficult for the Q-ships to find and attack their prey.

Commander Gordon Campbell, vanquisher of *U-68* in March the previous year, devised an effective, but highly dangerous, solution to this problem. He would deliberately invite an attack and allow his ship to be torpedoed; when the U-boat then surfaced to identify and finish off its victim, he would attack it. As a precaution, he filled his ship's cargo holds with wood, to act as a flotation aid.

Campbell was still in command of *Farnborough*, *Q-5*, and had gained a new first lieutenant, Ronald Neil Stuart RNR, a Liverpudlian professional merchant seaman with Allan Line before the war, who had joined up in 1914. On 17 February, Campbell was steaming forty miles to the south and west of Ireland, in the heart of the Western Approaches. At 0945hrs he sighted a torpedo track and altered speed and course so as to allow it to hit *Farnborough*. The missile duly hit aft by the engine room bulkhead; the blast injured an engineer sub lieutenant, knocked down Campbell and some of his men and, regrettably, blew the ship's cat overboard. But it also inflicted serious damage to the ship. The machinery spaces were so

---

* U-boat commanders were required to ascertain the identity and, if possible the cargo and destination of every merchant ship they sank.

flooded that the Engineer Lieutenant Len Loveless and his men had to lie on their faces on gratings at the top of the engine room compartment as she settled by the stern. The crew were well disciplined and the 'panic party' took to their boats with a great show of alarm and disorder. Campbell, Stuart, Loveless and his men and the gunners remained on board, lying prone on the deck out of sight.

The U-boat came closer, under water. She came so close that Campbell could see her outline only 20 or 30yds away from his ship. Then she surfaced about 300yds on the port bow, where none of *Q-5*'s guns could bear, and began to move towards the panic party's four lifeboats on the port quarter. As she came abeam Commander Campbell saw her conning tower hatch was open and her captain was on the bridge. It was a perfect set-up (if one ignored the fact that his ship was sinking). At 1010hrs he gave the order and some forty-five shells were fired at a range of 100yds. The very first shot decapitated the German captain, Bruno Hoppe, and the U-boat, *U-83*, was rapidly reduced to a wreck. Eight German sailors escaped the submarine before it sank but only two could be pulled from the water, one of whom subsequently died of his wounds. Hoppe had sunk six ships on this cruise and sixteen in his career. He would sink no more.

Farnborough was also sinking from her torpedo damage. Realising this, Campbell left the men in the boats, destroyed all confidential papers and radioed Queenstown for assistance. His somewhat unorthodox style came through in his message which read: '*Q-5* slowly sinking, respectfully wishes you goodbye.'[6] Bayly sent help; the destroyer *Narwhal* and the sloop *Buttercup* arrived and took the sinking *Farnborough* in tow. However, during the night a depth charge accidentally exploded on board, probably caused by the stern being underwater and activating the hydrostatic pistol, and she dropped the tow. Campbell ordered the twelve men who had remained on board into a lifeboat but stayed put himself, only to be driven off by the explosion of a second depth charge. As he prepared to leave his stricken vessel he discovered that Stuart had disobeyed his order and remained on board in order to make sure his captain disembarked safely. Later, the tow was again reattached and *Farnborough* and Campbell went once more on board. Eventually, she was beached at Mill Cove, west-south-west of Cork, pretty much wrecked. Campbell was awarded the Victoria Cross in recognition of the action, presented by King George V exactly a month later; and the crew shared £1,000 of prize money. Stuart and Loveless were both presented with the DSO. Campbell's plan had worked but it had cost a ship and could have cost lives too. It was a perilous way to sink submarines.

April

Sometimes death seems random. Thirty-four-year-old Lieutenant Commander William Hallwright was last met in this story commanding *Laburnum* and coming to the rescue of the besieged garrison at Galway. In early 1917 he had sought a transfer to the supposedly more exciting, and certainly more dangerous, role of captain of a Q-ship and took command of *Q-16*, the converted sloop *Heather*. On 21 April 1917 he was in action with a submarine when a shell splinter penetrated the deck and struck him on the head. He died at once. He had been nominated for the DSO for his service in the Queenstown force. It was gazetted posthumously twenty days later, on 11 May.

Q-21, or *Prize*, was an unusual type of Q-ship for she was a three-masted topsail schooner. She was named for the fact that she was the first prize taken by the Royal Navy on the outbreak of the First World War. Some hours after war having been declared, the German *Else* was in the English Channel on passage from Rio de Janiero to Falmouth, with a cargo of hides, when she was intercepted and taken as a prize of war by the old cruiser HMS *Diana*. She was then sold at auction to the Marine and Navigation Company owned by William Garthwaite,* who renamed the ship *First Prize*.

Informed that the Admiralty wanted the ship for 'special service', Garthwaite immediately placed her in their hands free of charge, and even offered to sail in her and pay for her fit out. This was politely declined (although he did, in fact, pay for the building of a number of minesweepers). She was converted at Falmouth where two 50hp motors were installed as well as a radio. The ship was also equipped with two 12pdr guns, a Lewis gun and a Maxim gun. The forward 12pdr was inside a collapsible deck house and the after one on a disappearing mounting below the hatchway covers of the after hold.

Prize was then sent to Milford Haven for stores where she was joined by her commanding officer, Lieutenant William Sanders RNR, a New Zealander who had been a seaman since age sixteen

---

* Created 1st Baronet Garthwaite of Durham on 19 May 1919.

and now became, at thirty-four years of age, one of the youngest officers to command a Q-ship. Another three officers and the ship's company of twenty-three ratings also came on board. Sanders had volunteered in New Zealand at the start of the war but was not called up, so he worked his passage in a troopship as second officer to get to England and then joined the RNR.

On Wednesday 25 April, Sanders formally commissioned *Prize* and early the next morning the ship sailed on its first patrol. Sailing ships were, as noted previously, easy prey for U-boats given their relative lack of manoeuvrability. So, although U-boat commanders now regarded steamers with suspicion, they saw sailing ships as easy meat. Sanders would prove them wrong.

U-93 was a large, modern submarine on her first war patrol, commanded by the impressively-named Freiherr Edgar von Spiegel von und zu Peckelsheim. By 30 April, she had already sunk ten ships, three of them that very day, and now lay 180 miles south of Ireland. Now Spiegel saw his chance for a fourth as *Prize* swam into his periscope, proceeding under sail at 2 knots. He surfaced some distance off the Q-ship's port quarter at about 2040hrs and opened fire. *Prize* was holed three times along the waterline, twice in the mainmast and her engine room was set on fire. She was without power and starting to sink. The cannonade had lasted twenty minutes. In that time a 'panic party' had cast off and Sanders had crawled along the schooners decks, under fire, to organise his men and his response. Thinking *Prize* to be sinking, *U-93* came to within 80yds of her. It was the moment of truth. The White Ensign flew to the mast top, the gun ports fell open and a withering fire poured into the U-boat. The German gun took a direct hit and the Lewis and Maxim guns swept sailors off the casing of the vessel. A shell wrecked the U-boat's conning tower and fires could be seen burning in her hull. Stern first, bow in air she slipped under the water. Spiegel, his navigating officer and one crewman, an engine room petty officer, had been blown into the water and were rescued by the schooner.

But *Prize* was in a bad way too. All hands, including the three prisoners, turned to pumping and plugging holes. The German navigator dressed wounds and the petty officer went into the engine room to help try to restart the engines. Somehow Sanders coaxed his broken ship back towards Ireland. On the afternoon of 2 May, the motor launch *ML-161* found her and towed her five miles to Kinsale, from where she was eventually taken back to Milford Haven.

For this action, Sanders was awarded the Victoria Cross, the second of Bayly's Q-ship commanders to receive the decoration. He was the first, and only, New Zealander to win the British Empire's highest military honour in a naval action. He was also given advanced promotion to the rank of lieutenant commander RNR.

Everyone, including Spiegel, thought that *U-93* was lost. But in fact it was discovered later that she had somehow made it back to Germany through outstanding seamanship by her first lieutenant and the remaining crewmen, even though she was unable to dive.

Her survival meant that Sanders would not enjoy his reward for long. On 14 August, *U-48* torpedoed *Prize* without surfacing, the Q-ship's true identity revealed to other German commanders by the survivors of *U-93*. She was lost with all hands.

June

Q-ship crews were always given the option of leaving after any voyage; but when Gordon Campbell (now VC and DSO for two confirmed 'kills') was offered a new Q-ship, almost the whole of the ship's company of *Farnborough* followed him to his new command.

Pargust was built in 1907 as a collier, and was originally named *Vittoria*. In 1917 she was requisitioned by the Royal Navy for use as a special service vessel and was converted for her new role at the Devonport naval base. The ex-collier was armed with depth charges, five guns (a 4in and four 12pdrs) and two torpedo tubes, all in concealed mountings. She was also fitted with a gun in plain sight. Many merchant ships were defensively armed by this stage of the war and she would have looked suspicious without one.

Campbell commissioned her on 28 March and in late May went to sea in the Western Approaches, again with the intention of being deliberately torpedoed. Well out to sea, a bird flew into his cabin, which he regarded as a good omen, for that had happened on the occasion of his two previous successes. Strange to think of this hard-bitten sailor being superstitious, but mariners often were.

And he was proved correct. The following day, 7 June, at 0800hrs, a torpedo was fired at *Pargust* at such close range that he could not have avoided it if he had tried to. The 'panic party' went away, carrying a stuffed parrot for effect. The U-boat closed in at periscope depth and circled *Pargust* and her boats in order to inspect her for any signs of concealed weapons. She then surfaced, intending to interrogate the boat crew, but the little lifeboat had been cleverly pulled away, around the steamer's stern, in order to bring the U-boat closer in. At 0836hrs, when the submarine was just 50yds away, Campbell opened fire.

Thirty-eight rounds were fired and at that range the gunners could hardly miss. With the conning tower damaged, the crew started to abandon ship, raising their hands in surrender. Campbell ordered cease-fire, at which the submarine, now identified as *UC-29*, started to move away on the surface, into the surrounding mist. With his own ship disabled and unable to manoeuvre, Campbell once more opened fire and continued firing until 0840hrs when *UC-29* blew up. Only two U-boat crewmen survived to be picked up. Commanded by Oberleutnant zur See Ernst Rosenow, the minelaying submarine had sunk eighteen ships in seven patrols, over and above those lost to its mines. Now its reign of terror was at an end.

Pargust meanwhile was lying helpless in the water, with Leading Stoker Isaac Radford killed and a sub lieutenant wounded. Campbell signalled Bayly 'Have sunk enemy submarine after being torpedoed. Totally disabled, need assistance.'[7] Bayly sent the sloops *Crocus* and *Zinnia* and the destroyer uss *Cushing*. *Zinnia* took on board the two German prisoners and resumed her patrol. Two days later she picked up three boats from one torpedoed ship and shortly afterwards the crew of a second. A total of sixty men were thus taken on board. Her captain, Commander Wilson, went to great lengths to ensure they were kept apart from the German U-boat prisoners. Meanwhile, *Crocus* managed to tow *Pargust* back to Queenstown, where her damage was found to be such that she was out of service until May the following year.

Joseph Taussig noted in his diary for 8 June that 'the submarines are very difficult to get and these special service ships which play the role of merchant steamers to decoy the subs are the best means of destroying them. The destroyers and sloops together with the auxiliary patrol vessels preserve the shipping by keeping the submarines down, but they are seldom able to engage one.'[8]

There was another £1,000 bounty to share and the King awarded the Victoria Cross to the whole ship, which meant that under Rule 13[*] there would be a ballot for a VC to be awarded to one officer and one seaman. The crew choose Lieutenant Ronald Neil Stuart RNR

[*] Clause 13 of the Victoria Cross Warrant of 28 January 1856 allowed those present at an action to choose one of their number to be awarded the VC to represent them all.

and Seaman William Williams RNR, who had physically held together a damaged gun shelter, preventing it from collapsing and revealing the ship for what she was. Campbell got a bar to his DSO.

August

Pargust paid off and Campbell took nearly all his old crew, excepting Stuart who went to command his own Q-ship, to his next vessel, *Dunraven*. She was also a collier, once of Cardiff, slightly bigger than his previous vessels. As replacement for Stuart he appointed his second lieutenant on *Pargust*, 32-year-old Charles George 'Gus' Bonner RNR, to be his new right-hand man. Campbell though that *Dunraven* was the best of all his Q-ships. She was 'a beautiful ship, and all her arrangements in every detail were as perfect as we could wish for'.[9]

Dunraven sailed from Devonport on 4 August and, knowing that U-boats were active in the Bay of Biscay, Campbell took a detour in that direction on his way to Queenstown. On 8 August, 130 miles south west of Ushant and with the ship disguised as the collier *Boverton*, Campbell spotted *UC-71*, another minelaying submarine, commanded by Oberleutnant zur See Reinhold Saltzwedel. *Dunraven*'s crew ignored the submarine which slipped below the waves and closed before resurfacing astern at 1143hrs and opening fire from long range.

Campbell made smoke, sent panicky distress messages and, using their one obvious defensive gun, made a deliberate bad fist of firing back. The submarine's firing was poor; in thirty minutes she made no hits, so when there was a near miss, Campbell simulated a hit, letting off steam and sending his 'panic party' away to try to draw the U-boat closer in. Unfortunately, *UC-71* suddenly discovered her accuracy and three shells hit the poop in quick succession. These set off the depth charges, one of which actually blew Bonner from his hiding place. He and Petty Officer Pitcher now had to stay hidden in the 4in gun hatch while fires blazed around them and in the ammunition store directly beneath them, the floor of their refuge glowing red hot.

Eventually, the magazine did indeed explode and all the men above it were blown into the air and the gun knocked off its mounting. Four men were wounded, as was Bonner himself. *Dunraven* was now exposed as a Q-ship. Campbell tried to bluff the U-boat by sending away a second panic party but to no avail. He also broadcast *en clair* for help. At 1320hrs a torpedo stuck the Q-ship near the engine room. Campbell sent a third 'panic party' away on a raft while the original one came back and picked up some more men, leaving only two guns manned. The poop deck was in flames and ammunition was exploding at regular intervals. *UC-71* then shelled her victim for another twenty minutes before diving at 1450hrs. Campbell fired two torpedoes at her periscope but they missed.

It would need a miracle to save *Dunraven* now; but one came as required. The U-boat had run out of torpedoes and could not risk surfacing again in case help was on the way – and it was. She slipped away under water. The old battleship *Implacable*, returning from the Mediterranean, had picked up the distress call and sent the destroyer *Attack* from her escort to investigate. It was her presence that drove Saltzwedel away. Eventually, the destroyer *Christopher* took *Dunraven* in tow but early on the 10th she started to sink, and in rough seas and darkness the destroyer bumped her nose against the sinking ship so that the Q-ship's crew could jump on board one by one, before sinking her with shells and depth charges. *Dunraven* went down with her White Ensign still flying.

Charles Bonner was awarded the Victoria Cross for the action and Petty Officer Ernest Herbert Pitcher was similarly decorated, under another Rule 13 ballot. Campbell gained a second bar to his DSO. Bonner, recovering from his wounds at Devonport Naval Barracks, received a letter of 'deep appreciation' from Walsall Town Council (his mother lived in Aldridge, Walsall) and from his former employers at Johnston Line gained a fulsome encomium that read 'it is exceedingly difficult to express in words what we all feel at this juncture, but we are proud that during our business careers we have been associated with one who unselfishly placed his country first and whose efforts have been such as to have justly merited so great an honour'.[10] And Admiral Sims later commented 'in my opinion ... *Dunraven* is the finest of all [Q-ship encounters] as a military action and the most deserving of complete success'.[11] In an amazing six months of action by the Queenstown Q-ships, Campbell had been decorated three times, six Victoria Crosses had been won, three U-boats sunk and two badly damaged.

For Campbell, Bayly decided enough was enough. A man can press his luck too far. When Campbell returned to Queenstown, Bayly told him that he wanted him to be his flag captain, replacing

Hyde, in command of the admiral's cruiser. His Q-ship days were done. As Bayly later noted, 'among the thirty-odd mystery ships who served under my flag, he [Campbell] was the only one who could stand the strain of mystery ship work over about a year and ten months in succession'.[12]

The Fight Continues, 1917

August started well for the Coast of Ireland Command. On the 4th, *UC-44*, a modern minelaying U-boat, blew herself up on her own mines whilst attempting to lay a minefield off the coast of Waterford.* Her commanding officer, Kurt Tebbenjohanns, was blown out of the conning tower by the explosion and was later picked up by a patrol vessel sent to investigate. The remaining twenty-eight crewmen died. She had sunk in shallow water so Bayly sent down divers and the submarine was salvaged and brought to port for examination. But the most important discovery came in the logbook and confidential documents that she carried and which were found intact.

When passed to the Admiralty these revealed to Rear Admiral 'Blinker' Hall, in charge of Naval Intelligence, orders which instructed U-boat commanders to transit to the Atlantic via the Dover Strait and thus through the Dover Barrage. 'Pass through at night and on the surface', it read, 'without being observed and without stopping. If forced to dive, go to forty metres and wait. Avoid being seen in the Channel ... on the other hand, those craft which in exceptional cases pass around Scotland are to let themselves be seen as freely as possible in order to mislead the English.'[1] The salvaged documents also seemed to indicate that 190 passages had been made in the six months between 23 December 1916 and 6 June 1917. These were chiefly carried out at night, and during these six months there were only eight reports of a net being touched and eight reports of being forced to dive to avoid patrols.

---

* Recent research shows that *UC-44* was lost on her own mines and not a mine laid by *UC-42* that had intentionally been left unswept, as had previously been asserted.

This reinforced Bayly's oft-expressed view that the Dover Barrage, intended to stop U-boats transiting from their Flanders bases into the Atlantic and Bayly's territory, did not work. The admiral commanding at Dover, Reginald Bacon, held strongly to the opinion that the Barrage was effective; the new evidence did not cause him to change his mind. As a result, the end of *UC-44* soon triggered the end of Admiral Bacon too.[*]

But despite the introduction of convoy on some routes, Allied and neutral losses to U-boats remained at the high level of 511,730grt in August, over three times the same month on the previous year. In the Western Approaches the sinkings continued. And Q-ships were not excluded.

HMS *Bracondale*

Thirty-two-year-old Lieutenant Douglas George Jeffrey, RNR, was typical of the merchant mariner reservists who had been enlisted in the navy in the early days of the war. Belfast-born and the son of a pastor, he had sailed six years in square-rigged sailing ships, gained his master's certificate and served in passenger, general cargo ships and tankers, before commanded the merchant ships SS *Strathearn*, *Scottish Borderer*, *Scottish Bard* and MS *Pamir*.

On 2 August, Jeffrey was in command of the new Q-ship, *Bracondale*, now named *Chagford*. She was a 2,100grt collier, built in Hartlepool in 1903 and converted to a Q-ship at Devonport, where she was armed with a 4in gun, two 12pdrs and a couple of torpedo tubes. Jeffrey had commissioned her in the June and now left his base at Buncrana (on Lough Swilly) looking for business.

At 0410hrs on 5 August, Jeffrey was 120 miles north-west of Tory Island, searching for two enemy submarines which had been reported the previous day. Out of seemingly nowhere, *Chagford* was hit just below the bridge by a torpedo. The explosion disabled both torpedo tubes and the 4in gun, shattered the boats on the starboard side and destroyed the captain's cabin and chart room. In addition, it wrecked all the voice-pipe connections to the torpedo tubes and guns, flooded the engine room and put the engines out of commission, killing one of the crew.

Jeffrey sent away the fake 'abandon ship' party. But just as the boats were getting away, a submarine surfaced on the starboard side

---

[*] See S R Dunn, *Securing the Narrow Sea* (Barnsley: Seaforth Publishing, 2017).

800yds away. As the enemy came to the surface, Jeffrey ordered 'open fire' at the top of his voice and both 12pdrs and the Lewis guns roared out, several direct hits being observed. The submarine then dived, and when submerged, fired a second torpedo at *Chagford*, which hit the ship abaft the bridge, again on the starboard side.

Jeffrey now ordered 'abandon ship' in earnest, recalled his boats and, placed the majority of his men into them. He, together with a lieutenant RNR, two sub lieutenants RNR, an assistant paymaster RNR and one petty officer remained on board, concealed on the poop and under hatches and hoping to get another crack at the U-boat. Periscopes were observed around them, and a submarine seen a long way off, but come the darkness no U-boat had shown itself. Lieutenant Jeffrey settled in for the night and posted sentries with machine guns around his ship.

But *Bracondale/Chagford* was in a bad way. Her main deck amidships was split from side to side, the bridge deck was badly buckled, and the whole ship was straining badly. And she was slowly settling into the water. Around midnight, the small remaining band of warriors slipped away from the ship. They rowed through the night and at 0730hrs were picked up by the armed trawler *Saxon*, probably not too soon, for submarines were known to be about still. The trawler attempted to tow the stricken Q-ship, but it was hopeless. At 0800hrs on the 7th, *Bracondale* sank.

There was a small element of cheer for Jeffrey and his men, however. They had damaged the U-boat, *U-44*, sufficiently for her to be unable to dive. She nonetheless kept on patrol, disguising her upper works as a fishing vessel. On 12 August, *U-44* was spotted off the coast of Norway by the destroyer HMS *Oracle*, which gave chase. The submarine was unable to submerge to escape and *Oracle* rammed and sank her. All forty-four men on board the U-boat died.*

HMS *Bergamot*

Forty-year-old Lieutenant Commander Percy Tennison Perkins, RNR, was another career merchant seaman, originally trained at HMS *Worcester* (the Thames Marine Officer Training School). He had

---

* After the war, Jeffrey was appointed navigating officer in *Quest* on the Shackleton-Rowett Antarctic Expedition, 1921–2 (led by Sir Ernest Henry Shackleton himself). Setting out from London on 17 September 1921, the expedition reached South Georgia where Shackleton suffered a heart attack and died on 5 January 1922. John Robert Francis Wild took command and the expedition continued, briefly exploring the South Sandwich Islands and the Weddell Sea before returning to Britain.

served at sea all his life and responded to the Navy's call when war came.

On 14 July 1917, Perkins had commissioned HMS *Bergamot*, designed as an *Anchusa*-class sloop but completed as a Q-ship. Four weeks later, on 13 August, he was at sea seventy miles north-west of Killybegs harbour when *Bergamot* was torpedoed without warning by *U-84*, commanded by Walter Rohr. The torpedo struck on the port side, entered the auxiliary engine room and destroyed the dynamo and the bulkhead separating the auxiliary engine room from the main one. All the lights went out and power was lost. Perkins tried to launch his 'panic party' in lifeboat No 1 but his ship was mortally hurt and lurched to port, then broke in half with both the bow and stern rising out of the water, and quickly started to sink.

The abandonment was now for real. There were thirty-one men in the first lifeboat and the remainder, including Perkins, in the second. The U-boat came amongst them, looking for the captain but, by bluff and subterfuge, the crew manged to conceal Perkin's identity, and the Germans questioned a ship's steward instead, misled that he was the captain as he wore a collar and tie!

At the moment of the explosion, *Bergamot*'s first officer, Lieutenant Frederick W Siddall, and her Surgeon Probationer, Robert Sydney Steele Cathcart Smith RNVR, were both in her wardroom. The explosion jammed the two watertight doors leading into it, and Siddall was knocked out by the blast. Smith built a tower of furniture to reach the skylight in the roof and then dragged the unconscious Siddall up and out of the compartment. Having reached the main deck, Smith treated both Siddall and a wounded petty officer, who was lying on the deck with a broken leg and arm.

It was clear to Smith that the ship was going to sink, so he inflated his charges' life vests and got them into the water. But as the vessel went under, the depth charges exploded, badly wounding Siddall and once again stunning him. Smith kept both injured men afloat and got them into lifeboat No 2, which now contained forty-seven men, where he continued to treat Siddall for twenty-five minutes, administering artificial respiration. In lifeboat No 2, Perkins set a course for Lough Swilly, about 100 miles away. It took forty-five hours of rowing before they were picked up by the Admiralty trawler *Lord Lister*. Number 1 lifeboat eventually reached the coast of County Donegal and was rescued by the Coastguard. For

Smith and Siddall it was a doubly unfortunate event; they had been on board *Salvia* when she had been torpedoed and sunk, six weeks previously (*vide supra*).

Fourteen men from *Bergamot* died in the attack. Probationer Surgeon Smith was awarded the Albert Medal for his actions (gazetted 20 November 1917). As for Perkins, the other forty-six crew members of lifeboat two presented him with the vessel's binnacle, inscribed;

> Binnacle from lifeboat no 2 Presented to Lt. Comdr P T Perkins RNR.
> Captain HMS *Bergamot*, torpedoed 13th August 1917.
> To commemorate his Skill and Fortitude in commanding Lifeboat No. 2 for 45 hours continuously.
> A token of admiration and respect from the survivors.

And Perkins was back on the job by October, in command of the new P-boat, *PC-43*, again completed as a Q-ship.*

In the month of August, five Q-ships were lost. The cost of killing submarines this way was high.

HMS *Cullist*

Cullist had started life as SS *Westphalia*, 1,030grt, launched in 1912 for the Leith, Hull & Hamburg Steam Packet Co Ltd. Shortly after the outbreak of war she was requisitioned by the Admiralty for service as a stores carrier and served the Grand Fleet in this humdrum role until early 1917. But Bayly's team saw potential in her as a Q-ship and in March she began her transformation into *Cullist*, armed with a 4in gun and two 14in torpedo tubes. Bayly appointed Lieutenant Commander Salisbury Hamilton Simpson RN to take charge of her. Simpson had been in command of the sloop *Jessamine* since October 1915; now he was to undertake more covert and dangerous work

On 12 June 1917 he sailed out of Berehaven for his first patrol in the Irish Sea and Western Approaches. The cruise was uneventful. That would change the following month. *Cullist* was operating between the French and Irish coasts on 13 July. It was a clear summer's day and some of the crew were lounging in the sunshine,

---

* After the war, Perkins became captain of his old school ship *Worcester*, and inaugurated a cricket field there (which became known as 'Perkins Field').

when at 1400hrs Simpson noticed a sail some four miles away; a sail which had not been there a moment ago. He sounded the alarm and as he did so, the sail disappeared and a gun flash revealed the presence of a U-boat on the surface, hitherto disguised.

The submarine fired thirty-eight rounds at long range without recording a hit. Simpson slowed down and allowed a straddle, then lit fires to simulate a hit. The U-boat came closer, still firing. After an hour she had discharged over seventy rounds and still not recorded a hit. But she was getting closer.

Then a little steamer swam into view, broadcasting for all she was worth that a submarine was attacking a merchant vessel. And two destroyers responded, racing towards the scene. Simpson was furious – this would drive away his prize. He opened fire and with his second salvo hit near the conning tower, but the U-boat slipped into the depths and safety. *Cullist* went to the spot where the U-boat had last been seen and dropped two depth charges; there was much oil and a floating corpse in seaman's dungarees, but there was no undeniable evidence that the Q-ship had sunk a submarine. Or at least that's what the Admiralty maintained despite Simpson and Bayly's claims otherwise.[*] Nonetheless, Simpson was awarded the DSO and four DSMs and three 'Mentioned in Despatches' were also granted.

Then on 20 August *Cullist* was attacked by another U-boat which fled after Simpson returned fire. The Q-ship received damage and two stokers were injured. Three DSMs were awarded for this action. On her arrival at Devonport, the vessel hit a jetty and was damaged, requiring time in dry dock.

But she was back in the Western Approaches by 28 September when she became involved in another firefight with a U-boat. This time Simpson was able to lure her to within 5,000yds before opening fire. *Cullist* fired thirteen rounds of which eight were direct hits. The submarine was seen to settle down by the bow while about 30ft of the stern was standing out of the water at an angle of around 30° to the horizon. After holding this position for some fifteen seconds she disappeared beneath the waves. But again there was no undeniable evidence of a sinking. Nonetheless, Simpson received a bar to his DSO for the engagement.

And in her final action of the year, on 17 November *Cullist* was

[*] And they were correct: no U-boat was sunk on that day.

attacked by a U-boat which opened fire at 8,000yds range. Within five minutes the enemy had the range and a shell bounced off the Q-ship's side, damaging one of the officer's cabins before bursting on the waterline. After disappearing in a bank of fog the submarine reappeared and continued to shell *Cullist* accurately for some fifty minutes. The decks and bridge were continually sprayed with shell splinters and drenched with water from near misses. In all, the U-boat fired ninety-two rounds. Simpson had returned fire at 4,500yds range, fourteen rounds, of which he thought six had hit home. But again, his prey turned away and dived to effect its escape.

So ended a frustrating and dangerous year for Lieutenant Commander Simpson and his crew; and in a moment of reflection, they might have given thanks for the very poor marksmanship exhibited by two of their three intended victims.

Q-ship *Lisette*

Lisette was a topsail schooner, converted during the summer of 1917 at Falmouth to a Q-ship. She was fitted with three 6pdr guns, two Lewis guns and a very inefficient Perkins engine. Amongst her crew was 58-year-old Commander Francis Fitzgerald Tower RNVR. Educated at Wellington and Trinity College, Cambridge, Tower was a gentleman of leisure and keen yachtsman who owned properties in London and on the Isle of Wight and had volunteered for service at the beginning of the war. Of independent means, Tower had married the daughter of Sir Thomas Butler, 10th Baronet Cloughgrenan in 1884 (and in 1915 had married his daughter Isolde to Fitzwalter George Probyn Butler, 17/27th Baron Dunboyne). He had served in the Dover Patrol, then as assistant to Captain V E B Phillimore in charge of auxiliary patrols from Falmouth. In August 1916 his 'old friend' Captain Charles Hope Robertson RNR, another recalled admiral (he had been on the retired list since 1909), asked him to join the armed yacht *Rovenski*, in which he made two cruises to the Mediterranean. And then, in the summer of 1917, he volunteered for service in Q-ships, joining *Lisette* for her maiden voyage.

Lisette's beat was around the Casquets and in the St George's Channel. Tower later described a typical night alert.

My place [was] the midships Lewis gun, which I took from its rack and waited at the foot of the ladder where the gun crews were collected waiting for orders down the speaking tube.

Soon came 'Lewis guns on deck' and this old gentleman in pyjamas and Lewis gun clambered, I am afraid somewhat stiffly, up the ladder and took up position amidships and waited.[2]

These evolutions did not trouble him half as much as the unsavoury conditions that he and his colleagues had to live in. 'My experience', he wrote, '[is that] the worst part of Q-ship work [was] the necessary confinement below deck which ... was not pleasant.'[3] And in heavy seas 'my cabin became a sort of shower bath'.[4] Despite their best efforts, however, *Lisette* never sank a U-boat.

But better news obtained elsewhere. On 12 September the Platypus Flotilla submarine *D-7*, Lieutenant Oswald Ernest Hallifax commanding, was on patrol to the north of Ireland. Lying on the surface in heavy seas and poor visibility she chanced to see *U-45* (Kapitänleutnant Erich Sittenfeld), closed up but on the surface. Hallifax ordered an immediate torpedo launch from the single stern tube at 800yds range and scored a direct hit. The U-boat blew up, taking forty-three men to the sea bed with it. There were two survivors picked from the sea by Hallifax. This was a humanitarian gesture denied to the crew of ss *Mariston*, whom Sittenfeld had left to be attacked and killed in the water by a school of sharks after had torpedoed the cargo vessel eighty miles west of the Fastnet the preceding July.

PC-61 was a brand new 'P'-class sloop (launched in June 1917), like many of her kind finished as a Q-ship, and based with some of her kindred at Pembroke Dock as part of Bayly's forces patrolling the St George's Channel and Irish Sea waters. On 26 September, she was on patrol under Lieutenant Commander Frank Arthur Worsley, RNR, a New Zealander who served on Ernest Shackleton's Imperial Trans-Antarctic Expedition of 1914–16 as captain of the *Endurance.* On his return he had joined the Navy, having been in the RNR since 1902, and was appointed to command *PC-61*, which he commissioned in July. She was equipped with a 4in quick-firing gun, hidden under a tarpaulin suspended from crane derricks. She also had hardened bows for ramming. On 26 September Worsley was on patrol to the south and east of Ireland when he observed the tanker ss *San Zefferino* suffer an on-board explosion. Assuming it to be from a torpedo, Wolsey tried to lure the submarine to the surface by making off, leaving the sea clear for the U-boat to surface and use its deck gun on its damaged victim. The attacker took the bait. Her commander, 26-year-old Oberleutnant zur See Alfred Arnold, was on only his second cruise as captain. He was perhaps too eager to claim his victory. As the U-boat showed itself, Worsley slewed his ship around and went to full speed to ram; Arnold sighted the British ship and desperately ordered a crash dive but it was too late. The P-boat's bow crashed into the U-boat amidships. She sank immediately, the only survivor being, ironically, Arnold himself. He was pulled from the water alive and later made a present to Worsley of his silver command whistle. It was a rare victory for Bayly's forces, one of only two in which the Pembroke PC-boats would participate. Worsley was awarded the DSO for his success.

Queenstown

Bayly's 'personal' cruiser, *Adventure*, had been almost permanently at two hours' notice since it had arrived on station and the cost of this now began to tell. On 10 August, Bayly wrote to Jellicoe that she needed a thorough overhaul and requested a replacement. He received *Active* the same month, a similar scout cruiser armed with ten 4in guns, and previously serving with the Dover Patrol.

By now, Bayly thought that he had sufficient resources, an unusual admission for him (or indeed any other Royal Navy commander at this time). He wrote on 22 August 'I think that when the convoys have been going three months, we shall require fewer escorts',[5] and three weeks later added 'the destroyers are just able to do the convoy work required at present with the help of the occasional sloop';[6] the sloops were still out on active patrolling. This remained a pretty futile activity. Even Admiral Sir David Beatty at Scapa was moved to write: 'It is a prodigious job, as it is like looking for a needle in a bundle of hay and, when you have found it, trying to strike it with another needle.'[7]

But if Bayley was satisfied with his convoy-escort ability, he was less sanguine about sub-hunting. By December he had *Active* out on patrol with the sloops and was begging Jellicoe for more light cruisers to aid his efforts.[8]

The U-boats change their plans

The Allied and neutral tonnage sunk by U-boats declined somewhat as a result of the adoption of convoy; September 351,748grt, October

458,558grt, November 289,212grt. It was still very high but at least not at the terrifying levels of April through August.

Convoys kept Queenstown busy. Outbound convoys from Queenstown were given 'OQ' designations. Homeward convoys were given an 'H' designation and their originating port, eg HH27 – Homeward Hampton Roads, Convoy 27. The port of destination was never given on these descriptors. Between August 1917 and January 1918 there were thirty-one OQ convoys for Bayly's team to escort. Of these, twenty-five left from Queenstown, one left from Milford Haven, one left from Rosslare via Queenstown, one departed from Rosslare direct and three were cancelled.

Germany's minelaying submarines frequently mined the entrances to Queenstown and the River Lee, more so when major convoys were forming up there. It was the job of the minesweeping force under Commander Heaton to keep the port free from such menace, both at Queenstown and at all the other harbours in naval use around the coast. The majority of this work fell on the trawlers, vessels such as *Morococala*, a 264-ton steel vessel built in Aberdeen in 1915. She had been taken up complete with her crew and skipper and put under the charge of a 24-year-old Glaswegian reservist, Lieutenant Alexander Allan RNR.

From June 1915, when she had arrived in Ireland, the converted trawler, armed with a single 6pdr gun, hunted U-boats and mines. She swept plenty of the later and in April 1917 nearly caught one of the former when she had an engagement with a surfaced U-boat, which escaped due to superior speed and firepower. Bayly noted that 'the *Morococala* was very skilfully handled by Lieutenant Alexander Allan RNR. His reports to me were clear and it was depressing to Lieutenant Allan to see his abilities wasted through the vessel being under-gunned. If a 12pdr gun could be spared to replace the 6pdr in this trawler she would make good use of it.'[9]

On 19 November 1917, a major convoy was due to leave Queenstown at 1100hrs. However, at 1500hrs the previous day a mine had been swept up in Y-channel and Bayly ordered Commander Heaton to organise a full sweep of the area before the convoy was due to depart. At 0700hrs on the 19th, *Morococala* was sent with seven of her sisters, all under the command of Lieutenant Allan, to sweep a clear passage to allow the convoy to transit the harbour later that day. They had to sweep and then buoy (mark out) the channel. *Morococala* formed a sweep pair with another trawler, *Indian Empire*, once of

Grimsby and a rescuer of the *Lusitania* survivors. Little did the trawlers know that the minelaying submarine *UC-31* had already been about its business.

The pair of sweepers set their wire at 0830hrs. Almost immediately a huge explosion rocked *Morococala* behind the bridge, hiding the stern in fire and smoke. Lieutenant Allan and Signalman William Bellman RNVR were seen to climb on top of the wheelhouse but a second explosion, due to collapsing bulkheads and water getting into the steam boilers, caused the bridge to cave in and pitched Allan and Bellman headfirst into the debris. Then the stern of the trawler rose upwards and she slipped under the waves, just one and a half miles south-east-by-south of the Daunt Rock light vessel. Skipper Alexander Stewart of the *Indian Empire* thought that she went down in about six seconds.

Stewart slipped his sweep and made over to the spot where *Morococala* had gone down, launching a small boat to help search for survivors; although he stayed there for twenty minutes he found none. All fourteen men aboard her died with the ship, Allan, eleven of her original crew, all RNR, and two signalmen RNVR.

At the subsequent court of enquiry into *Morococala*'s sinking it was concluded that 'she was completely destroyed and her total crew lost'.[10] Commander Heaton added that 'she was a most efficient trawler, commanded by a Lieutenant RNR who, in my opinion, was very keen on his job and as good as any we have and her crew was an excellent one'.[11]

Bayly was distraught. Six minesweeping trawlers were lost at Queenstown, four to mines. Of these, only four men survived from their combined crews. The admiral admired their courage and fortitude. Two days after the *Morococala* blew up he issued a note to 'the officers commanding armed trawlers and drifters on the Coast of Ireland Station'. He praised 'the devotion to duty and seamanlike ability of the trawlers attached to the coast of Ireland … [who] day after day go out to their duties with the one idea – to destroy their country's enemies who ruthlessly prey on helpless ships, showing neither honour, manliness nor self-respect in their cruel and brutal attacks … [I express] my wholehearted thanks and pride for what they have done in the past and my faith in their actions in the future.'[12] Bayly was a man who firmly repressed his emotions, but his depth of feeling about his little ships and their crews can be seen in his description of his enemies in this memorandum.

*   *   *

Two episodes in August and September 1917, both involving *Laburnum*, well illustrate the frustrations of convoy escort and the difficulties of protecting and saving merchant vessels. ss *Assyria* was a 6,399grt vessel sailing in convoy to New York with general cargo. Rounding Tory Island she was torpedoed. The damage was significant but not fatal and *Laburnum*, now operating out of Lough Swilly and detailed as part of the convoy escort, was ordered to escort her to safety. The merchant ship could manage only 5 knots which made her easy prey. Sure enough, she was torpedoed again, by *UB-61*, and sank. Her crew was picked up by a tug while the sloop dropped two depth charges without effect. A bitter Surgeon Lieutenant Mason confided to his diary '[it] well illustrates the impotence of sloops'.[13]

The following month, still operating in the north of Ireland, *Laburnum* was sent out on the 15th to meet an incoming convoy. At 1540hrs, as the convoy commodore's ship, the 6,764grt Alfred Holt Lines cargo vessel *Idomeneus*, entered the North Channel, she was attacked and torpedoed in the port side, near the engine room, killing an engineer and three Achinese firemen. She was wounded but still floating, not least because (it was said) her cargo of American cotton had expanded on contact with water and plugged some of the damage. It was decided to try to tow her to Buncrana. At 1700hrs *Laburnum* got a tow on board and with the 'R'-class destroyer *Rob Roy* acting as escort the sloop began the long journey to safety. But at 2100hrs the towing hook and rail carried clean away and the next three hours were spent trying to recover and refasten the tow. Weathering a false AQ (Action Quarters) alert at 0600hrs the following day, an hour later they got under way once more, this time attempting to reach the southern Hebrides. At 0900hrs the tow parted again. Now *Poppy* came up and at 1000hrs took over the tow, with *Laburnum* and *Rob Roy* as escort. The little convoy eventually reached Vatersay, at the extreme south of the Outer Hebrides, where the cargo ship was beached for later re-floating and repair.

Convoys were rarely-incident free. Sometimes fortune smiled on the submarine commanders, sometimes they planned well; and sometimes the fates combined both luck and planning. *U-79* was an *UE-1* class ocean minelayer built in 1916. She carried a 10.5cm deck gun and thirty-eight mines together with four torpedoes and, on 2 October 1917, was under the command of Kapitänleutnant Otto Rohrbeck. It was to prove a profitable day for the 34-year-old U-boat captain. He had laid his mines carefully, creating a field intended to sink ships in-bound to the north of Ireland channel from the transatlantic convoys, south-west of Bull Point, near Rathlin Island off the coast of Antrim. And here he lay in wait to see what might transpire.

Convoy HH24 had been escorted across from New York by ships including the armoured cruiser HMS *Drake*, over 14,000 tons displacement and the lead ship of her class when built in 1901. She had been in the reserve fleet at the outbreak of war but was reactivated and eventually sent to the North America command where she and her crew of 900 became a regular convoy escort ship.

On arrival at the north channel the convoy dispersed and *Drake* was sailing independently and unescorted when she swam into Rohrbeck's sights. He didn't hesitate. One torpedo was all that was necessary. The torpedo struck No 2 boiler room and caused two of her engine rooms and the space itself to flood, killing eighteen crewmen. The flooding gave her a list and knocked out her steam-powered steering. Additionally her bulkheads began to fail under the pressure from the inrushing sea.

Captain Stephen Herbert Radcliffe RN decided, erroneously as it proved, that the damage was containable and began to steam slowly for Church Bay on Rathlin Island. The ship was unwieldy and accidentally collided with the merchant ship SS *Mendip Range* before Radcliffe was able to reach the bay and drop anchor. *Mendip Range* was forced to beach herself lest she sink. *Drake* had made it into the bay but it was clear that she was finished and her crew were taken off; shortly afterwards she turned on her beam ends and sank.

The sloops *Poppy* and *Rosemary* had been part of the convoy escort for the latter part of the voyage. They picked up that *Drake* had been hit on their radios at 0930hrs and sped back to the area. On the way they also heard that SS *Lugano* had been sunk by mines near Rathlin Island; this they didn't need to be told for Sub Lieutenant Goodrich had observed the mine explode, sending a column of water '600ft into the air'.[14] Now they picked up the warning message 'mines off Bull Island' (*sic*) and saw the destroyer *Brisk*, also a victim of the minefield, being towed by two trawlers with her forepeak blown away. Goodrich sourly noted in his diary '*Rosemary* and *Poppy* organised a perfectly useless search for the submarine which we could not find'.[15] As for Rohrbeck, he had sunk three ships, including two warships, in a matter of hours and escaped.

On other occasions, U-boats simply waited in the routes the convoys had to take. As one example out of many, on 21 November OQ21, comprising six ships bound for New York plus escort, left Rosslare (the sole convoy direct from that port). After an hour's sailing the foremost ship, ss *Breynton*, 4,240grt, carrying empty barrels as ballast, was torpedoed by *U-67*. She was still capable of sailing and so uss *Fanning* and *Allen* were detailed to escort her back to Ireland. Bayly sent the rescue tugs *Cartmel* and *Stormcock*, and with their aid *Breynton* made it safely home.*

In November the Germans had announced an extension of their 'prohibited zone' where traffic would be torpedoed without warning. It now stretched to 30° West in the Atlantic and down to the Azores. But the relative success of the convoy system forced the U-boats to shift their operations from the Atlantic to the inshore waters of the Irish Sea, Bristol Channel and other coastal waters around Ireland and England. Here they could attack ships making for the convoy assembly points or sailing away from the dispersal ones. In the last three months of 1917, 33 per cent of losses to U-boats were vessels sailing independently from embarkation port to convoy assembly and 40 per cent were those proceeding from their dispersal point. This forced the Admiralty to abandon the practice of using Queenstown as the start point for convoys to the USA from the Clyde or Liverpool because of the danger to ships sailing through the Irish Sea. Instead they assembled at Lamlash on the Isle of Arran (and, eventually, during 1918 at Liverpool itself). The last OQ convoy was thus OQ31, which sailed from Milford Haven on Monday, 7 January 1918. Five large ships were escorted by uss *Duncan*, *Jarvis*, *Trippe*, *Paulding*, *Allen* and the sloop HMS *Zinnia*. In addition Bayly sent the Q-ships *Tamarisk* and *Aubrietia* to shadow the convoy.**

* The tugs received 'Naval Salvage Money' for the rescue, but not until three years later, when the award was gazetted on19 December 1920.

** Twenty-nine outbound convoys left Queenstown under escort with 209 ships escorted for a total of 954,503GRT. No ships were lost (Fayle, *Seaborne Trade*, Vol III, p 472).

***(page 189) Bayly was well aware of the dangers of collision when zigzagging, having issued an order on 1 August 1917 that captains must use their discretion as to when to zigzag but noting that 'on a dark night when there is little visibility, to zigzag means to greatly increase the risk of collision'. (Docs 4351, IWM). He called for his captains to balance the risk of being torpedoed with the risk of collision. On this occasion, *Benham* had decided that the risk of manoeuvre was worth taking; and suffered as a result.

The Americans are Blooded, 1917

The destroyer USS *Benham* had an adventurous start to her war. She had arrived at Queenstown on 24 May and was immediately involved in convoy escort work and submarine hunting. On 13 July she was seemingly attacked by three submarines at once. A total of three torpedoes were launched at her but by sharp manoeuvring she avoided them and attacked the presumed position of the U-boats with depth charges. Only weeks later, on 30 July and whilst returning to Queenstown, *Benham* spotted the wake of a torpedo some 1,500yds off and heading for her. General Quarters blared out and she attacked with depth charges and guns fired at the surface of the water. Later, her crew claimed to have sighted air bubbles and oil on the surface. The Lords of the Admiralty, eager to give the Americans early encouragement, commended her for probable damage to a German submarine, but post-war investigation proved no U-boat was lost on that day.

Three weeks later, at 2140hrs on 20 August, *Benham* and the sloop *Zinnia* collided in thick fog; the former ship had been zigzagging at 12 knots whilst both were escorting a convoy. *Benham*'s stern was badly damaged and sinking was a possibility. However, some smart work by *Zinnia* under Lieutenant Commander Wilson saved the day; he was able to take off the US ship's crew and get a tow on board. *Zinnia* towed her stricken victim back to Queenstown where she was moored up to the depot ship USS *Melville*, with her stern nearly awash.

At the subsequent investigation Bayly noted that 'this seems to be one where darkness was intermittent; therefore zigzagging became a matter of opinion.*** *Zinnia* was steering a steady course, *Benham* was zigzagging.'[1] He added 'I think the officers and men of both ships behaved remarkably well and the salving of the *Benham* was due to the smartness with which she was taken in tow. It was a very near thing with her.'[2]

Wilson received an 'appreciation' from Their Lordships at the Admiralty for the 'prompt manner in which USS *Benham* was taken in tow'. The USN vessel was repaired by the Haulbowline dockyard and its USN depot ship in time to move to Brest for duty in 1918.

USS *Cassin*

The first American sailors to lose their lives in the U-boat war around the British Isles were eight men of the armed guard on board the tanker SS *Montano*, sunk by *UC-47* on July 31 1917, twenty miles south-east of Start Point in the English Channel.

But it was to Queenstown-based destroyer USS *Cassin* that the doubtful honour went of being the first USN warship to be hit by, and lose men to, a U-boat. She had arrived in Ireland on 15 May, one of the second group of such ships to be despatched, and had immediately been put to work escorting transports and troopships.

On 15 October *Cassin* was engaged in just such duties, about twenty miles south of Mine Head Lighthouse, when she sighted *U-61* on the surface and raced towards her. The submarine dived and at 1330hrs the ship was just over the spot where they had seen the submarine submerge when *Cassin*'s watchmen saw a torpedo heading towards them. The captain, Commander Walter Vernou, rang for emergency full speed, turned hard to port and sounded General Quarters. It proved too little, too late. The torpedo struck on her port quarter. It was, in fact, a very lucky hit for the torpedo had been observed to have breached the surface of the water on two occasions and causing it to turn and follow the ship round and then it porpoised just before impact. The missile struck above the waterline causing considerable damage, blowing away the aft 4in gun and destroying part of the seamen's mess. There was, remarkably, only one casualty. When Gunner's Mate First Class Osmond Ingram saw the approaching torpedo, he ran to where the depth charges were and tried to throw them overboard, to prevent a catastrophic detonation. The explosion of the torpedo nonetheless ignited both of the charges and Ingram was killed outright. Nine other men were wounded.

Cassin's rudder had been blown off and her stern wrecked and she began to circle uncontrollably. Only one of her two engines would function and large pieces of her superstructure were dangling into the water. The U-boat closed to finish the job but was driven off by four rounds from the American vessel's 4in armament. With her radio damaged and out of action, *Cassin* had to jury-rig a system, but after an anxious hour made contact with USS *Porter* which came to give aid and protection – and to relay a message calling for assistance. This was much needed for *Cassin* was drifting towards Hook Head and certain disaster on the rocks of the headland if she was not secured in some way.

Bayly sortied his ships. First to arrive was the sloop *Jessamine* at 2100hrs. Then the Q-ship *Tamarisk*, commanded by Lieutenant Commander Ronald Neil Stuart VC, came alongside and spent the night attempting to get a tow on board *Cassin*. Twice they succeeded and twice it parted. Finally, *Tamarisk* got a line to hold and was able to prevent the American ship drifting further towards the rocks until, at daylight, the trawler *Heron* managed to pass a line on board and three trawlers started to tow *Cassin* towards Queenstown, at a snail-like 3 knots. Sixty miles out she was met by *Snowdrop* and the sloop fixed a tow, increasing the rate of advance to 7 knots. Eventually three tugs took over and *Cassin* was docked in the basin at Haulbowline Dockyard at 0800hrs on 16 October. She had lost 30ft of her stern and was flooded in three compartments. It took until July the following year to put her back into service. *Cassin* and her crew had been very lucky indeed.

Bayly thought it a fine effort by Stuart and went on board *Tamarisk* when she docked to congratulate the crew. The United States Navy agreed, awarding Stuart a US Distinguished Service Cross, their second highest award for bravery, to add to his burgeoning medal collection. As for Gunner's Mate Ingram, he received a posthumous Medal of Honor for his action and the destroyer USS *Osmond Ingram* (DD-255), launched in 1919, was later named in his honour.

USAT *Antilles*

The day after *Cassin* reached Queenstown and safety, sixty-seven American soldiers and sailors lost their lives when, at around 0600hrs, the troopship USAT (US Army Transport) *Antilles* was torpedoed to the west of the Bay of Biscay. It was the single greatest loss of American lives at sea to that point in the war.

Antilles, 6,879grt, had been taken up as a troopship from the Southern Pacific Steamship Company on 26 May. Under the command of Lieutenant Commander Daniel T Ghent USN, she had been among those vessels in the first troop convoy to depart for Europe on 14 June from the Hoboken Port of Embarkation (Commander Taussig in *Wadsworth* had been part of their 'welcoming party' in the Western Approaches). Three months later, on 24 September, she sailed again, in a four-ship convoy designated 'Group Number Eight'. The voyage was successfully completed and *Antilles* was three days out of St-Nazaire on the return trip, carrying some army personnel going back to the United States, when she was torpedoed by *U-105*, commanded by Kapitänleutnant Friedrich Strackerjan. It was the U-boat's first cruise and only her fourth 'kill'.

Antilles had been in a convoy of three troopships escorted by four American armed yachts, but in rough weather one escort had turned back and the others found station keeping difficult. Strackerjan had been able to creep up undetected and launch his weapon unimpeded.

The troopship's captain, Ghent, was washed overboard and as the ship sank was directly under the funnel, which he thought was going to strike him as it fell. But just before that could occur, the boilers exploded and the blast threw the smokestack clear. According to the *Chicago Sunday Tribune*, *Antilles* went down in five minutes.[3] 'The survivors underwent much suffering while exposed to the elements', the paper noted, 'many of them in their nightclothes'.[4] One hundred and seventy-eight survivors were plucked from rafts or the sea itself, 118 by the yacht USS *Alcedo* and fifty by USS *Corsair*. The latter, launched in 1898, had been owned by J P Morgan, the banker. The former had been purchased by the US Navy on 1 June from George W C Drexel of Philadelphia, another scion of a banking family; she was to be sunk on t5 November by *UC-71* with the loss of twenty-one of her crew. America was learning the hard way about the U-boat war.

USS *Fanning*

Revenge was not long in coming. USS *Fanning* was a modified *Paulding*-class destroyer, launched in 1912, equipped with five 3in guns and six 18in torpedo tubes. She was capable of a top speed of 29.5 knots on a good day and was named for Nathanial Fanning, who had served under John Paul Jones on the *Bonhomme Richard* when the latter had fought and captured the Royal Navy frigate *Serapis* in 1799.

On 17 November, *Fanning*, commanded by Lieutenant Arthur Schuyler Carpender USN, was escorting a convoy leaving Queenstown for the United States, in company with USS *Nicholson* and four other USN destroyers, plus the sloop *Zinnia* and Q-ship *Viola*. At 1615hrs the convoy was forming near to Daunt's light vessel with *Fanning* on its port side when in the fading light, her coxswain sighted the periscope of a submarine 400yds off her port bow. Officer of the deck Lieutenant Walter Owen Henry ordered full speed and an immediate attack. As she passed over the place where the U-boat had been sighted, flames and smoke belching from her four funnels, *Fanning* dropped her depth charges. The explosion of them was so violent that *Fanning*'s own generator was temporarily disabled. Now they waited; and waited; and suddenly the stern of a submarine shot into the air. *Nicholson* was charging in behind and dropped a depth charge alongside the submarine, loosing three shots from her main armament as well. The U-boat's bow rose from the water and she righted herself, only to begin to settle. *Fanning* fired a further three shots at what could now be seen was *U-58* and, thirteen minutes after the alert, the submarine's crew spilled out on deck, hands raised above their heads.

The submarine had in fact been mortally wounded by *Fanning*'s first attack and sunk to 278ft, from which unprecedented depth an emergency blow of the ballast tanks brought her back to the surface with motors, diving gear and oil feeds wrecked. It had been her first voyage under a new commander, Gustav Amberger, and they had arrived off Queenstown after a successful transit through the Dover Barrage. Amberger had sunk only a small wooden barquentine, *Dolly Varden* of 202grt, on the cruise thus far. *Fanning*, covered by *Nicholson*, moved in to pick up survivors and attempted to put a tow on board to capture her prize. But two Germans were observed to dart suddenly below and shortly afterwards the explosions of internal scuttling charges were heard. The U-boat began her last dive.

The crews of *Fanning* and *Cassin* pulled the German survivors from the water. Kapitänleutnant Amberger, wet and dripping, immediately walked up to Lieutenant Carpender, clicked his heels, saluted in a punctilious German fashion and surrendered himself, his officers and the crew. He also gave a parole, for himself and his men. The officers were put in separate cabins under guard and each of the crew was placed under the protection of a well-armed

American seaman. The U-boat had two men dead, the two brave (or foolhardy) souls who had gone below to scuttle her.

Carpender was a proud man that day. He wirelessed to Bayly 'Dropped depth charge on enemy submarine. Submarine surrendered. Returning to Queenstown with forty prisoners.'[5] Ensign Dwight Rudd, serving with the *Nicholson*, wrote 'to the *Fanning* went the credit and distinction of being the first American ship ... to get a submarine and take any prisoners at all. A wonderful piece of work from first to last.'[6] The prisoners, ill-shod due to leather shortages in Germany and speaking of constant problems getting fuel and supplies due to the Royal Navy's blockade, were held on the depot ship *Melville* before Bayly ordered them transferred to Milford Haven on one of the sloops, and hence to a POW camp. Once on board the sloop *Snowdrop* her captain, Lieutenant Commander George Ponsonby Sherston, put them on the upper deck, 10ft apart, had a chalk line marked around each man and placed a sailor with a rifle amidships; he then explained to his prisoners that anyone stepping over his mark would be shot. There was no trouble on the voyage.

As for *Fanning* and her crew, Bayly went on board when she docked and congratulated the officers and men on their achievement. He read out a telegram from the Admiralty; 'Express to commanding officers and men of the United States ship *Fanning* Their Lordships' high appreciation of their successful action against enemy submarine.'[7] And Admiral Simms added one of his own which concluded 'Go out and do it again'.[8]

Lieutenant Arthur Schuyler Carpender was awarded the British Distinguished Service Order, personally pinned his uniform by King George V at Buckingham Palace; he was also promoted to lieutenant commander. The *Cassin* and the *Antilles* had been avenged. And *Fanning*'s kill remained the only one by the United States Navy for the rest of the war.

USS *Jacob Jones*

USS *Jacob Jones* was a modern *Tucker*-class destroyer launched in 1915. Part of Bayly's Queenstown brood, she and her sisters were regularly employed escorting inbound US convoys to Brest. On 6 December, she was making the return voyage, alone and steaming in a zigzag pattern when at 1621hrs she swam into the sights of *U-53*, commanded by Kapitänleutnant Hans Rose and patrolling off the

Scilly Isles. The American ship's lookouts spotted a torpedo when it was 800yds away and her captain, Lieutenant Commander David Worth Bagley, went hard to port and rang for emergency speed, but to no avail. The torpedo struck to starboard, rupturing her fuel tanks, damaging her rudder, knocking out the engines and leaving her drifting and helpless. She was not even able to radio of her plight as there was no electricity for the W/T set.

As the ship began to sink by the stern, Bagley ordered all life rafts and boats launched. His depth charges had been set at 'ready' when the torpedo hit and would detonate when they slipped below the surface. Men tried to get off the doomed ship but her bow suddenly shot into the air and as she slipped backwards under the sea, the depth charges exploded, killing some of those who had yet to leave the ship. Eight minutes after she had been hit, she had gone under taking sixty-four men with her.

Lieutenant (jg) Stanton F Kalk had been officer of the deck when she went down and now worked in the cold Atlantic waters to get men into rafts and balance the loads in them. He died from exposure before he could complete the job. Thirty minutes after *Jacob Jones* sank, *U-53* surfaced and took on board two badly-injured American sailors. In a further act of by-now rare chivalry, Hans Rose also radioed to Queenstown with the approximate co-ordinates of the sinking before leaving the area.[*]

Bagley was of course unaware of this act of mercy and, leaving a lieutenant commander in charge of the rafts, set off with his executive officer and four crewmen in the motor dory to row to the Scillies and gain assistance. Meanwhile, throughout the night of 6/7 December the sloop *Camellia* and the liner ss *Catalina*, sent from Queenstown by Bayly, searched for the survivors; and found them. By 0830hrs on 8 December HMS *Insolent,* an ancient flatiron gunboat built in 1881, had picked up the last crewmen of *Jacob Jones*. Bagley had been found by *Camellia*. Sixty-six officers and men were lost in the sinking, out of a crew of 104, and *Jacob Jones* became the first-ever American destroyer to be sunk by enemy action. Kalk and Bagley received the Navy Distinguished Service Medal, the former posthumously.

---

[*] Rose was one of the most respected U-boat commanders and famous for his humanity and fairness. At times, when he torpedoed a ship he would wait until all the lifeboats were filled then throw a tow line, give the victims food and keep all the survivors together until a rescuing destroyer appeared on the horizon. Rose sank seventy-nine ships for a total of 213,987grt during his war service.

Jacob Jones was not the last US navy ship to be torpedoed in 1917. On 27 December, the armed yacht USS *Santee*, which had been converted into an American Q-ship, was torpedoed, probably by *U-105*, off Kinsale within twenty-four hours of her maiden cruise. It was not, however, a fatal wound; she was towed back to port with no casualties and remained the US Navy's only Q-ship on the station.

USN submarines

The United States Navy was anxious to gain submarine expertise, experience that had been hard won by British submariners over three years of war and in many theatres. In December 1917 seven American 'L'-class submarines[*] were despatched under Captain Thomas Charles Hart USN and, after a long and arduous Atlantic voyage, arrived in Ireland on 27 January 1918.

They were based at Berehaven and immediately put into the hands of Captain Martin Eric Nasmith VC, a war hero of great experience who had won his Victoria Cross for his exploits in the Dardanelles in the submarine *E-11*. He had been assigned to Bayly specifically to train up the American vessels. Nasmith's presence contributed to one of Bayly's favourite moments in the war. As he wrote to Jellicoe in December 'I was a very proud man walking along with two VC captains [Campbell and Nasmith, both under his command at that time].'[9]

The utility of submarines hunting U-boats with no sort of detection equipment can be questioned. In any case, when they finally were released to patrol duties in March 1918, Bayly would only allow one out at a time and insisted that all his officers should be informed that a US submarine was at sea; he wanted no politically-dangerous 'blue on blue' incidents. The USA was in the war, bloodied and a key part of the Allies' strategy.

---

[*] To avoid confusion with the British 'L'-class boats they were known as the 'AL'-class whilst on service in Ireland.

A Strange Sort Of Life

The Americans found Bayly's leadership congenial. Shortly before he went back to the USA, Commander Taussig confided his view of him to his diary.

> I think that most of us who have had the honour and pleasure of serving under Admiral Bayly consider him a most efficient officer. Although his manner is brusque at times, he has always treated me with the utmost courtesy and consideration. It has been a pleasure to serve under him directly, and in the numerous times when we have had to use our own initiative in deciding knotty questions, he has backed us to the limit and made commendatory remarks on our reports.
>
> There has not been the slightest sign of friction. Our relations have always been cordial. The co-operation between the two navies has been intimate and successful. Admiral Bayly is a man with the highest sense of duty — of a naturally retiring disposition but of quick perception and action.[1]

Some measure of Bayly's style and why it held such a strong appeal to capable commanders can be gained from Gordon Campbell's view of him.

> It would be impossible for me to say how much we got to love him; he was an ideal CinC in every way – he had our confidence and we thought that we had his. At first he used to give us sailing orders which were of the type that allowed the man on the spot to do his best, regardless of instructions; after

a few months I used to go to sea without any sailing orders and just report in each day what I was doing.[2]

Bayly struggled to show his emotions, a lifetime of 'keeping a stiff upper lip' and a strong sense of propriety perhaps constraining his humanity. But Taussig and the others recognised his fundamental decency. 'Although he undoubtedly feels deeply, he does not show it, and his manner belies the cordiality which I believe he really feels. I think the only two times he shook hands with me was when we first met and when I told him goodbye.'[3] Indeed when the Americans had first met Bayly, they nicknamed him 'Old Frozen Face' for his lack of emotion. This soon changed; instead, behind his back, the American officers came to call Bayly 'Uncle Lewis' and found it easy to confide in him on naval matters. Bayly also had strongly-held religious views, which were also apparent to the American sailors. 'He is very religious and I have often been impressed when talking with him that he is a Christian in heart and action', thought Joseph Taussig.[4] Some Royal Navy men found that Bayly belied his reputation too. Commander Tower noted that 'I was very much struck with him – a fine character'.[5]

Bayly had established a smallholding at Admiralty House, to provide fresh foodstuffs, and all the officers were invited to take a hand in working on it. Taussig reported that:

We walked around 'the farm' as the admiral calls the Admiralty grounds. They were looking very nice and fresh. The admiral said that he and Captain Price of the *Melville* had cut the front lawn grass that afternoon. The fruit is beginning to show, and the potatoes are nearly ready for digging. Peas will be ready for picking in about a week or ten days. We shut up the chickens and collected the eggs (eight) … I remarked about the large amount of space devoted to potatoes, and Admiral Bayly said it was necessary as his niece fed about half the poor of Queenstown.[6]

Bayly and Violet were, in fact, also active in looking after the victims of sinkings, who were deposited at Queenstown after rescue. Taussig again related their story. 'I was told that about ten days ago when a lot of survivors were brought in about midnight, they were taken to the Admiralty House and given a hot supper prepared by Miss Voysey. Vice Admiral Sir Lewis Bayly, KCB, CVO, then proceeded to wash the dishes and Rear Admiral Sims USN, a guest in the house, proceeded to dry them.'[7] Surely a less well-known and very human face of Anglo-American naval co-operation.

As previously noted, Bayly was at pains to ensure that his young captains were given the opportunity for civilised interaction and sleep in a proper bed. Commander Taussig remembered arriving for dinner when

the Admiral and Miss Voysey did not appear for fifteen minutes as they had been out somewhere. But we did not mind this as there is no ceremony at the Admiralty House, and everybody feels at home right away. The other guests were Miss French and Mr [name omitted in diary] making eight at table. The Admiral asked me if I would not like to stay all night in view of my sailing time being changed to noon. I said that I would, and Poteet [another American commander, captain of USS *Wainwright*] said he would like to, so the Coxswain of the barge was sent to bring our bags ... I again slept in a big double bed in a big front room with windows overlooking the Bay. The moon was full and the scene quiet and peaceful. I enjoyed the hot bath, the breakfast, and then the walk around 'the farm' with Admiral Bayly.

But of course reality quickly intervened. 'We then went into his office and he told me the *Wadsworth* would go on a special escort mission and that I could leave at 4 pm instead of noon.'[8]

Bayly's hospitality was particularly appreciated by the USN officers because they were perforce separated from their wives; many of the Royal Navy officers had moved their wives to Queenstown to be closer to their nearest and dearest. But British and American mixed happily from the admiral downwards. Bayly was unstinting in his praise for his New World charges. 'The Americans are splendid,' he wrote to Jellicoe in September 1917, 'and get on with our own people very well.' With a hint of future foreboding he added 'but the Irish have made a dead set at them and we may be in for big trouble later'.[9] And Commander Francis Tower noted 'I got on well with the Americans ... they were always ready in every way to help me as I tried to help them'.[10]

From the moment of their arrival and when time allowed the

American officers had plentiful opportunity for leisure refreshment, alcoholic or otherwise. The Cork Club had invited them to consider themselves 'Honorary Members' for the duration of the war; and the Royal Cork Yacht Club, the most prestigious in the area, wrote to Taussig on 4 May 1917 that 'the Committee and members of the RCYC 98 will be very much honoured if Lieutenant Commander J K Taussig and officers of the US Destroyer Flotilla will make use of the club premises as Honorary Members during their stay in harbour. If you would kindly make this offer progressive as far as future visiting ships of your fleet are concerned I shall be much obliged. With greetings from the club, signed H B Bruce, Secretary.'[11] Taussig's diary records that the invitees were not backward in availing themselves of these offers. And Queenstown had its own Freemasons' lodge which invited all American and British sailors who were of the Craft to join its ranks for the duration.[*]

There were some small issues, however. The Americans were in the majority and had built the better recreational facilities for their ratings (at Lynch Quay).[**] USN officers, aided by Bayly's grant of some land at Admiralty House, built a covered tearoom and other facilities. Sub Lieutenant Goldrich rather huffily noted that 'The Queens [a local hotel] was full of Yankee officers and I gather is no longer frequented by our crowd'.[12] One reason was the economic pressure exerted on price inflation by the mighty dollar. 'Whisky is two shillings a large tot and one shilling a half tot,' he added.[13] But he wasn't too proud to use the USN facilities. 'Next to the American concert and a Saturday night feature held at their gymnasium and swimming baths.'[14]

If American sailors serving under a Royal Navy admiral, and US and British personnel sharing mess and recreational facilities was considered unusual, then women serving with the Royal Navy must have seemed almost delusional at the time. The Woman's Royal Naval Service (WRNS) was founded in 1917 and 'Wrens' (as they became known) began to appear at Admiralty House. Eighteen-year-

---

[*] At the end of the war, on 12 December 1918, the British and American Masons presented a fine harmonium to the lodge, with a brass plaque inscribed 'presented to Lodge Neptune no. 190 I.C. Queenstown by the American and British brethren in appreciation of their being made honorary members while called in fighting for the love of truth and loyalty to freedom'.

[**] The facility held 200–300 ratings and had baths, reading rooms and a big hall for concerts. British ratings were made honorary members of it. The money was put up by US citizens in London.

old Mary Battersby joined Bayly's private navy at Queenstown in the same year. 'They wanted an English girl for decoding' she related.

> My mother thought girls should only work in canteens so she wouldn't sign my application form for the Wrens but my brother, an assistant paymaster at Queenstown, invited me over for a month's holiday and signed my form. I had a small room to myself under constant guard. The harbour was heavily mined and my work was connected with guiding our ships in and out – sloops, Q-ships, destroyers and minesweepers. I lived with my brother and I remember that [once] when we left the flat together and walked about fifty yards before going our separate ways to work, ten shillings was deducted from my pay as a fine for walking in public with an officer.[15]

A troubled land

All may have been well in relations between the Allies but Ireland was still a troubled land, especially in the area around Dublin and the south west. There had been demonstrations in Cork on the anniversary of the Easter Rising when Sinn Fein flags were flown and stones and paviours thrown, and there was a constant undercurrent of unrest. Bayly remained very aware that Queenstown was in hostile territory, writing '[Queenstown] containing many spies [doing] what they could to damage England's endeavours and where every ship or movement were closely watched'.[16]

Initially, the Irish revolutionaries had hoped that USN sailors of Irish extraction would support them; when this did not happen, Sinn Fein turned against the Americans. Many US sailors complained of a pro-German orientation amongst the Irish populace. One American historian reported a bluejacket as saying 'I'm Irish myself and yet I'd give a month's pay to crack the head of a Sinn Feiner'.[17] Sinn Fein responded by trying to turn the Americans against the British and Bayly in particular. Bayly wrote to Jellicoe in September

> I hear that there are many stories of friction [between US and RN personnel] here. I can quite understand it, the Sinn Feinians and other rebels have for a long time been getting hold of young American sailors in Cork and trying to persuade them that they are pulling chestnuts out of the fire for England while the English destroyers are doing nothing in English

harbours. Also for various reasons, the SF don't like me and hope to break up the merry party here by throwing mud and getting some to stick.[18]

British and American sailors going into Cork City for R&R frequently found themselves the target of abuse and assault, covert or overt, from revolutionary-minded Irishmen and were not backward in returning the favour. Some of the antipathy was due to nationalist fervour but some was also due to male competition for females. The relatively well paid and well off American sailors were an attractive proposition for the local colleens and a peacock-type competition for 'walking out' prerogatives resulted with the better tail-feathered Yankees winning. As one historian noted 'the Americans had more money than the Irish boys and could entertain the girls more lavishly'.[19] And a British naval officer wrote 'in the early days you would find US sailors walking along the streets of Cork with a girl on each arm and perhaps a third bringing up the rear hopefully'.[20]

It was not just in Cork that problems surfaced. John Aloysius McGinty was born and bred in County Donegal, had emigrated to America, and returned to Ireland as a radio operator on the tug USS *Genesee* as part of the USN forces at Queenstown. Granted leave, he travelled to his home town to visit relatives where he was spat on and had stones thrown at him as he was in uniform and 'either mistaken for a British sailor or reviled as an interfering American'.[21]

Back in Cork, a series of running battles developed on the streets between locals and naval personnel, and which reached a climax in September 1917 with five days of continuous rioting in the city. Amongst those caught up in the trouble on the 3rd of the month were local girls Margaret Ring and Mary Blackshields, who were making their way home from a night at the theatre with their American dates. They were attacked by a mob of young men who had been out harassing US servicemen. Their boyfriends ran off but the girls were assaulted and Margaret hit in the eye, whilst Rose was struck in the mouth. The events of the evening were only terminated by a police baton charge.

There was also trouble in Queenstown where a face-off between residents and USN personnel had to be broken up by American armed shore patrols. Between the first and the third of the month USN sailors were booed, hissed and stoned by the *soi disant* Cork

'Vigilantes' and several US sailors injured. 'This Irish-American fracas is an awful mess,' noted Lieutenant Lucien Green of USS *Tucker*, 'and it is a rotten shame the way our men are being treated.'[22]

Things got worse on the 7th. Fred Plummer was a painter at Haulbowline who had befriended USN Machinist's Mate J W Parente. While the two men enjoyed an evening promenade, Parente made a pass at Plummer's girl. They fought and Plummer was knocked down, striking his head on the kerbstone which killed him. British Intelligence noted that 'it caused considerable bad feeling amongst Queenstown residents and that this was reciprocated by the US sailors'.[23]

The animosity was clearly going to end in tears and when Bayly discovered that some US matelots were 'tooling up' by making knuckledusters and other weapons in the workshops of USS *Melville*, he put the whole city of Cork off limits. As Bayly wrote to Jellicoe 'the Americans hate the Irish now and if I were to let them go to Cork it is not the US sailors who would suffer'.[24] In fact it was the innkeepers and merchants of Cork who suffered, to the alleged tune of £4,000 per week according to Bayly.[25] A deputation from the city, led by the Lord Mayor, Thomas Butterfield, descended on Admiralty House to persuade him to lift the prohibition. He received them on stony silence, listened to their pleas and then asked one question – could they guarantee that there would be no attacks on his men in their city. The mayor havered and suggested they could not, at which point Bayly bid them a curt goodbye. Butterfield later told colleagues 'but by the grace of God I left through the door and not through the window'.[26] The ban had little impact on the more romantic of the sailors. There was a regular train service from Cork to Queenstown, by which the young ladies would travel down at the weekend; it became known as the 'Dove's Express', bringing a continuous cargo of eligible young Cork girls to the naval base.

There was a darker side to these *affaires d'amour*, however. As a port town, with a naval base and dockyard, there had always been prostitution in Queenstown, usually concentrated in the east of the town in an area known colloquially as 'Holy Ground'. With the advent of the US Navy, prostitutes now travelled to Queenstown in considerable numbers, not just from Cork but Dublin and even London. The Royal Irish Constabulary attempted to constrain the trade. Twenty-six women were convicted in Queenstown in 1918 of 'committing acts contrary to public decency on the street'. Under the Defence of the Realm Act (DORA, which required prostitutes not to frequent port areas) they were served with notices barring them from residing at Queenstown. In nine cases the order was disobeyed, and the women received sentences of three months' imprisonment.

The Roman Catholic Church expressed its customary dismay at such goings-on. One particularly vicious sermon from the pulpit of Queenstown Cathedral on 9 September 1917 inflamed the situation, blaming the lax morals of the young sailors for the corruption of Irish womanhood. The celebrant offered a strongly anti-naval message, urging parents to 'look after your daughters, especially since there had lately arrived on our shores hundreds of vultures, yea I might say thousands of them, preying upon the purity of our daughters of Queenstown'.[27] Bayly spoke with his friend the bishop and the rhetoric was toned down.

Nonetheless, there was a continued ill-will held against some of the Irish girls. There was a riot at Cork Railway Station on Monday 18 March 1918, for example. A mixed crowd, estimated at 300 people, gathered and attacked the women travelling on the train to Queenstown. They were beaten with sticks, stones were thrown at them and items of clothing were ripped off. The station master telephoned the police and the crowd was scattered with baton charges. The situation was repeated the following night and the police again had to use force to disperse the protesters.

Despite (or perhaps because of) this disapproval, some ninety-nine such marriages took place and young Irish girls were shipped off to the USA at the war's end. Amongst the highest-profile of such liaisons was the commander of the US seaplane base at Wexford, Lieutenant Commander Victor D Herbster, who married in Ireland and carried his bride, Cathleen Nolan, back to America at the end of his tour of duty. The Irish War Brides may have been reviled in County Cork, but they were welcomed in the USA. The *Washington Times* of 5 February 1919 reported that 'the highest average of comeliness is among the Irish brides. Few of the girls are of the high heeled variety, the majority having efficient acquaintance with household duties. The girls themselves are unanimous in pronouncing Americans persistent and gallant lovers.'

A good man returns home

The command lost a good man when Commander Joseph Taussig returned to America on 17 November 1917. The day before departing he said his farewells to Bayly and others and then went to see Violet. Their conversation was once more revealing about the intensely private nature of the admiral. As Taussig noted in his diary for that day 'I saw Miss Voysey and Lady Pinney. Miss Voysey gave me a little picture of Admiral Bayly. It is one of the few photographs of him in existence, as he has a great dislike of publicity. She said that Admiral Bayly had told her that Johnson and I might have pictures, but we were the only ones who should have them.'[28] As he departed, Taussig calculated that he and USS *Wadsworth* had steamed 47,456 miles to that point under Bayly's command. In eleven months of service he and his ship had been at sea for 206 days, roughly two-thirds of their time on station.

1 8

Difficult Times, December 1917

The weather off the Irish coast was a constant worry and dominated conversation at Queenstown. Patrol work could become impossible in the wrong sort of wind and sea. Aeolus frequently unlocked terrible gales.

On the Atlantic side the weather was driven in by strong westerlies. From late summer until autumn there would be former tropical depressions mixing in with the North Atlantic weather pattern depressions and producing severe storms. These were very significant weather events. Then Atlantic low-pressure systems became firmly established by December and depressions moved rapidly eastward in December and January, bringing strong winds with appreciable frontal rainfall to the coast of Ireland. In summer, incursions into the Atlantic by cold northerly air masses produced active depressions in late August and September. Warm air masses of high humidity and daytime heating sufficient to cause thunderstorms were a feature of mid- to late summer weather and in September the humid air was exposed to increasing periods of cooling by night, causing fog to form frequently on the coast and at sea, and was generally slow to clear. The Atlantic coast of Ireland thus offered Bayly's men all kinds of weather at all times of the year. Further out in the Atlantic the great rollers could wreck a ship with one wave, and the Bay of Biscay, part of the Western Approaches, was long famous for its violent seas, particularly in winter. Sometimes powerful storms would form when the pressure fell rapidly, travelling along the Gulf Stream at great speed like a hurricane, and finally crashing into the Bay with enormous power. One such storm occurred on 16 December 1917 when USS *Ammen* lost a funnel overboard, USS *Trippe* and *Jarvis* had men swept off deck, *Cummings* had three funnels battered out of shape and HMS *Achates* had to be escorted into Devonport with no bridge and only one funnel left out of three. The storm lasted for three days. The Irish Sea, between the western coast of Britain and the eastern coast of Ireland, also exhibited its own climatic conditions. Fog and mist were frequent hazards and short, sharp local storms would suddenly appear from nowhere.

It is said that the reason why the British talk about the weather is that they get so much of it; and that certainly held for the men of the Coast of Ireland Command, particularly the patrol vessels. Admiral Bayly noted that in 1917 'We had a succession of gales that winter and I was amazed at the way our small craft kept going, in spite of the discomfort and continuous work ... I was very proud of what they accomplished ... [and] the many acts of splendid bravery they performed.'[1] Others saw it in a slightly different light. Commander Tower thought that 'I shall not forget the bad weather – blowing and raining nearly all the time'.[2] And Robert Goldrich noted '[the] sea is really serious at times and the blinding squalls make navigation highly dangerous',[3] adding later that patrol work was constantly dangerous off the 'wild Irish coast, where the Atlantic winds howled like demons'.[4] When, after the war, a sailor who served with Campbell heard that he was writing a book on Q-ships, he sent his quondam captain a letter about the weather conditions. 'Don't forget to mention that winter in the Atlantic. It was the hardest few months I ever had in my life – as fast as we put things right the sea smashed them up again and however long the hours we worked you were never satisfied unless everything was exactly as you wanted.'[5]

With weather, the native population, constant patrol work and pressure and regularly mined harbours, Queenstown and the rest of the command was far from an easy billet. How some of the men must have envied the battleships swinging at anchor in Scapa Flow.

And December 1917 demonstrated that danger came not only from the German submarines. Weather and self-inflicted wounds also played a part.

At the end of November *Poppy* was at Belfast, defending the waters around the top of Ireland. The weather was atrocious. When orders came to go to Queenstown for repairs the weather was too fierce to even leave harbour. She finally arrived at the dockyard on 1 December. Bayly's early efforts to improve the efficiency of the dockyard had by now clearly paid dividends for Robert Goldrich was most impressed with its speed of action. 'We were no sooner secured than men flocked aboard and started work. The gun mountings were in the course of being dismantled and the boats surveyed within the first half-hour. It is in many ways a treat to come to a well organised base for a change.'[6]

By 12 December she was back on patrol, now operating out of Lough Foyle from the Londonderry base. Three sloops, *Poppy*, *Gladiolus* and *Rosemary* were in company with three destroyers, *Racoon*, *Harpy* (Senior Naval Officer) and the recently-arrived *Wolverine,* one of three *Beagle*-class destroyers (later renamed the 'G'-class) ordered from Cammell Laird as part of the 1908–9 ship-building programme. She could make 27 knots and was armed with a 4in gun and three 12pdrs together with two 21in torpedo tubes. Her captain was 26-year-old Australian-born Lieutenant in Command Frederick Langton Cavaye, who had been appointed to her only in September.

They were sailing to meet an inbound convoy with a rendezvous of 0900hrs. The ships had been disposed in two lines, sloops to the port of the destroyers but at 0530hrs the SNO ordered 'Form single line ahead' with the sloops now following the destroyers. *Wolverine* was the aftermost destroyer, two cables ahead of the leading sloop, *Rosemary,* which was slightly out of station being a little on the starboard quarter of the destroyer. The visibility was poor and there was fog around. Navigation lights were not in use.

At 0615hrs, some twenty-one miles from the rendezvous point, the SNO in *Harpy* hoisted a course alteration signal 'Leaders together, rest in succession'. The signalman on *Rosemary* confirmed the order to the Officer of the Watch who ordered the course change. Shortly thereafter, it was realised on board the sloop that the signal had not been made executive (i.e. confirmed by a further flag hoist). *Rosemary*, having turned to starboard, now tried to regain her original position, as she had manoeuvred before properly instructed, and turned to port.

Meanwhile, at 0625hrs *Harpy* made the signal executive and *Wolverine* began her turn to starboard. Her captain, Lieutenant Cavaye, was in the charthouse and the bridge was in the charge of the Gunner, Mr Carter. Disaster was about to strike. Moments after her turn, *Wolverine* sighted a vessel (*Rosemary*, although they did not know it) bearing 80° from right ahead. Gunner Carter yelled out 'Full speed ahead both', 'On navigation lights' and ordered a turn to port. On board *Rosemary* the looming disaster suddenly became clear. Officer of the Watch Acting Lieutenant William Gray RNR shouted for 'Full speed astern' and 'Hard-a-port' and sounded three blasts on the siren. A minute later *Rosemary* ploughed into the destroyer, sinking her stem into the bulkhead between the engine room and the after stokehold, starboard side. It was 0636hrs.

The rearward motion of the engines now pulled the sloop clear and water gushed into *Wolverine*; she drifted uncontrollably down the line of ships, past *Poppy* and towards *Gladiolus*. In a magnificent piece of seamanship, Lieutenant Commander Horace Walker RN of *Gladiolus*, ignoring the 12ft-high waves then running, put his ship forecastle to forecastle with the sinking destroyer and switched on his searchlights, thus allowing men to jump from the bows of one ships to the other and safety. Cavaye had ordered 'Abandon ship' and fifty men were thus able to cross to the sloop while *Wolverine* banged against her. Others jumped into the water and were picked up by *Gladiolus*'s whalers. Sub Lieutenant Goldrich on *Poppy* thought that 'excellent work it must have been to get so many men out of the water in time to prevent them dying of exposure', adding enviously, 'I believe *Gladi* has a decent sized hole in her side and a deck strained so they will get Christmas in dock'.[7] It was smart work by Commander Walker, for *Wolverine* sank within seven minutes of being rammed. Thanks to his efforts only two of the destroyer's crewmen were lost. Robert Goldrich, who had had a ringside seat to the disaster, had no doubt who was to blame and noted in his diary that '*Rosemary* was all over the place and fairly asked for trouble'.[8]

A court martial into the loss of the ship was convened by Admiral Miller at Buncrana. He sent for the Deputy Judge Advocate of the Fleet, Paymaster-in-Chief Frederick James Krabbe, who arrived post-haste from London and brought a freelance shorthand writer with him. It did not take the court long to agree with Goldrich. Lieutenant Cavaye was exonerated and the blame attached to Acting Lieutenant Gray of *Rosemary* for mistakenly altering course before the executive signal had been raised. Lieutenant Commander Walker was commended for his life-saving actions.[9]

Patrols had to continue. The day following the loss of *Wolverine*, *Poppy* was out again, this time looking for a convoy to escort. It took ages to locate it because 'as usual, the convoy was well to the north of where they thought they were'.[10] The 18th found *Poppy* back on active sub-hunting patrol. They were trying new tactics; two sloops sailed in line ahead while two destroyers kept station on either side, slightly forward of each sloop. But they didn't catch anything.

HMS *Arbutus* was an *Anchusa*-class sloop, completed as a Q-ship and based at Milford Haven. She had only just entered service, having been launched on 8 September. On 15 December she was on patrol some twenty-five miles off the Welsh coast in the St George's Channel under her captain, Commander Charles Herbert Oxlade RNR. Oxlade, born in 1876, was something of an adventurer having gained an aviator's licence in 1913 and served as a volunteer trooper in the Boer War. Now he was offering his ship as a target for U-boats.

The weather was filthy, blowing a gale and with rough seas, when *Arbutus* was hit by a torpedo from *UB-65*. Oxlade ordered abandonment, for real rather than deception as the ship was badly hit but stayed on board himself, along with his first lieutenant and a stoker party, to try to save his ship. Rescue vessels from Milford Haven attempted to tow *Arbutus* to safety but on the 16th, in continued foul weather she foundered and suddenly sank, taking Oxlade, his number one Lieutenant Charles Stewart RNR and six stokers with her. The remaining eighty-five crew survived. Another of Bayly's Q-ships had gone, its dangerous game lost.

Success did attend the sloop *Buttercup*, however, and on Christmas Day of all days. She was escorting Convoy HD15, Dakar to Liverpool, when the convoy was attacked by *U-87* under the command of Freiherr Rudolf von Speth-Schülzburg. Eighteen miles NWN of Bardsey Island in the Irish Sea, *U-87* torpedoed the steamship SS *Agberi* (4,821grt). But von Speth-Schülzburg, on his first cruise in command, stayed too long on the surface. The escorts spotted him and *Buttercup*, driven at full speed by her captain, Lieutenant Commander Arthur Collier Petherick, rammed into the U-boat; badly damaged, *U-87* could not submerge or escape. *PC-56*, a P-boat built as a Q-ship, was following up behind the sloop and sank the submarine with all hands, forty-four men in total.

But on 28 December, poor decision-making caused a convoy tragedy. The sloop *Primrose* was escorting a convoy past Malin Head, on the northern most tip of Ireland. Reports of an explosion were received and *Primrose* was ordered to disperse the convoy; she herself stayed with the leading ships. These made it to port successfully but the rear had to look after themselves and *U-19*, under Johannes Spiess, sank two of them, the Eagle Oil and Shipping Company oil-tanker ss *Santa Amalia* (4,309grt) and ss *Maxton*. Forty-three crewman of the former were lost, including the master. Sub Lieutenant Goldrich described it as 'a poor bloody exhibition'.[11]

A giant falls

Morale on the home front was not high. The continued slaughter on the Western Front brought pain and death to most families in the country. Merchant ships were seemingly sunk willy-nilly and food supplies had tightened. People had been asked to economise on foodstuff purchases and limited rationing was just around the corner. The Royal Navy was widely believed to have come off second best at Jutland and to lack an offensive spirit, lurking in harbour rather than taking the fight to the enemy. First Sea Lord Sir John Jellicoe was under frequent attack in some sections of the press and Lloyd George, Prime Minister since his putsch against Asquith in December 1916, had considerable reservations about Jellicoe's position.

But Bayly was optimistic. 'I am astounded at the gloom with which people in London seem to be shrouded,' he wrote to Jellicoe in December. 'The situation has never looked healthier to me. Germany has seen all countries at war with her and no possibility of regaining her overseas trade ... she sees herself bankrupt.'[12] In this statement he was to rather miss the point that Britain's finances were in a pretty parlous state too! Bayly was also self-congratulatory. 'I believe that you and I are the only admirals who have been on full pay since 1896', he added.[13]

In this he rather spoke too soon. Five days later Jellicoe was fired, on Christmas Eve and by letter. Jellicoe was highly respected and regarded in most of the higher echelons of the service and both the manner and the dismissal itself caused outrage in some parts of the navy. Rear Admiral Sir Dudley de Chair spoke for many when he was asked to join the new Board of Admiralty under Rosslyn Wemyss, Jellicoe's successor. He expressed the view that 'I was surprised that any naval officer on the Board of Admiralty could remain there, as it looked as if they condoned this action of Jellicoe's dismissal. In fact, I expressed myself forcibly, and let myself go, and left after a scene which did me no good and had disastrous results.'[14]

Bayly too was appalled. 'So they got rid of you at last', he wrote on 27 December. 'Well I am very glad indeed that you stuck to your post and showed that you were not afraid of them and their intrigues.'[15] And he invited Jellicoe to come and stay with him for two weeks.* 'My niece backs me up so do come', he enjoined.[16] And Admiral Sims, ill in bed in Queenstown, was also shocked and surprised. On 29 December he wrote to Jellicoe:

> Here I am at Admiralty House in bed since Christmas Eve with a rather painful attack of lumbago, and only just now being able to sit up a bit without considerable pain, otherwise I would have written before to say how much I was distressed to hear of your leaving the Admiralty, particularly when the effects of all your anti-submarine measures are showing such prominent results of complete success.
>
> I assume, of course, that the Government's action is based upon the supposed political necessity of responding to the pressure of the ignorant criticisms of the 'man in the street'— a danger to which all we military men must always be exposed in time of war. It would appear that when the public becomes impatient because the guns are not always firing, some of us have to sacrificed.[17]

As 1917 drew to a close, Bayly issued a memorandum to all ships under his command which reflected the confidence he had earlier expressed to Jellicoe.

> The Commander-in-Chief wishes to congratulate Commanding Officers on the ability, quickness of decision and willingness which they have shown in their duties of attacking submarines and protecting trade. These duties have been new to all, have had to be learned from the beginning and the greatest credit is due for the results.
>
> The winter is now approaching and with storms and thick weather the enemy shows an intention to strike harder and more often; but I feel perfect confidence that we shall wear him down and utterly defeat him in the face of all difficulties. It has been an asset of the greatest value that the two navies

---

* Jellicoe did make the visit. 'Everyone in the command was delighted to see him' reported Bayly (Bayly, *Pull Together*, p 236).

have worked together with such perfect confidence and with that friendship which only mutual respect can produce.[18]

But in the Western Approaches the ending of the year bought little relief. On the 29th the Norwegian cargo vessel SS *Tiro* (1,442grt) was sunk by *UB-57*, seven miles west-north-west of the Lizard. The following day the British SS *Zone* (3,917grt) on passage from Boulogne to Barry with a cargo of frozen offal, was torpedoed by *U-110* near St Ives. And the last ship to be sunk in Bayly's bailiwick in 1917 was another Norwegian ship, SS *Vigrid* (1,617grt), torpedoed by *U-95* ten miles north-west of the Lizard on 31 December. At the time of her sinking, she was sailing from Barry to Rouen with a cargo of good Welsh steam coal. Five members of the crew were lost, while the captain and thirteen other crewmen survived to land at Penzance. Of the five dead sailors, three were Swedish citizens and two Norwegian.*

---

* Norway was officially neutral throughout the war but her large fleet of merchant ships, over 2,000 strong, was in great demand by the Allies and suffered considerable harm from U-boat predation. The Norwegian merchant marine lost nearly half its ships and 1,892 sailors.

The Turning Tide, January – June 1918

The Royal Navy saw in 1918 in traditional style. On HMS *Poppy*, Sub Lieutenant Robert Goldrich noted that he 'heard the New Year born amid a blare of sirens, ship's bells and tin kettle drums'. He was however, unappreciative of his own crew's celebrations. 'The hands hurled their mess kettles down our ladders and marched down to wish us a Happy New Year. The stony silence defeated them and we were left to enjoy our well-earned repose.'[1]

The turning of the year brought no let-up in the work load of Bayly's forces. On 9 January, the *Beagle*-class destroyer *Racoon*, part of the 2nd Destroyer Flotilla based at Londonderry, was returning home through mountainous seas and a raging blizzard when she was wrecked east of Malin Head. *Poppy* was sent to hunt for survivors but in vain. Every single man aboard the destroyer, ninety-five in total, was lost. Goldrich was unsympathetic. 'If they attempted to pass through Inishtrahull Sound with the wind and seas that were running last night they asked for a nasty death and they appear to have got it.'[2]

The strain and demands of the last twelve months of activity with *Poppy* seemed to have introduced a more cynical note in Goldrich's diary entries. He dearly wanted a rest and it showed. 'No breakdowns yet unfortunately', he groaned. 'We have been on the run since Christmas and the sooner we join the *hors de combat* the better I will be pleased.'[3]

The Irish Sea Hunting Flotilla
The introduction of convoy had, as noted previously, caused the U-boats to seek targets closer inshore, after the convoys had dispersed, and particularly in the Irish Sea. To counter this new

tactic, Captain Gordon Campbell VC suggested the formation of a new 'hunting patrol' to cover the Irish Sea area specifically. The sterility of such tactics had surely by now been proven but aggressive patrolling appealed to Bayly's nature and he badgered the Admiralty for resources.

Under Jellicoe and Jackson the Navy had been accused in many quarters of taking an overly defensive stance. Now, the new team at the top favoured more aggressive approaches. Hunting patrols were seen as suitably offensive and Bayly's request was granted. Consequently, at the beginning of 1918, he was given the scout cruiser *Patrol*, launched in 1904 and badly damaged in 1914 when attempting to defend Hartlepool from bombardment by German battlecruisers, with Campbell himself as its captain. The cruiser, together with eleven old destroyers, an armed yacht, up to twenty or so motor launches, four airships, a squadron of aeroplanes and no less than eighteen PC-boats (P-boats completed as Q-ships) based at Pembroke formed the new force, designated the Irish Sea Hunting Flotilla. The destroyers were based at Kingstown (HMS *Earnest*, *Kestrel*, *Mallard*, *Seal* and *Zephyr*) and Holyhead (HMS *Albacore*, *Griffon*, *Lively*, *Orwell*, *Sprightly* and *Stag*) with *Patrol* at Queenstown. Under Campbell's energetic leadership, the Hunting Flotilla set about the task with vigour. Small Irish Sea convoys were also instituted to protect the ships sailing for ports after the main convoy had broken up.

The force continued in various guises until the end of the war; they did not sink any U-boats, although it is both possible and indeed likely that they deterred some from their intended destruction. Combing the seas looking for submarines was the apotheosis of searching for a needle in a haystack.

ss *Tuscania*

Since America's entry into the war, the safe conveying of US troops to Europe had been a major priority for Bayly and for the RN and USN forces under his command. Not a single inbound troopship or soldier had been lost in 1917. Long-range cruiser escorts brought the convoys across the Atlantic and when in range they were met by destroyers to reinforce the anti-U-boat-protection as they neared their destination.

ss *Tuscania* was a modern Anchor Lines passenger vessel, converted to trooping duties. Capable of 16 knots, of 14,348 tons and able to carry over 2,000 passengers, her 384 crew had embarked 2,235 US army personnel at Hoboken, New Jersey. These comprised companies D, E and F of the 6th Battalion, 20th US Engineers, some men from the 32nd Division and the 100th and 103rd Aero Squadrons.

On 24 January 1918 she sailed to Halifax, Nova Scotia, to join Convoy HX 20 heading for Liverpool. There were fourteen vessels in the convoy, including the White Star liners *Baltic* and *Ceramic*, also troop carrying, escorted by the armoured cruiser HMS *Cochrane*. The convoy formed five columns with the cruiser in the van and the collier USS *Kanawha* bringing up the rear.

Progress was slow, an average speed of only 12 knots, for a series of minor engine faults plagued *Tuscania*'s captain, Peter Alexander McLean, forcing him (and hence the convoy) to operate at reduced speed for much of the crossing. Nonetheless, after nine days at sea they were met by the close escort, comprising eight of Bayly's Londonderry-based destroyers from the 2nd Destroyer Flotilla. The following day, Tuesday, 5 February, they sighted Rathlin Island on the starboard bow and the Isle of Islay in the distance. They were almost there.

The convoy headed for the North Channel, with the escorts positioned all round it; *Beagle*, *Savage* and *Grasshopper to* starboard; *Badger*, *Pigeon* and *Mosquito* to port with *Harpy* (Commander Ernest Cardale, SNO destroyer escort) and *Minos* astern of *Cochrane* in the van. The weather was bad and getting worse, a force ten gale from the south west making sailing conditions difficult and visibility poor in the squally accompanying showers.

Unbeknown to anyone in the big ships, the convoy had been stalked since dawn by a U-boat, *U-77* under the command of Korvettenkapitän Wilhelm Meyer. All day he had looked for a firing position against the liners and at 1840hrs, with the light fading, Meyer decided that he had to take a shot. At 1,200yds range he fired two torpedoes. One missed; one didn't.

The torpedo hit *Tuscania* on the starboard side between the engine room and the stokehold. The first men to die were the thirty-nine stokers engaged in shovelling coal there; not a man survived. Others on board the ship felt it shudder and heard a dull thud accompanied by the sound of breaking glass. All the lights went out. The engine room compartments quickly filled with water and escaping steam while the force of the explosion threw a spout of debris and water high into the air, reaching as far as the lifeboats hanging in their davits. Several were damaged so badly as to render them useless.

It was obvious that *Tuscania* was mortally wounded. Captain McLean fired off his distress rockets and ordered 'abandon ship'. But the vessel had taken a 10° list to starboard and that made launching the boats difficult; on the port side it made it nigh on impossible. As they filled up with troops and were lowered, the waves battered them against the bilge of the liner. Oars were broken attempting to absorb the shock of the impact. Cracked and leaking, some drifted away empty; one lifeboat was accidentally dropped from its davits and fell on top of another, crushing its occupants.

The destroyers *Mosquito* and *Pigeon* were ordered to go to the stricken liner's aid; on the way, *Mosquito*'s Lieutenant Thomas Balfour Fellowes stopped to rescue some men clinging to an upturned boat. Meyer fired a torpedo at the destroyer but missed. Fellowes took his ship on a depth-charge run, before returning to the *Tuscania*, laying alongside so men could leap on board. But in heavy seas, some survivors in the water were caught in the wash of *Mosquito*'s propeller, as she tried to manoeuvre such that men could jump on to her decks; other men fell between the vessels and were crushed.

Grasshopper, commanded by Lieutenant John Smith, lay off the *Tuscania*'s starboard bow picking up survivors who had decided to swim for it but was then ordered away to provide anti-U-boat protection. The modern 'M'-class destroyer *Pigeon*, commanded by Lieutenant Commander Christopher John Francis Eddis, inched under the liner's starboard bow and using heaving lines was able to take 800 soldiers on board. The little ship was nearly sunk by the extra weight of the men rescued. Eddis lowered his ship's launch with Petty Officer John Jones in command of it to get men out of the water but then had to leave as he had received a submarine warning. Jones took charge of pulling together the eleven lifeboats still afloat until they could be collected, hours later, by the trawler *Elf King*, 375 men in total.

The liner took four hours to sink. During that time, *Grasshopper* had rescued 500 survivors, *Pigeon* over 800, *Mosquito* 200 and Petty Officer Jones 375. But there were still men struggling for life in the cold, cold seas; and many more that reached land did not survive the experience. Second Class Machinist's Mate Arthur Siplon was lucky. He had found himself in a lifeboat with forty other survivors when a mountainous wave hit and overturned it. Re-emerging from the waves, Siplon saw the upturned boat and dragged himself on top where he was joined by his friend Wilbur Clark. Their boat drifted towards the shore and just when it seemed they would be safe, another wave threw them against a rock; Siplon landed on his back, but Clark struck the rock with his head and then sank from sight without another sound. It was the same all along the coast of Islay; bodies were washed ashore and dashed against the rocky coast. Private William Smith was in lifeboat No 11 when it struck the coast, throwing its thirty occupants into the sea. 'I was carried over the rocks by a great wave', he later recounted, 'and wandered for six hours up and down the cliff. I have just seen the names of all the other occupants of the boat amongst the dead.'[4]

American newspapers predictably covered the story in detail. It was, after all, the story Secretary of the Navy Josephus Daniels had dreaded. The *Cornell Daily Sun* noted:

> In spite of the realization that the loss was remarkably small considering the number carried by the liner, the revised Admiralty report was received here with bitter disappointment. Press dispatches received here last night indicating that the dead, all told, might not exceed 100 had led to the hope that possibly not more than five per cent of the soldiers had perished. A cablegram received by the Navy Department during the day announced that 76 officers and 1,274 enlisted men of the army had been landed at Buncranna [*sic*], Ireland, that 91 soldiers are in hospitals in Londonderry, while 570 officers and men are at Islay. This is the total of 2,011 but does not include the scattering of survivors reported in official dispatches as having landed at ports in Scotland.[5]

When the final count was taken, the US army had lost 166 men; forty-four of the ship's crew were also killed. President Wilson sent a wreath. The unblemished record of transport success was finally broken.

Not all the American survivors were satisfied with the condition of their transportation or grateful to their rescuers. At the subsequent court of enquiry some alleged that there had been a lack of boat drills at mess times, an absence of instruction regarding the use of lifebelts and life preservers, and no night-time drills. Additionally it was suggested that the ropes of the davits were in poor condition and several of these had been painted over, making launching almost impossible. The physical condition of the lifeboats themselves was also criticised as was the attitude adopted by the officers and ship's crew towards the soldiery. True or false, no action was taken. The men lost on the *Tuscania* were victims of the exigencies of war. And that was all.

The loss of *Cullist*

Since the action of 17 November 1917 with an unknown U-boat, the Q-ship *Cullist* had continued to operate around the Western Approaches, still under the command of Lieutenant Commander Salisbury Hamilton Simpson. Q-ship work was inherently dangerous; to invite attack, to play possum in the hope of getting a chance to sink an opponent, who was more and more conscious of the risks posed by Q-ships, took a certain cold-blooded bravery. It also demanded a lot of luck.

In February 1918 Bayly ordered *Cullist* to the Irish Sea; on the 11th she was patrolling off the east coast of Ireland in Dundalk Bay, twenty-five miles east of Drogheda, when her luck ran out. She was torpedoed without warning by *U-97* and sank within minutes, never having the opportunity to use her concealed weapons.

Hans von Mohl, the U-boat commander, ordered his vessel to surface and the crew tried to locate Lieutenant Commander Simpson. Although he was injured and in the water, the submarine's crew could not locate him and thought he had been killed in action. Von Mohl took a number of sailors on board as prisoners of war, both as proof of his victory and for intelligence purposes, and left the survivors to their fate. Simpson was in fact alive, although with a badly dislocated shoulder. He, and the remaining sailors in the water (there had been no time to launch boats and no thought even of a 'panic party'), were later picked up by the trawler *James Green*. This rescue nearly resulted in disaster for the trawler found them at night and in the dark somehow mistook their raft for a U-boat. She prepared to open fire but Simpson and his men shouted out the song 'Tipperary' at the top of their voices and thus convinced the trawler skipper of their *bona fides*.

Of a crew of seventy, forty-three were lost. Simpson himself was considered so injured as to be fit for shore duty only and became an

Auxiliary Patrol officer at Plymouth. But in reality he spent much of that time convalescing, having eighty-two days of full-pay sick leave on the books of *Victory*, which had to be extended another month, before he was finally surveyed as fit 'for shore duty only, preferably in neighbourhood of London to enable him to continue the necessary treatment'.[6]

The list of men lost in the sinking makes interesting reading, for it displays in miniature the full Hegelian nature of the war at this point. The Prussian philosopher of Absolute Idealism, Georg Hegel, posited that the state had the right to demand that its citizens lay down their lives for its survival. The roll of honour for *Cullist* reflects the evidence that the British state was calling fully on its citizens worldwide and from all backgrounds.

The death toll was five officers, twenty-seven ratings, two Royal Marine Light Infantry and nine MMRs. Two of the dead were from Australasia. Engineer Sub Lieutenant Lewis Vincent Gully had been born in Nelson on New Zealand's South Island. Aged 28 he died with the ship in her engine room having travelled halfway round the world to join the fight. Signalman Frederick Thomas Whitchurch similarly journeyed from Australia and died aged 24.

There were RNR and RNVR men. Engineer Lieutenant Neil S MacKinnon RNR was one such and had already been decorated with the DSC and Mentioned in Despatches for services in *Cullist*'s previous actions against enemy submarines. He went down with the ship. Paymaster Robert Muir Hindley was another RNR reservist from Lime Grove, Newark, Notts.

Surgeon Probationer David John Whitton RNVR from Carlyle Road, Kirkcaldy, had been a medical student in training at the Royal Infirmary of Edinburgh when the war came. He left his studies and volunteered; and died.

Leading Seaman Ernest Robilliard, DSM, aged 28, had parents living in Guernsey. Able Seaman Raymond Victor John Jelfs was Worcestershire-bred. He was born in Bretforton and his parents received the news of his death at their new home in Redditch. Petty Officer Alfred Reginald Sheather, at 26 young for his rank, came from Hammersmith. William Ernest Lycett came from Wolverhampton; he died just 18 years old.

Cook's Mate Thomas Franklin Patten was born in Drayton, Somerset, the son of a carter. He had enlisted in 1916 for a twelve-year term and joined *Cullist* on 12 May 1917. He died aged 21.

Steward 3rd class Thomas Thompson Turner was killed aged just 18. One may wonder why a Q-ship needed officers' stewards, third class or otherwise? Ernest Woodall from Nether Poppleton, York, was a, Painter 1st Class, necessary for the constant changes of disguise. He was 24 when *Cullist* went down and left a wife Maud Marion.

And so the list went on. Men called from all backgrounds and regions and sacrificed to Moloch; and success still rare.

Manley and *Motagua*

Convoy escort continued to be a pressing need and a dangerous duty. On 4 March 1918 Convoy HD 26, had sailed from Dakar, West Africa, for British shores. As it neared its destination, the convoy consisted of ten cargo vessels escorted by the AMC HMS *Motagua*, formerly SS *Emil L. Boas*, built 1912 for Elders and Fyffes, of 5,977grt, and 426ft long, armed with six 6in guns. Bayly sent a strong escort to guide the precious cargo ships through the Western Approaches. On 19 March a mixed convoy escort of USN destroyers and British sloops approached the convoy, comprising USS *Beale*, USS *Patterson*, USS *Terry*, USS *Manley*, HMS *Tamarisk* and HMS *Bluebell*.

Manley carried orders for the captain of the *Motagua* (Captain Lawrence Leopold Dundas RN) and just before 0805hrs came close to her port bow with the intention of throwing a heaving line to pass despatches. Captain Dundas thought that the destroyer was too close and waved her off but as she turned to starboard her stern connected with the stern of the *Motagua*. The collision dislodged one of *Manley*'s depth charges, mounted in her Thornycroft thrower and it exploded. There followed a cataclysmic series of explosions; fragments from the blast pierced two 50-gallon drums of gasoline together with two tanks containing 100 gallons of alcohol on skid frames over the engine room hatch. The leaking fluids caught fire as they ran along the deck and then enveloped and destroyed the motor sailing vessel, the dory and punt and some wood stores, before setting fire to the after crew compartment. Her other depth charges cooked off in the heat and she was on fire from her bridge aft, with her stern blown off.

Motagua suffered collateral damage. Her poop and stern were wrecked with extensive damage caused to the whole upperworks, including the wireless cabin and aerial. She was, however, steerable. Captain Dundas set his men to collecting the wounded, clearing away debris and recovering the dead. *Bluebell* came alongside her to act as escort and later *Polyanthus* joined up too. At noon, Dundas was able to muster his men and discovered that Sub Lieutenant Rowland RNVR and seven men were missing and two officers (Lieutenant C S Wood RNR and Gunner Mr W J Lee RN) plus eighteen men were dead, one of whom was unidentifiable. There were also thirty-three wounded. He buried the dead at 1600hrs.

Manley was in a bad way, burning fiercely. Despite the fires, *Tamarisk* (still commanded by the saviour of the *Cassin*, Ronald Neil Stuart) edged up to the shattered destroyer and unsuccessfully tried to put a towline on board. She remained adrift until British-hired rescue tugs *Blazer* and *Cartmel* took her in tow after daylight on 20 March. *Manley* reached Queenstown at dusk the following day with more than 70ft of her hull awash or completely under water. She carried thirty-four dead sailors, including her executive officer, 29-year-old Lieutenant Commander Richard M Elliot Jr.

Bayly convened a court of enquiry at Queenstown; it took little time to decide that Commander Robert Lawrence Berry USN, captain of the *Manley*, should face a court martial on the charge of 'Culpable Inefficiency in the Performance of Duty'. The court, comprised as was Bayly's habit, of mixed USN and RN officers and convened on board USS *Melville* on 18 April. Berry was found guilty as charged. But, recognising the exigencies of wartime, five members of the court recommended clemency on the grounds that collisions of the nature of the one between the *Motagua* and *Manley* were commonplace by this time. It was the accident of the exploding depth charges that turned a small collision into a tragedy. The court accepted this view and Commander Berry was released from arrest and returned to duty. He took his damaged ship to Liverpool for repair.

A joint effort

Inspiration and success were sorely needed in April 1918. The Germans had opened a massive offensive on the Western Front, the Spring Offensive or *Kaiserschlacht*, Ludendorff and Hindenburg's final throw of the dice in search of a decisive victory. British forces were sorely pressed, and on the 11th Field Marshal Haig had issued his famous 'special order of the day' during the Battle of Messines: 'There is no other course open to us but to fight it out. Every position must be held to the last man: there must be no retirement. With our backs to the wall and believing in the justice of our cause each one of us must fight on to the end. The safety of our homes and the freedom of mankind alike depend upon the conduct of each one of us at this critical moment.' The war seemed on a knife edge.

At sea, Bayly's command was able to provide a nugget of success to stiffen the nation's resolve. *U-104* was a modern submarine, built by A G Weser in Bremen and commissioned in August 1917. By late April 1918 she was on her fourth patrol since launch, all of them under her commander, Kapitänleutnant Kurt Bernis. In *U-104*, Bernis had sunk seven ships; and on the 22nd he added an eighth. ss *Fern* was a small coastal steamer of 444grt, built in 1900 and belonging to the Laird Line of Ayr. She was sailing to Heysham, Lancashire from Dublin and was about five miles east of the Kish light vessel, off the coast of County Dublin, when she was torpedoed by *U-104* without warning. She sank with the loss of thirteen men.

Revenge was not long in coming, however. The following day, *U-104* was sighted in the Irish Sea by the destroyer uss *Cushing*, which immediately sounded General Quarters and turned to attack. Bernis dived for safety but *Cushing* dropped no less than fifteen depth charges over the spot that the submarine had disappeared and noted oil and debris rise to the surface. The U-boat was badly damaged and Bernis decided to make for home, sailing south to go back to his base via the Dover Strait.

Just like a Q-ship captain, a U-boat commander needed luck. Bernis's ran out at 0140hrs on Thursday 25 April. His damaged vessel was sailing at night and on the surface when it was spotted in the St George's Channel by the sloop *Jessamine*. She had served at Queenstown since being built in 1915, initially under Lieutenant Commander Salisbury Simpson. From March 1917, *Jessamine*'s captain had been Lieutenant Commander Sidney Arthur Geary-Hill. Now he had the chance to record his first U-boat 'kill'. *U-104*, damaged though she was, dived but at 0150hrs Geary-Hill attacked with depth charges, dropping six over the stricken submarine. A night attack was difficult and dangerous but was nonetheless fatal. The U-boat took all but one of her forty-two man crew to the sea bed with her; one survivor was picked up from the sea by *Jessamine* and subsequently transferred to uss *Rowan* and captivity. Geary-Hill received the DSO for his success 'for action with enemy submarines' (gazetted 11 June 1918) but the victory was really a joint one; the US and Royal Navies in partnership had done for *U-104*.

There was a strange sequel to the loss of the *Fern*. It emerged that ten of those who died with her were Irish workmen. This occasioned a question in the House of Commons on 28 October from the Irish Parliamentary Party MP for Dublin Harbour, Alfred 'Alfie' Byrne. He enquired of the Minister for Labour, George Roberts, concerning the status of the dead men's dependents. As *Hansard* recorded it:

> Mr. Byrne asked the Minister of Labour what Department or authority are responsible for the payment of compensation to the dependants of the ten Irish workmen who lost their lives owing to the sinking of the Dublin steamer *Fern* by enemy action on 23rd April [Byrne was incorrect about the date]; if he is aware that the Dublin Labour Exchange acted as agents and engaged these men for the British Dyes Company, Huddersfield, and provided them with travelling vouchers to proceed to Huddersfield on steamship *Fern*; and whether the Government, the shipping company, or the British Dyes Company will look after the dependants of these men, some of whom are now in receipt of relief from the Poor Law authorities?

Robert's gave a typical politician's reply.

> These workmen received the usual facilities offered by the Employment Exchanges in the way of bringing before them the offer of engagement by the British Dyes Company, and of advancing their rail and steamship fares. This does not render the Department liable to pay compensation in respect of the loss of life which unfortunately occurred *en route*. I am not in a position to advise as to the liabilities of the British Dyes Company or the shipping company.

Byrne persisted. 'Will the right hon. Gentleman answer the last part of the question, whether the Government will compensate dependants of the workmen who lost their lives through enemy action?' But he drew a stonewall reply. 'The hon. Member asked me whether I could say what Department or authority was responsible for the payment of compensation. I admit my inability to give that information.'[7] In other words, the government could admit no liability for any loss of life – for that would certainly open the floodgates to claims from far and wide.

The anti-conscription unrest

Ireland continued to seethe with unrest. On the second anniversary of the Easter Rising, memorial masses were held in Cork and the Royal Irish Constabulary thought it necessary for public safety to ban a planned nationalist protest demonstration in the city. And now a new reason for Republican fervour was simmering as the massive losses on the Western Front reopened the debate around Irish conscription.

Conscription – compulsory as opposed to voluntary military service – had been introduced in England, Scotland and Wales in a series of stages between March and May 1916.[*] But Ireland had always been omitted from the enabling legislation for fear of igniting Republican sentiment. Irish recruitment and (later) conscription had been a source of contention in Ireland since the beginning of the war. And not just in the south. After a bright start, particularly in the North of Ireland, rates of recruitment had fallen off. When Asquith visited Ireland after the Easter Rising the Lord Mayor of Belfast told him that the general feeling amongst Unionists was that 'we have sent the best of our manhood to the front; the Catholics of the south and west have contributed substantially less. If we now allow what remains of our available men to recruit we shall be left defenceless against a possible – even probable – invasion of our province. And our wives, our children, our homes, our religion will be at the mercy of our hereditary foes.'[8] In the South, Republicans saw no reason to fight and die for a country they saw themselves as at war with. And this untapped source of manpower caused resentment in the other home nations and among the politicians responsible for running the war effort. Minister without Portfolio Lord Lansdowne (Henry Charles Keith Petty-Fitzmaurice, 5th Marquess of Lansdowne), writing to the Cabinet in November 1916, noted that 'the inexhaustible supply of men is, they tell us, now very restricted and the

---

[*] Prime Minster Asquith had piloted the bill through Parliament in January 1916; most Irish Nationalist and a few dozen Liberal and Labour MPs voted against it.

number available can only be added to by a further reduction in industry. In the meantime Ireland still declines to add to the available supply the 150,000 men who would be obtainable from that country ...'[9]

But in 1918, with conscription now fully in place, and therefore a limited pool of future manpower available to replace the losses being incurred in the slaughter in the trenches of France, politicians and military men once more began to question the Irish exemption and to press for the tapping of this freely-available source of recruits. Bayly was one of these, writing to Jellicoe in December 1917 that he believed that Irish conscription was both necessary and just and may be beneficial to peace in Ireland itself.[10]

As a result Prime Minister Lloyd George decided to introduce compulsory military service in Ireland and the necessary legislation was passed in the House of Commons in April. In response a number of prominent nationalists, including de Valera (who had been released from prison in June 1917) formed the Irish Anti-Conscription Committee, which first met on 18 April. Simultaneously the Catholic bishops in Ireland came out against the new law. Both church and laity then developed a 'pledge' which was to be taken at every church door on the 21st and which read 'Denying the right of the British government to enforce compulsory service in this country, we pledge ourselves solemnly to one another to resist conscription by the most effective means at our disposal'. The rhetoric was fierce. One Father Murphy 'characterised Lloyd George's government as the successors to those "who in days gone by, by every means that human malice could devise, tried to extirpate the Irish race"'.[11]

A General Strike in Ireland followed on the 23rd and a series of rallies in April and May furthered the unrest. On 18 May Field Marshal Lord French (now Lord Lieutenant of Ireland), claiming evidence of a treasonable plot between Sinn Fein and the Germans, ordered the arrest of seventy-three Sinn Fein leaders, including de Valera, the other members of the Anti-Conscription Committee and Countess Markievicz. They were then sent to England and imprisonment from Kingstown by means of Bayly's vessels.

Commander Francis Tower was stationed at Kingstown at the time, in charge of the fourteen motor launches based there, and later wrote about what he had seen and thought.

One day orders came [from Bayly] with regard to putting some Sinn Fein rascals on board a vessel in conjunction with the soldiers and constabulary and a very successful deportation was carried out. Batches of the ruffians were brought to our base at Kingstown in military lorries, having been quietly taken at various places during the evening, arriving from late at night all through the dark hours. The warrant was read and the men put on board a sloop which had come in and was berthed alongside our quay.

A good haul it was including de Valera, the mad Countess Markievicz* and most of the principal leaders. A more feeble lot of malefactors I never expect to see. How this little lot could ever have come to be leaders of men, as they (Valera, etc) are, beats me completely after seeing them and the feeble exhibition they made of themselves.[12]

Tower had married into the Irish peerage, as had his daughter, so his political sympathies may not have lain with the Nationalists.

In fact the arrests inflamed things even more. And Lloyd George had made matters worse by linking the conscription legislation to a new Home Rule Bill, which had the effect of alienating both Nationalists and Unionists in Ireland. In the end the act was never implemented, the Cabinet coming to the view that it was more trouble than it was worth, and Ireland remained conscription free for the duration of the war.

The North Channel (again)

But at sea there was some good news. Although losses of Allied and neutral shipping to U-boats continued at high levels (January 306,658grt, February 318,957grt, March 342,597grt, April 278,719grt, May 295,520grt, June 255,587grt), these were less than half those of April, May and June in 1917. Convoy and escort had made a difference and just maybe Bayly's aggressive patrolling had too.

Which is not to say that men were not dying daily in the waters around Ireland. HMS *Calgarian* was an Allan Line passenger ship, intended for the Liverpool to Canada run, but taken up by the Royal Navy as an AMC in 1914. On 1 March she was escorting Convoy

---

* De Valera was sent to Lincoln gaol (from which he escaped in February 1919), and Markievicz to Holloway.

OB50, of thirty merchantmen, off the north coast of Ireland. In addition to her convoy duties, she was carrying a number of naval ratings who were being transferred to other stations or were going on leave. The convoy was outbound from the Clyde, heading into the Atlantic, and escorted, apart from *Calgarian*, by motor launches and airships to provide anti-submarine protection together with the sloops *Rosemary* and *Gladiolus* and the Q-ship sloop *Anchusa*. *Poppy* too had been sent to join the escort.

The relative success that convoy had in the Western Approaches caused the German naval command to decide upon a new and intensive submarine campaign directed against Allied shipping using the North Channel between Ireland and Scotland. *Calgarian* was to become the first victim of this concentration of effort.

As *Poppy* joined up with the convoy, *Calgarian* suddenly staggered and a loud explosion was heard. She had been torpedoed by *U-19*, under Johannes Spiess. The initial hit did not sink the liner and Captain R A Newton and his crew managed to contain the damage. *Rosemary* was despatched to take the liner in tow and armed trawlers came alongside to assist and protect from further attack. From *Poppy*, it seemed to Goldrich that trying to tow the 12,515grt vessel was 'an utterly lunatic procedure'. He was unimpressed to the point of fury. 'I do hope they won't lose her farting around. It is cruel the way well-meaning incompetents and hare brained lunatics are allowed to mess around with valuable, nay vital, ships and cargoes,' he confided to his diary.[13] She had taken a list which the wind made worse and could not steam. The towing hawser broke and Newton ordered abandon ship. Meanwhile, *Anchusa* was detailed to assist but as she reached the area she saw a periscope and attacked with depth charges.

Spiess, however, was undeterred. He fired a second and third torpedo, the blasts from which had the collateral effect of fatally damaging the armed trawler *Thomas Collard*, which was alongside the AMC assisting with evacuation. It stove in the side and bottom plates of the trawler, causing flooding which sank the vessel. Her depth charges had not been set to safe and, according to Goldrich, as she went down they went off, causing further damage to *Caligarian*. A second trawler, *Lord Lister*, had also been impacted by the torpedo hit and she limped away in poor condition. At 1800hrs the liner sank. Thirty-two of her crew, all MMR and from the stokehold, trimmers and firemen, died with her as did two RNR engineer officers. Two men also died on *Lord Lister*. *U-19*'s persistence had been well rewarded.

Despite the concentration on this North Channel area by the Germans, not all such attacks went unpunished. On the 15th of the same month, RMS *Amazon* (10,037 tons) was sailing from Liverpool to Brazil with twenty-four passengers and without an escort. She had left Liverpool the previous day but was forced to sail at slow speed due to a thick fog. At 0930hrs she was zigzagging some fifty-one miles off the north coast of Ireland, when she was hit by a torpedo in hold No 4. She sank stern first in just fifteen minutes but her calls for assistance had brought the destroyer HMS *Moresby*, part of Bayly's 2nd Destroyer Flotilla at Londonderry and she was able to rescue all the passengers and crew.

Amazon's assassin, *U-110*, had surprisingly remained in the area and now the hunter became the hunted as *Moresby* and her sister-ship *Michael* attacked with depth charges, damaging the U-boat and forcing her to surface before sliding back under the waves for the final time. The destroyers rescued nine Germans from the water; the other thirty-two crewmen died, including her captain, Korvettenkapitän Carl Albrecht Kroll.

And in May the Clyde-based steamer *Green Island* accounted for *UB-119* in the same North Channel area without the need of any naval assistance, British or American. On the 5th she was steaming west-north-west between Rathlin Island and the Irish coast when she sighted a periscope breaking the surface about 20yds off and turned to ram. The aim was true and the U-boat was crushed under the steamer's forefoot and sunk, lost with all hands. It was the submarine's first patrol and also the first command mission of her captain, 26-year-old Oberleutnant zur See Walter Kolbe. Perhaps his inexperience cost thirty-two men their lives.

Eventually, the German focus on the North Channel area finally ended when the American minelayer *Baltimore** laid four lines of deep mines across the middle of the channel, making transit too risky.

Ausonia and a courageous master

If a merchant vessel was torpedoed in the Western Approaches close to the coast of Ireland or England, the crew could entertain some hope

---

* An ancient protected cruiser of 1888 vintage, recalled to service and converted to a minelayer in 1913–14. She was despatched to the Clyde, arriving in early March 1918 to assist with mining operations.

of rescue or of saving themselves by their own efforts. But to be sunk over 600 miles into the Atlantic was a problem of a different order of magnitude and dreams of survival were often exactly that – dreams.

ss *Ausonia*, 8,163grt, was a passenger liner operated by the Cunard Steamship Company Limited. On Thursday 30 May 1918 she was on passage from Montreal to Avonmouth with general cargo, no passengers and a crew of 130, including one female stewardess, Theresa Edgar. At 1759hrs she was torpedoed without warning by *U-62*, commanded by the seemingly unstoppable Ernst Hashagen, 620 miles west and south of the Fastnet. The crew took to the lifeboats, seven in total. Hashagen brought his U-boat in amongst them to try to find the master, Commander Robert Capper RD, RNR, but he had removed his coat and they could not identify him. When the U-boat crew saw the stewardess, who had left the vessel wearing a kimono and a pink hat, in a boat they shouted 'You have a woman with you, clear away', and with that headed off, leaving the seven boats adrift in the dark. Two of them, under the care of the first officer and the bosun respectively disappeared during the night and were never seen again. Commander Capper managed to keep the remaining five lifeboats together for five days until a north-westerly gale blew up in the afternoon of Wednesday 5 June and they became separated, leaving Capper, Theresa Edgar, twenty men and a youth of 18, butcher's boy Matthew Robinson, who had suffered two broken legs when the torpedo had gone off under him, together in one lifeboat.

When Bayly heard of the sinking he had sent the sloops *Camellia* and *Zinnia,* together with HMS *Safeguard,* a coastguard cruiser, to look for survivors. It was a little like searching for a needle in a haystack, but they sailed down the likely track that survivors might have taken and prayed. Amazingly, on Saturday 8 June, *Zinnia* found Capper's boat just over twelve miles south east of Bull Light. 'The captain's boat was badly strained and leaking', Lieutenant Commander Wilson reported to Bayly, 'but it was obvious that she had been well fitted out and provisioned.'[14] He went on to heap praise on Capper; 'the officers and men of the boat spoke with great admiration of the skill and courage shown by their captain , , , for it was clear that it was only due to his leadership that five boats containing 108 people safely completed their voyage of nearly 600 miles. Captain Capper had had no sleep whatsoever for ten days but despite this he was in full possession of his faculties.'[15] The men (and woman) in the lifeboat were, however, demonstrably in a bad way, for Wilson continued 'I thought it unadvisable to tax the mental powers of the survivors more than was necessary to get an idea of the position of the missing boats'.[16] In fact *Safeguard* found three of them and *Camellia* one. Capper's outstanding stamina and authority had carried his men to safety. Young Robinson survived to be landed but died two days later, one of forty-four crewmen who lost their lives.

On 6 August Capper's efforts were recognised when he was gazetted with the Distinguished Service Cross. And Theresa Edgar, a resident of Oriel Road, Aintree, the young widow of a seafarer, went back to sea again on Cunard's liner *Orduna*, which was acting as a transatlantic troop transport.

The action of 31 May 1918

Even with a preponderance of forces, it was difficult to sink U-boats if there was no means of detecting them underwater. On 31 May, just off the south-west coast of Ireland, USS *Sterrett* (Lieutenant Commander Allan S Farquhar), a 742-ton *Paulding*-class destroyer launched in 1910, was detailed to escort the tanker *Ashrakhan* into Queenstown. As she neared the port, Farquhar sighted the periscope of a submarine. *Sterrett* immediately attacked with depth charges and oil and bubbles came to the surface, by which trail *Sterrett* was able to track the U-boat. She had no charges left, however, and called for help. Bayly sortied USS *Porter*, HMS *Jessamine* and three motor launches but *Porter* was short on fuel and had to give up the search. *Sterrett* continued to track the submarine until at 0435hrs the following day, the U-boat tired of the game, surfaced, and opened fire with its deck gun; *Sterrett* shaped to ram but before she could the U-boat dived once more.

Jessamine returned to the action and dropped two more depth charges with no apparent result. USS *Wilkes*, USS *Ericsson*, USS *Shaw*, and USS *Terry* now joined up and continued the search, but nothing further was seen. Six destroyers, a sloop and three motor launches had hunted one submarine; but no U-boat was reported missing that day. However, Farquhar received the Navy Cross, in part for this action, and he and his ship was given an official commendation from Bayly for their persistence.

The horror

Hospital ships were ships specially adapted to ferry the wounded back from the Western Front to a place of succour. Under the Hague Convention of 1907, they were supposed to be safe from attack by any combatant and allowed free passage. British hospital ships were designated 'HMHS' and, as under the Convention were painted white with yellow funnels, had a stripe of green round the sides and were illuminated with a row of green lights The Germans suspected Britain of using hospital ships under false pretences, something emphatically denied by the British government, and accused them of carrying arms and able-bodied soldiers. German commanders began to ignore the international dictats and, indeed, sixteen British and Empire such vessels were sunk during the war, fourteen of them being either torpedoed or mined by U-boats.

On 27 June 1918, the hospital ship *Llandovery Castle*, a former Union Castle liner, was on passage from Halifax, Nova Scotia, to Liverpool, where she would embark Canadian wounded soldiers for transportation home. She carried on board some 258 people, including ninety-four medical officers and nursing sisters of the Canadian Medical Staff. The fourteen nurses were under the charge of 33-year-old Matron Margaret Marjory (Pearl) Fraser, the daughter of Lieutenant Governor of Nova Scotia, Duncan Cameron Fraser.

It was 2130hrs and a fine but dark night. The ship was displaying the regulation Red Cross lights and was zigzagging at 14 knots, 116 miles west of the Fastnet rock. She was then hit by a torpedo fired by *U-86*, commanded by Oberleutnant Helmut Patzig. It blew a hole in the hospital ship's side, destroyed her Marconi radio apparatus together with several lifeboats and severed the bridge connection to the engine room, which meant that the ship continued to surge forward, going down by the head. Captain R A Sylvester, the master, ordered that the boats should not be lowered until the way came off the ship; but as she continued to go under, he decided to launch anyway. All those on board who had not been killed in the initial blast got off the vessel in boats or floats and the big liner sank ten minutes after she was hit.

Patzig now sought out Sylvester's boat; when he found it, he accused Captain Sylvester of having had eight American pilots on board. This was denied. Perhaps Patzig was now trying to exculpate himself for the sinking, for he now dragged a member of the medical staff, Major T Lyon, on board the submarine with such roughness as to break Lyon's foot. He was accused of being a Flight Officer and denied it. Captain Sylvester was then asked if he had wireless. He replied that he had been unable to use it. At this, both officers were allowed to return to the lifeboat.

Patzig's behaviour now seemed to be intent on one thing only – the obliteration of the evidence of his breach of convention and humanity. He first tried to ram Sylvester's lifeboat and was then observed to sail over to where the remaining boats were; whereupon the sound of deck gun firing and the immediate explosion of shells was heard and seen. Fourteen to twenty shells were reported. Patzig was murdering the survivors in the water. Sylvester's craft had now taken twenty-four souls on board. He rigged a sail and slowly the small vessel of shivering survivors began to edge towards the Irish coast. None of the nurses were with him.

Commander Francis Walter Despard Twigg was returning to Queenstown with the destroyer HMS *Lysander* when, twelve hours after the sinking, he chanced upon *Llandovery Castle*'s lifeboat and took on board its occupants. He radioed to Bayly that he was bringing them in and Bayly met them at Admiralty House. He and Violet gave them tea and food and listened to their story. Every fibre of Bayly's being was outraged. A hospital ship sunk, unarmed medical staff killed, women butchered in the seas on his watch; he was furious. He despatched *Snowdrop* and four US destroyers to the location of the sinking to search for more survivors. They found no-one. Bayly called off the search on 1 July.

But the AMC *Morea* found something. Returning from convoy duty, she suddenly found herself amongst a macabre tableau of dead bodies. Many years later an officer on her at the time, Kenneth Cummins, described the scene and his horror as he steamed through the nurses' floating corpses.

We were in the Bristol Channel, quite well out to sea, and suddenly we began going through corpses. The Germans had sunk a British hospital ship, the *Llandovery Castle*, and we were sailing through floating bodies. We were not allowed to stop – we just had to go straight through. It was quite horrific, and my reaction was to vomit over the edge. It was something we could never have imagined ... particularly the nurses: seeing these bodies of women and nurses, floating in the ocean, having been there some time. Huge aprons and skirts in billows, which looked almost like sails because they dried in the hot sun.

The sight stayed with Cummins for ever, to the point of being part of his obituary.[17]

War is terrible; but this seemed to so many people an atrocity too far. Reaction varied from a branch meeting of the National Sailors' and Firemen's Union held at Avonmouth, which passed a resolution demanding that hospital ships should now be armed, to a Canadian brigadier on the Western Front. Two of the nurses who died had come from the same town, Moose Jaw in Saskatchewan, as had he himself and many of his men. In the Brigade war diary, he wrote that he had given instructions to the Brigade that the battle cry should be '*Llandovery Castle*' and that that cry should be the last to ring in the ears of the Hun as the bayonet was driven home. A government fundraising advertisement carried a depiction of the tragedy with the slogan 'Victory Bonds will help stop this'.

Bayly finally abandoned his self-imposed ban on accepting honours for his service in mid-1918. On 3 June, in the King's Birthday Honours, he was appointed an Additional Member of the Second Class, or Knight Commander, in the Most Distinguished Order of Saint Michael and Saint George (KCMG). But, as will be seen, he still harboured his grudge regarding the loss of the *Formidable*.

The War from the Air

The first U-boat to be sunk by air attack was the UC II type minelayer *UC-66*. On 27 May 1917 she was attacked by a Royal Naval Air Service (RNAS) Curtiss H12 flying boat, No 8656, piloted by 35-year-old William Louis Anderson. *UC-66* was caught on the surface and attacked with bombs which inflicted terminal damage. All twenty-three men on board the U-boat perished.[*] Anderson himself described her sinking thus:

> 1018, sighted hostile submarine on starboard bow, altered course to attack. 1024, submarine opened fire with machine guns. 1025, dropped two 100-lb bombs, two direct hits observed forward of the conning tower. Submarine sank by the bows, stern coming out of the water at an angle of 60 degrees. Circled round position and observed bubbles and foam, considerable quantity of oil. 1028, set course south. Observed serious leak in starboard radiator. CPO Tadman climbed onto the wing root and plugged hole with handker-chief, remaining thus until return ... eight direct hits on seaplane.[1]

Anderson was based at Tresco in the Scilly Islands, part of Bayly's Western Approaches domain. The harbour near New Grimsby provided a suitable stretch of calm water where flying boats could take off and land. Here, Royal Naval Seaplane Base, Isles of Scilly, was established on a twenty-acre site on the waterfront. Hangars,

---

[*] Loss reassessed in 2013 by Dr Innes McCartney. *UC-66*'s previously recorded fate was that she was sunk on 12 June 1917 by depth charges from HMT *Sea King*, followed up by the explosion of her own mines.

offices, living accommodation and a wooden slipway were constructed and operations commenced in February 1917.

Initially there were six Curtiss H12 Large America seaplanes deployed, a type which had only recently entered RNAS service. American-built, these were twin-engine biplane flying boats with a wingspan of 92ft, and were modified for RNAS service by replacing their Curtiss engines with more powerful Rolls-Royce Eagles. They were relatively fast, well-armed (four Lewis guns, four 100lb bombs) and had an impressively long range due to an endurance of six hours. *UC-66* was their first 'kill'. Anderson received the DSC for his exploit* and after the war, perhaps moved by the destruction he had wrought, took holy orders, eventually becoming Bishop of Salisbury. Such attacks by flying boats were not without danger as Anderson's account makes clear. Just over a fortnight previously, on the 9th, three of his colleagues were killed when their flying boat attacked a U-boat, was fired on, crashed into the sea and exploded one mile south-west of the Scillies' Gush Island.

However, Bayly, in common with many of his peers and rather similar to his initial disdain for the submarine, did not really believe in air power. He had gone to sea in 1872, in the sail and steam frigate *Ariadne*. He did not serve in a recognisably modern ship until HMS *Colossus* in 1886. In 1903, when Orville Wright made the first aircraft flight with a petrol engine at Kitty Hawk Bay, Luigi was captain of the cruiser *Talbot* (launched in 1895) in the Far East. By the time that Commander Samson, flying a Short biplane, became the first man to take off from a moving ship by launching from HMS *Hibernia* while she steamed at 10.5 knots at the May 1912 Royal Fleet Review in front of King George V, Bayly was an admiral. He was not seized with enthusiasm for air power which he saw as just another fad, nothing to do with sea and wind and tide, perhaps suitable for scouting for the army, but not for the battle in the Western Approaches. As one historian of the air has written 'the Admiral commanding at Queenstown, Sir Lewis Bayly, had ... demonstrated a lack of interest in naval aviation'.[2] Indeed, when Bayly had first taken command at Queenstown, HMS *Empress* had joined his forces, a seaplane carrier converted from a cross-Channel packet ship. But air patrols in the south-western approaches were

---

* CPO Tadman was awarded the Conspicuous Gallantry Medal.

considered ineffective and in January 1916 she was sent to the Eastern Mediterranean.[*]

This was to ignore one of the key benefits that airpower brought. At the time the crow's nest on a battleship, perhaps 75ft above the sea, might provide visibility out to ten nautical miles in clear weather. From a P-boat the equivalent range might be five miles. But from an aircraft at 3,000ft the range of vision was some sixty miles. And that would make sub-hunting much easier all round.

It was perhaps as a consequence of Bayly's obduracy that, in September 1917, the Admiralty proposed to the Admiral Mayo mission[**] that the US Naval Air Service take over the existing seaplane bases in Ireland and run them themselves, including equipment, men and command, all under Bayly's oversight. The US Navy laid ambitious plans for 1,700 aircraft and 600 kite balloons but the eventual levels were more reasonable. In Ireland, the USN developed four flying boat bases, located at Queenstown (actually Aghada), Wexford, Lough Foyle and Whiddy Island. Additionally there was a kite balloon station at Berehaven. All of these sites came under the charge of Commander F R McCreary, located at Queenstown with Bayly's staff.

The USN force was established in February 1918 and all bases were completed by September 1918. The largest site, and headquarters for Ireland, was in Aghada, on the eastern side of Cork Harbour, on a site chosen and purchased by the Admiralty under DORA. From here, patrols covered areas from Cape Clear in the west, to the convoy channels to the east on the routes to France in the St Georges Channel. Aghada also served as the assembly premises for planes, and as a training station for pilots on the Ireland Station.

The seaplane base at Wexford was established under Lieutenant Commander Victor D Herbster, who reported on station on 28 March. Regular small drafts of USN men arrived from Queenstown, building to 20 officers and 406 men by October. The location of the

---

[*] Bayly's views were shared across the Atlantic too. Admiral Benson USN, Chief of Naval Operations stated that he could not 'conceive of any use the fleet will ever have for aviation' (Underwood, *The Wings of Democracy*, pp 11ff).

[**] Admiral Henry T Mayo was the CinC of the US Atlantic Fleet. He was sent by President Wilson to co-ordinate the American naval response with the Allied navy commanders. On his return he reported directly to the President and the Secretary of the Navy. The mission was not entirely altruistic, for the Americans were concerned that if Britain fell, as some believed developments at sea suggested it might, the US Navy would have to face the German High Seas Fleet on its own. It was not considered up to that task at the time.

station was strategically crucial; hence the focus on establishing it, for it lay directly at the southern entrance of the Irish Sea, within twelve miles of Tuskar Light. Tuskar Rock was one of the most important navigational marks in Irish waters but it had become a graveyard for merchant shipping, with many vessels sunk within view of the lighthouse.

Civilian contract labour was used to construct the road network, concrete hangar foundations, the aprons and slipway, the drainage systems, reservoir and reserve water tanks. They were also erecting the first hangars. Herein lay a problem for, perhaps unsurprisingly given the general unrest in Ireland by now, a strike was called and the delay thus caused meant postponements to the operational plans, a situation no doubt welcomed by U-boat commanders. Eventually four Curtiss H-16s arrived from Queenstown on 18 September. The next day, aircraft went out on their first patrols, and from then sortied every day, weather conditions permitting. By the war's end, eighteen H-16s were based at Wexford.

The seaplanes were soon in action. On 11 October 1918, the day after RMS *Leinster* was sunk (see Chapter 22) one of the USN planes sighted and bombed an enemy submarine in the area. This submarine showed signs of damage, and had trouble submerging. On 13 October, another submarine was bombed. On 16 October, a plane on patrol from Queenstown and heading for Wexford, manoeuvred for thirty minutes over a periscope sighting; it attacked but the first bomb dropped failed to explode, although the second was seen to explode very close to the periscope. That same day, a Wexford aircraft, crewed by Lieutenants John F McNamara and George Shaw with Queenstown-based Ensign James Roy Biggs, dropped bombs on a U-boat which disappeared under water leaving debris and oil. A reluctant Admiralty assessed it as only damaged not sunk; and they were correct. Operations at the base ceased after only eight weeks, as the Armistice took effect, but the Curtiss planes clocked up 312 patrol hours in ninety-eight flights in that time.

At Whiddy Island, at the head of Bantry Bay, work commenced on a flying boat base in December 1917 and the first personnel arrived in the following March. Under Commander J C Townshend, flying operations eventually began on 25 September 1918 when the first two Curtiss H-16s arrived. One crashed on 22 October while returning from a patrol, injuring four crewmen and killing one, Radio Operator Walford A Anderson. The remaining plane was supplemented by two sent from Queenstown and another two arrived just as the war ended, when there were five aircraft and 400 USN enlisted men at the base.

In the limited time they were operational, the US Naval Air Service had no success against U-boats. But this is to overlook the deterrent value of eyes in the sky. Kite balloons could provide (in good weather) visibility for tens of miles out to sea. Seaplanes could direct warships to a sighted submarine or fly over it to keep it below the surface where its slow speed and extremely limited visibility made it difficult for the U-boat to attack shipping. The German High Command became very wary of these air patrols and tried to route their flotillas round them wherever possible, which hampered operations by reducing the time that U-boats could spend in the most fertile waters for sinking merchant ships.

The other aspect of the war from the air was the use of airships, both rigid and non-rigid. For convoy escort work and for long endurance their low speed mattered little, and the RNAS operated airships on anti-submarine duty and convoy escort throughout the war (indeed it was their proud boast that no convoy had ever lost a ship to a U-boat whilst escorted by an airship). Jellicoe himself wrote that 'for actual escort work, airships were superior to heavier than air machines owing to their greater radius of action'.[3] There were RNAS airship bases covering the Irish Sea at Luce Bay in Scotland, Angelsey and Pembroke in Wales, and Mullion in Cornwall. However, these bases were too far from the Western Approaches to provide long-distance patrols. In Ireland itself there was only a mooring station in Malahide, County Dublin, offering basic tethering and maintenance facilities. In 1918 the decision was therefore made to build a major airship base near Cork, at Killeagh, and work progressed throughout the year. When the conflict ended, the station was still not complete (and in fact never became operational).

At some point, Bayly became a convert to airpower. He noted in his autobiography that 'I requested I might gain control of the air force on the west coast of England in order to obtain complete unity of command in the Irish Sea. This was granted, though I heard it caused some tribulation in certain circles.'[4] And in his final report to the Admiralty at the end of the war he noted that the USN seaplanes and kite balloons 'proved to be a valuable asset to the station'.[5]

A Hard Road, July – September 1918

By October 1918 there would be approximately 9,000 US naval personnel at Queenstown under Lewis Bayly. To support them, there were USN recreation facilities and a USN hospital, prefabricated in America and shipped over in pieces and which had been built on an estate called 'Whitepoint', acquired under DORA by the British authorities. US nurses were sent over to run it as the USN banned Irish staff since 'the proposition of having some Sinn Feiner in close proximity to the camp does not appeal very strongly'.[1] There was an American YMCA; Queenstown was a significant and growing American naval base. So when Assistant Secretary of the Navy Franklin Delano Roosevelt visited Europe in July, it was no surprise that he came to Queenstown. The future thirty-second President of the United States left New York on 9 July on board the brand-new destroyer USS *Dyer* and arrived at Plymouth on the 21st. From there he travelled to Queenstown on the 24th, in the company of British First Lord of the Admiralty Sir Eric Geddes, and both stayed with Bayly at Admiralty House for two nights.

Roosevelt gave an extemporaneous statement to the press on his arrival at the base in which he extolled the co-operation of British and American naval units in anti-submarine warfare and the efficient combination of British experience and American ability. He had been Assistant Secretary since 1913, a reward for loyalty from President Wilson, and had a strong interest in naval matters (he claimed to own 10,000 naval books). Roosevelt was more enthusiastic than his superior, Secretary Daniels, in supporting the creation of a large and efficient naval force and had actively canvassed for the initial deployment of ships to Queenstown. The building of significant numbers of new destroyers and sub-chasers (see below) was largely his doing. Here at Queenstown he could see the results of his work – under a Royal Navy admiral; work that continued in the same daily way.

The loss of *Anchusa*

HMS *Anchusa* was a sloop, launched in Walker-on-Tyne in April 1917 as the lead ship of an eventual class of twenty-eight convoy sloops, all finally completed as Q-ships. At 0900hrs on 14 July 1918 she had left Lough Swilly to reinforce the escort of a homeward-bound convoy by loitering around it, hoping to attract an unwary U-boat.

There was definitely at least one submarine stalking the convoy. Acting Commander S R Lane RNR, captain of the brand new '24-class' minesweeping sloop (all named for Derby winners) HMS *Ard Patrick*, was part of the convoy escort. North-west of Ireland, he had been hunting a U-boat all day of the 15th, in company with the hydrophone trawler *Vale of Lennox*, which had dropped depth charges at 2159hrs without any noticeable effect, and the destroyer *Mindful*. At 0200hrs on the 16th, Lane suddenly saw a flash in the sky 'like lightning' accompanied by the sounds of distant explosions. It was HMS *Anchusa* going to her grave.

She had been sunk by Oberleutnant zur See Hellmuth von Ruckteschell in *U-54*. He had already sunk nineteen Allied vessels (a total 32,500grt) when he had spotted *Anchusa*. Now he added a twentieth.

On board the stricken Q-ship it was chaos. Able Seaman G W H Loftus described what happened.

> I was in my hammock in number six mess ...and heard a frightful sound which woke me up ... [in the dark] I felt my way up on deck and as soon as I looked aft saw the stern was completely level with the water. At the same time I heard a second explosion which I took to be a [another] torpedo.
>
> The captain said 'get boats lowered' and asked what we were waiting for. He said 'get away from the ship'. We were just pushing off when the bows went right up into the air and the ship must have broke [*sic*] in two. There was another explosion [probably the boilers] and I felt myself going down through the water at a great rate and I could not stop myself. The next thing I was on the surface in a dazed condition.

There was no sign of the ship but I saw something in front of me which turned out to be a Carley Float.[2]

The ship sank in around two minutes. Loftus was a lucky man. Despite the freezing waters he survived three hours on the float to be rescued by Commander Loftus and *Ard Patrick*, one of only twelve from a crew of ninety-one to survive the sinking.

Admiral Miller at Buncrana thought the usual court martial for the loss of a ship unnecessary, writing to Bayly and the Admiralty that 'there are no surviving officers from *Anchusa* and in view of the difficulty of obtaining sufficient officers [to form the court] without seriously hampering movements of ships at a time when all available ships are required to deal with submarines, [I recommend] that a court of enquiry instead of a court marital be held'.[3] Bayly concurred. The enquiry found no one to blame. At the time of the enquiry there were three of the twelve survivors still in the County Infirmary Londonderry, four uninjured survivors given fourteen days leave and five injured men, given fourteen days sick leave. One imagines that they needed it.

Stock Force

Bayly continued to deploy his Q-ships around the Western Approaches. One of his recent acquisitions was the collier *Stock Force* (732grt), newly built by the Dundee Shipbuilding Company. She was spotted in Cardiff docks by her now captain and commandeered for conversion to a Q-ship, armed with two 4in guns and two 14in torpedo tubes.

On 30 July *Stock Force* was loitering some twenty-five miles to the west of Start Point. Her captain was 27-year-old Lieutenant Harold Auten RNR, born in Leatherhead, the son of a retired Royal Navy paymaster and in peacetime an officer with the P&O company. He was by now an experienced Q-ship sailor. When Lieutenant Commander Hallwright, captain of *Q-16* (HMS *Heather*), was killed (see Chapter 14), Auten had taken command of the vessel, one in which he had already won the DSC for bravery in action. Now he commanded in his own right and was hoping for further action – a wish as yet unfulfilled. But, as Auten himself later wrote, 'the charm of Q-boat warfare was its uncertainty'. That claim was about to be borne out.

At 1700hrs *Stock Force* was hit by a torpedo fired by *UB-80*. It struck the ship abreast No 1 hatch and entirely wrecked the fore part of the ship, including the bridge, wounding three ratings. Further damage followed from a storm cloud of planks, unexploded shells, hatches and other debris thrown up by the explosion which, on falling back down, wounded the first lieutenant and the navigating officer, and added to the injuries of the foremost gun crew and a number of other ratings. The ship settled down forward, flooding the fore magazine and between decks to the depth of about 3ft. *Stock Force* and her crew were in a bad way.

Lieutenant Workman, the first officer and another RNR volunteer, got the panic party away, despite his injuries, while Auten remained on board the slowly-sinking ship together with his gun crews and a skeleton engine room staff. They lay quietly out of sight whilst below them Surgeon Probationer George E Strahan RNVR, in peacetime a medical student and now working up to his waist in water, attended to the injured crewmen.

The submarine came to the surface ahead of the ship, half a mile away and remained there a quarter of an hour, watching the ship for any suspicious movement. Her commander, Kapitänleutnant Max Viebeg, was experienced; he was taking no chances, but he needed to get his proofs of success and the other details demanded by his superiors. The panic party began to row back towards their ship, hoping to draw the submarine in. Very slowly it followed them, coming onto the port side of the Q-ship, 300yds away. Still Auten waited. At 1740hrs, as the U-boat came abeam, where both of his guns could bear, Auten opened fire. The first shot carried away one of the periscopes, the second round hit the conning tower, blowing it away and throwing the occupants high into the air. The next round struck the submarine on the waterline, ripping her open and blowing out a number of the crew. The U-boat then slipped several feet into the water and her bows rose, presenting a target for all *Stock Force*'s weapons until she sank back into the water.

Auten thought that he had sunk his enemy but his more immediate problem was that his own ship was sinking too. He radioed for help and the whole of the crew worked hard to keep the vessel afloat. But at 2125hrs they gave up the unequal task. Two torpedo boats and a trawler took off the crew and *Stock Force* sank with colours flying, off Bolt Tail, Bigbury Bay. Auten was awarded the Victoria Cross for an action cited as one of the 'finest examples of coolness, discipline and good organisation in the history of "Q" ships'.[4] He became the seventh of Bayly's Q-ship sailors to win the decoration; a remarkable example of courage and determination in a dangerous trade. Trainee doctor George Strahan's medical commitment was recognised with the conferral of a Distinguished Service Cross.

But *UB-80* was not sunk,[*] although she was badly damaged. Viebeg nursed her back to his Flanders base and, repaired, the U-boat added two more cargo vessels to its catalogue of sinkings before the war ended.

The 'splinter ships'

On 21 August a group of small wooden US Navy ships sailed up the River Lee, past Haulbowline and arrived at moorings at Passage West. The sub-chasers had arrived.

They owed their genesis to the determination of Franklin Roosevelt to rapidly bring into service a class of vessel specifically designed to hunt and kill U-boats. Ordered in 1916, they were built in civilian dockyards, as the big naval yards were occupied building larger warships. They were constructed of wood as steel was in great demand and this led to their navy nickname – the 'splinter ships'. Thus far there had not been designed a truly effective anti-submarine vessel, for the difficulty was in fixing the enemy once under water and out of sight. Primitive forms of sound-detection equipment had been produced (see Appendix 3) but the existing sub-hunting plate hydrophones were non-directional. Thus, a captain might know that there was a U-boat somewhere, but not specifically where it was. In the sub-chasers three technologies came together which made it potentially a more effective U-boat killer: these were radio telephony, directional hydrophones and new depth-charge technology. They were 110ft long, powered by three petrol driven engines at a maximum speed of around 18 knots. Two officers and twenty-five men comprised the crew; the officers, in common with their Royal Navy equivalents in the motor launches, were all from the US Navy Volunteer Reserve. Armament consisted of a 3in gun forward and an aft-facing Y-gun depth-charge thrower, developed in America from a British design, which fired two bombs over the stern.

Under the command of Captain Arthur Jepy Hepburn USN,

---

[*] Although some sources continue to claim that she was.

thirty-six vessels were eventually deployed at Queenstown (there were another thirty-six in a different command at Plymouth), all of which had sailed across the Atlantic, a difficult exercise as they were not well suited to the rough Atlantic waters. Constant leaks from decks and windows, choking petrol fumes in the officers' quarters, and ever-present seasickness from the rolling motion, made them uncomfortable sea boats and in heavy weather they would be almost awash, with only the pilot house showing above the waves. The depth-charge racks were felt to be too heavy and made the little ships liable to take seas over the stern. Commander Tower appreciated them, however. 'I liked them as able to keep the seas in bad weather and capable of much ... good beam, strongly built and with a real good rubbing strake were points which appealed to me. A good gun, and a number of depth charges well-arranged gave an armament not to be despised.'[5]

The 'splinter ships' spent until the end of September under training in Bantry Bay and were then assigned to Queenstown, Berehaven and Holyhead, each port hosting a division of six vessels, while two divisions were held in reserve. Tactically they worked as a three-boat unit. One sub-chaser was designated the flagship, and this small group would patrol a pre-determined area, stopping their engines and drifting about a mile apart in an attempt to detect the underwater noise of submarine engines or propellers. In the event of a contact being made by one or more of the boats, the flagship would plot a fix using the directions given. Then a pattern of depth charges would be dropped to try to sink the submarine. Alternatively they worked in conjunction with a seaplane which spotted for them.

The sub-chasers at Queenstown finally went out on operational hunting patrols on 20 October. Less than a month later the war would be over and so their true potential was never revealed. Bayly thought that 'they would soon have become a great asset in working with the seaplanes off the coast'.[6]

Battleships at Berehaven
The sub-chasers were not the only USN vessels to arrive in Ireland in the summer of 1918. A division of battleships came too.

As more and more American troops crossed the Atlantic in troop convoys for service on the Western Front, the Navy Department became increasingly worried about the threat posed by large German surface raiders breaking out into the Atlantic. Chief of

Naval Operations Admiral William Benson, in particular, worried that if a German battlecruiser force got out into the Western Approaches and caught a troop convoy defended only by Bayly's small ships, then thousands of doughboys might be killed. The public outcry which followed might be difficult for the administration to handle.

Thus the Navy Department decided to send Battleship Division Six to Ireland's western coast to counter this threat, under the command of Rear Admiral Thomas Slidell Rogers. It comprised three dreadnought battleships, *Nevada* (ten 14in guns), *Oklahoma* (ten 14in) and *Utah* (ten 12in), which departed for Ireland on 12 August and were based at Berehaven. Their presence, however, aroused Bayly's grumpiness somewhat. Whilst welcoming the new force he was aggrieved that it did not come under his command (they reported directly to Admiral Sims in London) and that he was expected to sacrifice some of the Queenstown USN destroyers as an escorting force for the battlewagons, thus depleting the resources for what he believed was the primary task – escorting convoys and destroying submarines.

No sooner had the battleships arrived than, on 21 September, Rogers had to declare an epidemic of influenza, the first portent of the Spanish 'Flu outbreak which would wreak such havoc at the end of the war. Then, on 14 October, Rodgers was advised that German cruisers might have escaped into the Atlantic. Two troop convoys (HC-20 from Quebec and HX-51 from Hampton Roads) were approaching European waters and Rogers took Battleship Division Six to sea in order to provide additional escort through the Western Approaches danger zone. The weather was terrible and the kite balloons of *Utah* (struck by lightning) and *Oklahoma* (brought down by winds and sunk) were destroyed. Mission completed, they then returned to sea and escorted convoy HC-21 as well. But in fact no such breakout had occurred and this was the only raider warning issued to Rogers during the period on station. The three battleships never fired their guns in anger.

Mount Vernon and *Ticonderoga*

The danger to American troop transports came not from surface raiders but from the continued U-boat threat. The *Kronprinzessin Cecilie* had been built at Stettin, Germany, in 1906 as the last of four liners built for the North German Lloyd company. Her older sister,

Kaiser Wilhelm der Grosse, had been introduced in 1897 and was a great success. Her popularity on transatlantic routes prompted the company to construct three more superliners, *Kronprinz Wilhelm* (1901), *Kaiser Wilhelm II* (1903) and finally *Kronprinzessin Cecilie*. The first three named all served as AMCs from 1914 until their sinking or internment. But *Cecilie* had been caught unawares and unarmed by the outbreak of war and had sought safety in Bar Harbour, Maine. The United States government formally took possession of the ship in February 1917 and sent her to Charleston Navy Yard to be refitted as a troopship, now named USS *Mount Vernon*.

On 5 September she was outbound from Brest for New York in convoy with USS *Agamemnon*, another German liner converted to a troop carrier, once *Kaiser Wilhelm II,* with an escort of six Queenstown and Brest based destroyers. She had on board 900 crew, 350 sick and wounded soldiers (150 of whom were considered 'crippled') and about 200 other personnel, all under the command of Captain Douglas E Dismukes USN.

She was 250 miles west of Brest, off Ushant, and travelling at 18 knots when a periscope was spotted 500yds off the starboard bow by Seaman E B Briggs, manning the starboard bow 5in gun. Captain Dismukes had the guns manned and loaded for the passage and Briggs immediately opened fire at the sighting. Nonetheless the submarine came to the surface and fired a torpedo. The officer of the deck, Lieutenant George Milliken, shouted out for full right rudder and full speed but, as the huge ship began to turn, the torpedo stuck the starboard side, blowing a large hole in the hull and ripping a 5in gun off its mount. The weapon had struck at the junction of two firerooms; all of the men in one were killed, together with all but two in the other. The ship lost power, steerage way, communications and electricity; she was a sitting duck for the next shot.

The destroyers saved her. USS *Winslow, Conner, Nicholson* and *Wainwright* raced to the area where the submarine had been sighted and fired off multiple depth-charge patterns. Kapitänleutnant Heinrich Middendorff, commanding *U-82*, decided on discretion being the better part of valour and did not attempt to finish the job. Perhaps he felt that she would sink anyway. In fact, splendid damage-control procedures meant that after two hours she was able to proceed back to Brest at 15 knots and arrived with 10ft extra draught, thanks to the water taken in, at 0230hrs the following day.

She had thirty-five crewmen killed and thirteen wounded, one of whom died of his wounds. The medical staff had put the crippled injured into boats in case of need, but all were returned to harbour safely. At Brest the ship was patched up and she returned to Boston for major repairs, arriving on 28 October. It had been a considerable feat of seamanship by captain and crew.

Not every ship was as fortunate as *Mount Vernon*. Just over three weeks after she was attacked, the US Navy would suffer its worse loss of life at sea in the war. USS *Ticonderoga* had left New York on 22 September with a cargo of railway sleepers and the last-minute addition of a detachment of 116 soldiers bound for France. She was another ex-German ship, once the *Camilla Rickmers,* built in 1914 in Germany and had been seized by United States Customs officials in 1917. Handed over to the USN she was fitted out as an animal transport and commissioned at Boston in the Naval Overseas Transportation Service (NOTS) on 5 January 1918 under the command of Lieutenant Commander James J Madison, USNRF, a reservist volunteer, as were many of his crew. She was defensively armed with a 3in gun forward and a 6in at the stern.

Ticonderoga sailed as part of a 24-ship convoy escorted by the cruiser USS *Galveston*. On 30 September they were in mid-Atlantic, too far out to meet Bayly's escorts, when her engines began to give trouble and her speed was reduced to 3 knots. She quickly fell behind the convoy and was some five miles away from them when, at 0520hrs and in the darkness, a lookout spotted a submarine on the surface. Although Lieutenant Commander Madison could not know it, his opponent was one of the biggest and best armed submarines in German service. It was *U-152*, one of seven surviving U-boats designed and built to be large cargo submarines for shipping material to and from locations otherwise denied German surface ships by the Royal Navy blockade. They had all been converted to U-boat cruisers in 1917. She carried eighteen torpedoes and two deck guns, equivalent to 6in in calibre.

Calling for what little speed he could make, Madison turned to attempt to ram and cleared for action. *U-152* opened fire, at close range. The first shot hit the bridge, killing the helmsman and badly wounding Madison in the legs. The second shell destroyed the forward gun. Madison brought the ship about in order to engage the submarine with the larger aft gun. At this point *U-152* submerged to hide away only to surface ten minutes later, 2,000yds away, and resumed firing on *Ticonderoga*. *Galveston* had seen the gun flashes and made a half-hearted attempt to find out what was happening before firing a few shells in the direction of the gunfire and making off. The cargo vessel was on her own.

Madison could now only con the ship from the aft emergency steering position but for nearly two hours he and the U-boat kept up an artillery duel which only ended when, with men dead and dying littered around the American ship's deck, the submarine took off to three miles range and shelled the rear gun position with impunity, destroying it. She then closed to fire a torpedo and finally *Ticonderoga* began to sink. Madison was by now unconscious from loss of blood and his executive officer, Lieutenant Frank Muller, ordered 'abandon ship' under a white flag. The survivors had to cram onto just one boat and one raft as the other lifeboats had sunk upon launching. The comatose Madison was placed in the only lifeboat. After the cargo ship sank, the U-boat searched among the survivors on rafts and in the lifeboat looking, as per standard procedure, for senior officers to take prisoner. Kapitänleutnant Adolf Franz left Madison in the boat as he was too badly injured and instead took Muller and assistant engineer Lieutenant (JG) Junius Fulcher.[*]

It was four long days later when the British freighter ss *Moorish Prince* chanced upon the survivors in their little boat. Out of 237 men who set out from New York on *Ticonderoga*, only twenty-two survived to be landed in Britain (twenty-four if the two captured officers are included). The loss of 112 sailors and 101 soldiers was the greatest combat loss of any US Navy ship in the war. Madison survived to be awarded the Congressional Medal of Honour for his actions.[**]

Naval procedure
The war had been raging for over four years and the sloops had been in continuous action for almost as long, but back at Queenstown the naval niceties still had to be observed. On 1 October 1918 Bayly inspected Lieutenant Commander Wilson's *Zinnia* and filed a

---

[*] Muller and Fulcher were still aboard *U-152* when the boat returned to Kiel after the Armistice was signed. They were repatriated when the submarine surrendered.

[**] James Madison had his leg amputated owing to the wounds suffered on the *Ticonderoga*, and died from complications on Christmas Day in 1922 aged just 38. Before he died, he had been promoted to commander.

formal inspection report. 'Great credit is due to the Captain and Officers for their discipline and organisation and to the ship's company for their behaviour' he commented, adding 'a clean and smart ship.'[7] To be in such good order after all they had been through must indeed have been to their credit; for Bayly was not the sort of admiral to make any allowances.

Victory, 1918

As summer turned to autumn, it became clear that the German will to continue the war was failing. A combination of the Royal Navy's blockade, which was causing critical food and *materiel* shortages and a collapse of domestic morale, the ultimate failure of the great Spring Offensive on the Western Front and the increasing flow of American troops to the war zone, all led to a belief that Germany could not win the war. During October the new German government of Prince Maximilian of Baden began to seek an Armistice and on 5 October asked President Woodrow Wilson of the USA to mediate between all parties. One of Wilson's preconditions for an Armistice was that Germany should end its submarine war. In fact this had already begun to take place as, also on 5 October, the German Flanders Flotilla U-boats *UB-10*, *UB-40*, *UB-59* and *UC-4* all scuttled themselves off the Flemish coast, their strategic position deemed hopeless.

But while the politicians and military men dithered and argued, men still died.

uss *Shaw*

The danger of convoy escort duties did not come just from the threat of U-boat attack, or even of surface raiders. As has been previously described, collision was an ever-present danger when in convoy.

RMS *Aquitania* was one of the largest ships in the world when she made her maiden voyage to New York on 30 May 1914. At 45,747grt and carrying 3,236 passengers (618 first class, 614 second class and 2,004 third class) she was the pride of Cunard Line's fleet and known as 'Ship Beautiful'. At the outbreak of war, she was briefly employed as an AMC for all of two weeks before she collided with a Canadian steamer; she was just too vast and expensive to run for the task. Instead she became a troopship and by 1918 was conveying North American troops to Britain and wearing a spectacular dazzle paint scheme instead of Cunard's house colours. On one occasion *Aquitania* managed to transport over 8,000 men in a single trip.

uss *Shaw* was a *Sampson*-class destroyer of 1,125 tons displacement fully loaded. Commissioned in April 1917, she had arrived at Queenstown three months later, on 5 July. There she served as convoy escort and submarine hunter under Lieutenant Commander Milton Smith Davis, going about her long and tiring duties alongside her sister-ships. In early October 1918, uss *Shaw, Downes, Conyngham, Duncan* and *Kimberley* were ordered to escort the *Aquitania* through the Western Approaches to Southampton. *Shaw*'s commander observed the normal procedure of constant zigzagging around his charge, to make life difficult for U-boats. It was 9 October. Suddenly, *Shaw*'s rudder jammed as she was completing the right leg of a zigzag, leaving her directly on course towards the transport. Seconds later, the huge liner struck *Shaw* and cut off 90ft of the destroyer's bow, mangling her bridge and setting her on fire. *Aquitania* ploughed through the little ship as if she hadn't been there, her forefoot slicing the destroyer open to the seas.

Shaw's crew fought desperately to save their ship, none more so than her executive officer, Lieutenant George Fountain Parrott Jnr. He had been badly injured in the collision but insisted on helping to remove his wounded comrades from a damaged compartment, an action which exhausted him and exacerbated his wounds. The other destroyers took men off the damaged vessel and a skeleton crew of twenty-one men was left on board; somehow they got their ship forty miles to Portsmouth Harbour and safety. To refit her for sea again took until 29 May 1919. Twelve US sailors died in the accident, including Lieutenant Parrott;[*] it was a tragic waste.

The loss of *Leinster*

rms *Leinster* was a fast (24-knot) packet ship on the Kingstown to Admiralty Pier, Salt Island, Holyhead service. The service, operated by the City of Dublin Steam Packet Company, used four ships, each named after Ireland's provinces – *Connaught, Leinster, Munster* and *Ulster*. On board the ships was a post office, where mail was sorted

---

[*] George Fountain Parrott Jnr, from North Carolina, received the Navy Cross for his actions on 9 October, was posthumously promoted lieutenant commander and had a destroyer named after him in 1919.

by members of the Dublin Post Office Service for onward delivery once landed. The ships sailed unescorted as it was thought that their high speed provided sufficient protection. After the loss of *Connaught* in 1917 whilst on trooping duty, the remaining three ships had been painted in dazzle camouflage. They were also defensively armed with a 12pdr gun, manned by Royal Navy ratings.

On 10 October, *Leinster* was making her usual crossing from Kingstown. She had on board 771 souls, passengers and crew, under Dublin born Captain William Birch, a 61-year-old merchant master of long experience. The passenger manifest included 22 postal sorters and 180 civilians; but by far the greater number of passengers on board were military personnel, many of them going on leave or returning to duty. Among the former was Captain Hutchinson Ingham Cone USN, commander of US air forces in Europe and on Admiral Sims' staff.

When *Leinster* set sail at 0900 the weather was fine, but the sea was rough following recent storms. Earlier that morning a number of Royal Navy ships at sea off Holyhead had been forced to return to port due to the stormy conditions. Shortly before 1000hrs, about sixteen miles from Kingstown and four nautical miles east of the Kish light vessel, a few people on deck saw a torpedo approaching the port side of the ship. It missed, passing in front of the vessel. Soon afterwards a second torpedo struck the port side where the sorting room was located. It blew a hole in the ship there and the force of the explosion caused another to appear in the starboard side too.

Captain Birch turned his ship through 180° in an attempt to return to port. He ordered the lifeboats to be readied and was able to maintain a slow rate of progress. A third torpedo was then fired and struck on the starboard side, practically blowing the ship apart. The *Leinster* sank soon afterwards, bow first. In the water it was pandemonium. In lifeboats or clinging to rafts and flotsam in the rough seas, there now began a grim struggle for survival. Many passengers and crew died of exposure, or simple tiredness and drowned while awaiting help.

Rescue vessels were despatched from Kingstown and Holyhead. The first to arrive were the destroyers HMS *Mallard, Seal* and *Lively*, all with the Irish Sea Hunting Flotilla. Here was another U-boat which the force had clearly failed to find. Another soon on the scene was the yacht *Helga*, last noted shelling the rebels in Dublin. Bayly himself set out in a motor launch to see if he could assist.

As the survivors were brought home, and the dead bodies laid out, doctors, nurses and a fleet of 200 ambulances were rushed to Victoria Wharf, Kingstown. Those needing medical care were brought to St Michael's Hospital and several other Dublin hospitals. Those not requiring treatment were taken to local hotels and guest houses. The official casualty count was 501 dead; but more recent research suggests it was 529 at least. Twenty-one of twenty-two postal workers were killed; thirty-six of seventy-seven crew died; 115 of 180 civilians lost their lives. Two of the three RN gunners were lost. One hundred and forty-four military casualties were buried in Grangegorman Military Cemetery in Dublin. Amongst the dead was nineteen-year-old Wren Josephine Carr, a shorthand typist from Cork. She became the first WRNS member to die on active service.

Captain Birch had been wounded in the initial explosion. He was drowned when his lifeboat became swamped in heavy seas and capsized while trying to transfer survivors to HMS *Lively*. Captain Cone was injured while freeing lifeboats on deck but survived.[*]

Second Lieutenant Francis Kenvyn Lewis had survived the Somme, Ypres, Passchendaele and typhoid before being posted to Ireland with his regiment, the Royal Welch Fusiliers. Travelling home on leave, he had boarded the *Leinster* at 0900hrs and gone to his cabin to sort out his baggage. The purser appeared at his door with a message from his commanding officer, telling him to return to base, so with a heavy heart he left the ship. His survivor's luck was evidently still with him, for fourteen of his regimental comrades died in the sinking. And Commander Tower thought himself very fortunate. He had crossed on *Leinster* the day previously.

The U-boat responsible was *UB-123*, based at Zeebrugge. She did not survive to celebrate her achievement. The U-boat was probably lost to a mine in the Northern Barrage on her way back to base, on or about 19 October. The bodies of her commander, Oberleutnant zur See Robert Ramm, and his crew of two officers and thirty-three men were never recovered.

The loss of the *Leinster* was both the greatest ever loss of life in the Irish Sea and the highest ever casualty rate on an Irish-owned ship. And the war had only five weeks to run.[**]

---

[*] Cone was made an honorary commander of the Order of the British Empire for his actions.

[**] After the sinking, Foreign Secretary Arthur Balfour remarked in Cabinet 'brutes they [the Germans] were and brutes they remain'.

Armistice

Overriding the objections of Admiral Scheer, now Chief of the Imperial Naval Staff, Prince Max's government eventually conceded to Wilson's demands that U-boat attacks on merchant shipping cease on 20 October. The following day all U-boats at sea were recalled home. The seas began to empty of predators for the first time in four years.

The dying days of the war continued to claim victims, however. The coaster *Saint Barchan* was sunk by *UB-94*, four nautical miles off St John's Point, County Down, on the 21st. And the Spanish 'Flu was beginning to make its mark in Queenstown. On 2 November it carried off Skipper Henry W Plummer, of the minesweeping trawler *Freesia*, a 33-year-old Suffolk man, now destined to stay forever in Ireland

On 5 November the US armed cargo ship *Lake Harris* was attacked by a surfaced U-boat with gunfire and had to be beached near Penzance railway station. The Admiralty tug *Epic* joined her on the beach in trying to save her. This was the last attack on merchant shipping before the Armistice. Across the globe 'only' 118,559 tons of Allied and neutral shipping were sunk by U-boats in October and 17,682 tons in November. And trade flowed freely through the Western Approaches, the St George's Channel and the Irish Sea, past the Scilly Isles and Ushant, off Finisterre and through the mid-Atlantic wastes. It was over.

Admiral Bayly issued a memorandum 'From Commander in Chief to All Ships'. It read 'The Commander in Chief congratulates all British and United States officers and crews under his command on the splendid victory achieved, which their loyalty, ability and ever-ready energies have so greatly assisted. It will always be a source of great pride to him to have been so closely associated with them in this great war.'[1] In Cork bells were rung at 1100hrs on the 11th (but only in Protestant churches) and city workers and soldiers were given a day's holiday. That evening fistfights broke out between Republicans and British soldiers who used their belts on the 'shirkers', as they called the able-bodied Republicans who had not joined up. Bayly took an almost immediate leave, back to England. Lord French, Admiral Barlow and others attended a service of remembrance at St Patrick's Church of Ireland Cathedral in Dublin. Commander Tower represented the absent Bayly.

Admiral Sir Lewis Bayly had commanded over 8,000 US Navy

personnel as well as the British forces in his charge. Forty-seven US destroyers served under him, thirty sub-chasers, an American Q-ship, three US tugs, three depot ships and seven US submarines. Literally hundreds of Royal Navy ships, from cruisers to motor launches and trawlers were under his direction, as were some thirty Q-ships, not to mention seaplanes, airships and the like. He dealt with a hostile local population with firmness and some success. He might have permitted a small smile to cross his habitually expressionless face.

An admiral hauls down his flag

Bayly returned to Admiralty House and his post but it was to oversee the disassembly of the huge forces he had once commanded. The American ships began to leave almost immediately after the Armistice and Royal Navy vessels were quickly reassigned or mothballed. By May, all of the USN vessels had departed, excepting *Corsair*, the yacht of American billionaire J P Morgan, which had been lent to the navy for the war effort and had taken over from USS *Melville* as the base for the senior USN officer.

But before they left Queenstown for good, some forty of the USN commanding officers commissioned a silver half-model of a US four-funnel destroyer which they presented to Bayly. They called it USS *Pull Together* and each inscribed his signature on the dedication plate, which bore the additional information that it was presented by them to Admiral Sir Lewis Bayly in recognition of his command 'during the struggle to preserve the sea and make the world safe for democracy'.*

Bayley was able to relax a little and enjoy the trappings of his command. Commander Francis Tower was invited to stay with him and Violet and found the experience congenial. 'The Admiral and Miss Voysey met me and made me so welcome', he wrote later, 'giving me a charming room and taking me in the car to places around … and another day in the admiral's barge round the prettiest parts of the harbour.'[2]

Admiral Lewis Bayly struck his flag on 1 April 1919. His request for his service in Ireland to count as Foreign Service for leave purposes was refused. Which was odd, for the KCMG with which he had recently been invested was usually awarded for service overseas.

---

* In his will Bayly left the silver model to the Navy's torpedo school, HMS *Vernon*.

PART THREE
Bayly's Leaving and Achievements

Pain and Pleasure: An Admiral Takes His Leave

Bayly vs the Admiralty

When Bayly retired from the Service on 1 April 1919, he was laden with appropriate honours; these included the KCB and KCMG, the Danish Grand Cross of Danneborg, the United States Distinguished Service Order, the French *Légion d'honneur* and the Order Crown of Italy. His friends in the US Navy lauded him too. On 7 May he received a letter of commendation from Franklin D Roosevelt, still Assistant Secretary of the Navy; forwarded by 'Force Commander, US Navy forces', it read; 'The Department believes that, without exception, the feeling towards Ad Bayly of all United States Naval officers who have served during the war, either ashore or afloat, from the Queenstown base is not only unusual but unprecedented in the Allied warfare.'[1]

In his autobiography, written just before he died, Bayly claims that on hauling down his flag at Queenstown, he was offered by First Sea Lord Rosslyn Wemyss the post of CinC Portsmouth, the most senior port admiral position in the Royal Navy, but turned it down. It is uncertain if this was the case. The offer would more normally have come from the First Lord; the admiral who was awarded the post was Sir Cecil Burney who had seniority of more than a year over Bayly, and why would he refuse such a prestigious post anyway? In a letter to Charles Bonnor, written in August 1919, Bayly states 'I was sorry to leave the service but being told that there was no further intention of employing me, I saw no use in hanging on so settled down in the country.'[2] This is in direct conflict with the claim regarding Portsmouth made in his book.

What is certain is that he was still harbouring his grudge over what he perceived as his unfair treatment by Churchill and Fisher over the torpedoing of *Formidable*. The blame attached to him for the sinking and death of so many sailors clearly still rankled with Bayly. He wanted satisfaction. In March 1919, just before his retirement, he wrote to the Admiralty asking that the case be re-opened with a view to 'justice being publically done'[3] and in order that the official history of the War, being prepared by Sir Julian Corbett, correctly reflect his role.* In this letter, written from Admiralty House, he included all previous correspondence and noted once again that it was the Admiralty which had ordered the destroyers to leave him at Folkestone, a fact that he clearly saw as having grown in importance. It is indeed possible that he was by now being blamed for sending them away himself; certainly there are some accounts of the sinking which say he did, erroneously.

The matter of Bayly's letter was discussed at the Admiralty Board of 17 April but no one saw any reason to oblige him, and some good reasons not to, not the least being that a court martial now would set a precedent which could lead to many more such cases. Once again, his application was rejected. The Admiralty wrote to him at his home in Ermington, Devon, on 25 April. They pointed out that, as under Section 54 of the Naval Discipline Act, more than three years had elapsed since the incident so they were precluded from re-opening the case and further added that they did not feel justified in questioning the decision of a previous board. But they did re-iterate the sentiments of fullest appreciation of his services previously expressed in the consolation prize they had sent him on 5 April for his efforts as CinC at Queenstown. In that document, the Lords Commissioners of the Admiralty conveyed 'their appreciation of the manner in which you have carried out the important duties of that command and their satisfaction with the very high standards of efficiency maintained by HM Ships and Naval Establishment under your orders'. They concluded that 'your services have been of great value towards the successful prosecution of the war'.[4]

For Bayly, fine words were worthless. Determined and tough, single-minded and proud as a commander, he was not about to yield when retired. On 1 May he replied to the Admiralty in fulminating tones and scrawled handwriting. He railed that the Admiralty had not been 'unable' to accede to his request for a court martial, they

---

* In fact, Corbett attributed the loss as follows: 'In this particular instance the disaster was attributed to the neglect of ordinary precautions.'

were 'not prepared to'.[5] He dismissed the Section 54 argument with the comment that 'it only forms an excuse for not holding one'.[6] He concluded that 'it therefore appears that their Lordships consider it to be more just for an individual officer to be very severely punished unheard, than for a previous board decision to be re-opened'.[7]

Although Bayly was not to know it, behind the united front presented by the Admiralty to his request for a re-opening of the case there were some with sympathy for his plight, and who thought a greater injustice lay beneath the surface. When Bayly's letter of 1 May was circulated to the Board, the Deputy Chief of Naval Staff (DCNS) Rear Admiral Sidney Fremantle felt obliged to comment on it. In a handwritten note dated 9 May he wrote:

> I do not know if it is the intention to discuss this matter at a Board meeting – I cannot put all I should like to say on this subject on a circulating paper. I will, however, go so far as to say that I think the degree of blame which might be attributed to Admiral Bayly in <u>1915</u> is open to question; the decision to refuse his request for a court martial at the time most regrettable; and the tone and expression of some or most of the letters written to him by the then board still more so. I do not question the correctness of the view now taken, in any way, but I should welcome any solution which would remove the sense of injustice from which Admiral Bayly is suffering [the underlining is in the original].[8]

So Fremantle thought Bayly hard done by and that blame might lie elsewhere. Did he see or know that Churchill and Fisher had been desperate to allocate blame solely to Bayly? What did he not wish to say in a 'circulating' paper? In private, did he point the finger of blame in another direction?

The Second Sea Lord read the memorandum on 12 May. He suggested to the First Sea Lord (Rosslyn Wemyss) that they obtain the First Lord's (Walter Long) consent to agenda it at a Board meeting. Wemyss agreed. On 13 May he noted '... there are several circumstances connected with the case which are regrettable, but I see no way of rectifying them. I am of the opinion that in spite of Admiral Bayly's protests, the original decision must be adhered to.'[9]

They could find no way out of their difficulties. The Admiralty board considered Bayly's missive on 22 May. Their answer remained unchanged. Bayly could not resist a bitter final note; on 28 May he scrawled back 'my final experience in the Navy is that of injustice shewn [sic] to me by my official superiors'.[10] There was no reply. Bayly continued to quietly fume amongst his cottage garden flowers in Devon, his loyal niece by his side.

The admiral goes to America

Following the end of the war, the US Navy officers who had served at Queenstown founded the 'Queenstown Association', membership of which was only open to those USN officers who had served under Lewis Bayly for three months or more. The President of the Association was Admiral Sims, Bayly was appointed Vice President and the Secretary was Junius Morgan, who had served as a lieutenant (USNFR) aboard USS *O'Brien*. It is perhaps always wise when founding an organisation to have a number of wealthy participants and Morgan, the son of J P Morgan the American financier and banker, met that particular bill. Violet Voysey was appointed the only female honorary member and the association claimed a total participation of over 650 members.

In late 1920, Bayly and his niece arranged to cruise to Japan for a holiday. When this news reached the USA, the Queenstown Association insisted that he continue his journey to visit America as their guests. On arrival in Yokohama, they found that two large suites had been reserved for them at the Grand Hotel, free of charge. The owner was a former USN paymaster. From there they sailed on SS *Equados*, again free of charge, to San Francisco. As the ship entered harbour, at 0700hrs the captain sent for Bayly who arrived on the bridge in his pyjamas to find the liner surrounded by destroyers. The SNO enquired of Bayly by megaphone how he would like the escort placed. 'I placed in one on each bow one on each beam and one on each quarter and we proceeded into harbour' the admiral recorded.[11] As they passed the warships of the US Pacific Fleet, they all 'manned ship'. It is difficult not to think that a tear may have crept into the eyes of the curmudgeonly 63-year-old admiral and his niece.

From there they set off on what bore more than a passing resemblance to a royal tour. First to San Diego, where Bayly inspected the fleet; then to the cruiser USS *Birmingham*, which flew his flag (later presented to him) and gave a seventeen-gun salute. Next, on board SS *San Juan* to Balboa, where Lieutenant Commander Victor Herbster, he who had brought home an Irish bride, escorted them with seaplanes. Through the Panama Canal they passed, again escorted by Herbster, arriving in New York on 14 February. Here they were met, and escorted into harbour, by seven seaplanes and a dirigible; as they passed Governor's Island a salute was fired. Admiral Sims met them on the quayside.

Dinners and meetings followed including dining aboard the battleship *New York* and meeting Navy Secretary Daniels. From New York Bayly travelled to Annapolis to give a speech to 2,000 cadets (the subject was 'Traditions') and then back to New York City to stay at the Vanderbilt Hotel. Again, all expenses were paid for by the Queenstown Association.

On 19 February, there was a formal dinner for Bayly at the prestigious and ultra-snobbish New York Yacht Club, where Morgan's father had been commodore (and Junius would be too, in time). Captain Pringle, Bayly's American Chief of Staff in 1917–18, presented the old admiral with a silver rose bowl, inscribed with a dedication which included the statements 'to Admiral Sir Lewis Bayly RN, an honorary president and a master of his profession' and 'as a testimonial of loyalty and affection'.[12] Bayly responded later, in writing, declaring inter alia that 'I leave you with a deep affection, and I take away with me a proud recollection of the wonderful honour you have accorded us both'.[13] From New York, Bayly and Violet journeyed to Newport in company with Admiral Sims, where Bayly inspected the battleship USS *Tennessee*. They finally left for England on board RMS *Celtic* (mined twice in the Irish Sea on Bayly's watch) on 26 February. It had been a remarkable tribute. Bayly was a retired admiral, in no great grace with the Admiralty in Britain; but he had been afforded hospitality and acclamation more usually reserved for royalty.

A further, and surprising, honour was offered to Bayly ten years later. He was not, and had never been, a wealthy man, and was only just financially afloat in his Devon retirement. But Bayly would not compromise his principles to escape his genteel poverty; in retirement in Ermington, Devon, Bayly steadfastly refused to have any truck with personal publicity. Indeed, on 12 December 1921, he wrote to a Mrs Herbert declining her suggestion that he should write a book based on his war experiences. 'It requires as much training to write a book as it does to handle a ,' he noted, but gallantly added that if he had any intention of so doing he could put himself in no better hands than hers.[14]

He was not so impecunious as not to assist others, however. After the war an unseemly argument blew up between Norman Wilkinson of 'dazzle' fame and Professor John Graham Kerr as to who had actually invented the scheme. The Admiralty had given Wilkinson the credit but Kerr effectively accused him of stealing Kerr's own ideas. Eventually the matter went to 'court', or at least the Royal Commission for Awards to Inventors (RCAI), which had been established to give pecuniary reward to inventors who had helped the war effort. Both Kerr and Wilkinson retained barristers to represent them and Bayly was called as a witness for Wilkinson and on 16 October 1922 gave his opinion that Wilkinson did indeed deserve the credit, describing his work at Queenstown. Wilkinson won the case and an award of £2,000 (perhaps £90,000 today).

In 1922 Bayly had sought the Governorship of Jamaica, not least for the financial stability it would bring. His approach to the matter did not seem calculated to bring about the desired result. Despite his recent spat with the Admiralty upon his leaving the service, he wrote to the Secretary of the Admiralty from Ermington on 28 October: 'Sir. I would like to be appointed Governor of Jamaica when the post is vacant; and should the Lords of the Admiralty consider that it would be a good appointment from the country's point of view, I would be grateful if they would encourage my request.'[15] He went on to explain that Jamaica received many American visitors and that he got on with such people and understood them. The Admiralty forwarded his letter to the Colonial Office without comment; and one G Grindle replied to Their Lordships that a note had been made of Bayly's interest but that the post did not become vacant until summer 1924. Bayly heard nothing further about it. And in 1924 the post went to Brigadier Sir Samuel Herbert Wilson, an old Colonial Office hand.

Knowing of his financial situation, the Queenstown Association set up a fund in Bayly's favour made up from members' subscriptions, to allow him to purchase a house where he could live out the rest of his days. In 1930, Junius Morgan wrote to tell him that the fund had reached $15,000 and Morgan arranged for the money to be sent to Bayly's account at Lloyds Bank in Portsmouth. Bayly bought a house in Virginia Water, Surrey with the funds for Violet and himself to live in.

America Redux

In September 1932 Bayly's former Chief of Staff and quondam President of the Queenstown Association, Vice Admiral Joel Poinsett Pringle, died. Bayly determined to have a memorial to him in the USA and gained approval from the US Naval Academy in Annapolis that it be placed there.

Pressure was brought to bear on him by the members of the Association that he should unveil it personally and in May 1934 the admiral, now nearly seventy-seven years of age and in declining health, together with his niece Violet, boarded the *Aquitania* (the ship which had nearly done for USS *Shaw* in 1918) for New York. It was another triumph. Joseph Taussig, now an admiral and Assistant Chief of the Naval Staff sent a message of greeting as the liner arrived in harbour. 'Your comrades in the Queenstown Association ... are glad to welcome you to the United States and to offer recognition of your mission in coming to do honour of the past President of the Association.'[16]

Junius Morgan hosted them at his magnificent house 'Salutation' on Long Island and transported them on his 60ft, 25-knot petrol yacht *Shuttle*. They were wined and dined by various members of the Morgan dynasty. In Philadelphia they were met by Admiral Arthur Hepburn (who had commanded the 'Splinter Ships' at Queenstown), the senior surviving officer in the Association and shown round the Navy Yard and then dined at his official residence. From there to Washington for more entertaining, and thence to Annapolis for a dignified ceremony and round of speech-making to unveil the plaque. Back in Washington, President Franklin Roosevelt invited Bayly to lunch at the White House and Admiral Taussig gave the admiral and his niece dinner. Finally, Roosevelt invited Bayly to be his guest aboard USS *Indianapolis* for the Fleet Review of 31 May. They took lunch together in the wardroom and watched the review seated side by side. Afterwards, Roosevelt asked Bayly to convey his personal wishes for closer naval co-operation back to the Admiralty and King George V.

More feting and lunching followed, culminating in a dinner of the Queenstown Association in New York at the Harvard Club, attended by over 100 members and with the usual speeches of mutual affection.[*] Finally Bayly and Violet were given a presiden-

---

[*] The Queenstown Association was finally wound up in 1961, following the death of Junius Morgan the previous year.

tial police motorcycle escort to return to the *Aquitania* for the voyage home. *The Times* reported his tour on 30 June 1934 and Bayly delivered Roosevelt's message to the King in person. It was another remarkable tribute to a man of no official standing in his own country whatsoever.

In 1937, ill health caused Bayly to sell the house in Virginia Water and purchase a flat in London. Violet finally prevailed upon him to write his memoirs, which he did on the condition they should only be published posthumously. Just short of four years after his final visit to the USA, on 16 May 1938, Admiral Sir Lewis Bayly KCB KCMG CVO died. The Admiralty offered Violet a full naval funeral for him, but she declined. It was, she thought, unlike him to have wanted such ostentation. Instead, Bayly was cremated and his remains scattered in the Garden of Remembrance at Golders Green, north London. Violet sent all the flowers to the Cenotaph in Whitehall under the charge of a naval officer, with one exception. She placed the wreath from the Queenstown Association with his ashes.*

---

* Bayly left effects valued at £345 15 shillings and 5 pence (perhaps £22,000 at today's values).

Considerations and Conclusions

Bayly was a controversial appointment to the Coast of Ireland Command. If Fisher had continued in office, he would never have got the posting, or possibly any other. But Jackson and Balfour took a chance on him. Was it a successful decision?

This chapter will consider the answers to that question from four perspectives. Firstly, Bayly as leader; secondly, the strategies and tactics that he deployed; thirdly, success measured against the objectives that he set for himself and the command; and fourthly, the performance of the command in the context of the war as a whole.

Bayly as leader
Bayly was in many respects an unlikely leader. He was not a charismatic show-off like Beatty, a bombastic larger-than-life character like Beresford or Fisher, a self-promoter such as Keyes, or a technocrat like Jellicoe. Nor was he aristocratic as were, inter alia, Battenberg, Meux, Pakenham and so many others; nor even a country squire. He was an introspective man, forthright, repressed to the point of seeming shyness, and most comfortable out of the limelight doing what he knew best.

But these characteristics were bred into him by his background and the timing of his life in the Royal Navy. As one historian of the navy has written 'the stiff upper lip was, in the Senior Service, an essential requirement. Enduring months at sea, often in bad weather and continual danger, closed men in on themselves. Things that needed to be said in the navy were said briefly and bluntly. In confined space emotions had to be supressed.'[1] It seems that the men who served under him in Ireland recognised and accepted the causes of his, at times, anti-social behaviour; because, of course, they suffered in a similar way, each responding differently to the conditions.

Certainly he was not afraid to take quick and independent action. The apprehension of Roger Casement and the *Aud,* his despatch of his cruiser to Dublin at the outbreak of the Easter Rising and his actions in defending Galway were all determined and decisive actions.

And Bayly had those characteristics which, many centuries earlier, had been deemed necessary for the highest office. In mediaeval times, to be considered for election to the post of Holy Roman Emperor, a candidate must demonstrate 'leadership, justice, generosity and piety'.[2] In his own peculiar way, Bayly did just that.

The Americans loved him. If Bayly had one singular success as a leader it was the integration of the USN into the Command and the war. Many people feared he would make a hash of it. In fact he was a resounding success, to the point where the Americans appreciated him much more than did his own masters. There was a considerable cultural difference between the 'Mother of Empire' and the young growing democracy that was keenly felt by many Americans. And the US Navy certainly considered itself the junior partner in the naval war, at least in the beginning, and had an inferiority complex. They knew the weight of tradition behind the Royal Navy and they knew also of its ability to be smugly arrogant about its place in the world. Bayly confounded these expectations. He treated them as exact equals. Furthermore, there is a national trait possessed by Americans which is still one of the distinguishing characteristics of the country. They are open, frank, responsive to orders and dislike the rather indirect approach which can typify British upper-echelon behaviour. Bayly was always clear, authoritative, honest and forthright.

But he also had behaviours which work well for leaders today. He demonstrated trust, once it had been earned; he did not 'back seat drive'; he supported his men at all times; he fought to get them the rewards and comforts that he felt they deserved. He dealt face to face, not through memo and letter. Bayly worked through his men, rather than by dictat, and he demonstrated honest purpose. In this sense he was a very modern leader.

Bayly was childless, but in a way he seems to have seen these young men commanding his ships, all generally in their late twenties or early to mid-thirties, as his children. He created a family for them, with Bayly playing the paterfamilias and Violet the much-loved elder sister. They had a house to use, a garden to enjoy, a farm to work. Serving away from their own families, in a somewhat hostile land and in conditions of great discomfort, he made them feel that there was a home for them at Queenstown. And they uplifted him, giving him purpose, belonging, warmth and affection, which, although he tried not to show it, Bayly enjoyed. It is perhaps no surprise that, after he left that environment, he reverted to the grumpy and resentful person that many in the navy thought he was.

Judged solely as a leader of men, Bayly must be rated a success.

Strategies and tactics

On taking over the Command, Bayly inherited nothing more than a collection of trawlers and drifters with a few torpedo boats thrown in. With such forces he could hardly hope to catch any U-boat in the open seas and had to content himself with coastal defence, the laying of nets across headlands and estuaries and the escort of slow vessels through the waters near to Ireland.

Bayly's offensive capability was near to zero and it is no surprise that he lighted upon the Q-ship concept and made it his own. The Admiralty might not let him have any destroyers or other fighting ships but Q-ships could be requisitioned and converted in his own facilities or at Devonport and for limited sums of money. They thus became Bayly's first line of offence and it is telling that the first six U-boats to be sunk by the command were sunk by Q-ships. Not until May 1917 did a 'regular' warship achieve a sinking (see Appendix 4 for all the Command's successes against U-boats). Of course, it can be argued that the Q-ships were a double-edged sword. Once their tactics became known to the Germans, U-boat commanders were much more likely to attack merchant ships without warning and from under the water, giving less regard to the possible saving of lives.

When the sloops began to arrive in 1915–16, Bayly deployed them on area patrols, searching through a defined patch of water, hunting for U-boats; such a Sisyphean task demanded long hours and considerable seamanship but it was unlikely to produce much in the way of success, being the proverbial search for a needle in a haystack. Indeed, in the whole of the war the sloops sank a total of one-and-a-half U-boats. Bayly might argue that this nonetheless saved ships and lives by forcing the U-boats to stay submerged. In this belief he was later supported by the historian Arthur Marder who noted that 'sinking submarines is a bonus, not a necessity … what matters is that the ships deliver cargoes regularly and adequately ... it did not really matter how many U-boats the Germans had if they were forced to keep out of the way'.[3] In the end this is, of course, a case of *ignoramus et ignorabimus*, things that we do not know and cannot know. All that can be said is that it was possibly true but, given the area of sea involved in the Western Approaches, unlikely. The sloops were also used for escort duty but, in the main, they were escorting single ships only. This, as the example of convoy later demonstrated, was a misuse and waste of available resources.

When the destroyers arrived from the United States, Luigi's initial intention was to deploy them as he had deployed the sloops, on hunting patrols for U-boats. But convoy escort of the many troop and supply ships coming from the USA became their primary occupation instead. Bayly, like Admiral Benson in America, had opposed convoy (although he later dissembled). Sims claimed that it was his influence which forced the deployment of convoy for troop and supply ships in the Atlantic (from 24 May 1917 onwards). There may be truth in this but it is more likely that it was the political worry about the impact of a lost troopship on American public opinion which brought it about.

The USN destroyers did good work and escorted convoys proved a success. In the nineteen months that the USN was in the war, the Queenstown forces escorted 360 convoys and Bayly commanded ninety-two different US vessels. Two million US troops were safely ushered across the Atlantic. As U-boat hunters, however, the US destroyers achieved one solitary success; which was one more than the Irish Sea Hunting Flotilla, however.

Before convoy, the losses of merchant shipping in the Western Approaches were substantial. In February 1917 the German war aim for their unrestricted submarine campaign was to reduce British merchant shipping by 39 per cent. This required U-boats to sink 600,000grt of shipping each month. During the first three months of unrestricted U-boat attacks they sank 1,941,102grt (977 ships) of which 1,045,367grt were in the Western Approaches. When convoy was adopted, it forced the U-boats to operate closer inshore. But even here, attacks continued; between August and December 1917, 58 per cent of sinkings were within ten miles of the coast.

Bayly's neglect of naval aviation did not prove fatal as the Americans ably filled that gap once engaged. Whether he would have 'got there' under his own steam is, however, debatable. More certainly, his acquisition and use of experienced war commanders such as Nasmith and Evans gave the USN access to invaluable teachers at a formative stage.

In terms of strategy, Bayly possibly had been dealt a poor hand at the beginning, but drew good cards as the game progressed. It is perhaps fair to say that he played his hand at least as well as his experience and beliefs would allow.

Success vs objectives

Bayly defined the objectives of the Command as threefold. Firstly, sink submarines, secondly protect trade, and thirdly rescue survivors.

During the war, 202 U-boats were lost. Bayly's forces accounted directly for just fourteen of them. If one were being generous, that might be stretched to nineteen (see Appendix 3). The Command's Q-ships sank seven U-boats, plus another one-and-a-half sunk by PC-boats. Bayly might have claimed that his faith in the Q-ship was justified, or at least that it allowed his forces to obtain a level of success against the U-boat. But as this book has shown, the cost in life, *materiel* and sheer courage and stamina was considerable. The sloops can claim one-and-a-half U-boats sunk, submarines two and the USN one. But it is not a big haul for a navy which prided itself on the offensive, or for all the miles of area patrolling which Bayly's ships put in.

The sloops participated in many acts of rescue and mercy; there were numbers of merchant sailors who had cause to thank them for the seamanship and dedication that they demonstrated. *Laburnum* alone picked up 585 sailors from the sea during 1917.

Trade was better protected when convoy was introduced but the losses in the Western Approaches throughout the war were multiple, constant and, by early 1917, severe; it can hardly be claimed that the Command was successful in protecting trade beyond a certain low attainment.

The command in context

Without doubt, we can surely judge Bayly's overarching contribution to Great War history as being his successful integration of the British and US commands in Ireland. That this is in stark contrast to the experience of the Allied armies must, in part however, be chalked up to Admiral Sims.

The American supreme commander for Army forces, General

271

John 'Black Jack' Pershing, rejected British and French demands for American forces to be integrated with their armies and insisted that the American Expeditionary Force (AEF) would operate as a single unit under his command. The other Allies, desperate for men after three long years of attrition, wanted to feed soldiers wholesale into their lines. Pershing insisted that the AEF fight as complete units under American command, rather than being split up by battalions to bolster British or French brigades (although the US 27th and 30th Divisions were loaned, during the German 1918 Spring Offensive, to the Anglo-French Fourth Army).

Whilst this standoff may or may not have impacted on the successful prosecution of the war, it certainly did nothing to build Allied relationships and American troops were unnecessarily denied access to the learning that three years of war had brought. Pershing deployed massed infantry attacks supported by only limited artillery, a tactic then avoided by British and French commanders. The Meuse-Argonne offensive of September 1918, in which 1.2 million American soldiers participated, cost 26,277 lives, with 95,786 wounded, which made it both the largest, and the most bloody, AEF operation of the war. The inexperience of many of the troops, and the tactics used during the early phases of the operation, exacerbated the level of loss.

Sims, however, saw that a divided command could not work at sea and that his sailors had much to learn from their Royal Navy colleagues. And Bayly set up training programmes as soon as new men and ships arrived to ensure that these lessons were passed on. By the end of the war, Bayly's command was dominated by American forces but they were willing and happy to work under his direction with no thought of seeking a US commander to replace him.

American troopship losses were minimal. This in itself was a major achievement and saved Wilson and his advisers the headache of a backlash at home. Two million American soldiers were safely and successfully transported to Europe by sea. Bayly could claim a part of this success.

Perhaps the third claim on history that Bayly could make is that his Command became, by the war's end, the second or third largest in the Royal Navy, after the Grand Fleet and vying with the Dover Patrol for that distinction. Unlike the CinCs of these commands (Jellicoe and Beatty for the Grand Fleet, Bacon and Keyes for Dover) he was not feted or turned into a hero nor was he showered with honours and riches as they mostly were.* He may have been a reclusive character, but he would, one feels, have welcomed some recognition at home, particularly as he was never well off financially.

Staff

Unusually for an admiral of his age and background, Bayly appreciated the value of a staff. Not just any old collection though – if the right people were unavailable then he would make do until they were. He seemed to have a good eye for talent, and his choices for the staff positions in the Command were sound and enabled the operation to work as smoothly as it could. Paymaster Russell was clearly an important part of the machine but the addition of the experience of men like Herbert would have given the staff credibility in the eyes of the men of the Command, as did Campbell as his flag captain. Appointing Captain Joel Poinsett Pringle USN his Joint Chief of Staff was a masterstroke by Bayly and Pringle made a decided contribution to the running of the operation. Bayly said of him that 'Captain Poinsett Pringle would have been an outstanding officer in any navy'.[4]

As his other Joint Chief of Staff Bayly had several false starts with Hibbert and Carpendale both disappointing him. But in Captain Francis Martin-Leake he struck gold. When Leake died prematurely in 1928, Bayly wrote his *Times* obituary, noting that 'although Vice Admiral Martin-Leake was very little known outside the Service, it is true to say that no officer of or near his standing was so highly respected and more universally liked in the navy than he was … During his service as Chief of Staff in Queenstown he made a great reputation and friendship among the United States officers and men owing to his selfless tact and constant willingness to help all ranks and ratings of whatever nationality.'[5]

By 1917 the staff had expanded to include WRNS and many junior ranks as the example of Mary Battersby and her brother demonstrates. Marcus Victor Cumberlege was another of these unsung heroes. A thirty-year-old lieutenant commander RNVR he was unfit for sea service due to 'defective vision'. But he served aboard the depot ship *Colleen* as first lieutenant for three years. Martin-Leake thought highly of him. 'His duties have included dis-

---

* The King and Parliament granted Beatty a 'bonus' of £100,000 at the end of the war. Jellicoe received £50,000, Keyes £10,000. (£100,000 would be the equivalent of around £5 million today).

ciplinary arrangements of port depot establishment, harbour boat and night patrol services. Leave and patrol arrangements of the port. Liberty man received and handling of survivors from lost ships etc., etc. All these duties have been carried out with marked ability and without breakdown ... His work was of real value to the state ...'[6] A grateful nation awarded Cumberlege an OBE after the war. Such staff work would have been essential, for apart from warships, Bayly had a plenitude of small auxiliary vessels to manage. On I January 1918, there were 461 such vessels, including 162 trawlers and 194 drifters around the coast of Ireland and the Irish Sea, all of which required tasking, manning and direction (see Appendix 5). It seems clear that the calibre of the staff that Bayly surrounded himself with was an important factor in the success of the command.

* * *

Overall, Bayly undertook an important role and within the limits of his personality, naval education and background he did it successfully. He dealt well and fairly with all, he led from the front, he knew how to pick good men. Lewis Bayly has been largely ignored or mocked by history; in this, history would appear to be wrong.

Envoi

With Bayly's death in 1938, the story closes; but it would be remiss not to record the fates of three possibly unsung heroes of the war in the Western Approaches – William Sims, Violet Voysey and Admiralty House itself.

Sims was promoted to the rank of acting admiral in December 1918 but when reassigned back to the USA and his old position as President of the War College, he reverted to his pre-war status of rear admiral, a rank in which he continued until his retirement. In 1920 Sims published a book, *Victory at Sea,* which described his experiences during the war. A year later the book was awarded a Pulitzer Prize for History, making Sims the only career US naval officer to have gained such an accolade. In the book he was scathing regarding the activities of the Irish Republicans, noting the hostility to the USN by the Irish and that 'Irish republicans passed shipping intelligence to Germany, thus prolonging the war assisting German spies and costing American lives'.[1] Whilst still in the service, he became a vociferous critic of American naval policy and of Secretary Daniels in particular, which no doubt did his prospects of advancement no good at all. And he continued his attacks on Irish republicanism in speeches in which he blamed Irish-Americans for a 'great many of your sons at the bottom of the sea'.[2] Rear Admiral William Sims was placed on the retired list in October 1922, having reached the mandatory retirement age of sixty-four and died in Boston, Mass, thirteen years later. His role in winning the war is not as well-known as it deserves to be, even in his own country. Jellicoe certainly appreciated it, writing that 'it was fortunate indeed for the Allied cause that Admiral Sims should have been selected to command the United States forces in European waters, for ... he added a habit of speaking his mind with absolute fearless disregard of the consequences'.[3] Both Sims and Bayly were, in a sense, mavericks and suffered for it accordingly.

Violet Mary Annesley Voysey found herself in somewhat straitened circumstances after Bayly's death. A grateful nation had awarded her the OBE for services as 'President of the Queenstown War Work Fund and the Local War Pensions Committee' (gazetted 30 March 1920) but this did not pay the bills. The sale of the admiral's autobiography, *Pull Together*, had not reached the expected numbers and she had limited funds at her disposal. Once again the Queenstown Association came to the rescue. Members contributed to a fund which was deposited for her welfare for the remaining years of her life. Violet died on 19 November 1943; the balance of the fund was then returned to the Association.

Admiralty House in Queenstown had been the centre of Bayly's enterprise, home to him and his staff and a home-from-home for countless British and American naval officers. In 1922 Ireland was racked by civil war. The Irish Free State had been founded as a dominion within the British Empire by virtue of the Anglo-Irish Treaty of December 1921. The agreement was opposed by hard-line Republicans and a civil war broke out between the anti-treaty faction and the new government of Ireland. The area around Cork became the centre of the so-called 'Munster Republic', which was held by the anti-treaty Irish Republican Army. On 8 August 1922, 450 Irish Free State soldiers were landed by a converted passenger ferry at Passage West, between Queenstown/Cobh and Cork city, and proceeded to attack republican army positions. On the 10th, the defeated Irish Republican Army left Cork and its environs, burning buildings behind them as they departed. Amongst the buildings destroyed was Admiralty House, a symbol of the hated British rule and the Anglo-Irish treaty.

The Catholic Church later bought the gutted, roofless shell and refurbished it as a noviciate for the Sisters of Mercy. In 1993 the building was sold to another religious group, the Benedictine Order of nuns, and it is still used by them as a contemplative monastery, named St Benedict's Priory. But that is not quite the end of the story.

On 4 May 2017, the Port of Cork Company and Cork County Council, together with the Naval Order of the United States (NOUS), organised a 'Commemoration Ceremony to Mark 100 Years since the Arrival of the US Navy into Cork Harbour', which took place at the quondam Admiralty House, thrown open for the day by the nuns. Given that they are a closed order, this was a major concession. The great and the good of County Cork attended, as did representatives of the US Navy, the Irish Navy, NOUS, the American Legion, the Catholic clergy and the great-granddaughter of Commander Joseph Taussig, Ms Elizabeth Helmer. There was much speechmaking celebrating the American entry into the war and the great bonds of friendship that exist between Ireland and the USA – as one Irish speaker noted, 'after all, we built the place'. Bayly was mentioned twice, the Royal Navy not at all. NOUS dedicated and unveiled a plaque, to be placed at the entrance to the house, marking the US Navy's arrival and their deeds. It does not refer to the strong partnership that developed between the RN and the USN, under RN command. Nor does it recall the Royal Navy's four-year battle to protect life and trade off the Irish coasts. Just as in the UK, their sacrifice is forgotten.

*   *   *

A fitting tribute to the events described in this book may possibly be found in a work by two of Britain's greatest creative talents of the period. In 1911 Rudyard Kipling wrote a poem for children, *Big Steamers*, published in C R L Fletcher's *A School History of England* (Oxford: Clarendon Press, 1911). Edward Elgar set it to music in 1918, at the request of the Ministry of Food, to draw attention to the Mercantile Marine losses and the importance of their efforts. The last two verses seem a suitable epitaph for Bayly and his men and all the mariners they tried to defend.

'Then what can I do for you, all you Big Steamers,
Oh, what can I do for your comfort and good?'
'Send out your big warships to watch your big waters,
That no one may stop us from bringing you food.'

For the bread that you eat and the biscuits you nibble,
The sweets that you suck and the joints that you carve,
They are brought to you daily by All Us Big Steamers
And if any one hinders our coming you'll starve!"

The Principal Queenstown Sloops and their Commanders

Zinnia; Lieutenant Commander G F W Wilson RN.
Bluebell; Lieutenant Commander M A F Hood RN.
*Laburnum**; Lieutenant Commander W W Hallwright RN.
Poppy; Lieutenant Commander C B Hastings RN.
Snowdrop; Lieutenant Commander G P Sherston RN.
Rosemary; Lieutenant Commander R C Mayne RN.
Genista; Lieutenant Commander J White RN.
Sunflower; Lieutenant Commander J C Cole-Hamilton RN.
Jessamine; Lieutenant Commander S H Simpson, later S A Geary-Hill, both RN.
Myosotis; Lieutenant Commander W C Cochrane RNR.
Camellia; Lieutenant Commander R Richardson RN.

*Later converted to a Q-ship

The Queenstown VCs

Who	When	Where	Ship	Other
Commander Gordon Campbell DSO, RN	17 Feb 1917	W of Ireland	*Farnborough* (ex *Loderer*)	*U-83* sunk. Note Campbell got DSO for sinking *U-68* in the Atlantic 22 Mar 1916 in *Farnborough*
Lt Ronald Neil Stuart DSO, RNR	7 Jun 1917	Atlantic	*Pargust* (ex *Vittoria*)	*UC-29* sunk. Campbell commanding got bar to DSO Rule 13
Seaman William Williams DSM, RNR	do	do	do	Rule 13
Lt Charles George Bonner DSO, RNR	8 Aug 1917	Bay of Biscay	*Dunraven*	*UC-71* attacked Campbell commanding got second bar to his DSO Williams got bar to DSM Rule 13
PO Ernest Herbert Pitcher DSM, RN	do	do	do	Rule 13
Lt William Edward Sanders, RNR (born New Zealand	30 Apr 1917	180 miles S of Ireland	*Prize* (three-masted top sail schooner)	*U-93* (damaged, not sunk) *Prize* lost with all hands 14 August 1917
Lt Harold Auten DSC, RNR	30 Jul 1918	20 miles SW of Start Point	*Stockforce*	*U-80* (damaged not sunk)

Why Was It So Hard to Find a U-Boat?

Why was it so difficult to find and destroy the U-boats which ranged across the Western Approaches? The problem was to find them first.

In the early days of the war, U-boats would seek their prey on the surface, submerging only to hide from those that sought them. On the surface, low-lying and grey against a grey sea and grey sky, they were in any case difficult to detect from the bridge of a merchantman, sloop or destroyer. Submerged they were impossible to find. Initially, U-boats attacked on the surface, using their deck guns, or by putting boarding parties aboard to plant explosive charges and sink their captive. As the war wore on, and fear of Q-ships grew, ships were attacked from beneath the waves, using torpedoes, later marks of U-boat carrying more such weapons than the earlier ones could. The use of balloons, airships and aeroplanes made detection a little easier but the big problem still remained; how to 'see' a U-boat when it was submerged.

As it became clear that the submarine would not be conquered by traditional means, encouragement was given to those who were experimenting with 'new technology' to attack the U-boat menace. Some of Britain's greatest scientists were recruited to bring science to bear on the U-boat problem, not least the father and son combination of Professor Sir William Henry Bragg and his son William Lawrence, both of whom had been jointly awarded the 1915 Nobel Prize for Physics in connection with their work on crystal structure using X-ray spectrometry. William Lawrence did much work for the Army during the war on sound ranging methods for locating enemy guns. The father, William Henry, worked on methods of submarine detection, initially at Aberdour (see below), then at Harwich and finally at the Admiralty itself.

Bragg senior was involved in the invention of the hydrophone, a device for detecting underwater sound and thus identifying the presence of a submarine. Sir Ernest Rutherford (a Nobel laureate for Chemistry in 1908) had originally produced a paper suggesting that underwater microphones offered the best potential for experimentation and Bragg, working for the Board of Invention and Research (chaired by Fisher, brought back from retirement) co-operated with the Navy's own Hawkcraig experimental research station at Aberdour, HMS *Tarlair*, under the control of Commander (later Captain) Cyril Ryan RN and a staff of RNVR officers.

Here some 1,000–2,000 men were employed, a mixture of scientists and sailors. Starting with shore-based listening systems, then the non-directional 'Portable General Service' model, and finally the Mark II hydrophone, the Navy sought to solve the problem. These systems were non-directional; one could know that a U-boat was present but not in which direction or where. Triangulation was required to pinpoint the location and this required ships to drift with their engines off as their own engine noise would blank out that of the U-boat. Captains were nervous about such manoeuvres as it made their vessels a siting target for the U-boat they sought! In any case, the fact that the transmission of sound through water obeys the inverse-square law, i.e. its strength changes in inverse proportion to the square of the distance the sound has travelled, means that the noise made by a submarine falls off fast.

Bayly's ships, and especially trawlers and drifters, were equipped with these devices but they brought scant reward. The 'Splinter Ships' which arrived at Queenstown just before the war's end were all equipped with an American version of the underwater hydrophones.

The USN was also enamoured of the MV system (Multiple Unit Variable Compensated Acoustic Tubes) which, in simple terms, consisted of sound detecting tube nipples (and later, microphones) fitted into the hull of a vessel. Sims was so impressed that in November 1918 he had suggested that all US destroyers under his aegis should be fitted with them. However, they did not seem to be particularly effective in practice. The American troopship *Tuscania*, sunk on 5 February 1918 by *U-77* was so fitted and still went to her doom without ever detecting her attacker.

But for both British and American vessels, the lack of a

directional hydrophone meant that their ability to detect an underwater foe was limited. This lack was finally overcome by the invention of ASDIC (not named after the Anti-Submarine Detection Investigation Committee, as popular myth would have it, but a way of making A/S Division into a catchy word) which was a prototype developed by June 1917 but not used until after the end of the war.

Note: Bayly and his men might, granted the blessing of time travel, have felt better about their inability to find U-boats if they had been able to observe exercises off the coast of Florida, conducted in 2015, when the French nuclear submarine *Saphir* eluded US sub-hunters and their sophisticated sensors sufficiently to 'sink' the newly-overhauled aircraft carrier USS *Theodore Roosevelt* (reported in *The Economist*, August 6–12 issue, 2016).

U-boats Sunk in the Western Approaches by Vessels under Bayly's Direct Orders

U-boat	When	Sunk by
U-27	19 Aug 1915	*Baralong* (Q)
U-41	24 Sep 1915	*Baralong* (Q)
U-68	22 Mar 1916	*Farnborough* (Q)
U-19	30 Nov 1916	*Penshurst* (Q)
UB-37	14 Jan 1917	*Penshurst* (Q)
U-83	17 Feb 1917	*Farnborough* (Q)
U-81	1 May 1917	HMS *E54* (Vulcan Flotilla)
UC-29	7 Jun 1917	*Pargust* (Q)
U-45	12 Sep 1917	HMS *D-7*
UC-33	26 Sep 1917	HMS *PC-61*
U-58	17 Nov 1917	USS *Fanning*
U-87	25 Dec 1917	HMS *Buttercup* and *PC-56*
U-110	1 Mar 1918	HMS *Moresby*
U-104	25 Apr 1918	HMS *Jessamine*

In addition, Bayly might claim some responsibility for *UC-44* and *UC-42* which both sank in his area through explosions of their own mines, and for *UB-119* rammed by SS *Green Island*. *U-49* was lost in the Bay of Biscay when rammed by SS *British Transport* but it would be a stretch of the truth to allocate its loss to any action by Bayly's forces, as would the loss of *U-36*, rammed by the French steamer *Moliere* off Ushant.

APPENDIX 5

Auxiliary Vessels based on the Coast of Ireland and Irish Sea, 1 January 1918

Base	1	2	3	4	5	6	7	8	Total
Yachts	3	3	3				1	1	11
Trawlers	47	19	26	28	6	8	15	13	162
Drifters	61	14	69	15		4	17	14	194
MLs	8	12	12		8	6	16	6	68
Boom Defence	3	1	1	4		1	5		15
Minesweeping trawlers			4				7		11
									Total 461

Bases
1. Milford Haven
2. Kingstown
3. Lough Larne
4. Lough Swilly
5. Galway Bay
6. Berehaven
7. Queenstown
8. Holyhead

Principal German U-boat Types

The Coast of Ireland Command had to contend with most German U-boat types. In all the Germans deployed 375 submarines of thirty-three different classes. The principal types encountered are listed below (number constructed in brackets)

Ocean-going diesel-powered torpedo boats
Typically, six torpedoes, 8.8cm deck gun, 17 knots on surface, 7–9 knots submerged
U-19 (4), *U-23* (4), *U-27* (4), *U-31* (11), *U-43* (8), *U-51* (6), *U-57* (12), *U-63* (3), Large Ms. (4), *U-81* (6), *U-87* (6), *U-93* (22)

UB coastal torpedo boats
Typically, type UB-II six torpedoes, 8.8cm deck gun, 6-9 knots on surface, 5–6 knots submerged; type UB-III ten torpedoes and ran at 14 knots surfaced and 8 knots submerged; type UB-I carried no deck gun and only two torpedoes.
UB-I (17), UB-II (30), UB-III (89)

UC coastal minelayers
Typically, type UC-I twelve mines, no deck gun, 6 knots surfaced, 5 knots submerged. Type UC-II, eighteen mines, seven torpedoes, 8.8cm deck gun, 12 knots surfaced, 7 knots submerged. Type UC-III, very similar but fourteen mines
UC-I (15), UC-II (64), UC-III (16)

Author's Note

When I started writing this book I had two preconceptions – that I did not like Lewis Bayly and that the campaign in the Western Approaches was largely a failure. In the first assumption I proved myself wrong; I came to admire the admiral. His very old-fashioned-ness and introverted nature became attractive, as the men who served under him also found. He was also a much more complex man than previous writers of naval history have given him credit for.

As to the success of the campaign, I have less certainty. Many merchant ships and civilian seaman were lost in the Western Approaches and the strategies deployed against their attackers, until the introduction of convoy, were of limited value. But I did come to appreciate the bravery of the merchant sailors who risked their lives bringing vital supplies to Britain and her Allies; their sacrifice should be remembered as of equal worth to those of the men who served in the armed forces.*

In any case, I hope that I have told the story of the Western Approaches and the men of the Coast of Ireland Command fairly and well. Their story is often neglected in the standard histories of the war and they deserve better; this book is an attempt to provide a fitting memorial for them.

The writer of historical works in the UK is helped immensely both by the quality and the availability of archives and by the skill of the archivists who manage them. To the staff and trustees of the following institutions I owe a debt of thanks. The National Archives, Kew; the Imperial War Museum, London; The National Museum of the Royal Navy, Portsmouth; the Churchill Archive, Churchill College, Cambridge; the National Maritime Museum, Greenwich; the British Library London; the Liddle Collection, Leeds University; the Cobh Museum, Cobh; Arklow Maritime Museum, Co Wicklow; the National Library of Ireland, Dublin. In addition, those who maintain on-line resources, such as the incomparable www.naval-history.net deserve my gratitude.

Heather Johnson at the National Museum of the Royal Navy helped me track down some of Bayly's and Jackson's correspondence with great efficiency. Yvonne Allen, the curator of the Cobh Museum (though sadly for researchers, trying to retire) was extremely helpful and gave me heaps of uncatalogued papers to read through, to my benefit. Jim Rees, curator of the Arklow Maritime Museum, was both kind and co-operative and provided some rare imagery for me.

The Irish maritime historians Sean T Rickard and Daire Brunicardi generously made reading suggestions by email and I was able to enjoy an instructive coffee with Sean in Cobh.

I have, as always, been greatly assisted by the advice of Julian Mannering of Seaforth Publishing, who commissioned this book, my third with that esteemed house.

And finally, my thanks go to Vivienne, without whose support and advice none of my books would ever have happened.

Most books contain errors of commission and omission. If there are errors or solecisms the fault is mine and I should like to hear of them; *errare humanum est.*

---

* In total some 12,000 men of the Merchant Marine lost their lives in the First World War. Their names are inscribed on the walls of the Merchant Marine Memorial in Trinity Square Gardens, London, EC3 (also known as the Tower Hill Memorial).

Notes

The following abbreviations will be used for brevity.

Institutions

BL	British Library, London.
CAC	Churchill Archive, Churchill College, Cambridge.
IBMH	Buro Staire Mileata (Irish Bureau of Military History), Dublin.
IWM	Imperial War Museum, London.
NA	National Archives, Kew.
NMM	National Maritime Museum, Greenwich.
NMRN	National Museum of the

Royal Navy, Portsmouth.

Papers

JP	Jellicoe papers, British Library.

Books

FDTSF	Marder, *From the Dreadnought to Scapa Flow*.

It is the convention that page numbers be given for citations. This is not always possible in the modern world. Some digitised documents lack page numbering and some archives hold unnumbered single or multiple sheets in bundles under one reference or none at all. Thus, page numbers will be given where possible but the reader will understand that they are not always available or, indeed, necessary.

Preface
1. Smith, *Yellow Admiral*, p 54.
2. Marder, *Fear God and Dread Nought*, Vol 1, p 147.

Chapter 1
1. Wilson, *Empire of the Deep*, p 300.
2. ADM 203/99, NA.
3. Beresford, 'Home Rule and Naval Defence', p 191.
4. Marder, *FDTSF*, Vol 1, p 358.
5. Dunn, *Blockade*, p 21.
6. Wilson, *Empire of the Deep*, p 503.
7. Nolan, *Secret Victory*, p 25.
8. Ibid, p 27.

Chapter 2
1. Letter to Lulu C, 15 May 1915, GBR/0014/Hood 6-6, CAC.
2. Letter to *The Times*, 7 July 1914.
3. Draft paper of 11 July 1914, RIC/1/9, NMM.
4. Marder, *Fear God and Dread Nought*, Vol 2, p 505.
5. Churchill, *World Crisis*, Vol 2, p 280.
6. Scott, *50 Years*, p 201.
7. CHAR 12/61/86, CAC.
8. CHAR 13/61/94, CAC.
9. *The Times*, 15 January 1915.
10. *Argus*, 19 January 1915.
11. CHAR 13/60/124, CAC.
12. *Connaught Tribune*, 15 March 1915.
13. Stewart, *Carson*, pp 94–5.
14. Jeffrey, *1916*, p 7.
15. ADM 137/592, NA.
16. Brunicardi, *Sea Hound*, p 29.
17. Docs 114498, 4 October 1914, IWM.

Chapter 3
1. Marder, *FDTSF*, Vol 2, p 358.
2. Ibid.
3. Letter to Lulu C, 15 May 1915, GBR/0014/Hood 6-6, CAC.
4. CHAR 13/64/53-54, CAC.
5. Nolan, *Secret Victory*, p 68.
6. CHAR 13/64/29, CAC.
7. CHAR 13/64/31, CAC.
8. Letter to Lulu C, 15 May 1915, GBR/0014/Hood 6-6, CAC.
9. *Cork Examiner*, 6 February 1946.
10. CHAR 13/64/34, CAC.
11. CHAR 13/64/68, CAC.
12. CHAR 13/64/64, CAC.
13. CHAR 13/64/65, CAC.
14. Nolan, *Secret Victory*, p 83.
15. Borgonovo, *Dynamics of War*, p 29.
16. Letter to Lulu C, 15 May 1915, GBR/0014/Hood 6-6, CAC.

17. CHAR 13/64/53-54, CAC.
18. CHAR 2/66/11, CAC.
19. Winton, *Victoria Cross at Sea*, p 115.
20. Jellicoe to Browning, 7 July 1917, JP Add MS 49036 f.36, BL.
21 Marder, *FDTSF*, Vol 2 p 361.
22. Ibid, p 362.
23. Ibid, p 361.
24. Bayly, *Pull Together*, p 181.
25. Letter 9 January 1915, MSS 255/6/20, NMRN.

Chapter 4
1. Bayly, *Pull Together*, p 92.
2. De Chair, *The Sea is Strong*, p 115.
3. ADM 196/87, NA.
4. 'Lamda', *Naval Review*, May 1939, p 314.
5. Bayly, *Pull Together*, p 121.
6. 21 November 1908, King-Hall diary.
7. Marder, *FDTSF*, Vol 2, p 98.
8. Quoted in Marks and Potts, *Before the Bells*, p 97.
9. Marder, *Portrait of an Admiral*, p 134.
10. Ibid, p 136.
11. Bayly, *Pull Together*, p 176.
12. Ibid, p 182.
13. 2 August 1915, MSS 255/6/2, NMRN.
14. Ibid.
15. 12 August 1915, MSS 255/6/4, NMRN.
16. Bayly, *Pull Together*, p 185.
17. Ibid, p 186.
18. Ibid, p 185.
19. 12 August 1915, MSS 255/6/4, NMRN.
20. MSS 255/6/8, NMRN.
21. Bayly, *Pull Together*, p 213.

Chapter 5
1. MSS 255/6/5, NMRN.
2. MSS 255/6/8, NMRN.
3. Keeble-Chatterton, *Danger Zone*, p 73.
4. Ibid.
5. Bayly, *Pull Together*, p 193.
6. *The Jewish Ex-Serviceman's Magazine* (February 1935), p 11.
7. MSS 255/6/8, NMRN.
8. Bayly, *Pull Together*, p 193.
9. MSS 255/6/8, NMRN.
10. MSS 255/6/4, NMRN.
11. MSS 255/6/8, NMRN.
12. Ibid.
13. Oliver, *Memoirs*, Vol 2, pp 125–6.

14. MSS 255/6/8, NMRN.
15. Keeble-Chatterton, *Danger Zone*, p 76.
16. Ibid, pp 76–7.
17. www.naval-history.net/OWShips-WW1-18-HMS_Jessamine.htm.
18. Keeble-Chatterton, *Danger Zone*, p 106.
19. Marder, *Portrait of an Admiral*, p 22.
20. CHAR 13/27/20, CHAR 13/64/20, CAC.
21. CHAR 13/66/20, CAC.
22. CHAR 13/70/37-38, CAC.
23. Ibid.
24. Bayly, *Pull Together*, p 194.
25. Ibid.
26. Dunn, *Blockade*, p 23.
27. Marder, *Portrait of an Admiral*, pp 134–5.
28. MSS 255/6/4, NMRN.
29. MSS 255/6/7, NMRN.

Chapter 6
1. *Argus*, 21 August 1915.
2. Ibid.
3. MSS 255/6/15, NMRN.
4. MSS 255/6/14, NMRN.
5. Ibid.
6. Ibid.

Chapter 7
1. Jeffrey, *1916*, p 306.
2. *Evening World*, 31 January 1916.
3. Jeffrey, *1916*, p 309.
4. Schmidt, *The Folly of War*, p 79.
5. *Sydney Sunday Times*, 9 January 1916.
6. Campbell, *Mystery Ships*, p 32.
7. Lake, *Smoke and Mirrors*, p 116.

Chapter 8
1. *New York Sun*, 17 March 1916.
2. Ibid, 29 March 1916.
3. MSS 255/6/30, NMRN.
4. Ibid.
5. *The Times*, 25 and 26 April 1916.
6. MSS 255/6/30, NMRN.
7. Quoted in Brunicardi, *The Sea Hound*, p 36.
8. Quoted in Cameron, *1916*, p 80.
9. Brunicardi, *The Sea Hound*, p 44.
10. Bayly, *Pull Together*, p 206.
11. Borgonovo, *Dynamics of War*, p 41.
12. Doc 406, IBMH.

13. Ibid.
14. Jeffrey, *1916*, p 105.
15. *London Gazette*, General Maxwell's Despatch, 21 July 1916.
16. MSS 255/6/30, NMRN.
17. Quoted in Townsend, *Easter 1916*, p 241.
18. *London Gazette*, 21 July 1916.
19. De Courcy Ireland, *The Sea and the Easter Rising*, p 22.
20. Ibid, p 23.
21. Brunicardi, *Haulbowline*, p 128.

Chapter 9
1. MSS 255/6/30, NMRN.
2. Ibid.
3. MSS 255/6/31, NMRN.
4. Ibid.
5. Hankey, *Supreme Power*, Vol 2, p 489.
6. *Kalgoorlie Miner*, 13 May 1916.
7. Docs 11440 Pt 2, p 21, IWM.
8. Keeble-Chatterton, *Danger Zone*, p 188.
9. Bayly, *Pull Together*, p 208.
10. Sloan, *Geopolitics*, p 141.
11. MSS 255/6/42, NMRN.
12. Ibid.
13. Ibid.
14. MSS 255/6/49, NMRN.
15. MSS 255/6/52, NMRN.
16. MSS 255/6/55, NMRN.
17. Ibid.
18. Bayly, *Pull Together*, p 190.
19. Ibid.
20. Ibid, p 191.
21. *Aberdeen University Review* (1937), p 97.
22. MSS 255/6/61, NMRN.
23. MSS 255/6/62 , NMRN.
24. *The Times*, 25 November 1916.
25. Cameron, *1916*, p 163.
26. JP MS 49009, Vol XXI, 4 December 1916, BL.
27. Hough, *The Great War at Sea*, p 196.
28. MSS 255/4/64, NMRN.
29. JP MS 49009, Vol XXI, 4 December 1916, BL.
30. Jones, *A Naval Life*, p 233.
31. Ibid, p 235.
32. Ibid, p 236.
33. Bayly, *Pull Together*, p 199.
34. Jones, *A Naval Life*, p 238.
35. 2009.39/1/31, NMRN.

Chapter 10
1. Docs 11165, IWM.
2. Diary 14 January 1917, docs 11165. IWM.
3. Ibid.
4. Diary 26 July, docs 11165, IWM.
5. Diary 29 January, docs 11165, IWM.
6. Diary 29 and 31 January, docs 11165, IWM.
7. Diary 8 February, docs 11165, IWM
8. www.presidency.ucsb.edu/ws/index.php?pid=65393
9. German Ambassador Count Johann von Bernstorff to Robert Lansing, U.S. Secretary of State, Washington D.C., 31 January 1917, firstworldwar.com.
10. Heckscher, *Woodrow Wilson*, pp 428–9.
11. Diary 26 February, docs 11165, IWM.
12. Green and Tanner (eds), *The Strange Survival of Liberal England*, p 108.
13. Jellicoe, *The Naval Crisis*, p 111.
14. Cobh Library, 'Irish Lights' exhibition 2016.
15. ADM 156/120, NA,
16 Keeble-Chatterton, *Danger Zone*, p 220.
17. Churchill, *World Crisis*, Vol 2, p 1233.
18. Marder, *FDTSF*, Vol IV, p 127.
19. ADM 137/1322, NA.

Chapter 11
1. Fayle, *Seaborne Trade*, Vol III, p 92.
2. Docs 4531, IWM.
3. Ibid.
4. Newbolt, *Naval Operations*, Vol V, pp 21–4.
5. Van Ellis, *America and WW1*, p 97.
6. Nolan, *Secret Victory*, p 157.
7. Sims, *The Victory at Sea*, pp 1–2.
8. Ibid, p 7.
9. Ibid, p 27.
10. Ibid, pp 28–39.
11. Ibid, p 53.
12. Ibid, p 54.
13. *Reveille*, 1 July 1938, p 10.
14. Keeble-Chatterton, *Danger Zone*, p 309.

15. JP, Vol XXI, 4 July 1917, MS 49009, BL.
16. Marder, *FDTSF*, Vol V, p 123.
17. Nolan, *Secret Victory*, p 182.
18. JP, Vol XXI, 23 May 1917, MS 49009, BL.
19. Marder, *Portrait of an Admiral*, p 247.
20. Bayly, *Pull Together*, p 219.

Chapter 12
1. Sims, *The Victory at Sea*, p 40.
2. Taussig, *The Queenstown Patrol*, p 11.
3. Ibid, p 16.
4. Ibid, p 18.
5. Ibid, p 19.
6. Ibid, p 20.
7. *Relevance*, Spring 2004 Issue, Volume 13, Number 2: article Paul Halpern.
8. Keeble-Chatterton, *Danger Zone*, pp 245–6.
9. Ibid, pp 245–6.
10. Bayly, *Pull Together*, p 214.
11. *Relevance*, Spring 2004 Issue, Volume 13, Number 2: article Paul Halpern,
12. Ibid.
13. Ibid.
14. Sims, *The Victory at Sea*, p 61.
15. Halpern, *A Naval History*, p 359.
16. JP, Vol XXI, 1 September 1917, MS 49009, BL.
17. Sims, *The Victory at Sea*, p 32.
18. Ibid, p 93.
19. Ibid, p 97.
20. Halpern, *A Naval History*, p 362.
21. Bayly, *Pull Together*, p 239.
22. Van Ells, *America and WW1*, p 98.
23. Sims, *The Victory at Sea*, p 49.
24. Liddle/WW1/RNMN/311, Liddle Collection.

Chapter 13
1. 28 April 1917, docs 1278, IWM.
2. Docs 4531, IWM.
3. Ibid.
4. Ibid.
5. Diary 18 May, docs 11165, IWM.
6. Liddle/WW1/RNMN/311, Liddle Collection.
7. Taussig, *The Queenstown Patrol*, p 61.

8. Jones, *A Naval Life*, p 245.
9. Bayly, *Pull Together*, p 252.
10. Ibid.
11. Sims, *The Victory at Sea*, p 68.
12. Taussig, *The Queenstown Patrol*, p 62.
13. Keeble-Chatterton, *Danger Zone*, p 252.
14. JP, Vol XXI, 4 July 1917, MS 49009, BL.
15. Ibid, 23 May 1917.
16. Ibid, 4 July 1917.
17. Ibid, 10 July 1917.
18. Ibid, 4 July 1917.
19. Ibid, 10 August 1917.
20. 21 July 1917, docs 1278, IWM.

Chapter 14
1. JP, Vol XXI, 22 August 1917, MS 49009, BL.
2. Jones, *A Naval Life*, p 241.
3. Ibid, p 240.
4. Ibid, p 245.
5. Ibid, pp 258–9.
6. Winton, *The Victoria Cross at Sea*, p 6.
7. Taussig, *The Queenstown Patrol*, p 52.
8. Ibid.
9. Winton, *The Victoria Cross at Sea*, p 133.
10. Letter 19 October 1917, docs 14178, IWM.
11. Sims, *The Victory at Sea*, p 164.
12. Campbell, *Mystery Ships*, p xxix.

Chapter 15
1. Lake, *Zeebrugge and Ostend Raids*, p 2.
2. Docs 11440, Pt 2, p 15, IWM.
3. Ibid, p 16.
4. Ibid, p 17.
5. JP, Vol XXI, 22 August 1917, MS 49009, BL.
6. Ibid, 10 September 1917.
7. Halpern, *Naval History*, p 367.
8. JP, Vol XXI, 10 December 1917, MS 49009, BL.
9. Nolan, *Secret Victory*, p 114.
10. ADM 137/3267, NA.
11. Ibid.
12. Ibid.
13. Diary 26 August 1917, docs 11165, IWM.
14. Docs 1278, IWM.
15. Diary 2 October 1917, docs 1278, IWM.

Chapter 16

1. Docs 4531, IWM.
2. Ibid.
3. *Chicago Sunday Tribune,* 28 October 1917.
4. Ibid.
5. Keeble-Chatterton, *Danger Zone,* p 304.
6. Ibid, p 306.
7. Sims, *The Victory at Sea,* p 133.
8. Ibid, p 13.
9. JP, Vol XXI, 10 December 1917, MS 49009, BL.

Chapter 17

1. Taussig, *The Queenstown Patrol,* p 174.
2. Campbell, *Mystery Ships,* p 79.
3. Taussig, *The Queenstown Patrol,* p 174.
4. Ibid.
5. Docs 11440, Pt 2, p 23, IWM.
6. Taussig, *The Queenstown Patrol,* pp 49–50.
7. Ibid.
8. Ibid.
9. JP, Vol XXI, 10 September 1917, MS 49009, BL.
10. Docs 11440, Pt 2, p 24, IWM.
11. Taussig, *The Queenstown Patrol,* p 26.
12. Diary 1 December 1917, docs 1278, IWM.
13. Ibid.
14. Ibid.
15. Stuart-Mason, *Britannia's Daughters,* p 22.
16. Campbell, *Mystery Ships,* p xxix.
17. Van Ells, *America and WW1,* p 100.
18. JP, Vol XXI, 1 September 1917, MS 49009, BL.
19. Van Ells, *America and WW1,* p 100.
20. Borgonovo, *Dynamics of War,* p 122.
21. Letter from his son 11 October 2005, Cobh Museum Archive.
22. Borgonovo, *Dynamics of War,* p 126.
23. Ibid, p 129.
24. JP, Vol XXI, 19 December 1917, MS 49009, BL.
25. Bayly, *Pull Together,* p 233.
26. Borgonovo, *Dynamics of War,* p 128.
27. Sloan, *Geopolitics,* p 160.
28. Taussig, *The Queenstown Patrol,* p 173.

Chapter 18

1. Bayly, *Pull Together,* p 246.
2. Docs 11440, Pt 2, p 23.
3. Diary 8 January 1918, docs 1278, IWM.
4. *Jewish Ex-Serviceman's Magazine* (February 1935), p 10.
5. Campbell, *Mystery Ships,* p 95.
6. Diary 1 December 1917, docs 1278, IWM.
7. Ibid, 14 December 1917.
8. Ibid, 12 December 1917.
9. ADM 156/85, NA.
10. Diary 13 December 1917, docs 1278, IWM.
11. Ibid, 28 December 1917.
12. JP, Vol XXI, 19 December 1917, MS 49009, BL.
13. Ibid.
14. De Chair, *The Sea is Strong,* 238.
15. JP, Vol XXI, 27 December 1917, MS 49009, BL.
16. Ibid.
17. JP, MS 49036, BL.
18. Bayly, *Pull Together,* p 246.

Chapter 19

1. Diary 1 January 1918, docs 1278, IWM.
2. Ibid, 9/10 January 1918.
3. Ibid.
4. *Chicago Daily Tribune,* 13 February 1918.
5. *Cornell Daily Sun,* 9 February 1918.
6. ADM 196/49/280, NA.
7. Hansard 28 October 1918 Vol 110 cc1113-4.
8. Asquith paper to Cabinet, Part II, MCKN 5/12, CAC.
9. Cabinet papers, MCKN 5/12, CAC.
10. JP, Vol XXI, 19 December 1917, MS 49009, BL.
11. Borgonovo, *Dynamics of War,* p 192.
12. Docs 11440, Pt 2, p 22, IWM.
13. Diary 1 March 1918, docs 1278, IWM.
14. Diary 8 June 1918, Docs 4531, IWM.
15. Ibid.

16. Ibid.

17. *Independent*, 18 December 2006.

Chapter 20

1. www.rafmuseum.org.uk/blog/
flying-boats-over-the-westrn-
approaches/#sthash.pcv0N6us.dpuf

2. Abbatiello, *Anti-Submarine Warfare*, p
96.

3. Jellicoe, *Naval Crisis*, p 70.

4. Bayly, *Pull Together*, p 248.

5. Ibid, p 252.

Chapter 21

1. Borgonovo, *Dynamics of War*,
p 133.

2. ADM 137/3445, NA.

3. Ibid.

4. *The London Gazette* (Supplement) No.
31021, p 13695, 20 November 1918.

5. Docs 11440, Pt 2, p 24, IWM.

6. Bayly, *Pull Together*, p 252.

7. Docs 4531, IWM.

Chapter 22

1. Bayly, *Pull Together*, p 249.

2. Docs 11440, Pt 2, p 25, IWM.

Chapter 23

1. Bayly, *Pull Together*, p 286.

2. Bayly to Bonnor, 28 August 1919, docs
14178, IWM.

3. Bayly to Admiralty, 17 March 1919,
ADM 178/33, NA.

4. Bayly, *Pull Together*, p 285.

5. Bayly to Admiralty, 1 May 1919, ADM
178/33, NA.

6. Ibid.

7. Ibid.

8. MS note 9 May 1919, ADM 178/33, NA.

9. Ibid, 13 May 1919.

10. Bayly to Admiralty, 28 May 1919,
ADM 178/33, NA.

11. Bayly, *Pull Together*, p 259.

12. Ibid, p 265.

13. Ibid, p 266.

14. Autograph letter in private collection.

15. CO 137/763, NA.

16. Bayly, *Pull Together*, p 268.

Chapter 24

1. Wilson, B, *Empire of the Deep*,
p 463.

2. Wilson, H, *The Holy Roman Empire*, p
338.

3. Marder, *FDTSF*, Vol V, p 103.

4. Bayly, *Pull Together*, p 223.

5. *The Times*, 27 January 1928.

6. ADM 171/87.

Chapter 25

1. Borgonovo, *Dynamics of War*,
p 137.

2. Ibid, p 138.

3. Jellicoe, *Naval Crisis*, p 116.

Bibliography

The following books have been cited in the main text. The place of publication is London unless otherwise stated.

Abbatiello, J, *Anti-Submarine Warfare in World War 1* (Routledge, 2006).

Bayly, L, *Pull Together* (George G Harrap and Co, 1939).

Beresford, C, 'Home Rule and Naval Defence', in *Against Home Rule* (F Warne and Co, 1912).

Borgonovo, J, *The Dynamics of War and Revolution; Cork City 1916-1918* (Cork: Cork University Press, 2013).

Brunicardi, D, *Haulbowline; the naval base and ships of Cork harbour* (Dublin: History Press Ireland, 2012).

――――――――, *The Sea Hound* (Cork: The Collins Press, 2001)

Bywater, H, and Ferraby, H, *Strange Intelligence* (Constable, 1931, republished Biteback, 2015).

Cameron, J, *1916, Year of Decision* (Oldbourne, 1962).

Campbell, G, *My Mystery Ships* (New York: Doubleday, Doran and Co, 1929).

Churchill, W, *The World Crisis* Vol 2 (Thornton Butterworth, 1923).

De Chair, D, *The Sea is Strong* (George G. Harrap and Co, 1961).

De Courcy Ireland, J, *The Sea and the Easter Rising* (Dublin: Maritime Institute of Ireland, 1966).

Dunn, S R, *Blockade; Cruiser Warfare and the Starvation of Germany* (Barnsley: Seaforth Publishing, 2016).

Evans, R, *The Pursuit of Power* (Allan Lane, 2016).

Fayle, C E, *Seaborne Trade* Vol III (Sussex: Naval and Military Press, facsimile edition; originally John Murray, 1924).

Green, E, and Tanner, M (eds), *The Strange Survival of Liberal England* (Cambridge: Cambridge University Press, 2007).

Halpern, P, *A Naval History of World War I* (UCL Press, 1994).

Hankey, M, *Supreme Command,* 2 vols (George Allen and Unwin, 1961).

Heckscher. A, *Woodrow Wilson* (Connecticut: Easton Press, 1997).

Hough, R, *The Great War at Sea* (Oxford: Oxford University Press, 1983).

Jeffery, K, *1916, A Global History* (Bloomsbury, 2015).

Jellicoe, J, *The Crisis of the Naval War* (New York: George H Doran Company, 1920).

Jones, M (ed), *A Naval Life* (Somerset: Persona Press, 2007).

Keeble-Chatterton, E, *Danger Zone* (Rich and Cowan, 1934).

Lake, D, *Smoke and Mirrors* (Stroud: Sutton Publishing, 2006).

――――, *The Zeebrugge and Ostend Raids 1918* (Barnsley: Pen and Sword Military, 2015).

Marder, A, *Fear God and Dread Nought*, 2 vols (Jonathan Cape, 1952).

――――――, *Portrait of an Admiral; the life and papers of Sir Herbert Richmond* (Cambridge, Mass.: Harvard University Press, 1952).

――――――, *From the Dreadnought to Scapa Flow*, Volumes I–V (republished Barnsley: Seaforth Publishing, 2013).

Newbolt, H, *Naval Operations*, Vol V (Longmans Greens and Co, 1931).

Nolan, L, and Nolan, J, *Secret Victory* (Mercier Press, 2009).

Potts, M, and Marks, T, *Before the Bells Have Faded* (Sussex: Naval and Military Press, 2004).

Schmidt, D, *The Folly of War: American Foreign Policy 1898-2005* (New York: Algora Publishing, 2005).

Scott, P, *50 Years in the Royal Navy* (John Murray, 1919).

Sims, W, *The Victory at Sea* (John Murray, 1920).

Sloan, G, *The Geopolitics of Anglo-Irish Relations in the 20th Century* (Leicester: Leicester University Press, 1997).

Smith, H, *A Yellow Admiral Remembers* (Edward Arnold, 1932).

Stewart, A, *Edward Carson* (Dublin: Gill and Macmillan, 1981).

Stuart-Mason, U, *Britannia's Daughters* (Barnsley: Pen and Sword, 1992).

Taussig, J, *The Queenstown Patrol, 1917*, ed W Still (Newport, Rhode Island: Naval War College Press,1996).

Townshend, C, *The Easter Rising* (Penguin, 2006).

Underwood, J, *The Wings of Democracy: The Influence of Air Power on the Roosevelt Administration, 1933–1941* (College Station: Texas A&M University Press, 1991).

Van Ells, M, *America and WW1* (Massachusetts: Interlink Books, 2015).

Wilson, B, *Empire of the Deep* (Weidenfeld and Nicolson, 2014).

Wilson, H, *The Holy Roman Empire* (Allen Lane, 2016).

Winton, J, *The Victoria Cross at Sea* (Michael Joseph, 1978).

Archival Documents

Private Papers of Rear Admiral Sir Horace Hood, GBR/0014/Hood, Churchill Archives Centre, Cambridge.

Churchill Papers, CHAR 13, Churchill Archives Centre.

McKenna Papers, MCKN 5/12, Churchill Archives Centre.

Keyes papers, Add 82414, British Library, London.

Jellicoe Papers, MS 49009, MS 49036, British Library.

Private Papers of Admiral Henry Jackson, MSS 255, National Museum of the Royal Navy, Portsmouth.

Private Papers of Admiral John Locke Marx, 2009.39, National Museum of the Royal Navy.

Memoirs of Admiral Sir Henry F Oliver, 2 vols, 1946 (unpublished), OLV/12, National Maritime Museum, Greenwich.

Private papers of Admiral Sir Herbert Richmond, RIC/1/9, National Maritime Museum.

Papers of Captain F S W de Winton, Liddle/WW1/RNMN/311, Liddle Collection, Leeds University Library.

Private Papers of Lieutenant C G Bonner RNR, Docs 14178, Imperial War Museum, London.

Private Papers of Commander F F Tower RNVR, Docs 11440, Imperial War Museum.

Private Papers of Commander R Goldrich RN, Docs 1278, Imperial War Museum.

Private Papers of Captain A G D Twigg RN, Docs 11498, Imperial War Museum.

Private Papers of Captain G F W Wilson RN, Docs 4531, Imperial War Museum.

Private Papers of Surgeon Probationer W E Mason, Docs 11165, Imperial War Museum.

Testimony of Frank Hardiman, Doc 406, Buro Staire Mileata, Dublin.

General Archive, Cobh Museum, Co Cork.

Magazines and Newspapers

Aberdeen University Review (1937).

Argus (Melbourne).

Atlanta Constitution.

Chicago Daily Tribune.

Chicago Sunday Tribune.

Connaught Tribune.

Cork Examiner.

Cornell Daily Sun.
Evening World (New York).
Hansard.
Independent.
Jewish Ex-Serviceman's Magazine.
Kalgoorlie Miner (Western Australia).
Naval Review.
Reveille.
Relevance (the quarterly journal of the Great War Society).
Sun (New York).
Sunday Times (Sydney).
The Economist.
The Times.
Washington Times.

On-line Resources
www.naval-history.net
www.dreadnoughtproject.org
www.corkshipwrecks.net

Other
Cobh library exhibition 2016, 'Irish Lights'

Index

Abosso, RMS 130–1
Aboukir, HMS 32
Aburi 130
Achilles (cargo ship) 85
Achilles, HMS 162
Active, HMS 183
Addah, SS 159–60
Admiralty, the 29, 43, 49, 211; and Bayly 55, 57, 67–8, 91, 97, 105, 127, 129, 138, 259–62, 266; Churchill's sacking from 48; and Coke 36, 44, 45–6, 47; and convoys 150–1, 152; and Hood 43; and Marx 165; and Q-ships 66, 67, 127, 168; signals intelligence 91; and Sims 135–6
Adventure, HMS 57, 63, 79, 95, 96, 100, 105, 183
Agamemnon, USS 247
Aghada 237
Ahern, William 26, 45
air warfare 93, 235–9, 270; *see also* airships; seaplanes/flying boats
airships 93, 215, 228, 239, 280
Aislaby, SS 115
Aitkin, Max 95
Albacore, HMS 215
Albermarle, HMS 97
Albion, HMS 97, 100
Alcedo, USS 192
Alexandria, SS 107–8
Algonquin 121
Alide 155
Allan, Alexander 184, 185
Allen, USS 188
Alyssum, HMS 106, 123
Amazon, RMS 229
Amberger, Gustav 193
American Expeditionary Force (AEF) 272
Ammen, USS 206
Anchusa, HMS 228, 241–2
Anderson, Walford A 238
Anderson, William Louis 235, 236
Anglo-Californian, SS 49–50
Anglo-Columbian 76
Anglo-Irish Treaty 276
Anti-Conscription Committee, Irish 226
anti-submarine nets 40–1, 47, 60–1
Antilles, USAT 191–2
Antwerp, RMS 72

Aplin, Henry F 94, 95, 102
Aquitania, RMS 251–2, 265, 266
Arabic, SS 70–1, 77, 83
Arbutus, HMS 210
Archimède 71–2
Ard Patrick, HMS 241, 242
Ariadne, HMS 236
Aries 120
armed merchant cruisers (AMCs) 13, 31, 33, 221–2, 227–8, 233; German 14
Armistice, the 251, 255
Arnold, Alfred 183
Artist, SS 130
ASDIC 282
Asgard 101
Asquith, H H, 25, 48, 69, 105, 211, 225
Asquith government 25, 48–9
Assyria, SS 186
Aster, HMY 48
Athenry 98–9
Atlanta, SS 37
Atlantic trade 13
Attack, HMS 173
Aubrietia, HMS 114–15, 156, 160, 164–5, 188
Aud, SS 90–3, 268
Ausonia, SS 230–1
Auten, Harold 242, 243–4

Babcock, John V 135, 146
Bacon, Reginald 29, 176
Badger, HMS 216
Bagly, David Worth 195
Balfour, Arthur James 49, 50–1, 91, 113, 137, 254n
Ballarat, SS 131
Baltic, SS 216
Baltimore, USS 229
Baralong, SS 71, 72–3; as *Wyandra* 76
Barlow, Charles James 'Billy' 40, 255
Barnson, SS 65
barrage 41
Battersby, Mary 200–1, 273
Bauer, Hermann 32
Bayhall, SS 115
Bayley, Charles James 'Billy' Bayly, Henrietta Charlotte 53
Bayly, Henrietta Mary, née Voysey 56
Bayly, Sir Lewis 16–17, 33, 106–7, 138–9, 185, 197–9, 204, 205, 207, 212–13; and the Admiralty 55, 57, 67–8,

91, 97, 105, 127, 129, 138, 259–62, 266; and airpower 236–7, 239, 270; and Asquith 105; attitude to submarines 55; and the *Aud* 91–3, 268; background and pre-Queenstown career 53–6; Borkum plan 68; and Campbell 86, 87, 173–4, 197–9; and Churchill 54, 55, 56, 68, 162, 259–60, 261; Coast of Ireland Command *see* Queenstown, Coast of Ireland Station and Command; and convoys 152, 162, 183, 184–5, 270; correspondence 57, 59, 60, 62, 63, 68, 78–9, 102, 105–6, 107, 145, 150, 183, 199, 201–2, 203, 211, 212, 226, 260, 264; death 266; and the Easter Rising 95, 96, 97, 99–100, 101, 102, 268; efforts to gain recognition for his men 109; and *Fanning* 194; fight against U-boats 62, 65–8, 76, 79–80, 84–5, 127 *see also* patrolling, anti-submarine *and* Q-ships; and Fisher 55, 56, 259–60, 261; and *Formidable* 55, 70, 162, 234, 259–60, 261; and *Genista* 108; at Greenwich RN College 55–6; holiday (June 1917) 160–1; honours 234, 259; and the hunting flotilla 215; and Irish conscription 226; and Jackson 51, 57, 58, 59, 60, 62, 63, 68, 78–9, 102, 105–6, 107, 113; and Jellicoe 17, 59, 113, 139, 150, 162, 183, 199, 201–2, 203, 211, 212, 226; as leader 267–9; and *Llandovery Castle* 233; and Marx 114–15, 165; and Miller 148; and MLs 104–5; and the *Motagua/Manley* collision 222; naval procedure and inspection 249–50; post-war visits to America 262–6; posted as Admiral responsible for Western Approaches 50–1, 56–9; and Pringle 150; *Pull Together* (autobiography) 259, 266, 276; and Q-ships *see* Q-ships; recognition

from USN 256, 268; recom-
mendation for heavily-
patrolled trade routes 127;
rescue missions instigated
by 79–80, 84, 108, 167, 188,
191, 195, 230, 233, 253;
retirement 259; and Sims
138–40, 153, 160–1, 162,
199, 263; and Sinn Fein
201–2, 226, 227; staff 161–2,
273–4; strategies and tactics
269–71 *see also* patrolling,
anti-submarine *and* Q-ships;
success vs objectives 271;
and Taussig 145, 146, 197,
198–9, 265; and US
submarines 196; victory
memorandum 255; and
White 108; and Wilkinson
154; and the working of
united RN/USN command
149–50, 153–4, 197–200,
268, 272; and zigzagging
ships 188n, 189–90
Beadnell, Frank E 103
Beagle, HMS 216
Beale, USS 221
Beatty, Sir David 50, 183
Bee, W H A 92
Begonia 80, 84; as *Q-10* 84–5
Belfast 51
Bellman, William 185
Benham, USS 153, 188n,
189–90
Benson, William 148–9, 151,
152, 245–6, 270
Benvorlich, SS 69
Berehaven 23, 51, 80, 196,
237, 245–6
Beresford, Charles William de
la Poer, 1st Baron 25, 29
Bergamot, HMS 177–9
Bergensfjord 33
Berger, Gerhard 119–20
Berlin, SS 32, 33
Bernis, Kurt 223
Bernstorff, Johann, Count von
77–8, 90, 91, 117–18
Berry, Robert Lawrence 222
Bertun, Captain 114
Beryl, HMY 114
Bethell, Sir Alexander 55
Bethmann-Hollweg, Theobald
von 14, 78, 90
Biggs, James Roy 238
Birch, William 253
Birmingham, HMS 32
Birmingham, USS 262
Bittern, HMS 85
Blackshields, Mary 202
Blazer 222
blockade of Germany 34,
35–6, 77, 117, 251;
American displeasure at 78,

82, 117, 149
Bluebell, HMS 92, 221, 222
Boadicia II, HMY 94, 95
Bolivia 35
Bonner, Charles George 'Gus'
172, 173
Borkum island 68
Boyle, Robert Francis 41
Bracondale, HMS 176–7
Bragg, Sir William Henry
280–1
Bragg, Sir William Lawrence
280
Brandon, SS 130
Breitung, Edward N Jr 35
Breynton, SS 188
Bridgeman, Sir Francis 29, 54
Briggs, E B 247
Brisk, HMS 187
Bristol Channel 35, 40, 43,
51, 60, 122, 188, 233–4
British Duke, SS 109
British Expeditionary Force
(BEF) 31
Brodrick, William St John, 1st
Earl of Midleton 101
Browne, Robert 58
Brunicardi, Daire 101
Bryan, William Jennings 81,
83
Bullock, H H 129
Burney, Sir Cecil 259
Burrows, USS 153
Buttercup, HMS 106, 167, 210
Butterfield, Thomas 203
Byrne, Alfred 224–5

Cabotia 107
Cairnhill, SS 133
Calgarian, HMS 227–9
Callaghan, George 68
Camellia, HMS 80, 195, 230,
231
Campbell, Gordon 85–7, 114,
166–8, 170–4, 215, 273; on
Bayly 197–8
Canadian, SS 129
Capper, Robert 230–1
Carbery, Ellen 73–4
Carbineer, HMT 104
Cardale, Ernest 216
Caronia, HMS 31
Carpendale, Charles Douglas
57, 79, 146, 148, 162, 273
Carpender, Arthur Schuyler
193–4
Carr, Josephine 254
Carson, Sir Edward 38, 113,
162
Carter, Gunner 208–9
Cartmel, HM Tug 188, 222
Casement, Sir Roger 90, 91,
92, 93, 268
Cassin, USS 190–1

Castro, SS 90–1 *see also Aud*,
SS
Catalina, SS 195
Cavaye, Frederick Langton
208, 209
Cawley, George 126–7
Cayo Romano 43
Celtic, RMS 153, 263
Centurion, SS 43
Ceramic, SS 216
Chagford, HMS 176–7
Chanaral 88
Chancellor 76
Chase, Irwin 104
Chatterton, Edward Keeble
104n
Chevington 66–7
Childers, Erskine 101
Chivas, Captain 119
Churchill, Winston 127; and
Bayly 54, 55, 56, 68, 162,
259–60, 261; and Coke
48–9; Dardanelles affair 48,
69; and Fisher 30, 48;
Gallipoli disaster 48; and
Leake 25n; and Q-ships 66;
sacked from Admiralty 48;
and submarines 30
City of Exeter 45
City of Memphis 121
Clark, Wilbur 218
Clearfield, SS 130
Clintonia 69
coal 66–7, 130
coalition government 48–9
Coast of Ireland Station *see*
Queenstown, Coast of
Ireland Station and
Command
Cochrane, HMS 216
Cock O'the Walk 107
Cockman, G W 131
Cohalan, Daniel 105
Coke, Sir Charles Henry 24,
26, 27, 33, 35, 36, 44, 45–6,
47, 50; and Churchill 48–9;
fired 51–2; and Jellicoe 50
Cole-Hamilton, John Claud 75
Colleen, HMS 25, 57
Colossus, HMS 236
Colville, Sir Stanley 127
commerce warfare 13, 15,
26–7, 30; prize rules 13, 14,
30, 32, 37, 88, 103, 115
Cone, Hutchinson Ingham
253, 254
Connaught, RMS 252–3
Conner, USS 247
conscription 89, 121; unrest
in Ireland 225–7
Constant, Georges 115
convoy escorts 150–3, 158–9,
162, 210–11, 216, 221,
227–8, 231, 241–3, 246,

251–2, 270, 271; with airships 239; U-boats adapting to 183–8, 214
Conyngham, USS 143, 252
Corbett, Sir Julian 260
Cork 22, 123, 201–3, 225, 255, 276; Easter Rising 97–8; Railway Station riot 204; 'Vigilantes' 202–3
Cormorant 100
Corsair, USS 192, 256
Costello 70
Cove 22–3 *see also* Queenstown, Coast of Ireland Station and Command
Cranmore, SS 132
Cressy, HMS 32
Crocus, HMS 171
Croft, Thomas Charles 126
Cullist, HMS 179–81, 219–21
Cumberlege, Marcus Victor 273–4
Cummings, USS 207
Cummins, Kenneth 233–4
Curragh Mutiny 25
Curtiss aircraft 235, 236, 238–9
Cushing, USS 223
Cymbeline, SS 73
Cymric, SS 103–4

Dacia, SS 35–6
Daniel O'Connell 45
Daniels, Josephus 135, 151, 152, 263, 275
Dardanelles 48, 69
Dare, Charles Holcombe 40, 96, 109
Davis, Milton Smith 252
Davis, USS 144
dazzle paint camouflage 154
de Chair, Sir Dudley 54, 211
de Valera, Eamon 97, 226, 227
de Winton, Francis Stephen W 153, 158
Dee, HMS 95–6
Defence of the Realm Act (DORA) 204, 237, 240
destroyers, RN 29, 129, 147, 158, 215, 229, 233; 2nd Flotilla 214, 216, 229; 6th Flotilla 31; Harwich Force 31
destroyers, USN 143–6, 147, 148, 149–54, 158–9, 183, 221, 223, 231, 240–1, 246, 247, 256, 270
Dewar, Kenneth 55
Diana, HMS 168
Dictator, SS 75
Dismukes, Douglas E 247
Dixie, USS 150

Dohna-Schlodien, Nikolaus zu 83
Dolly Varden 193
Dolphin, G R 126, 127
Doris, HMS 31
Dorman, Thomas Stephen 147
Douro, SS 75
Dover Barrage 175–6
Downes, USS 252
Doyle, Sir Arthur Conan 27
Drake, HMS 187
Drexel, George W C 192
drifters 36a, 41, 124
Dublin 201, 203, 255; Easter Rising 93–7
Duncan, USS 188, 252
Dundas, Lawrence Leopold 221, 222
Dunraven, HMS 172–3
Dunslee, SS 70
Dyer, USS 240

Earl of Latham 43
Earnest, HMS 215
Easter Rising 93–101, 268; Cork/Queenstown 97–8, 139; Dublin 93–7; Galway 98–100
Eddis, Christopher John 217
Edgar, Theresa 230, 231
El Zorro 79, 80
Elco Company 104
Elf King 217
Elgar, Edward 277
Elizabeth 45
Elliot, Richard M Jr 222
Emerson, Francis 126
Empress, HMS 236–7
English Channel 34, 36
Englishman, SS 84
Enniscorthy 96
Epic, HMS 255
Epsom, HMS 128
Equados, SS 262
Ericsson, USS 153, 231
Eridge, HMS 128
Evans, Arthur 123, 124
Evans, Edward ('Teddy') 145, 146, 271

Fairfield, Arthur P 143
Falaba, RMS 37–8
Falcon 119
false-flag deception *see* Q-ships
Fanning, Nathanial 192
Fanning, USS 188, 192–4
Farnborough, HMS 86–7, 166–8
Farnham, SS 157
Farquhar, Allan S 231
Fastnet 42, 43, 65, 84, 119, 122, 129, 157

Feldkirchner, Johannes 32
Fellowes, Thomas Balfour 217
Fern, SS 223, 224–5
Finch, William 70
Fisher, Elizabeth 74, 75
Fisher, John Arbuthnot 'Jackie', 1st Baron 14–15, 27, 69, 281; and Bayly 55, 56, 259–60, 261; and Churchill 30, 48; naval reforms 24; resignation 48; and submarines 29, 30
Fleswick 43
flying boats *see* seaplanes/flying boats
Foreign Office 45
Formidable, HMS 55, 70, 234, 260
Forstner, Georg-Günther von 69–70
Frampton, Captain 120
France 22, 23, 83
Franz, Adolf 249
Fraser, Margaret 'Pearl' 232
Freemasons 200
Freesia 80, 255
Fremantle, Sidney 261
French, John, 1st Earl of Ypres 101, 226, 255
Frohman, Charles 46
Frost, Wesley 46

Gafsa 124–5
Gage, Alfred 110
Gage, Edward 110
Galgate 103
Galgorm Castle 120, 121
Gallipoli 48
Galveston, USS 248, 249
Galway, Easter Rising 98–100
Gamble, Edward Harpur 53
Garthwaite, William 168
Geary-Hill, Sidney Arthur 223–4
Geddes, Sir Eric 162–3, 240
Genista, HMS 107–9
Georg, Carl-Siegfried Ritter von 108, 124
George V, King 131, 136, 167, 171, 194, 236, 265, 266
George, Robert 158
German navy: development after 1871 unification 24; High Command 239; High Seas Fleet 13–14, 26; mine-laying 32, 34 *see also* U-boats: minelaying; submarines *see* U-boats
Germany: Armistice 251, 255; Britain's declaration of war on 37; declaration of unre-stricted submarine warfare 117–19; emigrants to US 82;

and Irish nationalists 90–3, 275; merchant fleet 35; prohibited zone 188; RN blockade of *see* blockade of Germany; ships registered to 34; Spring Offensive, 1918 (*Kaiserschlacht*) 222, 251, 272; 'Turnip Winter' (1916/17) 117; US trade with 82–3
Ghent, Daniel T 192
Gladiator 72
Gladiolus, HMS 106, 208, 209, 228
Glaister, Robert 100, 101
Glendevon 66–7
Glenholm 47–8
Glitra, SS 32
Gloucester, HMS 91, 97, 99–100
Golden Effort 102
Goldmouth 85
Goldrich, Robert 62, 155–6, 163, 200, 207–8, 209, 211, 214, 228
Goodrich, S.Lt 187–8
Gordon, Charles George 53
Goulfar 115
Grasshopper, HMS 216, 217
Gray, Francis 100
Gray, William 209
Great Southern, SS 99
Great Yarmouth 93
Green, Lucien 203
Green Island, SS 229
Greenwich RN College 55–6
Grenfell, Francis Henry 111–12, 166
Greta, HMY 79, 80
Grey, Sir Edward 27
Griffon, HMS 215
Grindle, G 264
Guildford Castle, HMHS 130
Guillemot (South Arklow Light Vessel) 125–6
Guillimot, HMT 99
Gully, Lewis Vincent 220
Gunther, Paul 165–6
Güntzel, Ludwig 87
Guthrie, Percy 74, 75

Hague Convention (1899) 28, 30
Hague Convention (1907) 30, 232
Haig, Sir Douglas 162, 222–3
Haldon, HMS 128
Hall, Sir William Reginald ('Blinker') 175
Hallifax, Oswald Ernest 182
Hallwright, William Wybrow 99, 168, 242
Halsey, William Frederick ('Bull') Jr 153

Hanan, Francis W 98–9
Hankey, Maurice 102
Hansen, Claus 76
Hardiman, Frank 99–100
Harpy, USS 208, 216
Hart, Thomas Charles 196
Hartmann, Richard 120
Harwich 93; Force/Patrol 31
Hashagen, Ernst 132, 156, 230
Haulbowline Island 22–4, 57, 59, 66, 84, 97, 190
Hay, John 54
Healdton 121
Healy, Tim 95
Heaton, Gervase W H 128, 184–5
Hectoria 131
Helga, HMY 94, 96, 97, 253
Helmer, Elizabeth 277
Heneage, HMT 91–2
Henry, Walter Owen 193
Hepburn, Arthur Jepy 244, 265
Herbert, Godfrey 71–3, 161–2, 273
Herbster, Victor D 204, 237, 262–3
Heron 191
Hersing, Otto 119
Hesione 76
Hesperian, RMS 73–5, 78, 83
Hewitt, George Osbourne 157
Hibbert, Hugh Thomas 24, 33, 57, 273
Hibernia, HMS 236
Hindley, Robert Muir 220
Hogue, HMS 32
Holland 1 28
Holyhead 60
Hood, Sir Horace 29, 42–3, 44–5, 47
Hope, George Price Webley 135
Hopkins, Albert L 46–7
Hoppe, Bruno 167
Horgan, J J 47
Hornby, Robert Stewart Phipps 31
hospital ships 33, 130, 232–4
Hoy, Elizabeth 120
Hoy, Mary 120
Hubbard, Elbert 46
Huronian 79–80
Hurst, HMS 128
Hutton, George B 35
Hyde, Fred 121
Hyde, George 57, 95, 97
Hyde, Harry 121
hydrophones 244, 281–2

Ibex, SS 112
Idomeneus, SS 186
Illinois, SS 121

Imberhorne 155
Implacable, HMS 173
Ina Williams, HMT 42, 158
Indian Empire, HMT 45, 184–5
Indianapolis, USS 265
Ingram, Osmond 190
Insolent, HMS 195
Inverclyde, John Burns, 2nd Baronet 114
Invergordon 24
Inverlyon 87
Iolanda 114
Ipswich 93
Ireland 21, 24–5, 89–90, 201–4, 276; Anglo-Irish Treaty 276; anti-conscription unrest 225–7; Asquith in 105, 225; Catholic Church 39, 204, 276; civil war 276; Easter Rising *see* Easter Rising; fishing industry 36a; General Strike (1918) 226; Germany and Irish nationalists 90–3, 275; Home Rule 25, 27, 38, 227; nationalists and the *Aud* 90–3; nationalists modelling themselves on Boers 90; at outbreak of war 38–9; Protestant Ascendancy 24–5; Queenstown *see* Queenstown, Coast of Ireland Station and Command; RN pre-war activity and facilities in 22–7; War Brides 204
Irish Citizen's Army 93
Irish Republican Army 276
Irish Republican Brotherhood 39
Irish Revolutionary Brotherhood (IRB) 93
Irish Sea 22, 43, 51; 1914 burst of sinkings in 37; navigation lights 68; net barrage 40, 41; patrols *see* patrolling, anti-submarine; U-boats in *see* U-boats; weather 64, 206–7, 210, 246; Western Approaches *see* Western Approaches
Irish Sea Hunting Flotilla 214–15, 253
Irish Volunteers 25, 27, 38, 39, 90, 93, 96–8, 99, 102
Irishman, SS 133
Isis, HMS 31
Ivrig 155

Jackson, Sir Henry 49, 51; and Bayly 51, 57, 58, 59, 60, 62, 63, 68, 78–9, 102, 105–6, 107, 113
Jacob Jones, USS 153, 194–5

Jamaica 264
James Green, HMT 219
Jarvis, USS 188, 206–7
Jeffrey, Douglas George 176–7
Jellicoe, Sir John 15, 63, 66, 113, 123, 133–4, 136, 162, 211; and Bayly 17, 59, 113, 139, 150, 162, 183, 199, 201–2, 203, 211, 212, 226; and Coke 50; fired 211–12; and Sims 136, 212; and Taussig 145
Jenkins, USS 159
Jessamine, HMS 64–5, 191, 223, 231
John Hardie 76
Johnson, Alfred P 143
Jones, John 217
Jones, John Paul, Captain 192
Jorgen Olsen 156
Jose de Larrinaga, SS 155
Juno, HMS 31, 42, 43, 44
Jürst, Hellmuth 84
Jutland, Battle of 211

Kaiser Wilhelm der Grosse 247
Kaiser Wilhelm II 247
Kalk, Stanton F 195
Kanawha, USS 216
Kariba, SS 130
Keats, Sir Richard 53
Kerr, John Graham 264
Kerr, Walter Talbot 53
Kestrel, HMS 215
Killeagh 239
Kimberley, USS 252
King-Hall, George 54
Kingstown 26, 36, 51, 60, 93–5, 100, 105, 215, 226–7
Kinsale 22, 45
Kish, SS 132–3
kite balloons 237, 239, 246
Kolbe, Walter 229
Krabbe, Frederick James 209
Kroll, Carl Albrecht 229
Kronprinz Wilhelm 247
Kronprinzessin Cecilie/USS *Mount Vernon* 246, 247–8

Laburnum, HMS 99, 116–17, 119, 120, 129, 157, 159, 186
Lacey, Ernest 106
Laconia, RMS 120
Lacy, Captain 145, 162
Lady Patricia, HMS 157
Lake Harris, USS 255
Lambert, Cecil 102
Lane, S R 241
Lansdowne, Henry Petty-Fitzmaurice, 5th Marquess of 225–6
Lansing, Robert 78, 83, 118
Larne 26, 36, 41, 51, 60

Lavender, HMS 62, 147
Law, Andrew Bonar 95
Le Marchant, Evelyn Robert 40
Leake, Francis Martin 25n, 162, 273–4
Lee, W J 222
Leinster, RMS 252–4
Lewis, Francis Kenvyn 254
Lewis, Norman McCrea 132
Lincoln 93
Lisette, HMS 181–2
Lively, HMS 215, 253, 254
Liverpool 21, 34, 40, 48, 51, 77
Llandovery Castle, HMHS 232–4
Lloyd George, David 37, 111, 152, 162, 211, 226, 227
Loderer, SS 86
Loftus, G W H 241–2
London, Treaty of 36
Lord Lister, HMT 178, 228, 229
Lough Swilly 23
Loveless, Len 167, 168
Lowestoft 93
Lugano, SS 187
Lusitania, RMS 43–7, 72, 75, 77, 83
Lycett, William Ernest 220
Lyon, T 232–3
Lysander, HMS 233

Mac Curtain, Tomás 98
McCreary, F R 237
McDougal, USS 143, 153
McGinty, John Aloysius 202
McKenna, Reginald 89
Mackinder, Sir Halford John 15
MacKinnon, Neil S 220
McLean, Peter Alexander 216, 217
McMullen, Lt 102
McNamara, John F 238
MacNeill, Eoin 39
Madison, James J 248–9
Main, William 73, 74, 75
Malahide 239
Malcolm, K B 103
Mallard, HMS 215, 253
Malmanger, SS 124
Manchester Citizen, SS 131
Manchester Commerce, SS 32, 131
Manchester Inventor, SS 131
Manley, USS 221, 222
Mantola, SS 119
Marder, Arthur 14–15, 26, 269–70
Marie Pierre 115
Marina 110
Mariston, SS 182
maritime law 34

Markievicz, Constance, Countess 226
Martha Edmonds 70
Martin, Captain 87
Marx, John Locke 113–15, 160, 164–5
Mary Rose, HMS 129, 145
Mason, William 116–17, 120, 157, 159, 186
Maxton, SS 211
Mayo, Henry T 237
Melville, USS 149, 154, 194, 222
Mendip Range, SS 187
Mentor, HMS 49
Mercantile Marine Reserve (MMR) 121
merchant ships/sailors: armed cruisers *see* armed merchant cruisers (AMCs); Compulsory Convoy Act (1798) 22; losses to U-boats *see* U-boats: merchant shipping losses to
Meux, Hedworth 66n
Mexico 118
Meyer, Wilhelm 216
MFA 1463 133
Middendorff, Heinrich 247
Midland 107
Midland Queen 70
Midleton, William St John Brodrick, 1st Earl of 101, 138–9
Mignonette, HMS 106, 123–4
Milford Haven 26, 36, 41, 51, 60, 105, 109, 129, 168–9, 188
Miller, Francis Spurston 147, 148, 209, 242
Milliken, George 247
Mimosa 73
Mindful, HMS 241
Minerva, HMS 31
mines 32, 123, 124, 129, 130, 158, 229; Dover Barrage 175–6; German fields off Queenstown and Kinsale 123–4; merchant shipping losses to 32; minelaying U-boats 112, 123, 158, 171, 172, 175, 184–5, 186–8, 285; in Queenstown harbour 140, 184, 201; Tory Island minefield 32–4
minesweepers/minesweeping 33, 106, 123–4, 140, 158, 184–5; 3rd Flotilla 128
Minos, HMS 216
Miranda, HMS 49
Mohl, Hans von 219
Montano, SS 190
Moorish Prince, SS 249
Morea, HMS 233

Moresby, HMS 229
Morgan, J P 192, 256, 263
Morgan, Junius 262, 263, 264, 265
Morning Star, HMS 97
Morococala, HMT 184–5
Morton, Leslie 44
Mosquito, HMS 216, 217
Motagua, HMS 221–2
motor launches (MLs) 104–5, 124, 147, 215, 226, 228, 231; *ML-161* 169; *ML-181* 145; *ML-325* 145
Mount Vernon, USS 247–8
Möwe 83–4
Munster, RMS 252–3

Narwhal, HMS 129, 153, 167
Nasmith, Martin Eric 196, 271
National Volunteers (Ireland) 39
Nebeker, Mr 70
Nebraskan, SS 48
neutral ships 14, 34, 37, 77, 111, 117, 119, 121, 129, 136–7, 163, 176, 227
Nevada, USS 246
New York, SS 135
New York City 70
New York Times 103
Newton, R A 228
Nicholson, USS 193, 247
Nicosian, SS 71, 72–3
Nictator, HMS 97
Noake, Basil Stratford 84
Nolan, Cathleen 204
Noodt, Erich 112
Norbreck 42
Norma, SS 165
North Channel 41, 186, 187, 216, 227–9
North Wales 110
Norway 213n
Norway, Mary Louisa 100
Norwich 93
NOUS (Naval Order of the United States) 277

O'Connell, Daniel 23
Oklahoma, USS 246
Oliver, Sir Henry F 63, 68
Oliver, William O 79
Olphert, Wybrants 160
Onslow, HMS 97
Oracle, HMS 177
Orduna, SS 231
Orwell, HMS 215
Osmond Ingram, USS 191
Ossory, HMS 97
Oxfordshire, HMHS 33
Oxlade, Charles Herbert 210

P-boats (coastal sloops) 67,
95, 122–3, 271; *P-39* 123; *P-46* 123; *P-53* 123; *P-67* 123; *PC-43* 179; *PC-56* 210; *PC-61* 182–3; PC class 123, 182, 183, 215, 271
Page, Walter Hines 81–2, 136–7
Pallada 28
Parente, J W 203
Pargust, HMS 170–2
Parker, USS 153
Parrott, George Fountain Jnr 252
Parry, Joseph 44
Parslow, Frederick Daniel 49, 50
Parslow, Frederick Jr 49–50
Parthian, HMS 129, 144–5
passenger liners attacked by U-boats 43–7, 70–1, 73–5, 77–8, 83, 103–4, 120, 129, 130–1, 230
Patella, SS 65
Patey, Sir George Edwin 66, 67
Pathfinder, HMS 25n, 32
Patrol, HMS 215
patrolling, anti-submarine 36, 41–2, 47, 60–1, 65–7, 85, 127, 151, 156, 157–60, 183, 206, 227; Irish Sea Hunting Flotilla 214–15, 253
Patten, Thomas Franklin 220
Patteron, USS 221
Patzig, Helmut 232–3
Paulding, USS 153, 188
Pearse, Patrick 93
Penshurst, SS 111–12, 166
Perkins, Percy Tennison 177–9
Pershing, John 'Black Jack' 271–2
Petherick, Arthur Collier 210
Peyton, HMS 129, 133
Phillimore, Valentine E B 79
Pigeon, HMS 216, 217
Pilar de Larrinaga, SS 155
Pitcher, Ernest Herbert 172, 173
Plummer, Fred 203
Plummer, Henry W 255
Polyanthus, HMS 222
Poppy, HMS 106, 155, 163, 186, 187–8, 207–10, 214, 228
Porter, USS 143, 153, 191, 231
Portia 70
Poteel, Fred H 144
Primrose, HMS 210–11
Pringle, Joel Roberts Poinsett 150, 263, 265, 273
Prize, HMS 168–70
Prize Courts 35–6
prize/cruiser rules 13, 14, 30,
32, 37, 88, 103, 115
prostitution 203–4

Q-ships 65–7, 71, 72–3, 76, 84–5, 86–7, 106, 107, 113–15, 122, 123, 127, 131–2, 164–74, 176–83, 188, 196, 210, 215, 219–21, 228, 241–4, 256, 269, 271; camouflaged 154; *Q-1* 107; *Q-5* 86–7, 166–8; *Q-7* 111–12, 166; *Q-12* 131–2; *Q-13* 114–15, 156, 160, 164–5, 188; *Q-14* 133; *Q-15* 160; *Q-16* 168; *Q-21* 168–70; *Q-25* 157; *Q-36* 126–7
Queen, HMS 54
Queen Mary, SS 130, 132
Queenstown, Coast of Ireland Station and Command: 1914 base 31, 36, 38, 39; 1915, before Bayly's arrival 43, 44–5; American/British relations *see* United States Navy: British relations at Queenstown; arrival of USN 137, 143–54; auxiliary vessels (1 Jan. 1918) 284; Bayly makes base at 51, 56–9; Bayly's RN command till April 1917 56–140; Bayly's RN and USN command from May 1917 143–256, 268, 271–3; convoy escorts *see* convoy escorts; departure of USN 256; and the Easter Rising 95, 96, 97, 99–100, 101, 139, 268; and Irish nationalism 39, 95–101; men's unwavering efforts 15; origins as Cove 22–3; ships, 1915, allocated to 60–7; ships, 1916, allocated to 104–5; ships, 1917, allocated to 122–3, 128, 129 *see also* destroyers, USN; ships, 1918, allocated to 244–5; staff 161–2, 273–4; united command formed with USN 148–50; Victoria Crosses 50, 167, 170, 171, 173, 196, 243–4, 279; Whitepoint 240
Queenstown (town) 50, 201, 202–4; Admiralty House 16–17, 24, 57, 58, 63, 106, 138, 145, 146, 161, 198–9, 200, 203, 240, 276–7; Cork Club 200; dockyard 57–8, 67; Easter Rising 97–8; harbour mined 140, 184, 201; hospitality to officers

of the united Command 200; lifeboat 45; Old Church Cemetery 47; prostitution 203–4; Royal Cork Yacht Club 200

Queenstown Association (American organisation) 262, 263, 264, 265, 266, 276

Racoon, USS 208, 214
Radcliffe, Stephen Herbert 187
Radford, Isaac 171
Raikes, Robert Henry 148
Raleigh, Sir Walter 26
Ramillies, SS 163
Ramm, Robert 254
Ranza 69
Rappahannock, SS 110
Rathlin Island barrier 41
Ravenhill 87–8
Raymond Ester 155
Redmond, John 25, 27, 38–9, 89
Retvizan 28
Reventlow, Ernest von 121
Rewa, HMHS 130
Rhydwen, SS 133
Richmond, Herbert 29–30, 41, 55, 66, 68, 139
Ring, Margaret 202
Rob Roy, HMS 186
Robarts, Marjorie Campbell 74
Roberts, George 224–5
Robertson, Charles Hope 181
Robilliard, Ernest 220
Robinson, Matthew 230, 231
Rockingham 155
Rocky Island 22
Rogers, Thomas Slidell 246
Rohr, Walter 178
Rohrbeck, Otto 187, 188
Roman Catholic Church 39, 204, 276
Roosevelt, Franklin Delano 240–1, 259, 265, 266
Roosevelt, Theodore 54, 81, 121, 134, 148
Rose, Hans 194, 195
Rosemary, HMS 106, 187–8, 208–9, 228
Rosenow, Ernst 171
Rossiter, James 126
Rosyth 31
Rovenski, HMY 181
Rowan, USS 223
Rowland, S.Lt 222
Royal Fleet Reserve (RFR) 121
Royal Irish Constabulary 203–4, 225
Royal Marines 72, 97, 106
Royal Naval Air Service (RNAS) 235–6, 239
Royal Naval Reserve (RNR) 121
Royal Naval Volunteer Reserve (RNVR) 104, 116
Royal Navy: 1914 dispositions 31; and anti-submarine nets 40–1, 47, 60–1; anti-submarine patrols by Queenstown Command *see* patrolling, anti-submarine; blockade of Germany *see* blockade of Germany; centralisation 24; Coast of Ireland Station *see* Queenstown, Coast of Ireland Station and Command; destroyers *see* destroyers, RN; divided command structure around Irish coast 40; Fisher's reforms 24; Grand Fleet 13, 158; minelaying 34; minesweepers *see* minesweepers/minesweeping; motor launches *see* motor launches (MLs); Northern Division 147–8; pre-war activity and facilities in Ireland 22–7; pre-war role and state 14; Q-ships *see* Q-ships; sloops *see* sloops; submarines *see* submarines, RN; torpedo boats 26, 45, 60, 79, 123; trawlers *see* trawlers
Royal Navy War College 54
Ruckteschell, Hellmuth von 241
Rudd, Dwight 194
Rundell, Nicholas 120
Russell, H Robert 59, 138, 139, 161, 162, 273
Rutherford, Sir Ernest 281
Ryan, Cyril 281

Saalwächter, Alfred 115
Safeguard, HMS 230, 231
sailing ships 47–8, 120
Saint Barchan 255
St George's Channel 22, 31, 35–6, 41, 51, 181, 182, 210, 223, 255
St Olaf 70
Saltzwedel, Reinhold 172
Salvia, HMS 160, 179
Salvin, Anthony 23
Samson, Charles Rumney 236
Samuel S Morse 109
San Hilario 130
San Juan, SS 262–3
San Urbano, SS 148
San Zefferino, SS 182
Sanders, William 168–70
Santa Amalia, SS 211
Santee, USS 196
Savage, HMS 216
Saxon, HMT 177
Saxon Prince, SS 83–4
Scaduan HMY 160
Scapa Flow 24, 31, 33, 59, 158, 207
Scheer, Reinhard 88, 93, 102, 255
Schneider, Rudolph 70, 79
Schwanden 87
Schwieger, Walther 44, 74, 75, 78, 103
Scilly Isles 26, 51, 60, 79, 122, 235–6
Scott, Sir Percy 27, 30
Seadaun, HMY 48
Seagull 43
Seal, HMS 215, 253
Sealark II, HMT 94
seaplanes/flying boats 63, 112, 235–6, 238, 239, 263; bases 204, 235–6, 237, 238
Senator, HMT 158
Settee II 91
Shaw, George 238
Shaw, USS 153, 231, 252
Sheather, Alfred Reginald 220
Shee, Commander 45
Sheerness 31
Sherman, Mr (US Vice Consul) 146
Sherston, George Ponsonby 109, 162, 194
Shuttle 265
Siberia, SS 84
Siddall, Frederick W 178–9
Silvership, SS 65
Simpson, Salisbury Hamilton 63–4, 179–81, 219–20, 223
Sims, William Sowden 134–8, 139–40, 148–9, 151–2, 154n, 173, 246, 262, 270, 271, 272, 275–6, 281; and Bayly 138–40, 153, 160–1, 162, 199, 263; commanding in Bayly's absence 160–1; and Jellicoe 136, 212; *Victory at Sea* 275
Sinn Fein 25, 39, 89, 93, 94, 201–2, 226
Siplon, Arthur 217–18
Sittenfeld, Erich 182
Skerries 95–6
Slade, Edmond 54
Slapp, Charles 158
sloops 61–5, 67, 84, 85, 91, 92, 99, 106, 109–10, 119, 122, 123, 124, 127, 132–3, 147, 156, 171, 183, 186, 187–8, 210–11, 223, 228, 230, 241–2, 269, 271; camouflaged 154; coastal *see* P-boats; principle

302

Queenstown sloops and their commanders 278
Smith, John 217
Smith, Robert Sydney 178–9
Smith, William 218
Snowdrop, HMS 84, 99, 100, 129, 191, 194, 233
Southland, SS 159
Spanish 'Flu 246, 255
Speth-Schülzburg, Rudolf von 210
Spiegel, Edgar von 169, 170
Spiess, Johannes 211, 228
Spike Island 22
Spindler, Karl 91–2
Sprightly, HMS 215
Stafford, Brigadier General 98
Stag, HMS 215
Starkey, Anthony 130
Steinbrinck, Otto 125–6
Stella, Giuseppe 56
Stella, Henrietta, née Voysey 56
Stephens, Frances 75
Sterret, USS 153, 231
Stewart, Alexander 185
Stewart, Charles 210
Stileman, Harry Hampson 40
Stock Force, HMS 242–4
Stormcock, HM Tug 44, 45, 188
Strachan, Alexander L 108–9
Strackerjan, Friedrich 192
Strahan, George E 243, 244
Stuart, Ronald Neil 166, 168, 171–2, 191, 222
sub-chasers ('splinter ships'), USN 240–1, 244–5, 256, 281
submarines, German see U-boats
submarines, RN 28, 29–30, 85; A-4 71; and Bacon 29; D-5 71; D-7 182; 'D'-class 71, 147, 182; E-54 148; 'E'-class 147–8; and Fisher 29, 30; Platypus Flotilla 147, 182; Vulcan Flotilla 147
submarines, USN 196, 256
Sunflower, HMS 75, 106
supply chains 13, 26–7, 36–7, 38, 119
Sussex, SS 88
Sussex pledge 88, 110
Sutlej, HMS 31
Sutphen, Henry 104
Swabey, George Thomas 106
Swansea 60
Sylvester, R A 232, 233

Talbot, HMS 236
Tamarisk, HMS 188
Tamarisk, USS 191, 221, 222
Tara 41

Tarlair, HMS 281
Taussig, Joseph Knefler 143–6, 153, 158–9, 161, 171, 192, 197, 198–9, 200, 205, 265
Tebbenjohann, Kurt 175
Tennessee, USS 263
Terek, SS 109
Terestchenko, Elizabeth 114
Terry, USS 221, 231
Teutonic 84
Thomas Collard, HMT 228
Thresher, Leon 38
Ticonderoga, USS 248–9
Tiro, SS 213
Tirpitz, Alfred von 14, 78
Toft, James Thomas 131
Toro, SS 130
torpedo boats 26, 45, 60, 79, 123, 285
torpedoes 28, 30, 41, 43–4 69–70, 123, 147, 164; and German submarine warfare see U-boats
Torrington, SS 130
Tory Island 122, 147, 186; minefield 32–4
Tower, Francis Fitzgerald 105, 181–2, 199, 207, 226, 227, 245, 254, 255
Townshend, J C 238
trade war see commerce warfare
Travers, Robert H 78–9
trawlers 36a, 41, 60, 85, 91, 94–5, 99, 122, 124, 158; armed 36, 41, 42, 45, 47, 58, 91–2, 94, 96, 104, 158, 228; minesweeping 33, 124, 158, 184–5, 215
Trevone, SS 130
Trippe, USS 153, 188, 206–7
Tsesarevich 28
Tulip, HMS 131–2
Turner, Maud Marion 220
Turner, Thomas Thompson 220
Turner, William 43, 44, 45, 47
Tuscania, SS 215–19, 281
Tuskar Rock 155, 238
Tweedmouth, Edward Marjoribanks, 2nd Baron 54
Twigg, Alan George Despard 39
Twigg, Francis Walter 233

U-boats 14, 15, 27, 31; 1914 warfare 32, 36–8; 1915 warfare 41–8, 50, 60–1, 62, 65–7, 69–71, 72, 73–80, 83; 1916 warfare 84–5, 86–8, 102, 107–8; 1917 start of joint operations against 155–60; 1917 unrestricted

warfare 117–37, 155–60, 163, 164–73, 175–96, 210–11, 213, 270; 1918 unrestricted warfare 214–21, 223–4, 227–34, 241–4, 246–9; adapting to convoys 183–8, 214; airpower used against 235–9; and anti-submarine nets 40–1, 47, 60–1; and the Armistice 251, 255; arrival around Irish coast 36–8, 39; Atlantic trade targeted by 13, 14; Bayly's early under-estimating of threat 55; campaign suspension, autumn 1915 77–80; campaign suspension spring 1916 88, 102; difficulties in finding 280–2; and the Dover Barrage 175–6; hospital ships attacked by 130, 232–4; liner attacks by 43–7, 70–1, 73–5, 77–8, 83, 103–4, 120, 129, 130–1, 230; merchant shipping losses to 15, 37, 51, 72–3, 76, 79, 85, 87, 88, 102–4, 107, 110–12, 119–20, 121, 127, 129, 130, 131, 155, 159–60, 163, 211, 213, 238, 270; minelaying 112, 123, 158, 171, 172, 175, 184–5, 186–8, 285; neutral ships attacked by 14, 34, 37, 111, 121, 129, 136–7, 163, 176, 227; principal types 285; Queenstown patrols against see patrolling, anti-submarine; sailing ships targeted by 47–8, 120; sunk in Western Approaches by vessels under Bayly's direct orders 283; and the Sussex pledge 88, 110; U-1 28, 37–8; U-13 32; U-15 32; U-17 32; U-19 211, 228; U-20 42–4, 74, 75, 103; U-21 32, 36, 119; U-24 55, 70, 79; U-27 72; U-28 69–70, 84; U-32 84; U-33 73, 76; U-34 42; U-38 36, 70; U-39 49; U-41 76; U-43 84, 131; U-44 84, 85, 176–7; U-45 182; U-46 115, 157; U-48 170; U-50 119–20, 158; U-53 194–5; U-55 110, 130, 133; U-57 108, 124–5, 157; U-58 163, 193; U-60 132; U-61 130; U-62 132, 156, 230; U-63 106, 107, 110; U-65 155; U-66 87, 132n; U-67 87–8, 188; U-68 86–7; U-69 87, 107, 110; U-70 84, 159; U-73 87;

U-77 216; *U-79* 186–8; *U-80*
158; *U-81* 148, 155; *U-82*
247; *U-83* 167; *U-84* 178; *U-86* 232; *U-87* 210; *U-93* 169,
170; *U-95* 213; *U-97* 219; *U-104* 223; *U-105* 192, 196; *U-110* 213, 229; *U-152* 248–9;
UB-10 251; *UB-19* 112; *UB-29* 88; *UB-32* 131; *UB-37*
165–6; *UB-39* 107; *UB-40*
107, 251; *UB-57* 213; *UB-59*
251; *UB-61* 186; *UB-65* 210;
UB-80 242–3, 244; *UB-94*
255; *UB-119* 229; *UB-123*
253–4; *UC-4* 251; *UC-10*
148; *UC-21* 121; *UC-29* 171;
UC-31 185; *UC-44* 175, 176;
UC-65 125–7; *UC-66* 121,
123, 235, 236; *UC-69*
159–60; *UC-71* 172–3, 192;
and the US 77–8, 81
Ulster, RMS 252–3
Ulster, SS 95
Ulster Division 38
Ulster Volunteer Force (UVF)
25, 27, 38
United States Naval Air
Service 237–9
United States Navy: arrival in
Queenstown 137, 143–54;
Battleship Division Six 246;
British relations at
Queenstown 197–200 *see
also* Queenstown
Association (American
organisation); departure
following Armistice 256;
destroyers *see* destroyers,
USN; facilities at
Queenstown 240; flying-
boat bases in Ireland 237–8;
MV sound-detecting system
281; recognition of Bayly
256, 268; sub-chasers
('splinter ships') 240–1,
244–5, 256, 281;
submarines 196, 256; united
command with RN formed
at Queenstown 148–50
United States of America: in
1916 81–3; American
Expeditionary Force (AEF)
272; anti-German rioting on
sinking of *Lusitania* 77; and
the Armistice 251; Bayly's
post-war visits 262–6; enters
war 121–2; exports during
early months of the war
82–3; German/Austro-
Hungarian immigrants 82;
German relations and
reluctance to declare war
47, 81, 82, 117, 118–19; and
Germany's declaration of

unrestricted submarine
warfare 117–19; neutrality
77–8; and the *Sussex* pledge
88; trade with Germany
82–3; troops ('doughboys')
150, 246; and U-boats 77–8,
81, 117–19; and the
Zimmermann Telegram 118
Urbino, SS 76
Utah, USS 246

Vale of Lennox 241
Valentiner, Max 70
Van Stirum, SS 79
Vanderbilt, Alfred 46
Venus, HMS 31
Vernou, Walter 190
Veronica, HMS 62
Vickers 104
Victoria Crosses 50, 167, 170,
171, 173, 196, 243–4, 279
Viebeg, Max 131, 243, 244
Vigilancia 121
Vigrid, SS 213
Viknor, HMS 33–4
Volturno 110
Voysey, Annesley Wesley 56
Voysey, Charles Francis 56
Voysey, Violet Mary 56, 139,
161, 198–9, 205, 233, 256,
262, 263, 264, 265–6, 268,
276

Wade, G F 56, 92
Wadsworth, USS 143, 145,
153, 205
Wagenführ, Paul 84
Wainwright, USS 144, 153, 247
Walker, Horace 209
Wanderer 45
War Brides 204
War Risks Insurance Scheme
37
Warley Pickering, SS 119
Warner, HMS 127
Warrior, HM Tug 44, 84
Wassner, Erwin 159–60
weather 64, 206–7, 210, 246
Wedel, Count Botho von
('Rosato Spero') 33–4
Wemyss, Rosslyn 35, 211,
259, 261
Werner, Wilhelm 130
Western Approaches 13, 14,
21–2, 23, 26–7, 73, 103,
106, 155, 163, 255; battle
for 15, 50, 62, 65–8, 76–7,
79–80, 84–5, 122, 129–37,
155–73, 175–96, 270 *see
also* patrolling, anti-
submarine; U-boats; Bayly
made responsible for 50–1,
56–9; Coast of Ireland
Command *see* Queenstown,

Coast of Ireland Station and
Command; convoy escorts
see convoy escorts
Wexford 237–8
Whiddy Island 237, 238
Whitchurch, Frederick
Thomas 220
White, Arnold 27
White, Edward 45
White, John 108
Whitton, David John 220
Wild, John Robert 177n
Wilhelm II, Kaiser 13–14, 26,
78
Wilhelms, Ernst 110
Wilkes, USS 231
Wilkinson, Norman 154, 264
Williams, William 172
Williamson, James 147
Willie 84
Wilmot-Smith, Andrew 76
Wilson, Sir Arthur 29
Wilson, Ben 21
Wilson, Graham F W 109,
124–5, 132, 133, 156–7,
171, 189, 230, 249–50
Wilson, Sir Samuel Herbert
264
Wilson, Woodrow 47, 77, 81,
82, 83, 104, 117, 118–19,
121–2, 218, 251, 255, 272;
reluctance to enter war 47,
81, 82, 117, 118–19
Wimborne, Ivor Guest, 1st
Viscount 96
Winslow, USS 247
Wolverine, USS 208–9
Women's Royal Naval Service
(Wrens) 200–1, 254, 273
Wood, C S 222
Workman, Lt 243
Worsley, Frank Arthur 182–3
Wortman, Ward K 143
Would, Jesse 74
Wright, Orville 236
Wyandra, SS 76 *see also
Baralong*, SS
Wyatt, Henry Joseph 100–1

Zarefah, HMY 39
Zent, SS 87
Zephyr, HMS 215
zigzagging 188n, 189–90, 252
Zimmermann, Arthur 90
Zimmermann Telegram 118
Zinnia, HMS 64, 84, 92,
109–10, 124–5, 132–3, 154,
156–7, 171, 188, 189–90,
230, 249–50
Zogbaum, Rufus 144
Zone, SS 213